The Romance of the Rose

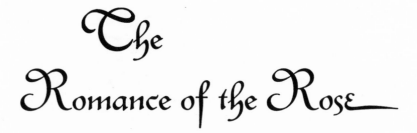

The Romance of the Rose

BY GUILLAUME DE LORRIS

AND JEAN DE MEUN

TRANSLATED BY CHARLES DAHLBERG

UNIVERSITY PRESS OF NEW ENGLAND

Hanover and London

UNIVERSITY   PRESS   OF   NEW   ENGLAND

BRANDEIS   UNIVERSITY
BROWN   UNIVERSITY
CLARK   UNIVERSITY
DARTMOUTH   COLLEGE
UNIVERSITY   OF   NEW   HAMPSHIRE
UNIVERSITY   OF   RHODE   ISLAND
TUFTS   UNIVERSITY
UNIVERSITY   OF   VERMONT

Printed in the United States of America

LIBRARY OF CONGRESS CATALOGING IN PUBLICATION DATA

Roman de la rose. English.
The Romance of the rose.

Translation of: Le Roman de la rose.
Bibliography: p.
Includes index.
I. Guillaume, de Lorris, fl. 1230.   II. Jean,
de Meun, d. 1305?   III. Dahlberg, Charles, 1919–
IV. Title.
PQ1528.A43   1983   841'.1   83-40017
ISBN 0-87451-267-0 (pbk.)

5 4 3

TO MY FATHER AND MOTHER

CONTENTS

The Romance of the Rose

viii   *Contents*

ILLUSTRATIONS

THE illustrations follow p. 450. The line number refers to the line immediately following the miniature's position in the manuscript; captions are in most cases adapted from the manuscript rubrics where they exist. All illustrations are reproduced here in their actual sizes.

PREFACE

*C*HIS translation of the *Romance of the Rose*, the first in modern English prose, is one of nearly a dozen volumes during the past decade to present an edition, a translation, or a major commentary on the Old French poem. The aim of this book is to provide a clear, readable text that is as faithful as possible to the original, particularly in terms of imagery. Because translations have their pitfalls and because thirteenth-century assumptions about the use of imagery, indeed of poetry, are very different from ours, I have provided a variety of materials that may help the reader to approach the poem with an approximation of the perspective of that time. The introduction, notes, and illustrations are designed primarily to elaborate and clarify such a view of the poem.

If the book fulfills such an aim, it will do so in large part because of the help that many people have given, help that has forestalled errors and infelicities in both text and commentary; those that remain are mine alone. D. W. Robertson, Jr., has given freely of time, insight, erudition, food, and good fellowship; my debt to him will be obvious on page after page. John V. Fleming was generous of comment, particularly on the illustrations, in the later stages of the preparation of the manuscript. Without their encouragement and that of other friends and colleagues, progress would have been even more glacial than it has been. Mrs. Linda Peterson and Mrs. Polly Hanford of Princeton University Press have been most helpful and encouraging at every stage of the book's preparation; and the readers of the manuscript have made many valuable suggestions.

Various institutions have contributed their help in one way or another. Some of the preliminary work took place during a predoctoral Fulbright Fellowship; the bulk of the manuscript was completed in draft during a sabbatical leave from my post at Queens College; and the final stages occupied much of a later short leave. At all stages the Librarian, Professor Morris Gelfand, and the staff of the Paul Klapper Library at Queens College have been cooperative in every possible way. In Paris, I have enjoyed the most cordial assistance from the staffs at the Bibliothèque Nationale

Preface

and the other major collections in the city. The Institut de Recherche et d'histoire des Textes of the Centre National de la Recherche Scientifique was particularly helpful in getting manuscripts from provincial libraries for use in Paris. Princeton University provided two grants toward the expenses of obtaining photographs and microfilms.

The third volume of the Lecoy edition appeared too late to permit its use in the Introduction or Notes to this volume, but I have been able to correct the Bibliography and Appendix to acknowledge its existence.

My wife is due thanks for much beyond the hours that we have shared in working on the manuscript; they have all been good hours. My fundamental and continuing debt is one that I am glad to acknowledge in the dedication.

Scarsdale, N.Y., 1969-70   CHARLES DAHLBERG

PREFACE TO THE 1983 EDITION

𝒯HIS paperback edition provides the opportunity to correct minor errors and to make a few additions to the bibliography. I have not attempted a thorough update of the bibliography, since Maxwell Luria's recent *A Reader's Guide to the Roman de la Rose* has a convenient bibliography as part of an excellent guide. The Bibliographical Supplement, however, lists works that I mention in this preface and several that I omitted from my earlier Bibliography. Among these is Marc-René Jung's critical bibliography of 1966, "Der Rosenroman in der Kritik seit dem 18. Jahrhundert." New editions and translations include André Lanly's French translation and Karl A. Ott's edition with facing German translation.

During recent years, a number of writers have reemphasized the contrast between the two authors in their treatment of the poem's allegory. Such is the case even in the relatively small space devoted to the poem in Jung's important book on Latin and French allegory, a work that parallels the series of essays by Hans Robert Jauss on the origins and development of allegorical poetry up to the *Romance*. In Paul Piehler's survey of medieval allegory through Dante and *Pearl*, he contrasts Guillaume and Jean in their balancing of landscape and dialogue. In works specifically on the *Romance*, Daniel Poirion contrasts Guillaume's narrative dream allegory with Jean's amplified discursive allegory. René Louis's essay on the interpretation of the poem's erotic allegory opposes Guillaume's idealized, refined love to Jean's emphasis on the sexual and procreative aspects. Jean Charles Payen sees Jean's concern as sexual revolution and the longing for the ideal communal social order. And Paul Zumthor establishes distinctions among emblem, symbol, and allegory, as well as among allegorical functions (didactic, deictic, narrative); with these distinctions, he sees Guillaume's part of the *Romance* as narrative (*récit*), in contrast to Jean's, which he views as antinarrative, a "deconstruction" that remakes Guillaume's work "on the level of explicative discourse" (1974, p. 204).

Such contrasts are traditional in *Romance* criticism. Others, however, see a greater degree of unity than has often been granted. Karl D. Uitti, on the basis of medieval attitudes toward myth and poetry, argues for the unity of the two parts. John Took, in the course of his work on the *Fiore*, supports the idea of the integrity of the *Romance* as a whole. And Maxwell Luria's edition of an important sixteenth-century gloss, in the Collins manuscript of Philadelphia, offers a medieval view of allegory, one that supports a unified reading.

The *Romance*'s fourteenth-century reputation is the subject of Pierre-Yves Badel's recent book, an extended survey of allusions to the poem through the quarrel of the early fifteenth century. Other treatments of the quarrel appear in Eric Hicks' edition, in Peter Potansky's analysis, and in Joseph L. Baird and John R. Kane's translation of the documents. Interest in Christine de Pisan has helped to encourage this area of *Romance* scholarship, as had John V. Fleming's 1965 article "The Moral Reputation of the *Roman de la Rose* Before 1400."

Much of the controversy in the fifteenth-century debate centered on the validity of the character Reason, and the question is still with us. Fleming's book, *The Roman de la Rose: A Study in Allegory and Iconography*, has of course provoked a good deal of comment, not only from several of those whom I have cited above, but also from those who question his assumption that Reason's voice is authorial. Michael D. Cherniss, Winthrop Wetherbee, and Thomas D. Hill are representative of this skepticism and, with George D. Economou, reflect in different ways the notion of "naturalism" or "generation" as Jean's imperative. Fleming has presented his position more fully in a recent book, *Reason and the Lover.*

For help with corrections and many other matters I am grateful to John Benton, Alfred David, John Fleming, and Maxwell Luria. Mistakes and infelicities that remain are my responsibility.

Queens College, CUNY   C. D.
May 1983; revised October 1986

BIBLIOGRAPHICAL SUPPLEMENT

This supplement contains works referred to in Preface to the 1983 Edition and in a note to lines 10830–31. For fuller bibliography, see Maxwell Luria's *Reader's Guide*.

Badel, Pierre-Yves. *Le Roman de la Rose au XIVe siècle: Etude de la réception de l'œuvre*. Geneva: Droz, 1980.

Baird, Joseph L., and John R. Kane. *La Querelle de la Rose: Letters and Documents*. Chapel Hill: University of North Carolina Press, 1978. English translations.

Cherniss, Michael D. "Irony and Authority: The Ending of the *Roman de la Rose*." *Modern Language Quarterly*, 36 (1975), 227–38.

———. "Jean de Meun's Reson and Boethius." *Romance Notes*, 16 (1975), 678–85.

David, Alfred. "How Marcia Lost Her Skin: A Note on Chaucer's Mythology." *The Learned and the Lewed* (B. J. Whiting Festschrift), ed. Larry D. Benson (Cambridge: Harvard University Press, 1974), pp. 19–29.

Economou, George D. *The Goddess Natura in Medieval Literature*. Cambridge: Harvard University Press, 1972.

Fleming, John V. *Reason and the Lover*. Princeton: University Press, 1984.

Fleming 1965, 1969. See p. 432.

Guillaume de Lorris and Jean de Meun. *Le Roman de la Rose, traduction en français moderne*. Trans. André Lanly. 3 vols. Paris: Champion, 1971–76.

———. *Der Rosenroman*. Ed. and trans. Karl A. Ott. 3 vols. Munich: Fink, 1976–79. Edition with facing German translation.

Hicks, Eric, ed. *Le Débat sur le Roman de la Rose*. Paris: Champion, 1977. Edition and French translation of documents by Christine de Pisan, Jean Gerson, Jean de Montreuil, Gontier Col, and Pierre Col.

Hill, Thomas D. "Narcissus, Pygmalion, and the Castration of Saturn: Two Mythographical Themes in the *Roman de la Rose*." *Studies in Philology*, 71 (1974), 404–26.

Jauss, Hans Robert. "Entstehung und Strukturwandel der allegorischen Dichtung." *La littérature didactique, allégorique, et satirique*, ed. Hans Robert Jauss, 2 vols., Grundriss der romanischen Literaturen des Mittelalters, vol. 6, parts 1 and 2 (Heidelberg: Carl Winter, 1968–70), 1:146–244, with bibliography in 2:203–80.

———. "La transformation de la forme allégorique entre 1180 et 1240: d'Alain de Lille à Guillaume de Lorris." *L'humanisme médiéval dans* *les littératures romanes du XIIe au XIVe siècles* (Paris: Klincksieck, 1964), pp. 107–42. Has references to his earlier articles of 1960 and 1962.

Jung, Marc-René. *Etudes sur le poème allégorique en France au moyen âge.* Berne: Francke, 1971.

————. "Der Rosenroman in der Kritik seit dem 18. Jahrhundert." *Romanische Forschungen,* 78 (1966), 203–52.

Lanly 1971–76. See Guillaume de Lorris... 1971–76.

Louis, René. *Le Roman de la Rose: Essai d'interprétation de l'allégorisme érotique.* Paris: Champion, 1974.

Luria, Maxwell. *A Reader's Guide to the Roman de la Rose.* Hamden, Conn.: Archon, 1982.

————. "A Sixteenth-Century Gloss on the *Roman de la Rose.*" *Mediaeval Studies,* 44 (1982), 333–70. Edition, with commentary, of the glosses in MS. Philadelphia Museum of Art, Collins Collection, 45–65–3.

Ott 1976–79. See Guillaume de Lorris ... 1976–79.

Payen, Jean-Charles. *La Rose et l'Utopie.* Paris: Editions sociales, 1976.

Piehler, Paul. *The Visionary Landscape: A Study in Medieval Allegory.* London: Arnold, 1971.

Poirion, Daniel. *Le Roman de la Rose.* Paris: Hatier, 1973.

Potansky, Peter. *Der Streit um den Rosenroman.* Munich: Fink, 1972.

Quarrel (querelle, débat, Streit) of the *Roman de la Rose.* See Baird and Kane; Hicks; Potansky.

Roman de la Rose. Editions and translations. See Guillaume de Lorris ... 1971–76, 1976–79.

Took, John. "Towards an Interpretation of the *Fiore.*" *Speculum,* 54 (1979), 500–527.

Uitti Karl D. "The Myth of Poetry in Twelfth- and Thirteenth-Century France." *The Binding of Proteus: Perspectives on Myth and the Literary Process* (Colloquium ... Bucknell), ed. Marjorie W. McCune, Tucker Orbison, and Philip M. Withim (Lewisburg, Pa.: Bucknell University Press, 1980), pp. 142–56.

Wetherbee, Winthrop. "The Literal and the Allegorical: Jean de Meun and the *De Planctu Naturae.*" *Mediaeval Studies,* 33 (1971), 264–91.

————. *Platonism and Poetry in the Twelfth Century: The Literary Influence of the School of Chartres.* Princeton: University Press, 1972.

Zumthor, Paul. "Narrative and Anti-Narrative: Le Roman de la Rose." *Yale French Studies,* 51 (1974), 185–204. Trans. Frank Youmans from "Récit et anti-récit: Le *Roman de la Rose,*" *Medioevo Romanzo,* I (1973) 5–24. See also his *Essai de poétique médiévale.* Paris: du Seuil, 1972.

INTRODUCTION

𝒯HE *Romance of the Rose* was, for nearly three hundred years after its composition in the thirteenth century, one of the most widely read works of the French language. Since French was the official language of the English court for many years, it was nearly as important there as in France. The decline of its popularity after the sixteenth century can be attributed to a major shift in taste, one in which allegory came to be regarded as a somewhat simplistic, arbitrary vehicle for pious works. Recently, a renewed interest in medieval allegory, beginning perhaps with C. S. Lewis's *Allegory of Love* in 1936, has prompted a revaluation of the poem which sees it as a serious work of art that offers rich rewards to the attention of modern readers.

THE TWO AUTHORS

The *Romance* exists in two portions of unequal length, composed by the two authors at more than a forty-year interval. Our evidence for their authorship, even for much of their lives, comes largely from the poem itself. The first 4058 lines are by Guillaume de Lorris, who, according to his name, was born in Lorris, a village east of Orléans; the longer portion (4059-21780) is by Jean de Meun. In a long speech (10495-678), Jean has the God of Love tell us that Guillaume began the *Romance* but died before he had finished it. Then, more than forty years later, says the God of Love, Jean Chopinel, born in Meung-sur-Loire (a village southwest of Orléans), will continue the story.

The poem refers further (6631-740) to a contemporary struggle between Charles of Anjou and his opponents, Manfred and Conradin, for the Kingdom of Sicily; and it assumes in line 6643 (Charles "is now king of Sicily") that Charles is still alive. Jean's continuation must therefore have been written between 1268, the year of the struggle, and 1285, the year of Charles's death. The most recent editor of the poem, Félix Lecoy, has also pointed out that lines 12130-38, at least, must have been drafted before 1274; for the Friars of the Sack, referred to at 12137, were suppressed by the Council of Lyon in that year and were probably absorbed by the Augustinians.[1] An approximate date of 1275 will serve for this portion and 1230-35 for Guillaume's portion, written more than forty years before.

Both authors came from the neighborhood of Orléans, "the center of humanistic studies" during the first half of the thirteenth century.[2] We know no more of Guillaume than the poem tells us, but Jean apparently migrated to Paris, the dominant intellectual center during his lifetime, when "literary studies had declined" in Orléans.[3] He was undoubtedly connected in one way or another with the University of Paris; we are reasonably certain that he lived from 1292 until his death in 1305 in a house on the Rue Saint-Jacques, about a kilometer from the Seine and a few hundred yards from the house where in 1253 Robert de Sorbon had established a college for poor theology students of the University of Paris, the house that has metamorphosed into the Sorbonne, the present-day Faculties of Letters and Sciences of the University.[4]

Jean produced other works besides the continuation of the *Romance*. Manuscript tradition attributes to him a *Testament* and *Codicile*, both presumably late works written after his translation of Boethius. In the Preface to this work, *Li Livres de Confort de Philosophie*, he lists the following translations: Vegetius's book on *Chivalry*, the book of *The Marvels of Ireland* (by Giraud de Barri), the *Letters of Abelard and Eloise*, and the book *On Spiritual Friendship* by Aelred of Rievaulx.[5] Of these, three survive, the Boethius, the Vegetius, and the *Letters*. Boethius is an important influence on the *Romance*, and Aelred's conception of friendship and natural love parallels that offered by Jean through the character Reason (4686 ff., 5763 ff.).

THE UNITY OF THE
TWO PARTS

The existence of two authors separated in time gave rise quite naturally to the question of whether or not the two parts form a unified whole. The question had not disturbed earlier critics, but

---

[1] Lecoy 1968. The Sack Friars did not, however, disappear as quickly as Lecoy suggests, since the order continued, without novices, and the Paris house of the order existed until at least 1289. See Emery 1960.

[2] Paëtow 1914, p. 17. [3] Ibid., p. 18.

[4] Lecoy 1965, p. viii. [5] Jean de Meun 1952, p. 168.

in the nineteenth century the obvious disparity in the length of the
two parts, the differences in scale and style of treatment, and perhaps the unconscious assumption of the uniqueness of the individual
literary artist led to the now conventional judgment that Guillaume
and Jean were opposed in intent and treatment.[6] This attitude sees
the earlier part, by Guillaume, as a joyous celebration of "courtly
love," fresh and lyrical, and the longer second portion, by Jean
de Meun, as an "anti-Guillaume," a brilliant, but encyclopedic and
digressive, denunciation of the ideals of courtly love and a celebration of a naturalistic doctrine of a sort of philosophical liber-
tinism. Gérard Paré's *Les Idées et les lettres au XIIIe siècle*, a
detailed analysis of the *Romance* in the light of scholastic terminology, is perhaps the leading recent exposition of this viewpoint.
For English readers, C. S. Lewis's *Allegory of Love* was a most
influential study of "courtly love" and its allegorical vehicles in
poetry from Chrétien de Troyes to Spenser; and his treatment of
the *Romance* has given wide currency to the notion of a fundamental opposition in the two parts of the poem.[7]

A major challenge to this position came from Alan Gunn, in a
Princeton dissertation later expanded and published as *The Mirror
of Love*. Gunn argued that the poem was unified as a treatise on
love, that Jean de Meun understood Guillaume's purpose, and
that he fulfilled it in a greatly amplified continuation, an extended
psychomachia or "grand debate" in which the various personifications reflect the poet's conflicting attitudes on the subject of love.[8]
For Gunn, this "love" is essentially the sexual union symbolized by
the rose; and he relates the poem's development to a "philosophy
of plenitude" which involves the continued regeneration of species,
including man. Although Gunn sees unity, he does not, as we shall
see, distinguish between the opinions of the characters and those of
the poets.

A more radical challenge was that of D. W. Robertson, Jr.,
who in 1951 characterized the *Romance* as "a humorous and witty
retelling of the story of the Fall."[9] Through analysis of the tradi-

---

[6] See, for example, Paulin Paris 1856; Gaston Paris 1914; Faral 1926;
Thuasne 1929; Lewis 1936; Cohn 1961; Hatzfeld 1962.

[7] For further detail, see Dahlberg 1961.

[8] Gunn 1952, pp. 21-22 and *passim*.

[9] Robertson 1951, p. 43. Cf. Robertson 1962, pp. 91-104, 196-207, and
elsewhere.

tional associations of the garden imagery of the poem, he established a framework for understanding the subject of love in terms of Christian doctrine. In 1961 I followed Robertson in suggesting that, different as the two authors are in style, they had a common understanding of their material and its allegorical trend, and that a coherently developed structural pattern stems from this common understanding, a pattern based upon the traditional analysis of the Fall: suggestion to sense, delight of the heart, and consent of reason.[10] Evidence of a basic allegorical intent lies in the opening of the poem, where Guillaume cites Macrobius as one "who did not take dreams as trifles"; for an examination of Macrobius's doctrine on dream-allegory leads to the conclusion that Guillaume's citation indicates that he is using a fabulous narrative (*narratio fabulosa*) to conceal, and reveal, an art or developed doctrine of love. In such an art, the clear sexual symbolism of the rose has its place as one of the kinds of love. But to interpret the poem simply as an erotic dream would violate the Macrobian and medieval concept of dream-allegory. Macrobius puts erotic dreams into the category of nightmares, which are "not worth interpreting," and Jean de Meun develops this idea of Macrobius in a passage in the sermon of Nature (18343-424). The citation of Macrobius's doctrine by the two authors indicates a scheme in which the sexual symbolism gains its significance from its relationship to other kinds of love.

Recent work has tended to reinforce the idea that the poem is unified. In her last book, Rosemond Tuve presented a detailed and convincing analysis of Jean de Meun's allegorical technique and in doing so came independently to conclusions that parallel those of Robertson.[11] John Fleming, in an important recent book, has studied the poem anew in the light of the manuscript illuminations and its early literary reputation and has supported the notion that the poem shows a basic unity.[12] Both of these books emphasize the element of irony in the poem, and this emphasis, important in itself, may point at the same time to a major source of difference among those who have written about the poem, the varying attitudes taken toward its irony.

[10] Dahlberg 1961.
[11] Tuve 1966, pp. 232-80, particularly pp. 262-63, n.
[12] Fleming 1969.

THE TECHNIQUE OF IRONY

The recognition of irony can never depend solely upon the close examination of the text; it must arise from the acceptance of a set of values or assumptions that are necessarily implicit. Swift's *Modest Proposal* exists as irony only because of certain implicit moral assumptions about infanticide and cannibalism. While such acceptance is still relatively easy in the case of *A Modest Proposal*, it is by no means so in that of the *Romance*, where the proposition that a young lover in pursuit of *pudendum* is necessarily not only funny but irrational, and therefore sinful, is a very difficult one for an age whose ideas on what is funny, rational, and sinful differ markedly from those of the thirteenth century. Yet the *Romance* goes much farther than does *A Modest Proposal* in elaborating the assumptions that are necessary to its understanding. Much of this elaboration occurs in Reason's discourse, and the failure to take seriously the implications of what she says has allowed most critics of the last century to take overseriously the discourses of other characters—Friend, the Old Woman, Genius, for example—and to conclude that such characters express the poets' opinions. This somewhat uncritical assumption lies at the root, it seems to me, of the major difficulties in understanding the poem. Paré's discussion of the poem's "philosophie de la vie religieuse" tends to equate the characters with the poet, Jean, and to see irony, strangely enough, only in his direct statements that his remarks do not apply to the truly religious (15195-302, 11017-22).[13] Gunn regards the speeches of the various characters as externalizations of the Lover's—and presumably the poet's—inner turmoil, as contributions to a "grand debate" that presents Jean's composite view of love as a principle of plenitude. Thus he takes the Old Woman's opposition to the religious life, on the ground that it destroys natural liberty, as an expression of the poet's view (13967-78).[14]

Robertson, Tuve, and Fleming provide the major exceptions to this tendency.[15] They do not assume such general identity between

---

[13] Paré 1947, pp. 187-90. Cf. his Chapter VII (298-346), which has the same basic assumption that Jean expresses his own ideas directly through his characters.

[14] Gunn 1952, pp. 363-65, 374-95, 468, and elsewhere.

[15] Cf. Tuve, p. 249 n.; Fleming, pp. 50-53, 69, 110; Robertson, as cited above; Friedman 1959; Dahlberg 1969, pp. 568, 583-84.

the poet and his character; Reason seems to be the only unexceptionable voice, but even she exists *primarily* as an allegorical character, however much the poets may favor her. In other words, we may learn more about the poem by taking it in its own terms than by trying to see it in the light of unprovable assumptions about the authors' subjective identification with their characters. By following such a procedure, these three critics have found that irony is a basic literary technique in the poem, a device that fulfills the allegorical intent that Guillaume establishes at the very beginning with his citation of Macrobius. It may be worthwhile to call attention in further detail to the pervasiveness of this technique in both parts of the poem.[16]

At the point where the God of Love is about to give his commandments, there is a passage (2057-76) which shows how Guillaume establishes an ironic framework, in an apparently straightforward address to the reader-listener, through a series of shifts in point of view between the poet and the Lover, the character that the poet has created. The passage opens with the point of view of the Lover ("The God of Love then charged me"), but immediately establishes that of the poet ("exactly as you have heard"), shifts back to the Lover's ("word for word, with his commandments") and again to the poet's ("This romance portrays them well"), where it remains to the end of the passage. The effect is to establish a distinction between the two points of view that encourages the reader to examine critically whatever the Lover says from another perspective, that of the poet. Thus the poet's exhortation to "those who wish to love" slyly echoes the Lover's point of view in a mock-appeal to those who want to love in the way that the Lover does; but it suggests that there are other ways of loving when it speaks of the dream's true significance, which is to be revealed as the *Romance* progresses. Guillaume echoes his opening lines when he says "the truth, which is hidden, will be quite open to you when you hear me explain this dream, for it doesn't contain a lying word."

The statement, however, is both direct and ironic. It is ironic in that the entire romance is a literary lie, an example of Macrobius's *narratio fabulosa*. It is true in that a *narratio fabulosa* may

---

[16] For fuller elaboration of irony in the poem as a whole, see Fleming, *passim*.

conceal truth; if so, the dream type is the *somnium*. But this particular dream, on its first level of allegorical significance, is an erotic dream, the kind that Macrobius puts in the category of *insomnium*, or nightmare, and labels as "not worth interpreting."[17] In the sense of erotic dream, then, the *Romance* is deceiving. Thus Guillaume's statement becomes doubly ironic as well as direct in a basic sense.

For a parallel passage in which Jean de Meun speaks on this primary, apparently direct level, we may turn to lines 15133-302. Earlier, at 15103, it is clearly the Lover's voice that we hear: "The porters would have killed me without fail if the men of the host had not come." Now, as prologue to his mock-heroic battle between the forces of the God of Love and those of the castle of Jealousy, Jean switches abruptly to the voice of the poet: "From now on we will come to the battle. . . . Listen now, loyal lovers. . . ." Apparently unlike Guillaume, he does not shift point of view quickly back and forth so as to establish the binocular perspective which reveals in depth the layers of direct and ironic utterance; but in fact, Jean uses the same technique in a different form by transferring the Lover's voice to the poet and by setting up the contrast in such a way that the poet, now with two voices instead of one, can say things both directly and ironically.[18]

Thus the command "Listen now, loyal lovers, so that the God of Love may help you" shows the voice of the poet and the point of view of the Lover; but the iconographical detail which follows, that of the dogs pursuing the rabbit, forces us back to another point of view, a traditional one which sees the detail as symbolic of the sexual hunt of Venus and contrasts it with Adonis's sterner hunt of the boar, the more difficult pursuit of charity, a different kind of love.[19] The ironic contrast between the two points of view continues throughout the passage and reaches a hilarious climax in Jean's protest that he does not write against good women or the good religious and that he submits his work to the judgment of Holy Church (15195-302). This is the passage that Paré thinks ironic and that Pierre Col considered the only one in which Jean

---

[17] Dahlberg 1961, pp. 575-76, citing Macrobius 1952, I. ii-iii (for the Latin text, see Macrobius 1962).

[18] Jean uses the technique elsewhere; cf., e.g., 15751-64.

[19] Fleming 1969, pp. 186-87, citing Arnulfe d'Orléans in Ghisalberti 1932, p. 223. See also 15138-42 n., 15675-750 n.

spoke directly in his own person. My own reading agrees funda-
mentally with that of Col, but even in this most nearly direct of
passages, Jean's wit sparkles with continued ironies. The important
task is to separate the strains of direct and ironic utterance and to
see how they complement each other.

The poet can state his intention directly:

> . . . my writing . . . is all for our instruction. . . . We have
> set these things down in writing so that we can gain knowl-
> edge. . . . It is good to know everything. . . . For, as the text
> witnesses, the whole intent of the poets is profit and delight.
> . . . I take my bow and bend it . . . to recognize . . . the un-
> lawful people. . . . And if I make any utterance that Holy
> Church may consider foolish, I am ready at her wish to
> change it if I am capable of making the change.

Yet even here there is an echo of the Lover's voice in the idea
that the "instruction" is in erotic love; but the echo stands in
ironic contrast to the Horatian context of profit and delight, and
such "instruction" could only appear trivial to Holy Church.
Moreover, these passages mingle with others that reinforce them
through further irony:

> I pray all you *worthy* women [are there many?] . . . please
> do not blame me. . . . I certainly never said anything . . .
> against any woman *alive* [but rather against abstractions, sins
> rather than sinners]. . . . Besides, *honorable* ladies, . . . don't
> consider me a *liar*, but [understand the nature of a literary
> fiction, a "fable," and] apply to the authors who . . . have
> written the things that I have said and will say. I shall never
> *lie* in anything [except of course in the persons of my char-
> acters and in the fact that this entire poem is an elaborate
> literary lie, a fabulous narrative]. . . . It was never my in-
> tention to speak against any *living* man who follows holy
> religion [False Seeming is not living, but a personification
> of abstract evil, again, sins not sinners].

In short, the poet, through his two voices and through the ironic
echoes set up by his technique, can say the same things both directly
and ironically.

Such complexity exists on the simplest level, that of the first-person narrator, Dreamer or Lover, through whose voice alone we hear those of the other characters. To take even this voice as consistently that of the poet is dangerously misleading; to take those of the other characters as such is to compound the danger of abandoning the literary controls that the two poets have established. Lionel Friedman, in his 1959 article, " 'Jean de Meung,' Antifeminism, and 'Bourgeois Realism,' " revealed this danger through an analysis of lines 9155-56: " ' "All you women are, will be, and have been whores, in fact or in desire." ' " The passage comes from the speech of the Jealous Husband, which forms part of the discourse of Friend; we are three narrative levels away from the poet, let alone Jean de Meun, and to ascribe this sentiment to him is to invite contradiction with other portions of the poem—the passage cited above, for example—and to ignore the primary critical task. Even if it were Jean's opinion, how that opinion operates in this context must be our question; and Fleming has shown that the words form part of the tirade of a character whom Friend introduces to "illustrate the rightness of his views on the marital hierarchy," but who instead "exemplifies evils which arise from its breakdown or inversion as its chains snap with the forces of passion and avarice."[20]

A parallel case of a speech at four removes from Jean de Meun is that of the wife who worms her husband's secrets from him (16402-536). It occurs in Genius's long discourse on, and offers a specific example of, the vices of women. That speech occurs just as Nature is about to confess to her "priest," Genius, and it postpones her confession by some 400 lines. Jean de Meun would certainly have been either inept or feeble-minded if he wrote this section with no intent of irony. Genius starts by calling Nature "My lady, queen of the world"; says that he believes her misdeed a great one; anticipates the confession by assuming that the misdeed is one committed *against* her and warns her against the "feminine" vice of wrath; goes on from there to an increasingly vehement warning against the vices of women (the wife's speech is exemplary of such vices); and wanders finally into a warning, not to his interlocutor, Nature, but to "Fair lords," to protect themselves from women (sleep with them but don't talk to them). At 16701 Jean de Meun disingenuously "remembered" that Genius was

---

[20] Fleming 1969, pp. 155-57.

speaking to Nature and has him say that he had not said these things on her account. But of course he had. Certainly this passage establishes the proper comic tone for the parody of religion that Fleming has characterized neatly as "a spectacle of Nature making a 'confession' which is not a confession of a 'sin' which is not a sin to a 'confessor' who is not a confessor."[21] It also serves at the outset to establish the nature of the parody by assuring the reader of Genius's false credentials. His discourse on women parallels that of Friend, and both make similar use of the Golden Age motif.[22]

With no historical basis for accusing Jean de Meun of holding the varied opinions of all his characters and with a clear literary basis for discarding such an assumption, it becomes possible to see the play of ironies directed toward the consistent development of a theme. However hilarious they become, they are directed, more simply in Guillaume's case, more elaborately in Jean's, toward the revelation of the Lover's headstrong folly in his pursuit of the rose-sanctuary-*con*.

STYLE AND THEME

That characters in a literary work should voice opinions appropriate to them rather than to their creator is an elementary matter of literary decorum, the neglect of which may lead to mistaken history as well as questionable criticism. There is another aspect of decorum—stylistic decorum—which is less well recognized in, but central to, our understanding and evaluation of the *Romance*; in this case the principle involved has become so much a part of our literary folklore that it is a neglected cliché: the notion that a sublime subject may gain strength from a simple style. We forget that the principle may lead to a corollary: a seemingly inappropriate surface may call attention to and strengthen a theme of great importance.

Erich Auerbach has called our attention to the difference between this and the classical notion of stylistic decorum and has identified Augustine of Hippo, convert from classical rhetoric to Christianity, as the theoretician and practitioner of this new kind of rhetoric.[23] In the *Christian Doctrine*, Augustine recognized the three traditional Ciceronian levels of style but rejected the principle of

---

[21] Ibid., p. 207.   [22] See 8355-9664 n., 20033 n.
[23] Auerbach 1965, pp. 27-66.

decorum which assigned each to a corresponding category of subject matter. The reason for this important change in rhetorical theory was that the "Christian orator's subject is always Christian revelation, and this can never be base or in-between."[24] As a result, the "humblest" things could be treated in a sublime style and, conversely, the most "elevated" in a simple style. Auerbach points out that such a development arises from the Christian conception of the fusion of the humble and sublime in Christ's Incarnation and Passion, a fusion which confounds traditional categories and establishes a mode of discourse that affected Christian literature throughout the Middle Ages.[25] The *Divine Comedy*, of course, is Auerbach's candidate for "the greatest document of this Christian sublimity."

Yet Dante's poem may be less apt than the *Romance of the Rose* as an illustration of the new principle of decorum to which Auerbach has called our attention, for in the classical categories, "the comic and frivolously erotic, the satirical, realistic, and obscene" were all "subjects . . . assigned to the lowest class."[26] The appearance of such subjects in the *Romance* has misled modern critics into applying the Ciceronian rather than the Augustinian principle of decorum and, as a result, into regarding the *Romance* and the *Comedy* as antithetical. Yet, as John Fleming points out, Laurent de Premierfait (ca. 1400) thought that the *Romance* was the actual model for the *Comedy*.[27] Although Laurent was probably wrong historically, his reasons for thinking so are important: Jean painted a *mappemonde* of all things in heaven and earth; in his book there is a full description of the heaven of the good and the hell of the wicked. Clearly Laurent implies that the two poems are alike in meaning, not in form.[28] He is judging the similarity on the basis of the Augustinian rather than the Ciceronian principle of decorum. In Ciceronian terms, the *Romance* is at best a great satire, but to consider it only as that is to neglect the Augustinian possibility of conveying an elevated theme in such a manner. The corollary is also true: the humor cannot exist without the serious background that gives it point.

---

[24] Ibid., p. 35. See Augustine, *On Christian Doctrine*, IV. xvii-xix (34-38), trans. Robertson 1958, pp. 142-46.

[25] Auerbach 1957, pp. 131-32; 1965, pp. 65-66.

[26] Auerbach 1965, p. 37.   [27] Fleming 1969, pp. 17-19.

[28] Ibid., p. 20.

It is probably such a principle that can be of greatest help in understanding both the nature of the poem's unity and the basis of its ironic technique. It would also account most readily for the stylistic distinction between the two parts, a distinction that Fleming has characterized as a shift from predominantly iconographical abstraction in Guillaume's poem toward an increasing degree of verisimilar exemplification in Jean's portion.[29] Note that Jean's *exempla* are no less iconographic than Guillaume's abstractions; the style changes but the theme remains unified. It is to that theme, and its linear development, that we must now turn.

THE THEME OF LOVE

It is a commonplace, often neglected, that love is a central doctrine of Christianity and, as a theme, occupies a dominant place in much medieval poetry. Guillaume and Jean are quite explicit about the centrality of this theme, and interpretation diverges principally over the question of the variety of love which controls the poem's development. I have argued elsewhere that traditional Christian analyses of love offer the best background for our understanding of the theme and its structural development.[30] They offer a range of definition that at the same time gives a comprehensive background for Reason's treatment of the subject, accounts most satisfactorily for the linear articulation of the poem's parts, provides a spacious framework for possibilities of ironic technique within the allegory, and justifies the authors' Macrobian concept of dream-allegory as a literary form.

These traditional analyses had encouraged an important ambiguity in the use of the word *amor*. At least from the time of Augustine, this term—and often the term *dilectio*—came to be used for both charity and cupidity. Alanus de Insulis reflects this tradition when, in his *Distinctiones dictionum theologicalium*, he defines *amor*, "in the strict sense," as cupidity, but also as charity, as the Holy Spirit, as Christ, and, most importantly, as "natural affection."[31] This natural affection is the "other love, a natural one," that Reason describes to the Lover (5763 ff.). Although, as she suggests, the Lover is not interested in this love, it is his starting

---

[29] Ibid., pp. 29-32.   [30] Dahlberg 1961, 1969.
[31] *PL* 210, col. 699. Cf. *Regulae Theologicae*, cols. 673-74; *Summa de arte praedicatoria*, cols. 152-53.

point, even for the cupidinous course that he pursues; it can lead upward to charity or downward to cupidity. This position is Augustinian and Boethian, but the idea that the love of God is natural and that it begins in just such a natural love is of great antiquity and was given a special impetus in the twelfth century by Saint Bernard and his Cistercian followers. Thus, in Bernard's *De diligendo Deo*, we find that love is one of the four passions given us by nature, that it is, in its first degree, a carnal love, by which man loves himself for himself.[32]

There is reason to think that this basic concept is important to Jean and to the poem. Reason says that Nature has given this love to man and beast and that it has no merit in itself and deserves neither praise nor blame (5764, 5770-80). Jean also takes over the figures of Nature and Genius from Alanus, a fact that gives "nature" a prominent place in relation to love. And the development of the poem places these figures at the service of the Lover's self-seeking interpretation of the function of natural love. If it may lead in two directions, there is no mistaking the direction that the Lover wants it to take. Jean's use of Alanus's oxymoronic description of love (4293 ff.) shows his awareness of the opposites generated by this natural force in man. In a mounting series of oppositions Reason says that love is a sin touched by pardon but a pardon stained by sin (4315-16). Although this is clearly a description of the torments of cupidinous love, it reflects the other kinds that Alanus had spoken of in his *Distinctiones*.

Reason's exposition is thus firmly rooted in the tradition represented in Alanus's types of love. After the opening description from Alanus's *Complaint of Nature*, Reason gives Andreas Capellanus's definition from the *De amore*, a definition of cupidinous love (4377-88), and contrasts this love with the legitimate wish to continue one's divine self through propagation by taking the delight that Nature has implanted in order to ensure the continuation of the species.[33] She tells the Lover that the love which holds him is not this legitimate natural love but one which holds out to him the prospect of carnal delight (4600-28, 5789-94). When the Lover asks for elaboration, Reason explains other varieties of love.

---

[32] *PL* 182, cols. 987-88. Cf. Aelred of Rievaulx, *De spirituali amicitia*, *PL* 195, col. 663; Pierre de Blois 1932, pp. 124-26.

[33] For the Augustinian parallel, see 4403-21 n.

First she gives the definition of charity according to the concept of *amitié*, and she indicates that she wishes the Lover to follow this love and avoid the other that she has described at length (4685-768). She then describes (4769 ff.) another kind of cupidity, the love which arises from the desire for gain, the love which comes from Fortune (4783) and causes men to love the rich (4803-8). Those who follow it subject themselves to Fortune, and he who does so is a wretched, naïve fool, for, as Boethius says, earth is not our country (4837-5040). A long passage on this love leads Reason to advise the Lover to renounce loving *par amour* (5369). Next, in response to the Lover's objection that the good love to which she counsels him has been impossible on earth since the giants put the gods to flight (5375-433), Reason counsels him to practice this love by loving generally rather than particularly, by loving what is common to all and by acting in accord with the Golden Rule (5434-58). There follows a discussion on Justice; it derives its force from charity, but judges have become corrupt (5459-692).

After a short passage, Reason closes her explanation of the kinds of love with the definition of natural love, common to man and beast, that we have examined as the starting point for other kinds of love. The passage serves as a bridge between the explanation of the different kinds of love (4293-5794) and an extended development of the unreasonableness of the love of Fortune (5795-6900). After she tells the Lover that she knows that he is not interested in the natural love (5789-94), Reason advises him to take her as his sweetheart and contrasts the love of reason with that of fortune and of the God of Love (5842-46, 6884-90); to establish the contrast, she develops the theme of Fortune with many examples and an extensive borrowing (5921-6172) of the description of Fortune's dwelling in Alanus de Insulis's *Anticlaudianus*.

If we grant that Reason's discussion of love presents its kinds in terms of a series of contrasting definitions, with a transitional definition of the natural love from which the others begin, and a long recapitulation in terms of the love of Fortune, we must still see clearly that among these loves, that of the Lover is a cupidinous love, not the "simple physiological function" that in itself is neutral. There is ample evidence that it is cupidinous. Reason identifies his love as foolish (e.g., 2997-3072, 4147-50, 4242, 10249-60), and she is seen throughout the poem as opposed to the love which the Lover follows. At the close, when the Lover possesses his rose, he says that he did not remember Reason, who had given him a lot of trouble for nothing (21760-61). Taken literally, the Lover's desire for the rose is the classic form of cupidity, a love of an earthly object for its own sake rather than for the sake of God. The linear progress of that desire through the poem follows the pattern of cupidinous love, the love inspired by Cupid, the poem's God of Love.

It was Robertson who first identified that pattern with the Fall,[34] that prototypical sin which was thought to fall into three parts, corresponding to the three protagonists: suggestion to sense (Satan), delight of the heart (Eve), and consent of the reason (Adam). Such an analysis is commonplace in medieval thought;[35] and in the *Romance*, the process is suggested by Jean's use, in the speech of Reason, of Andreas's definition of love (4377-84): Love is a malady of thought (reason), coming from an ardor (delight) born of disturbed vision (sense).[36] In this process, the important feature is that there is a reversal of the right ordering of the faculties: where Reason, the image of God, should govern the body and the senses, it is governed by them. The first of these three steps, suggestion or involvement of the senses, is strongly indicated by the dreamer's experience up to the time when the God of Love pursues him. The imagery of Chapter 1 emphasizes the role of sense impressions. Sight images predominate and underline the idea that love begins with sight, "disordinate glances." The two crystal stones in the fountain of Narcissus suggest the eyes, and Sweet Looks is the name of the allegorical character who carries the two bows and ten arrows for the God of Love (904-84). Five of the arrows encourage love and five others discourage it. The series of the five encouraging arrows, while it does not correspond in detail to the series of the five bodily senses, begins and ends with names that suggest sight. Beauty, lying in the beholder's eye, leads through advancing degrees of intimacy—Simplicity, Openness, Company—to the subjective sight impression of Fair Seeming.

It is from the sight of the mirrored image of the rosebush in the

---

[34] Robertson 1951, p. 43.   [35] Dahlberg 1961, p. 578 n.
[36] Cf. Robertson 1953, pp. 152-53.

Narcissus-fountain that the Lover conceives the "ardor" which leads to his "malady of thought." The second stage, delight of the heart, is objectified by the passage describing the pursuit and capture of the Lover by the God of Love. The arrows pierce his heart, usually entering the eye in the traditional manner. When the Lover has received five arrows, the God of Love announces, "Vassal, you are taken!" (1884), and the Lover performs the act of homage in the best feudal fashion, kneeling before his captor with joined hands and receiving the kiss on the mouth (1955-57). With his catechism of love, the course of his "ardor" is well begun. But all is not yet lost, since his reason is not involved. After a temporary repulse in his quest, Reason admonishes him, but he refuses to follow her counsel and returns to his quest, only to be repulsed again and to find himself in despair.

Such is the structure of Guillaume's poem, a structure in which the progression of imagery and narrative is seen most coherently as a succession of stages of involvement in sin. Jean de Meun, in finishing the poem, has developed the third stage, the involvement of reason, at great length, and the effect of his detailed and leisurely elaboration is to enlarge the scope and significance of the fundamental issues of Guillaume's poem. He performs this feat principally by the introduction of personifications who illuminate the process of the overthrow of reason from several standpoints and who serve as reflectors of the inner state of the Lover as he continues in his rejection of Reason.[37]

Recently, Lionel Friedman has suggested that the progress of the *Romance* corresponds to the five steps of love—sight, conversation, touching, kissing, and *factum* (or *coitus*)—of a very widespread tradition that appears in Alanus as well as elsewhere. Guillaume, he says, "leads the lover up four of the five steps," and "Jean took over at the stage of *factum*." The topos of the five steps, the *gradus amoris*, thus "served to order the narrative sequence in the *Roman de la Rose* within the conventions of personification."[38] Clearly this is a significant parallel tradition that reinforces that of the three-step analysis above.[39] Jean himself says

[37] Cf. Tuve 1966, pp. 239, 259.

[38] Friedman 1965, pp. 174, 175, 177. See note to 924-25, 935 ff.

[39] See Fleming 1969, pp. 99-103. For another parallel tradition, that of the five bodily senses and five spiritual senses, arranged in two different

in the Preface to his translation of Boethius that in the *Romance* he had "taught the way to seize the castle and pluck the rose."[40] Even in addressing his king, Jean reflects the irony of his poem, for an essential part of his teaching method was to establish first the intellectual framework which gives point and significance to the Lover's *factum,* and the first of the personifications that he uses for this purpose is Reason, that faculty involved in the third of the three steps.

It is Reason who uses Andreas's three-step definition of love, who establishes firmly the context for the understanding of the poem when she speaks of the different kinds of love at the same time that, in doing so, she is fighting a losing battle for the Lover. The Lover's rejection of Reason (6901-27) has amusing consequences in the passage immediately following, where he objects to her use of the word *testicles* (coilles). This hilarious passage shows one aspect of his prudish irrationality. He had shown the same attitude before (5697-724), and he later chooses his own euphemisms for penis and testicles, the pilgrim's staff and sack of two hammers (21346 ff.), and thus fulfills the God of Love's prohibition against *ribaudie* (2109-14). The Lover's rejection of "the sentences, fables, and metaphors of the poets" (7190-92) is a literary extension of this literalist attitude and parallels False Seeming's position (11216); in fact, False Seeming objectifies the Lover's attitude of pretense.[41]

Next, Friend appears to abet the Lover in his rejection of reason and to further the course of his love. His worldly advice, at first repugnant to the Lover (7795-818), establishes the pattern that he follows subsequently when the God of Love assembles the barons for their assault on the Castle of Jealousy. Friend's counsels of deceit and trickery, a mockery of true friendship, become more and more grotesque and bear fruit in the figures of False Seeming and the Old Woman. These passages, often thought of as digressive displays of Jean's encyclopedic erudition, are in fact central

---

orientations, toward charity or cupidity, see Dahlberg 1969, pp. 575-76, citing Davy 1953, p. 97, n. 1; Rahner 1933; Augustine, *Sermo CLIX,* iv (4), *PL* 38, col. 869; Guillaume de Saint-Thierry, *De natura et dignitate amoris,* ed. Davy 1953, p. 94; Saint Bernard of Clairvaux, *Sermo X de diversis,* 2-4, *PL* 183, cols. 568-69.

[40] Jean de Meun 1952, p. 168.   [41] Cf. 7153-80 n.

to the intrigue because the speakers represent qualities characteristic
of cupidinous love: the deceitful exterior and flagrant self-seeking,
among others. At the same time, they reflect in their perversity
the value of the reason that is being overthrown.

False Seeming, for example, presents the theme of reason's fall
in the ironic confession of a corrupt pretender to the prelatical
status of the Church, that status which, in medieval thought, stood
highest among men (allegorically), as reason stood highest within
man (tropologically).⁴² Where reason guides and instructs the individual, members of the prelatical status were to guide and instruct
the members of the Church. False Seeming's perversion of the
prelatical functions is the central theme of his confession and, at
the same time, a reflection of the perversion of the Lover's reason.
His action in the Lover's behalf—the rear-gate deception and
murder of Foul Mouth, which opens the way to the Old Woman
and Fair Welcoming—fulfills both Friend's advice and False
Seeming's own self-portrait in his confession, a model for that of
Chaucer's Pardoner.

The third in the series of grotesques that follow upon the Lover's
denial of Reason is the Old Woman, the literary ancestress of
Chaucer's Wife of Bath and Prioress as well as of Juliet's Nurse.
Her long speech to Fair Welcoming, urging him to receive the
Lover, is a hilarious exposition of rapacious mercantilism in love,
an ironic condemnation of her futile sentimentality over her own
past. Through the Old Woman, the Lover gains access to Fair
Welcoming, but is again repulsed by Resistance when he stretches
his hand toward the Rose (14808 ff.). The ensuing battle of
abstractions, a mock-heroic paradigm of the *psychomachia*, establishes a period in the Lover's progress when a truce is taken (15627-
58). After Venus's aid is invoked, the final action takes place. The
attack, repulse, and battle, which relate directly to the Lover's
quest, stand between the three grotesques—Friend, False Seeming, and the Old Woman—and the cosmic personifications Nature
and Genius.

Nature again reflects the overthrow of reason when she laments
the fallen state of man. To understand her significance, we may
recall Augustine's distinction between two natures, a nature rightly

⁴² Robertson and Huppé 1951, pp. 13, 20-21, 28-29; Paré 1947, pp.
160-87.

created in the beginning and a nature corrupted by sin, a formulation given currency for the later Middle Ages by Peter Lombard.[43] Man's task is the restoration of this fallen nature. As Gilson puts Saint Bernard's formulation, "The love of God is first in right, and carnal love is first in fact. How to return from the state in which we stand in fact, and recover the state in which we ought to stand as of right? There lies the whole question."[44] This emphasis in earlier writing upon the point from which we start accounts for the development of the *Romance* in terms of the pattern of the Fall and for the place occupied in that development by the concept, and personification, of Nature.

The portrait in Alanus's *Complaint of Nature* is clearly Jean's source, but Jean makes certain that we understand that his Nature is the fallen variety, for her job is to reproduce the species in the post-lapsarian manner described by Augustine,[45] and she admits her ignorance of any other method of reproduction (19146 ff.). While the Lover is interested in the gifts of Nature—his staff and the sack with its hammers (21346-96)—he has no interest in the work of Nature; in fact, his emphasis on breadth of experience (21551), on luxury (21553), his neglect of Nature in his final thanks to the God of Love and Venus (21753), and his rejection of Reason (21760-61) convey the idea that his principal interest in Nature is to enlist her aid in his *con*-game. That, in fact, is the essentially antirational trend of the action. To use Nature without the guide of Reason is to reproduce the pattern of the Fall.

The position that the *Romance* celebrates a naturalistic doctrine of love, as we saw above, rests on the dangerously uncritical assumption that the Lover represents Jean de Meun and that the personifications express his opinions. It also assumes that the Lover's antics are "natural." But part of Jean's effect is to portray the Lover's addled wits by revealing a series of illogicalities. For example, Genius appears as Nature's priest, and she makes her confession to him (16272 ff.). It is true that his sermon on the Park of the Lamb (19931 ff.) presents a valid and important contrast to the Garden of Diversion, but this same sermon preaches the

---

[43] Augustine, *De trinitate*, XIII. xii [16]; Peter Lombard, *Sentences*, III. xx. 1. Cf. the *Summarium* to Alanus de Insulis, *Anticlaudianus*, ed. Bossuat 1955, p. 199.
[44] Gilson 1940, p. 38.   [45] See 4403-21 (and note), 15891-976.

doctrine that the Park will be the reward of those who work conscientiously with their plows, styluses, and hammers at the task of natural reproduction; as Paré puts it, "the contemplation of the Trinity is promised to those . . . who faithfully observe [Nature's] laws."[46] But we cannot, with Paré, conclude that this is Jean de Meun's doctrine, and its obvious deficiencies are reinforced by other details.[47] Genius, we are told, represents natural inclination, or *naturalis concupiscentia*,[48] and our first encounter with the figure in the *Romance* (16272 ff.) reinforces this identification in a startling way, for it turns out that the Mass that he sings is not a new one,[49] but a recitation of "the representative shapes of all corruptible things" (16281-82). He is "the god and master of places" (16286). His function is thus appropriate to the identification *naturalis concupiscentia*, but it is at variance with the priestly expression of it in the form of a Mass and with his priestly robes. When he sets out to help lovers (19428 ff.), he takes off these robes, but when he arrives at the council of barons, he receives the inappropriate robes of a bishop from the inappropriate hands of the God of Love (19477 ff.). After his sermon, he throws down his torch and vanishes so that no one knows what has become of him. The action of the rest of the poem is dominated not by Genius but by Venus, who takes up his torch and spreads her fire.

It seems clear that Jean de Meun cannot be seriously accused of spreading, let alone believing in, these ponderous illogicalities, particularly since they accord much more with the mentality of the Lover in the poem than with Jean's evident sophistication. They serve to introduce the Lover's perversion of the idea of natural love, they illustrate his lack of reason, and thus they reinforce the already obvious development of the theme of ludicrous and cupidinous love.

In the description of the final assault there is a passage in which the image in the shrine is compared with the statue that Pygmalion made. This comparison occasions a retelling of the Pygmalion story (20817-21214), which is a clear reflection, in miniature, of the structure of the whole of the poem, with its three stages; for

[46] Paré 1947, p. 325; translation mine. Cf. Tuve 1966, p. 279.

[47] Cf. Robertson 1962, pp. 200-2.

[48] Ibid., pp. 199, 107; the identification is that of Guillaume de Conches, in his commentary on Boethius's *Consolation of Philosophy* (*De cons.*).

[49] Cf. ibid., pp. 127-30.

Pygmalion goes through essentially the same process as does the Lover. Like the Lover, who falls in love when he sees the rosebush reflected in the fountain of Narcissus, Pygmalion is the victim of a manifestation of self-love when he falls in love with the statue of his own creation. His folly develops quickly into a very clear loss of reason with comic, pathetic, and tragic consequences.

More than ever in this latter part of the poem, the comedy is a fundamental part of the poem's meaning, for the very blasphemy of the mock religiosity of the Lover's quest, figured in terms of an aberration of the celestial pilgrimage, shows the depth and extent, as well as the ridiculousness, of the full and final overthrow of reason, where everything is turned upside-down and black seems white. The futility of such a perversion is hinted at in the closing lines of the poem—"straightway it was day, and I awoke"—which suggest that the Lover's *insomnium* is fleeting and insubstantial.

But if the Lover's love is empty, it is so only in the context of that charity which is the only true "cosmic force of generation," the chain of love that Boethius sang and Jean echoed in French prose.[50] To understand the Lover's love, we must turn to the theologians for illumination. We turn to Augustine, to Bernard and Alanus not because Guillaume and Jean *copy* an explanation of charity from them but because their explanations clarify the ludicrousness of the Lover's headstrong course. The *Romance* is a poem, not a tract. This fact should make it clear that there is no incongruity in turning to theological sources for an understanding of the vernacular love poetry of the twelfth and later centuries, and that to do so involves no disagreement with Gilson's contention that there is no filiation between "courtly love" and Bernard's mysticism.[51] An allegorical poem like the *Romance* may appear to be "secular," and therefore removed from Bernard's development of charity, but it is far less meaningful as an expression of "humanism" or "naturalism" than as a complex development of a traditional theme, the folly—and attractiveness—of cupidinous love. It is more meaningful precisely because this development includes and depends upon dimensions of love—natural love, fortune, amity, and the charity that is the source and goal of the other forms—

[50] *De cons.*, 2, m. 8. Cf. Jean de Meun 1952, pp. 204-5.
[51] Gilson 1940, pp. 170-85. On courtly love, see Robertson 1953 and 1962, Chapter 5; Benton 1961; Schoeck 1951.

that give it a meaningful context. The poetic development gives form to the idea that cupidinous involvement grows in stages of increasing gravity; proceeding by means of irony, the poem presents these stages in terms of increasing levity until we reach the dream's conclusion. The defiant joy of the Lover over the possession of the rose gives way to the light of day, and the dream vanishes.

THE ILLUSTRATIONS

It is no accident that recent studies which emphasize the importance of the poem's ironic technique are also those that for the first time have revealed the importance of manuscript illustrations. Following on the pioneering work of Robertson, Fleming has provided an excellent guide to the significance of the manuscript illustrations of the *Romance*. Of more than two hundred manuscripts that have survived, many are beautifully illustrated and exceptionally rich in iconographic materials, but modern critical editions have totally neglected these materials. Charles Dunn selected a series of fifteen miniatures from three manuscripts in the Morgan Library, New York, as illustrations for the Robbins translation, but the major modern collections since Kuhn's are those of Robertson, Tuve, and Fleming. The latter, a series of forty-two figures from twenty-seven manuscripts, is the fullest collection designed specifically to document a detailed reading of the text of the *Romance*. There remains unpublished a great store of valuable and beautiful material that deserves presentation in color and in unbroken groupings from individual manuscripts.

The present translation offers, for the first time since Kuhn's early study, the full schedule of illustrations from a single manuscript; this series of twenty-eight miniatures, covering Guillaume's portion only, comes from one of the two earliest illustrated versions, the thirteenth-century Paris MS. B. N. fr. 378. The other major group of illustrations, covering Jean's portion, comes from a late fifteenth-century manuscript, Douce 195 in the Bodleian Library; and the last sixteen of this group form a complete sequence of all the miniatures from about line 20,000 to the end of the poem. The last six miniatures illustrate special points in the notes; one, from B. N. fr. 1559, represents the other earliest illustrated manuscript, and the remaining five are from manuscripts dated 1329, 1352, and ca. 1365. Thus there are representative illustrations from a chronological spectrum of two hundred years, and they provide evidence of stylistic developments during that period.

In general, they help to document further many of Fleming's conclusions. The two major groups of figures illustrate, in a manner but little exaggerated by the two-century difference in time, the stylistic distinction between Guillaume's abstract iconography and Jean's increasing use of exemplification, particularly in the humanistic materials. The long sequence of nine miniatures on the Pygmalion story (Figs. 47-55) illustrates both Jean's use of the material and the miniaturist's sensitivity to the ironies involved in its use. Other individual miniatures provide further examples of the various ways in which the illuminations serve as a form of gloss to the text.

In particular, certain ones confirm the notion, explored above, that the ironic technique depends upon two points of view, those of the Lover in the poem and of the poet or reader outside. Fig. 43, as Miss Tuve has shown, recognizes this form of irony by revealing through its calculated blasphemy that point of view of the Lover that is implicit in Genius's misapplication of Trinitarian imagery in his description of the Fountain of Life.[52] In this case, of course, the text itself provides the poet-reader point of view in the traditional religious imagery.

The rose, the major symbol of the poem, is a recurring iconographic device that subsumes the two points of view, for its traditional associations were already ambivalent.[53] Its appearances in the illustrations quite properly show its associations with carnality: Fig. 64, for example, shows both the literal and symbolic action of plucking the rose. In Fig. 57, the lady of the sanctuary wears a rose-chaplet, and the Lover's "sack" bears rosette decorations. The chaplet of course had been the Lover's gift in Fig. 36. And in Fig. 42 the rose appears in the head of the bishop's crozier, which the God of Love has given to Genius. But at the same time, the association with the religious symbols of the crozier and the pilgrim's sack reinforces the ironic point of view.

[52] Tuve 1966, p. 277.
[53] See 895-96 n.; Dahlberg 1969, pp. 577-78, 581.

Fig. 1 develops the religious associations of the rose in a somewhat more complex manner. I have discussed elsewhere the parallels between this type of opening miniature and contemporary Nativity representations.[54] The position of the rose tree behind the bed on which the Dreamer lies recalls the position of the cradle in many of the Nativities, but the tree is also reminiscent, as Kuhn noted long ago, of the tree of Jesse, the source, in one sense, of the Nativity. The form of the rose tree is appropriately parodic of the tree of Jesse in that its curves, instead of being erect and bisymmetrical, are asymmetrical and involute or downward, like those of the conventional *arbor vitiorum* rather than the *arbor virtutum*.[55]

Another feature of Fig. 1, however, illustrates even more clearly both the existence of the two points of view in the text and the illustrator's recognition of them. The figure at the foot of the bed represents the character Resistance (Dangier), and the club on his shoulder is his identifying attribute. His position corresponds to that of Joseph in the Nativities, but the parallel with Joseph is apparently at variance with the situation in the poem, where Resistance appears as the Lover's opponent in his quest for the rose, not his protector, as Joseph was for Mary. Thus the miniature makes the point that the Lover's situation is parodically unlike the Nativity. But although Resistance in the text is the Lover's opponent and appears as a coarse, hairy, violent churl (*vilain*), the Resistance in this miniature is a beardless, tonsured young clerk who bears a close resemblance to the Dreamer in the bed. The suspicion that he *is* an aspect of the Dreamer becomes a certainty when we read Fleming's penetrating observation that Dangier is "a moral category which manifests itself in psychological restraint."[56] Fig. 1, in common with a number of early illustrations, makes this point by showing Resistance without a beard.[57] Such a recognition depends upon a point of view different from that of the text, for there Resistance is seen consistently from the Lover's

---

[54] Dahlberg 1969, pp. 578-81, citing Kuhn 1911, pp. 12-14 (1913-14, pp. 20-24), who uses this style of opening miniature as the basis for his Group I.

[55] See Hugh of Saint Victor's *De fructibus carnis et spiritus*, PL 176, cols. 1007-10.

[56] Fleming 1969, p. 189.

[57] Cf. Kuhn 1913-14, Figs. 2, 3, pp. 16, 18; Fleming 1969, Figs. 10-11.

point of view—as resistance, in fact—and this point of view produces a hairy, bearded character, distinct from the Dreamer, in the miniatures of other manuscripts.[58] Clearly the reader sees such a character differently from the way in which he sees the Resistance of Fig. 1; but it is also clear that the Lover's point of view is hardly trustworthy, since "resistance" helps to inflame the Lover's desire by denying him immediate satisfaction of the rose, and in this sense helps to further the cause of the forces of the God of Love. The illustrator of Fig. 1, in short, clarifies a double point of view that relates external "resistance" to internal "restraint."

The awareness of the double point of view persisted in the traditions of manuscript illumination. Two centuries after Fig. 1 was produced, a beardless young Resistance appears as a knight in Fig. 38, an illustration of one of the opening phases of the *psychomachia* in Chapter 8. Here he is subduing Openness, to whose aid appears Pity, who tries to retard Resistance's club. An interesting feature of this miniature is the position of Openness's horse, which appears to be kneeling before Resistance's onslaught. Now the horse is another iconographical detail with traditionally ambivalent associations (see 19787 n.); if the rider controls the horse by means of the reins, the image may represent a right order, one in which reason restrains the passions, but an uncontrolled horse may suggest the upset of this right order. The attitude of the horse in Fig. 38 then seems to confirm that point of view which sees Resistance as reasonable restraint, a point of view which contrasts with that of the Lover, who of course wishes to be restrained in no way by Reason.

Not every horse that appears to be controlled by reins represents a similar point. In Figs. 33 and 37, for example, we see the Lover on horseback, holding the reins of his mount. From the standpoint of the total iconography, however, this detail is subordinate to others: the Lover himself, his clothing, curled hair, his dog, the hawk on his wrist in Fig. 33, the nature of the interlocutor —Wealth in Fig. 33 and the Old Woman in Fig. 37—all these

[58] Cf. Kuhn 1913-14, Figs. 4, 10, 14, 15, 26, pp. 19, 26, 29, 30, 41; MS B. N. fr. 802, fol. 1 R; B. N. fr. 1560, fol. preceding 1 R; B. N. fr. 1575, fol. 1 R; B. N. Rothschild 2801, fol. 1 R. The beard may also have been encouraged by the Nativity scenes, which usually show a bearded Joseph.

details indicate that the Lover is engaged in the hunt of love, in "venery," and that the horse, though directed, is misdirected.[59]

With these few examples of some of the ways in which the illustrations may serve as guides to the poem's irony, we may turn to the problems that face the translator.

THE PRESENT TRANSLATION

It is clear that much of the irony of the poem depends upon the imagery, and it was partly in the hope of maintaining such imagery for its iconographic significance that the present translation was undertaken. I am aware that the result of such an approach may seem at times unnecessarily awkward or wordy, and I cannot in good conscience plead that my authors were sometimes so. But it has seemed important primarily to preserve the accuracy of the diction, the imagery, even when it might not appear to be crucial to a given passage.

The same principle has governed the choice of the prose medium. This translation, the first in English prose, follows upon those of F. S. Ellis (1900) and Harry W. Robbins (1962), the one in four-stress couplets and the other in blank verse. It is based upon the edition of Ernest Langlois (1914-24). I had completed the translation in draft before the appearance of the first volume of the new edition by Félix Lecoy (1965–   ), and I provide in the Appendix a concordance of line numbers in the two editions, in so far as M. Lecoy's has appeared. In the Notes, I shall call attention to any major differences between the two editions.

The basic difference is one of editorial method and will not be readily observable in translation. Briefly, Langlois's aim was to reconstruct a critical, "archetypal" text on the basis of the surviving manuscripts; Lecoy's purpose is to select the best surviving manuscript and to use it as the basis of a diplomatic text. One result of Lecoy's procedure is a text, based on MS Paris, B. N. fr. 1573, with more marked dialectal characteristics than will be found in Langlois's normalized archetype. Further, since Lecoy numbers his lines to agree with the base MS, his count totals thirty fewer than Langlois's, although he supplies twenty-four of these lines within his text as emendations and gives the other six in his textual

---

[59] See 15675-750 n.

variants (see Appendix). The marginal numbers in this translation refer the reader to the line numbers of the Langlois edition.

The chapters into which I have divided the translation reflect the divisions of the poem as I have analyzed it above and represent an attempt to relate the steps in the love intrigue to the structural pattern as I have presented it, with the so-called digressions forming a reasoned part of that structure.

PART I

BY GUILLAUME DE LORRIS

The Dream of
Love

I

THE GARDEN, THE FOUNTAIN,

AND THE ROSE

MANY men say that there is nothing in dreams but fables and lies, but one may have dreams which are not deceitful, whose import becomes quite clear afterward. We may take as witness an author named Macrobius, who did not take dreams as trifles, for he wrote of the vision which came to King Scipio. Whoever thinks or says that to believe in a dream's coming true is folly and stupidity may, if he wishes, think me a fool; but, for my part, I am convinced that a dream signifies the good and evil that come to men, for most men at night dream many things in a hidden way which may afterward be seen openly.

In the twentieth year of my life, at the time when Love exacts his tribute from young people, I lay down one night, as usual, and slept very soundly. During my sleep I saw a very beautiful and pleasing dream; but in this dream was nothing which did not happen almost as the dream told it. Now I wish to tell this dream in rhyme, the more to make your hearts rejoice, since Love both begs and commands me to do so. And if anyone asks what I wish the romance to be called, which I begin here, it is the Romance of the Rose, in which the whole art of love is contained. Its matter is good and new; and God grant that she for whom I have undertaken it may receive it with grace. It is she who is so precious and so worthy to be loved that she should be called Rose.

I became aware that it was May, five years or more ago; I dreamed that I was filled with joy in May, the amorous month, when everything rejoices, when one sees no bush or hedge that does not wish to adorn itself with new leaves. The woods, dry during the winter, recover their verdure, and the very earth glories in the dews which water it and forgets the poverty in which the winter was passed. Then the earth becomes so proud that it wants a new robe; and it knows how to make a robe so ornate that there are a hundred pairs of colors in it. I mean, of course, the robe of grass and flowers, blue, white, and many other colors, by which the earth enriches itself. The birds, silent while they were cold and the weather hard and bitter, become so gay in May, in the serene weather, that their hearts are filled with joy until they must sing

74 or burst. It is then that the nightingale is constrained to sing and make his noise; that both parrot and lark enjoy themselves and take their pleasure; and that young men must become gay and amorous in the sweet, lovely weather. He has a very hard heart who does not love in May, when he hears the birds on the branches, singing their heart-sweet songs. And so I dreamed one night that I was in that delicious season when everything is stirred by love, and as I slept I became aware that it was full morning. I got up from bed straightway, put on my stockings and washed my hands. Then I drew a silver needle from a dainty little needlecase and threaded it. I had a desire to go out of the town to hear the sound of birds who, in that new season, were singing among the trees. I stitched up my sleeves in zigzag lacing and set out, quite alone, to enjoy myself listening to the birds who were straining themselves to sing because the gardens were bursting into bloom.

103 Happy, light-hearted, and full of joy, I turned toward a river that I heard murmuring nearby, for I knew no place more beautiful to enjoy myself than by that river, whose water gushed deep and swift from a nearby hill. It was as clear and cold as that from a well or fountain, and it was but little smaller than the Seine, but was spread out wider. I had never seen a stream so attractively situated, and I was pleased and happy to look upon that charming place. As I washed my face and refreshed myself with the clear, shining water, I saw that the bottom of the stream was all covered and paved with gravel. The wide, beautiful meadow came right to the edge of the water. The mild morning air was clear, pure, and beautiful. Then I walked out away through the meadow, enjoying myself as I kept to the river bank in descending the stream.

129 When I had gone ahead thus for a little, I saw a large and roomy garden, entirely enclosed by a high crenelated wall, sculptured outside and laid out with many fine inscriptions. I willingly admired the images and paintings, and I shall recount to you and tell you the appearance of these images as they occur to my memory.

139 In the middle I saw Hatred, who certainly seemed to be the

one who incites anger and strife. In appearance the image was choleric, quarrelsome, and full of malice; it was not pleasing, but looked like a woman crazy with rage. Her face was sullen and wrinkled, with a pug nose; she was hideous and covered with filth and repulsively wrapped up in a towel.

Beside her, to the left, was another image of the same size. I read her name, Felony, beneath her head. 152

I looked back to the right and saw another image named Villainy, who was of the same nature and workmanship as the other two. She seemed a creature of evil, an insolent and unbridled scandalmonger. He who could produce an image of such a truly contemptible creature knew how to paint and portray; she seemed full of all sorts of defamation, a woman who knew little of how to honor what she should. 156

Covetousness was painted next. It is she who entices men to take and to give nothing, to collect valuable possessions; it is she who, in her great passion for heaping up treasure, loans money at usury to many. She excites thieves and rascals to theft; and it is a great evil and sorrow that in the end many of them must hang. It is she who causes people to take the goods of others, to rob, to ravish, to commit fraud, to keep false accounts, and to tally falsely. It is she who leads people to the trickery and trumped-up litigation by which boys and girls have often been defrauded of their rightful inheritances. This image had hands that were clawlike and hooked, appropriate to Covetousness, who is always in a fever to get the possessions of another. She understands nothing else, but esteems most highly what belongs to another. 169

There was another image, called Avarice, seated side by side with Covetousness. This image was ugly; dirty, badly shaped, thin and miserable-looking, she was as green as a shallot; she was so discolored that she looked sick. She seemed a thing dying of hunger, one who lived on bread kneaded with strong, bitter caustic. She was not only thin but poorly clothed: she had an old coat, torn as if it had been among dogs, that was poor and worn out and full of old patches. Beside her, on a little thin clothespole, hung a mantle and a coat of sleazy material. The mantle had no fur linings, but very poor and shabby ones of heavy, shaggy black lamb. Her dress was at least ten years old, but, in anything to do with clothing, Avarice rarely had any desire to hurry. It weighed 195 heavily on her to use the dress at all, for when it was worn out and tattered, she would be very distressed over a new one and would suffer great privation before she would have another made. In her hand Avarice held a purse which she hid and tied up so tightly that she had to wait a long time before she could draw anything out of it. But she would have none of it; she went to the purse hoping only that she might take nothing away from it.

235 Envy was portrayed next. She never laughed in her life nor enjoyed anything unless she saw or heard a report of some disaster. Nothing could please her so much as unhappiness and misfortune. She is very pleased when she sees misfortune fall on any good man, and she rejoices in her heart when she sees a great ancestral house fall from its eminence or come into shame. But she is deeply wounded when anyone rises to honor through his intelligence and ability. Understand that she must be angry when good things happen. Envy is so cruel that she bears no loyalty to any companion. However closely a relative may hold to her, she has none to whom she is not an enemy; for, certainly, she would not want good fortune to come even to her father. But understand too that she pays a heavy price for her malice. When men do good she is in such terrible torment and grief that she is just short of melting in the heat of her passion. Her wicked heart so cuts her in pieces that God and men are revenged on her. Envy finishes no hour without imputing some evil to blameless men. I believe that if she knew the noblest gentleman here or beyond the sea, she would want to defame him; and if he were so well trained that she could neither entirely ruin his reputation nor bring him into low esteem, then she would want at least to deprecate his ability and, through her gossip, to minimize his honor.

279 Then I saw, in the painting, that Envy had a very ugly appearance: she looked at everything obliquely, and she had this bad habit because she could not look anything straight in the face, but closed one eye in disdain; for she burned and melted with rage when anyone at whom she looked was either wise, fair, or noble, or was loved or praised by men.

291 Next, quite close to Envy, Sorrow was painted on the wall. Her color seemed to show that she had some great sorrow in her heart. She looked as though she had jaundice, and Avarice was nothing like as pale and gaunt as she. The dismay, the distress,

the burdens and troubles that she suffered, day and night, had made her grow yellow and lean and pale. Nothing in the world ever lived in such martyrdom nor was ever so greatly enraged as it seemed that she was; I believe that no one ever knew how to do anything for her that could please her. She did not even want to be consoled at any price nor to let go of the sorrow she had in her heart; she had angered her heart too much, and her grief was too deep-rooted. She seemed to sorrow immeasurably, for she 313 had not been slow to scratch her whole face, and she had torn her dress in many places, until it was practically worthless, as though she had been in a violent rage. Her hair, which she had torn out in bad temper and anger, was all unplaited and lay straggling down her neck. And know truly that she sobbed most profoundly. There was no one so hardhearted who, seeing her, would not have felt great pity as she tore and beat herself and struck her fists together. The grief-stricken wretch was completely occupied in creating woe. She took no interest in enjoyment, in embraces and kisses, for whoever has a sorrowful heart—know it as the truth —has no talent for dancing or caroling. No one who grieved could ever bring himself to have a good time, for joy and sorrow are two contraries.

Old Age, shrunken by a good foot from her former stature, was 339 portrayed next. She was so old, so far fallen into her second childhood, that she could hardly feed herself. Her beauty was spoiled and she had become very ugly. Her entire head was as white with age as if it had been decked with flowers. If she had died, it would have been neither a great loss nor a great wrong, for age had already dried up her body and reduced it to nothing. Her face, once soft and smooth, was now withered and full of wrinkles. She had mossy ears, and she had lost so many teeth that she had none left. Her age was so great that, without a crutch, she would not have gone as far as four fathoms. Time, who goes away night and day, without rest and without interruption, who parts from us and steals away so quickly, seems to us to be always stopped at one place, but he never stops there at all. He never ceases passing away, so that no man, even if you ask learned clerks, can tell you what time it is that is present, for before he had thought, three moments would already have passed. Time, who cannot stay, but 373 always goes without returning, like water which is always descending, never returning a drop backward; Time, before whom nothing endures, not iron nor anything however hard, for Time destroys and devours everything; Time, who changes everything, who makes all grow and nourishes all, who uses all and causes it to rot; Time, who made our fathers old, who ages kings and emperors and will age us all, unless Death cuts us off; Time, who has it in his power to age all mankind, had aged Old Age so cruelly that, in my opinion, she could not help herself but was returning to her infancy. Certainly, I think she had no more power, force, or intelligence than an infant of one year. Nevertheless, to my knowledge, she had been wise and sensible in her prime; but now, I think, she was no longer wise, but had lost all reason. As I remember, she had clothed her body very well and protected it against the cold with a fur-lined coat. She was dressed warmly, for otherwise she would have been cold. These old people, you understand, are very cold by nature.

407　　Next was traced an image of what seemed to be a hypocrite; it was called Pope-Holiness. It is she who, in secret, when no one can watch her, is not afraid to commit any evil. In public she looks as if butter would not melt in her mouth; her face is simple and sad, and she seems a saintly creature. But there is no wickedness under heaven that she does not think of in her heart. The image resembled her very much; it was made in her likeness. The face was simple, and she was shod and clothed as if she were a nun. In her hand she held a psalter, and she took all kinds of trouble, you may know, to make feigned prayers to God and to call upon all the saints. She was not gay nor merry, but she appeared to be completely occupied in doing good works; she had put on the hair shirt. Know too, that she was not fat, but seemed worn out from fasting; her color was pale and deathly. To her and hers the door to Paradise was forbidden, for, as the Gospel says, these people disfigure their faces for praise among men and for a little vain glory which God and his kingdom will carry off from them.

441　　The last portrayed was Poverty, who wouldn't have a penny if she had to hang herself. Even if she could sell her dress, she would fare no better, for she was as naked as a worm. I think that if the weather had been a little bad she would have perished of cold, for she had only an old thin sack, full of miserable patches, as her coat and her mantle. She had nothing else to wear, but she

had plenty of opportunity for shivering. She was a little apart
from the others; she crouched and cowered like a poor dog in a
corner. Anything poor, wherever it may be, is always shamed and
despised. Cursed be the hour in which a poor man was conceived,
for he will never be well fed, well clothed, nor well shod; he is
neither loved nor advanced in fortune.

I looked over the images well, for, as I have described, they   463
were done in gold and azure, painted all along the wall. The wall
itself was high and formed a perfect square; it took the place of a
hedge in enclosing and shutting off a garden where no shepherd
had ever entered. This garden stood in a very beautiful place, and
I would have been very grateful to anyone who had been willing
to lead me inside, either by ladder or over steps; for, to my belief,
no man ever saw such joy or diversion as there was in that garden.
The birds' dwelling was not to be scorned, nor was it cheap. No
place was ever so rich with trees or songbirds: there were three
times as many birds as in the whole kingdom of France. The harmony of their moving song was very good to hear; all the world
should enjoy it. For my part, I was so overjoyed when I heard
them that I would not have taken a hundred pounds, if the way
into the garden had been open, not to enter and see the flock of
birds (God save them!) who sang the dances of love in melodies
that were sweet, courteous, and charming.

When I heard the birds singing, I began to go out of my mind   497
wondering by what art or what device I could enter the garden.
But I could never discover any place where I could get in; you
see, I didn't know whether there were opening, path, or place by
which one might enter. There was not even any one there who   506
might show me one, for I was alone. I was very distressed and
anguished until at last I remembered that it had never in any way
happened that such a beautiful garden had no door or ladder or
opening of some sort. Then I set out rapidly, tracing the outline
of the enclosure and extent of the square walled area until I found
a little door that was very narrow and tight. No man entered there
by any other place. Since I didn't know how to look for any other
entrance, I began to knock on the door. I knocked and rapped a
great deal and listened many times to see whether I might hear
anyone coming. Finally a very sweet and lovely girl opened the
wicket, which was made of hornbeam. She had hair as blond as a

copper basin, flesh more tender than that of a baby chick, a gleaming forehead, and arched eyebrows. The space between her eyes
was not small but very wide in measure. She had a straight, well-
made nose, and her eyes, which were gray-blue like those of a
falcon, caused envy in the harebrained. Her breath was sweet and
savory, her face white and colored, her mouth small and a little
539   full; she had a dimple in her chin. Her neck was of good proportion, thick enough and reasonably long, without pimples or sores.
From here to Jerusalem no woman has a more beautiful neck;
it was smooth and soft to the touch. She had a bosom as white as
the snow upon a branch, when it has just fallen. Her body was well
made and svelte; you would not have had to seek anywhere on
earth to find a woman with a more beautiful body. She had a pretty
chaplet of gold embroidery. There was never a girl more elegant
or better arrayed; nor would I have described her right. Above the
chaplet of gold embroidery was one of fresh roses, and in her
hand she held a mirror. Her hair was arranged very richly with a
fine lace. Both sleeves were well sewn into a beautifully snug fit,
and she had white gloves to keep her white hands from turning
brown. She wore a coat of rich green from Ghent, cord-stitched
all around. It certainly seemed from her array that she was hardly
busy. By the time that she had combed her hair carefully and prepared and adorned herself well, she had finished her day's work.
She led a good and happy life, for she had no care nor trouble
except only to turn herself out nobly.

575   When the girl with gracious heart had opened the door to me,
I thanked her nicely and asked her name and who she was. She
was not haughty toward me, nor did she disdain to reply.

582   "I am called Idleness," she said, "by people who know me.
I am a rich and powerful lady, and I have a very good time, for
I have no other purpose than to enjoy myself and make myself
comfortable, to comb and braid my hair. I am the intimate acquaintance of Diversion, the elegant charmer who owns this garden
and who had the trees imported from Saracen land and planted
throughout the garden.

595   "When the trees were grown, Diversion had the wall, that you
have seen, built all around them, and on the outside he arranged
to have portrayed the images that are painted there. They are
neither elegant nor delightful, but, as you saw just now, sad and

mournful. Many times Diversion and those who follow him, and who live in joy and comfort, come to this place to have a good time in the cool shade. Without doubt, he is at this moment still there within, listening to the song of the nightingales, the mavises, and other birds. There, with his followers, he enjoys and comforts himself, for he could find no better place or spot to indulge in pleasure. The fairest people that you ever found anywhere, you know, are the companions of Diversion, who leads and guides them."

When Idleness had told me these things, and I had listened   619
closely to all of them, I then said to her, "Lady Idleness, never doubt any of these things, since Diversion, the fair and gentle one, is now in this garden with his people, and, if it lies in my power, I shall not be robbed of the chance of still seeing this assembly today. I must see it, for I believe that this company is fair, courteous, and well instructed."

Then I entered into the garden, without saying another word,   631
by the door that Idleness had opened for me, and, when I was inside, I was happy and gay and full of joy. Believe me, I thought that I was truly in the earthly paradise. So delightful was the place that it seemed to belong to the world of spirit, for, as it seemed to me then, there was no paradise where existence was so good as it was in that garden which so pleased me. There were many singing birds, collected together, throughout the whole garden. In one place were nightingales, in another jays and starlings; elsewhere again were large schools of wrens and turtledoves, of goldfinches, swallows, larks, and titmice. In another place were assembled the calender-larks, who were tired out from singing in spite of themselves; there, too, were blackbirds and redwings, who aspired to outdo the other birds in singing. Elsewhere again were parrots and many birds that, in the woods and groves where they lived, had a wonderful time with their beautiful songs.

These birds that I describe to you performed a lovely service: 661
they sang a song as though they were heavenly angels. Know well that I was filled with great joy when I heard it, for mortal man never heard so sweet a melody. It was so sweet and beautiful that it did not seem the song of a bird; one could compare it rather with the song of the sirens of the sea, who have the name *siren* on account of their clear, pure voices. The little birds were intent on

their singing, and they were neither unskillful nor ignorant. Know, then, that when I heard the song and saw the burgeoning green of the place, I was seized with joy; no one had ever been so happy as I became then, full of gaiety as I was over the garden's delectable charm. Then I realized and saw that Idleness, who had placed me in the midst of this delight, had served me well. My love was due her when she unlocked the wicket gate of the branching garden.

691   From now on, I shall recount to you, as well as I know, how I went to work. First I want to tell you, without any long story, about what Diversion served and about his companions, and then I will tell in a full and orderly way about the appearance of the garden. I cannot speak of everything together, but I will recount it all in such order that no one will have any criticism to make.

701   The birds went along performing their wondrously sweet and pleasing service, in which they sang love lays and elegant songs, one high, the other low. Without joking, the sweetness and melody of their singing brought great joy to my heart. But when I had heard the birds just a little, I couldn't hold myself back from going off then to see Diversion, for I wanted very much to see how he carried on and what he was. I went off then straight to the right, by a little path full of fennel and mint, and I found Diversion nearby when I penetrated to a secluded place where he was. There he enjoyed himself, and with him he had people so fair that, when I saw them, I did not know where people so beautiful could have come from, for, in absolute truth, they seemed winged angels. No man born ever saw such beautiful people.

727   These people of whom I tell you were formed into a carol, and a lady called Joy was singing to them. She knew how to sing well and pleasingly; no one presented her refrains more beautifully or agreeably. Singing suited her wonderfully, for she had a clear, pure voice. Moreover, she was not vulgar, but knew how to move her body well in dancing, to kick up her heels and enjoy herself. Everywhere she went, she was, customarily, always the first in sing-ing, for singing was the activity that she performed most willingly.

743   Then you would have seen the carol move and the company dance daintily, executing many a fine farandole and many a lovely turn on the fresh grass. There you would have seen fluters, min-strels, and jongleurs. One was singing *rotrouenges*, another an air

from Lorraine, for in Lorraine they have more beautiful airs than in any other kingdom. There were also many lady tumblers thereabouts. There were tambourine jugglers, expert players who never stopped throwing the tambourine into the air and catching it on a finger without ever missing. In the middle of the carol, Diversion, with great nobility, directed the dancing of two darling young ladies dressed only in kirtles, with their hair in single braids. It is useless to speak of how quaintly they danced: each one came very prettily toward the other, and when they were close they thrust their mouths forward in such a way that it would have seemed to you that they were kissing each other on the face. They knew well how to move their bodies. I don't know how to describe it to you, but I never would have wanted to move as long as I could see these people bestirring themselves to carol and to dance.

I stood there motionless, watching the carol, until a very lively   777 lady noticed me. She was Courtesy, the worthy and debonair (may God keep her from harm!), and she called out to me then:

"Fair friend, what are you doing there?" said Courtesy. "Come   784 here and, if it pleases you, join in the carol with us." Without delaying or stopping I joined the carol, where I was by no means at a loss. You may know of course that I was very pleased when Courtesy asked me and told me to join the carol, for I was eager and longing to carol if I had dared. I began then to look upon the bodies, the dress and the faces, the expressions and the manners of those who were caroling there, and I shall tell you which they were.

Diversion was handsome, tall, and straight. Never among men   801 will you come upon any place where you will see a more handsome man. His face, like an apple, was red and white all over, and his person was cunningly and beautifully adorned. His eyes were blue-gray, his mouth fine, his nose most carefully shaped. His hair was blond and curly. Somewhat broad in the shoulders and narrow in the waist, he was so elegant and full of grace, so well formed in all his limbs, that he looked like a painting. He was lively, valiant, and active; I have never seen a more agile man. He had neither beard nor mustache, except for a very little down, for he was a young man. His body was richly clothed in samite decorated with birds and beaten gold. His dress was highly ornamented; in several places it was cunningly slashed or cut away. He was shod with great skill in low-cut, laced shoes. His sweetheart had, with loving care, made for him a chaplet of roses, which suited him beautifully.

831   And do you know who his sweetheart was? It was Joy, who hated him not at all, the gay girl, the sweet singer, who, when she was no more than seven years old, had given him the gift of her love. In the carol, Diversion held her by the finger, and she him. Each suited the other well, for he was handsome and she was beautiful. Her color made her look like a new rose; and her skin was so tender that one could tear it with a tiny thorn. Her forehead, white and gleaming, was free of wrinkles, her eyebrows brown and arched, her gay eyes so joyful that they always laughed regularly before her little mouth did. I don't know what to tell you about her nose: no one ever made a better one out of wax. Her mouth was tiny and ready to kiss her lover. Her head was blond and shining. Why should I go on telling you? She was beautiful and beautifully adorned. Her hair was laced with a golden thread, and she had a brand new chaplet of gold embroidery. I have seen twenty-nine of them, and never had I seen a chaplet so beautifully worked in silk. Her body was dressed and adorned in a samite worked in gold, the same material that her lover wore, only she was much more proud of it.

865   On the other side the God of Love stayed near to her. It is he who apportions the gifts of love according to his desire, who governs lovers, and who humbles the pride of men, making sergeants of seigneurs and servants of ladies, when he finds them too haughty. In his bearing the God of Love did not resemble a boy. His beauty, indeed, was greatly to be valued. But I fear that I should be grievously burdened in describing his dress, since it was not of silk but of tiny flowers made by delicate loves. The gown was covered in every part with images of losenges, little shields, birds, lion cubs, leopards, and other animals, and it was worked with flowers in a variety of colors. There were flowers of many sorts, placed with great skill. No flower born in the summertime was missing from it, not even the flower of the broom, the violet, the periwinkle, or any yellow, indigo, or white flower. Intermingled in places there were large, wide rose leaves. On his head he wore a chaplet of roses; but the nightingales that fluttered around his head kept knocking them down to the earth. He was

completely covered with birds, with parrots, nightingales, calender-larks, and titmice. It seemed that he was an angel come straight
from heaven. He had a young man, called Sweet Looks, whom
he kept there beside him.

This young fellow watched the carols and kept the two Turkish 907
bows that belonged to the God of Love. One of these bows was
made of the wood of a tree whose fruit tastes bitter. The bow was
filled, below and above, with knots and burls, and it was blacker
than mulberry. The other bow was made from the trunk of a
shrub, a little long and of fine workmanship. It was well made,
planed smooth, and very well ornamented. All over it were painted
gay and clever ladies and young men. Sweet Looks, who seemed no
lowborn fellow, held, along with the two bows, ten of his master's
arrows. Five of them he held in his right hand, and these five
arrows had flights and nocks that were very well made, and all
were painted gold. The points were strong and sharp and keen for
piercing well, but without iron or steel, for there was nothing that
was not made of gold, except the feathers and shaft. These arrows
were tipped with barbed golden points.

Of these arrows, the best, the swiftest, the most beautiful, and 935
the one with the best feathers fixed on it, was named Beauty. And
the name of that one which wounds the most was, in my opinion,
Simplicity. Another of them was called Openness; this arrow was
feathered with valor and courtesy. The name of the fourth was
Company, an arrow that, because of its very heavy point, was not
prepared to travel very far, but if anyone wanted to fire it at close
range he could do a lot of damage. The fifth had the name Fair
Seeming, and, although it was the least harmful of all, nevertheless, it made a very large wound. However, he who is wounded
by this arrow may expect good grace: his pain is of good use, for
he can soon expect health, and by it his sorrow must be cured.

There were five arrows of another sort, as ugly as you like. 957
The shafts and points were blacker than a devil from hell. The
first had the name Pride. The second, worth no more, was called
Villainy, and it was all stained and poisoned with felony. The
third was called Shame, the fourth, Despair, and the last, without
doubt, was called New Thought. These five arrows were of one
sort, all alike. The one bow that was hideous and full of knots and
burls was very suitable; it should indeed shoot such arrows. Un-

doubtedly, the power of these five arrows was contrary to that of the other five, but I shall not now tell all about their force and power. I shall indeed recount to you the truth about them and their significance, and I shall not forget to do so; before I finish my story I will tell you what all this signifies.

985   I shall come back now to my account, for I must tell of the countenances, the array, and the appearances of the noble people of the carol. The God of Love was well accompanied: he was very closely joined to a lady of great worth whose name, like that of one of the five arrows, was Beauty. She had many good qualities: neither dark nor brunette, she shone as clear as the moon, to which the other stars are like tiny candles. Her flesh was as tender as dew; she was as simple as a bride and white as the *fleur de lis*. Her face was clear and smooth, straight and somewhat thin. It was not rouged or painted, for she had no need to adorn or decorate herself. She had long, blond hair that reached to her heels. Her nose, her eyes, her mouth, were all well made. So help me God, my heart is touched with great sweetness when I remember the arrangement of her every limb, for there was no woman so beautiful in all the world. Briefly, she was a delightfully pleasing young blonde, openly coquettish, nicely elegant, and slender and plump together.

1017   Wealth, a lady of great dignity, worth, and moment, stayed next to Beauty. Whoever dared, in word or in deed, to harm her or hers would have been not only overweening but also very brave, since she can both harm and help a great deal. The great power of rich men to bring both aid and trouble is not just a thing of today and yesterday: all the greatest and humblest have done honor to Wealth. All hoped to serve her for the love of deserving well of her, and each one called her his lady, for everyone feared her: the whole world was in her power. To her court came many a flatterer, many a traitor, and many an envious man, those who are eager to belittle and to blame all who are more successful in loving. Outwardly these flatterers praise men in order to please them; they anoint everybody with words. But secretly their flatteries pierce men to the bone, for they denigrate the merits of good men and decry those who are praised. Flatterers, by their flattery, have denounced many good men, for they alienate from court those who should be intimate. May misfortunes fall upon these flatterers full of envy, for no worthy man loves their existence.

Wealth had a purple robe. Now don't take it as a trick when   1053
I tell you truly and assure you that nowhere in the world was there
a robe so beautiful, so costly, or so gay. The purple was covered
with gold embroidery which portrayed the stories of dukes and
kings. The collar was very richly edged with a band of gold
decorated with black enamel. And you may know for certain that
there was a great plenty of precious stones which emitted flashes of
brilliant light. Wealth had a very costly belt which encircled her
outside the purple robe. The buckle was made of a stone that had
great power and virtue, for he who wore it on himself feared
nothing from any poison; no one could poison him. One would do
well to love such a stone; it was worth more to a rich man than all
the gold of Rome. The clasp was made of another stone, which   1077
cured toothache and which had a virtue so great that whoever saw
it on an empty stomach could, just from seeing it, be protected for
the whole day. The studs on the cloth woven with gold threads
were made of purified gold and were large and heavy, each one
a good bezant. On her blond tresses Wealth had a golden circlet.
No such beautiful one was ever yet seen. It was made of pure gold,
cunningly worked. But he who knew how to describe all the
stones that were in it would be an expert at the art of description,
for one couldn't estimate the worth of the stones that were set
in the gold. There were rubies, sapphires, jargons, and emeralds
of more than two ounces. In front there was a carbuncle, set with
great skill, and this stone was so clear that, now that night was
falling, one could see his way well enough for a league ahead. Such
brilliance came from the stone that Wealth's face and head, with
everything round about, shone radiantly from the light.

Wealth held by the hand a young man, full of great beauty, one   1109
who was her true lover. He was a man who took delight in living
in fine mansions. He was well shod and clothed, and had valuable
horses. He thought that he might just as well be accused of murder
or theft as to have a poor horse in his stable. Therefore he cherished his acquaintance with Wealth and her benevolence toward
him; for he always thought to live a life of lavish spending, and
she could furnish the means and support his expenses. Indeed, she
gave him coins as if she drew them out of granaries.

Next was Generosity, who was well trained and instructed in do-   1127
ing honor and distributing gifts. She was of Alexander's lineage

and took joy in nothing so much as when she could say, "Here, take this." Even the wretch Avarice was not so intent on grasping as Generosity was on giving. And God made all her goods increase, so that she did not know how to give away as much as she had. She was highly esteemed and praised. She had done so much with her fair gift that she held both fools and wise men completely in her power. As a result, I believe that if there were anyone who hated her, she would make a friend of him through her services to him. Therefore she had the love of both rich and poor at her will. The great man who is a miser is a great fool, and a man in high place can have no vice so harmful as avarice. A miserly man can conquer neither lands nor lordships, for he does not have a plenti-

1155 ful supply of friends with whom he may work his will. Whoever wants to have friends must not love his possessions but must acquire friends by means of fair gifts; for, in the same way that the loadstone subtly draws iron to itself, so the gold and silver that a man gives attract the hearts of men. Generosity wore a completely new robe of Saracen purple. Her face was lovely and well formed, but her neck was disclosed, since, not long before, she had at that very place made a present of her neck-clasp to a lady. However, it did not suit her badly that her collar was open and her throat disclosed so that her soft flesh showed its whiteness across her shirt.

1175 Generosity, worthy and wise, held the hand of a knight of the lineage of the good King Arthur of Britain who carried the banner and standard of valor. He is still of such renown that they tell stories of him before both kings and counts. The knight next to Generosity was but recently come from a tournament where he had made many an assault and jousted for his lover. He had uncircled many a green helmet, pierced many a bossed shield, and struck down many a knight and overcome him by strength and courage.

1191 After all these came Openness, who was neither brown nor swarthy, but white as snow. She did not have an Orléans nose, for hers was long and straight. Her eyes were gray-blue and laughing, her brows were arched, her hair was long and blond, and she was as simple as a dove. She had a heart that was sweet and good-natured. She would not have dared to say or do to anyone anything that she should not; and if she knew a man who was tormented on account of his affection she would have taken pity on him, believe me, for her heart was so full of compassion, so sweet and so agreeable that she would have been afraid of committing a very base act if anyone were to suffer on her account, and she did not come to his aid. She was wearing a smock that was not made of canvas; there was no richer one between there and Arras. It was so well gathered and fitted that there was not a single tuck that was not properly placed. Openness was very well dressed, for no dress is so pretty on a young lady as a smock. A woman is quainter and more delightful in a smock than in a kirtle. The smock, which was white, signified that she who wore it was sweet and open.

Next, side by side with Openness, was a young bachelor. I didn't know his name, but he was as fair and noble as if he had been the son of Windsor's lord, come to life again.   1224

Courtesy was next in the ring; since she was neither proud nor silly, she was much esteemed by everyone. It was she—may she be given grace—who, rather than anyone else, called me into the carol when I came there. She was neither foolish nor distrustful in her fair replies and fine speeches, but wise and reasonable, without excess. She never gave anyone cause to feel injured, nor did she hold rancor toward anyone. She was a gleaming brunette, with a clear and shining face; I know no more pleasing lady. She was worthy to be an empress or a queen in any court. She held the hand of a knight who was easy to know and pleasant of speech, and who knew how to accord due honor to people. He was handsome and noble, skillful at arms, and well loved by his sweetheart.   1229

Lovely Idleness came next, holding close to me. I have given you an accurate account of her size and appearance, and I will tell you no more of her, for it was she who gave me so great a bounty when she opened to me the wicket of the flowering garden.   1251

Next, according to my knowledge, came Youth, with a clear and laughing face, who, as I believe, was not yet much more than twelve years old. She was naïve and did not suspect the existence of any evil or trickery. She was very happy and gay, for, as you well know, a young thing is troubled by nothing except play. Her sweetheart was so intimate with her that he kissed her whenever he pleased, in sight of all those in the carol. They were never ashamed, no matter what anybody said of the two of them. Rather you might see them kissing each other like two turtle doves. The   1259

boy was young and handsome, of the same age and spirits as his
sweetheart.

1279   Thus these people, along with others of their households,
danced their carols there. All together they were warm, open
people, well instructed and beautifully trained. When I had seen
the appearances of those who led the dances, I then had a desire
to go see and explore the garden, to contemplate those lovely
laurels, the pines, cedars, and mulberry trees. Already they were
stopping the carols, for most of them were going off with their
sweethearts to shelter under the shade of the trees in order to make
love. God! What a good life they led! He who does not long for
such a life is a fool. He who could have such a life might dispense
with a greater good, since there is no greater paradise than to have
one's beloved at one's desire. At this point I left there and went
off alone to enjoy myself here and there throughout the garden.

1304   Immediately the God of Love called Sweet Looks. Now he no
longer cared to have him keep his golden bow: without waiting
further he commanded him to string the bow, and Sweet Looks did
not delay in doing so. Immediately he strung the bow and gave it
to him along with five arrows, strong and shining, ready to shoot.
Straightway the God of Love began to follow me, bow in hand,
from a distance. Now may God protect me from a mortal wound if
he goes so far as to shoot at me! Knowing nothing of all this,
always enjoying myself, I went along quite freely through the garden, while the God of Love set his intent on following me; but
he did not stop me in any place until I had been everywhere.

1323   The garden was a completely straight, regular square, as long
as it was wide. Except for some trees which would have been too
ugly, there was no tree which might bear fruit of which there were
not one or two, or perhaps more, in the garden. There were apple
trees, I well remember, that bore pomegranates, an excellent food
for the sick. There was a great abundance of nut trees that in their
season bore such fruit as nutmegs, which are neither bitter nor
insipid. There were almond trees, and many fig and date trees
were planted in the garden. He who needed to could find many a
good spice there, cloves, licorice, fresh grains of paradise, zedoary,
anise, cinnamon, and many a delightful spice good to eat after
meals.

There were the domestic garden fruit trees, bearing quinces,   1347
peaches, nuts, chestnuts, apples and pears, medlars, white and black
plums, fresh red cherries, sorb-apples, service-berries, and hazel-
nuts. In addition, the whole garden was thronged with large laurels
and tall pines, with olive trees and cypresses, of which there are
scarcely any here. There were enormous branching elms and, along
with them, hornbeams and beech trees, straight hazels, aspen and
ash, maples, tall firs, and oaks. Why should I stop here? There
were so many different trees that one would be heavily burdened
before he had numbered them. Know too that these trees were
spaced out as they should be; one was placed at a distance of more
than five or six fathoms from another. The branches were long
and high and, to keep the place from heat, were so thick above
that the sun could not shine on the earth or harm the tender grass
for even one hour.

There were fallow-deer and roe-deer in the garden, and a great   1375
plenty of squirrels, who climbed among the trees. There were
rabbits, who came forth out of their burrows for the whole day and
in more than thirty ways went scampering around one another on
the fresh green grass. In places there were clear fountains, without
water insects or frogs and shaded by the trees, but I couldn't tell
you the number of them. In little brooks, which Diversion had had
made there as channels, the water ran along down, making a
sweet and pleasing murmur. Along the brooks and the banks of the
clear, lively fountains, sprang the thick, short grass. There one
could couch his mistress as though on a feather bed, for the earth
was sweet and moist on account of the fountains, since as much
grass as possible grew there.

But the thing that most improved the place was the appearance   1399
that, winter and summer, there was always an abundance of flowers.
There were very beautiful violets, fresh, young periwinkles; there
were white and red flowers, and wonderful yellow ones. The
earth was very artfully decorated and painted with flowers of various colors and sweetest perfumes.

I won't offer you a long fable about this pleasant, delectable   1411
place, and it is now time for me to stop, for I could not recall all
of the beauty and great delight of the garden. However, I went so
far, to left and to right, that I searched out and saw the entire

condition and nature of the garden. And the God of Love followed me, watching me all the time, as does the hunter who waits until the animal is in good position before he lets fly his arrow.

1425   At last I arrived at a very good spot, when I found a fountain under a pine. Not since the time of Charles or Pepin has such a fair pine been seen. It had grown so tall that no tree in the garden was taller. Nature, with consummate skill, had placed the fountain under the pine within a marble stone, and in the stone, on the border of the upper side, had cut small letters saying that there the fair Narcissus died.

1439   Narcissus was a young man whom Love caught in his snares. Love knew so well how to torment him, to make him weep and complain, that he had to give up his soul. For Echo, a great lady, had loved him more than anything born, and was so ill-used on his account that she told him that she would die if he did not give her his love. But he, because of his great beauty, was so full of pride and disdain that he did not wish to grant her his love, for all her tears and prayers. When she heard him refuse, her grief and anger were so great and she held him in such great despite that she died without delay. But just before she died she prayed to God and asked that hardhearted Narcissus, whom she had found so indifferent to love, might one day be tormented and burned by a love from which he could expect no joy, and that he might know and understand the grief of those loyal lovers who are so basely

1467   denied. Since the prayer was reasonable, God confirmed it: one day when Narcissus was returning from hunting he came by chance to rest at the clear, pure fountain under the pine. He had endured such labor in pursuing the hunt by hill and valley that he was very thirsty, what with the fierce heat and the fatigue that had left him out of breath, and when he saw the fountain, covered by the branches of the pine, he thought that there he would drink. Lying flat on his stomach over the fountain, he began to drink from it and saw his face, his nose and mouth, clear and sharp. Then he was struck with wonder, for these shadows so deceived him that he saw the face of a child beautiful beyond measure. Then Love knew how to avenge himself for the great pride and the resistance that Narcissus had directed toward him. And Narcissus was well repaid: he mused so long at the fountain that he fell in love with his own reflection and died of his love in the end. This was the outcome of the affair, for, when he saw that he could not accomplish his desire and that he was captured so inescapably that he could in no way take any comfort, he became so distressed that he lost his reason and died in a short time. Thus did he receive his deserved retribution from the girl whom he had scorned. You ladies who neglect your duties toward your sweethearts, be instructed by this exemplum, for if you let them die, God will know how to repay you well for your fault.

When the inscription had made clear to me that this was indeed   1511
the true fountain of the fair Narcissus, I drew back a little, since I dared not look within. When I remembered Narcissus and his evil misfortune, I began to be afraid. But then I thought that I might be able to venture safely to the fountain, without fear of misfortune, and that I was foolish to be frightened of it. I approached the fountain, and when I was near I lowered myself to the ground to see the running water and the gravel at the bottom, clearer than fine silver. It is the fountain of fountains; there is none so beautiful in all the world. The water is always fresh and new; night and day it issues in great waves from two deep, cavernous conduits. All around, the short grass springs up thick and close because of the water. In winter it cannot die, nor can the water stop flowing.

At the bottom of the fountain were two crystal stones upon which   1537
I gazed with great attention. There is one thing I want to tell you which, I think, you will consider a marvel when you hear it: when the sun, that sees all, throws its rays into the fountain and when its light descends to the bottom, then more than a hundred colors appear in the crystals which, on account of the sun, become yellow, blue, and red. The crystals are so wonderful and have such power that the entire place—trees, flowers, and whatever adorns the garden—appears there all in order. To help you understand, I will give you an example. Just as the mirror shows things that are in front of it, without cover, in their true colors and shapes, just so, I tell you truly, do the crystals reveal the whole condition of the garden, without deception, to those who gaze into the water, for always, wherever they are, they see one half of the garden, and if they turn, then they may see the rest. There is nothing so small, however hidden or shut up, that is not shown there in the crystal as if it were painted in detail.

1571   It is the perilous mirror in which proud Narcissus gazed at his
face and his gray eyes; on account of this mirror he afterward lay
dead, flat on his back. Whoever admires himself in this mirror can
have no protection, no physician, since anything that he sees with
his eyes puts him on the road of love. This mirror has put many a
valiant man to death, for the wisest, most intelligent and carefully
instructed are all surprised and captured here. Out of this mirror a
new madness comes upon men: Here hearts are changed; intelligence and moderation have no business here, where there is only
the simple will to love, where no one can be counseled. For it is
here that Cupid, son of Venus, sowed the seed of love that has
dyed the whole fountain, here that he stretched his nets and placed
his snares to trap young men and women; for Love wants no other
birds. Because of the seed that was sown this fountain has been
rightly called the Fountain of Love, about which several have
spoken in many places in books and in romances; but, when I have
revealed the mystery, you will never hear the truth of the matter
better described.

1603   I wanted to remain there forever, gazing at the fountain and the
crystals, which showed me the hundred thousand things that appeared there; but it was a painful hour when I admired myself
there. Alas! How I have sighed since then because of that deceiving mirror. If I had known its powers and qualities, I would never
have approached it, for now I have fallen into the snare that has
captured and betrayed many a man.

1615   Among a thousand things in the mirror, I saw rosebushes loaded
with roses; they were off to one side, surrounded closely by a
hedge. I was seized by so great a desire for them that not for Pavia
or Paris would I have left off going there where I saw this splendid
thicket. When this madness, by which many other men have been
seized, had captured me, I straightway drew near to the rosebushes.
Mark well: when I was near, the delicious odor of the roses penetrated right into my entrails. Indeed, if I had been embalmed,
the perfume would have been nothing in comparison with that of
the roses. Had I not feared to be attacked or roughly treated, I
would have cut at least one, that I might hold it in my hand to
smell the perfume; but I was afraid that I might repent such
an action, which might easily provoke the wrath of the lord of the
garden. There were great heaps of roses; none under heaven were

as beautiful. There were small, tight buds, some a little larger, and some of another size that were approaching their season and were ready to open. The little ones are not to be despised; the broad, open ones are gone in a day, but the buds remain quite fresh at least two or three days. These buds pleased me greatly. I did not believe that there were such beautiful ones anywhere. Whoever might grasp one should hold it a precious thing. If I could have a chaplet of them, I would love no possession as much.

Among these buds I singled out one that was so very beautiful   1655
that, after I had examined it carefully, I thought that none of the others was worth anything beside it; it glowed with a color as red and as pure as the best that Nature can produce, and she had placed around it four pairs of leaves, with great skill, one after the other. The stem was straight as a sapling, and the bud sat on the top, neither bent nor inclined. Its odor spread all around; the sweet perfume that rose from it filled the entire area. And when I smelled its exhalation, I had no power to withdraw, but would have approached to take it if I had dared stretch out my hand to it. But the sharp and piercing thorns that grew from it kept me at a distance. Cutting, sharp spikes, nettles, and barbed thorns allowed me no way to advance, for I was afraid of hurting myself.

2

THE GOD OF LOVE AND THE AFFAIR
OF THE HEART

1681   The God of Love, who had maintained his constant watch over me and had followed me with drawn bow, stopped near a fig tree, and when he saw that I had singled out the bud that pleased me more than did any of the others, he immediately took an arrow and, when the string was in the nock, drew the bow—a wondrously strong one—up to his ear and shot at me in such a way that with great force he sent the point through the eye and into my heart. Then a chill seized me, one from which I have, since that time, felt many a shiver, even beneath a warm fur-lined tunic. Pierced thus by the arrow, I fell straightway to the earth. My heart failed; it played me false. For a long time I lay there in swoon, and when I came out of it and had my senses and reason, I was very weak and thought that I had shed a great quantity of blood. But the point that pierced me drew no blood whatever; the wound was quite dry. I took the arrow in my two hands and began to pull hard at it, sighing as I pulled. I pulled so hard that I drew out the feathered shaft, but the barbed point called Beauty was so fixed inside my heart that it could not be withdrawn. It remains within; I still feel it, and yet no blood has ever come from there.

1721   I was in great pain and anguish because of my doubled danger: I didn't know what to do, what to say, or where to find a physician for my wound, since I expected no remedy for it, either of herbs or roots. But my heart drew me toward the rosebud, for it longed for no other place. If I had had it in my power, it would have restored my life. Even the sight and scent alone were very soothing for my sorrows.

1733   I began then to draw toward the bud with its sweet exhalations. Love selected another arrow, worked in gold. It was the second arrow and its name was Simplicity. It has caused many a man and woman all over the world to fall in love. When Love saw me approach, he did not threaten me, but shot me with the arrow that was made of neither iron nor steel so that the point entered my heart through my eye. No man born, I believe, will ever dislodge it from there, for I tried, without any great joy, to pull the shaft from me, but the point remained within. Now know for a truth that if I had been full of desire for the rosebud before, my wish was greater now. As my woes gave me greater distress, I had an increased desire to go always toward the little rose that smelled sweeter than violets. I would have done better to go farther away, but I could not refuse what my heart commanded. I had to go perforce, always where it aspired to be. But the bowman, who strove mightily and with great diligence to wound me, did not let me move without hurt in that direction. To madden me further, 1765 he caused the third arrow, called Courtesy, to fly to my heart. The wound was deep and wide, and I had to fall in a swoon beneath a branching olive tree. I lay there a long time without moving. When I was able to stir, I took the arrow and straightway removed the shaft from my side, but, no matter what I might do, I could not draw out the point.

There I sat, in deep distress and thought. My wound tormented 1777 me very much and urged me to approach the rosebud that pleased me. But the bowman frightened me away, as indeed he should, for he who has been scalded must fear all water. However, necessity is a powerful force; even if I had seen it raining stones and crossbow bolts as thick as hail, I would still have had to go toward the rosebud, for Love, who excels all other things, gave me the strength and heart to perform his commandment. I rose then to my feet, as feeble and weak as a wounded man, and made a great effort to move forward, nothing daunted by the archer, toward the rosebush where my heart longed to be. But there were so many thorns, thistles, and brambles, that I hadn't the power to pass through the thicket of thorns and reach the rosebud. I had to remain near the hedge, which was next to the rosebushes and made of very sharp thorns. But it was a delight for me to be so near that I smelled the sweet perfume that came from the rosebud, and I was very pleased with what I could see freely. My reward at this sight was so great that I forgot my woes in my delight and joy. I was greatly healed and comforted; nothing ever pleased me as 1813 much as to rest in that place. I would never have sought to leave it. But after I had been there a long time, the God of Love, who had shattered my heart in making it his target, made a new assault upon me. To my discomfort he shot another arrow and made a new wound in my heart, under my breast. This arrow's name was Company, and there is none that subdues a lady or young man more quickly. Immediately the great anguish of my wounds began again. I swooned three times in a row.

1831   When I revived, I wailed and sighed, for my anguish was growing so much worse that I had no hope, either of cure or of relief. I would rather have been dead than alive, for, in my opinion, Love would make a martyr of me in the end. I could not part from him by any other means. Meanwhile he had taken another arrow, one that I value highly and consider very powerful. This arrow is Fair Seeming; it does not allow any lover to repent of serving Love, no matter what woes he may suffer. It has a point for piercing and an edge as keen as a steel razor. But Love had anointed it very well with a precious unguent so that it might not hurt too greatly. He did not want me to die but to be relieved by the power of the unguent, one which was full of healing comfort. Love had made it with his own hands to comfort pure lovers and to help them support their troubles. When he shot the arrow at me he made a great wound in my heart, but the ointment, spreading throughout the wound, gave me back the heart which I had lost. Without the sweet ointment I would have been dead and in an evil plight.

1864   Then I drew the shaft from me, but the head, newly polished, remained inside. Thus five of them were so well embedded that they would never be removed. Although the ointment was worth a great deal to me, nevertheless my wound hurt so much that the pain made me change color. This arrow has an unusual property; it brings both sweetness and bitterness. Indeed I felt and understood that it helped me at the same time that it harmed; while the point gave me anguish, the ointment gave relief. One part heals, the other pains, and thus it helps and harms.

1881   Then straightway Love came toward me with quick steps, and as he came he cried out: "Vassal, you are taken. There is no chance for escape or struggle. Surrender without making any resistance. The more willingly you surrender the sooner will you receive mercy. He is a fool who resists the one whom he should flatter and before whom he would do better to beg. You cannot struggle against me, and I want to teach you that you can gain nothing through folly or pride. Rather submit yourself as a prisoner, as I wish, in peace and with a good will."

I replied simply: "Sir, I surrender willingly, and I shall never defend myself against you. May it never please God for me even to think of ever resisting you, for to do so is neither right nor reasonable. You may do with me what you wish, hang me or kill me. I know very well that I cannot change things, for my life is in your hand. Only through your will can I live until tomorrow, and, since I shall never have joy and health from any other, I await them from you. If your hand, which has wounded me, does give me a remedy, if you wish to make me your prisoner or if you do not deign to do so, I shall not count myself deceived. Know too that I feel no anger whatever. I have heard so much good spoken about you that I want to give my heart and body over to your service, to be used entirely at your discretion, for if I do your will I cannot complain of anything. I still believe that at some time I shall receive the mercy that I await, and under such conditions I submit myself prostrate before you."

With these words, I wanted to kiss his foot, but he took me by the hand and said, "I love you very much and hold you in esteem for the way that you have replied here. Such a reply never came from a lowborn fellow with poor training. Moreover, you have won so much that, for your benefit, I want you to do homage to me from now on: You will kiss me on my mouth, which no base fellow touches. I do not allow any common man, any butcher, to touch it; anyone whom I take thus as my man must be courteous and open. Serving me is, without fail, painful and burdensome; but I do you a great honor, and you should be very glad—since Love carries the standard and banner of courtesy—that you have so good a master and a lord of such high renown. His bearing is so good, so sweet, open, and gentle, that no villainy, no wrong or evil training can dwell in anyone who is bent on serving and honoring him."

Immediately, with joined hands, I became his man. And you may understand that I grew very proud when his mouth kissed mine; this gift gave me great joy. Then he required sureties from me: "Friend," he said, "I have received many homages from one

1898

1926

1955

and another person by whom I was later deceived. These criminals, full of falsity, have tricked me many times. I have heard many a complaint about them, and they know how much they burden me. If I can get them into my power, I shall sell them dearly. Now, because I love you, I wish to be very certain of you and to bind you to me so that you may not repudiate your promise or covenant with me nor do anything you ought not to do. Since you seem loyal to me, it would be a sin if you were to play me false."

1977   "Sir," I said, "hear me. I don't know why you ask pledges or surety of me. Already you know for a truth that you have so ravished and captured my heart that without your permission it could do nothing for me even if it wished to do so. This heart is yours, not mine, for it is bound, for good or ill, to do your pleasure, and no man can dispossess you of it. You have placed within it a garrison that will guard and rule it well. Beyond all that, if you fear anything, make a key for it and carry it with you. The key will serve in place of a pledge."

1994   "By my head," said Love, "that idea is not a wild one, and I agree to it. He who has command over the heart is sufficiently lord of the body; and he who asks more is unreasonable." Then from his purse he drew a small, well-made key made of pure, refined gold. "With this," he said, "I shall lock your heart, and I require no other guarantee. My jewels are under this key; it is smaller than your little finger, yet it is the mistress of my jewel-box, and as such its power is great." Then he touched my side and locked my heart so softly that I hardly felt the key.

2011   Thus I did all his will, and when I had put him out of doubt, I said:

2013   "Sir, I have a great capacity for doing what you wish. But, by the faith that you owe me, receive my service with thanks. I do not say so out of weakness, for I do not fear your service in any way, but because a sergeant exerts himself in vain to perform worthy service if it does not please the lord for whom he does it."

2023   Love replied, "Now do not be distressed. Since you are installed in my household, I shall take your service with thanks and raise you to high station if some wickedness does not steal it from you. Perhaps, however, such elevation will not come immediately. Great fortunes do not come in a few hours; pain and delay are necessary for them. Wait and endure the distress that now pains and wounds you, for I know very well by what potion you will be brought to your cure. If you maintain your loyalty I shall give you a marsh mallow unguent that will heal your wounds. By my head, it will certainly appear if you serve with a good heart, and it will depend on how you fulfill, night and day, the commandments that I prescribe for pure lovers."

"Sir," I said, "for the grace of God, before you move from here charge me with your commandments. I am in good heart to perform them, but perhaps if I didn't know them I could go astray immediately. Therefore, since I don't want to be mistaken in anything, I desire very much to learn them." 2043

Love replied: "What you say is very good. Now listen and remember them. A master wastes his effort when the disciple does not turn his heart toward retaining what he hears so that he might remember it." The God of Love then charged me, word by word, with his commandments; this romance portrays them well. Let him who wishes to love give his attention to it, for the romance improves from this point on. From now on one will do well to listen to it, if he is one who knows how to recount it, for the end of the dream is very beautiful, and its matter is new. I tell you that he who will hear the end of the dream can learn a great deal about the games of Love, provided that he wishes to wait while I tell the tale in French and explain the dream's significance. The truth, which is hidden, will be quite open to you when you hear me explain the dream, for it doesn't contain a lying word. 2051

"First of all," said Love, "I wish and command that, if you do not want to commit a wrong against me, you must abandon villainy forever. I curse and excommunicate all those who love villainy. Since villainy makes them base, it is not right that I love it. A villain is cruel and pitiless; he does not understand the idea of service or friendship. 2077

"Next, guard well against repeating anything about other people which should be kept quiet. Slandering is not a good characteristic. Take, for example, the seneschal Kay: in former days, he was hated on account of his jeers, and he had a bad reputation. Just as men praised Gawain, who was well trained, on account of his courtesy, so they blamed Kay because he was wicked and cruel, insolent and evil-tongued beyond all other knights. 2087

"Be reasonable and easy to know, soft-spoken and just toward 2099 men of both high and low rank. Cultivate the habit, when you go along the streets, of being the first to greet other people; if someone greets you first, before you have opened your mouth, take care to return his greeting without delay.

2109   "Next, take care not to utter dirty words or anything bawdy. You should never open your mouth to name anything base. I do not consider any man courteous who names anything that is filthy or ugly.

2115   "Honor all women and exert yourself to serve them. If you hear any slanderer who goes around detracting women, take him to task and tell him to keep quiet. If you can, do something that is pleasing to ladies and girls, so that they will hear good reports told and retold about you. By this means you can rise in people's esteem.

2125   "After all this, guard against pride, for pride, rightly understood and considered, is madness and sin. He who is tainted with pride cannot bend his heart to serve nor to make an entreaty. The proud man does the contrary of what a pure lover should do.

2133   "He, however, who wants to take trouble for love must conduct himself with elegance. The man who seeks love is worth nothing without elegance. Elegance is not pride. One is worth more for being elegant, provided that he be empty of pride, so that he is neither foolish nor presumptuous. Outfit yourself beautifully, according to your income, in both dress and footwear. Beautiful garments and adornments improve a man a great deal. Therefore you should give your clothes to someone who knows how to do good tailoring, who will seat the seams well and make the sleeves fit properly. You should have fine laced shoes and small boots and get new ones often, and you must see that they are so close-fitting that the vulgar will go around arguing over the way you are going to get into or out of them. Deck yourself out with gloves, a belt, and a silk purse; if you are not rich enough to do so, then restrain yourself. You should, however, maintain yourself as beautifully as you can without ruining yourself. A chaplet of flowers that costs little, or of roses at Pentecost—everyone can have these, since great wealth is not required for them.

2165   "Allow no dirt on your person: wash your hands and scrub your teeth. If the least black shows under your fingernails, don't let it remain there. Sew your sleeves and comb your hair, but do not rouge or paint your face, for such a custom belongs only to ladies or to men of bad repute, who have had the misfortune to find a love contrary to Nature.

"Next, you should remember to keep a spirit of liveliness. Seek   2175
out joy and delight. Love cares nothing for a gloomy man. It's a courtly disease through which one laughs, plays, and has a good time. It is thus that lovers have hours of joy and hours of torment. At one hour they feel that the sickness of love is sweet, at another, bitter. The disease of love is very changeable. Now the lover is playful, now tormented, now desolated; at one hour he weeps and at another sings. If, then, you can produce some diverting entertainment by which you might be agreeable to people, I command you to do so. Everyone in all places should do what he knows suits him best, for such conduct brings praise, esteem, and gratitude.

"If you feel yourself active and light, don't resist the impulse   2195
to jump; if you are a good horseman, you should spur your mount over hill and dale; if you know how to break lances, you can gain great esteem from doing so; and if you are graceful at arms, you will be ten times loved for that quality. If you have a clear, sound voice and are urged to sing, you should not try to excuse yourself, for a beautiful song is very pleasing. Moreover, it is very advantageous for a young fellow to know how to play the viol, to flute, and to dance. By these means he can further himself a great deal.

"Don't let yourself be thought miserly, for such a reputation   2211
could be very troublesome. It is fitting for lovers to give more freely of what they have than do those vulgar, stupid simpletons. No man who doesn't like to give can ever know anything about love. If anyone wants to take pains in loving, he must certainly avoid avarice, for he who, for the sake of a glance or a pleasant smile, has given his heart away completely should certainly, after so rich a gift, give his possessions away without any reserve.

"Now I want to recall briefly what I have told you so that you   2225
will remember, for a speech is less difficult to retain when it is short. Whoever wants to make Love his master must be courteous and without pride; he should keep himself elegant and gay and be esteemed for his generosity.

"Next, I ordain that night and day, in a penitential spirit and   2233
without turning back, you place your thought on love, that you think of it always, without ceasing, and that you recall the sweet

hour whose joy dwells so strongly in you. And in order that you may be a pure lover, I wish and command you to put your heart in a single place so that it be not divided, but whole and without deceit, for I do not like division. Whoever divides his heart among several places has a little bit of it everywhere. But I do not in the least fear him who puts his whole heart in one place; therefore I want you to do so. Take care, however, that you do not lend it, for if you had done so, I would think it a contemptible act; give it rather as a gift with full rights of possession, and you will have greater merit. The favor shown in lending something is soon returned and paid for, but the reward for something given as a gift should be great. Then give it fully and freely, and do so with an easy manner, for one must prize that which is given with a pleasant countenance. I would not give one pea for a gift that one gave in spite of himself.

2265   "When you have given your heart away, as I have been exhorting you to do, things will happen to you that are painful and hard for lovers to bear. Often, when you remember your love, you will be forced to leave other people so that they might not notice the suffering which racks you. You will go all alone to a place apart; then sighs and laments, shivers, and many other sorrows will come to you. You will be tormented in several ways, one hour hot, another cold, ruddy at one time and pale at another. You have never had any fever as bad, neither daily nor quartan agues. Before this fever leaves you, you will indeed have tested the sorrows of love. Now it will happen many times, as you are thinking, that you will forget yourself and for a long time will be like a mute image that neither stirs nor moves, without budging a foot, a hand, or a finger, without moving your eyes or speaking. At the end of this time you will come back in your memory and will give a start of fright upon returning, just like a man who is afraid, and you will sigh from the depths of your heart, for you well know that thus do those who have tested the sorrows that now so torment you.

2299   "Next, it is right for you to remember that your sweetheart is very far away from you. Then you will say: 'Oh God, how miserable I am when I do not go where my heart is! Why do I send my heart thus along? I think constantly of that place and see nothing of it. I cannot send my eyes after my heart, to accompany it; and if my eyes do not do so, I attach no value to the fact that they see. Must they be held here? No, they should rather go to visit what the heart so desires. I can indeed consider myself a sluggard when I am so far from my heart. God help me, I hold myself a fool. Now I shall go; no longer will I leave my heart. I shall never be at ease until I see some sign of it.' Then you will set out on your way, but under such conditions that you will often fail of your design and spend your steps in vain. What you seek you will not see, and you will have to return, thoughtful and sad, without doing anything more.

"Then you will be in deep misery and be visited again by sighs, 2325 pangs, and shivers, that prick more sharply than a hedgehog. Let him who does not know this fact ask it of those who are loyal lovers. You will not be able to calm your heart, but will continue to go around trying to see by chance what you long for so much. And if you can struggle until you attain a glimpse, you will want to be very intent on satisfying and feasting your eyes. As a result of the beauty that you see, great joy will dwell in your heart; know, too, that by looking you will make your heart fry and burn, and as you look you will always quicken the burning fire. The more anyone looks upon what he loves, the more he lights and burns his heart. This fat lights and keeps blazing the fire that makes men love. By custom every lover follows the fire that burns him and lights him. When he feels the fire from close by, he goes away by approaching closer. The fire consists in his contemplation of his sweetheart, who makes him burn. The closer he stays to her the more avid he is for love. Wise men and simpletons all follow this rule: he who is nearer the fire burns more.

"As long as you see your joy thus you will never seek to move, 2359 and, when you have to leave, you will remember the whole day afterward what you have seen. And you will think yourself very vilely deceived in one respect, that you never had a heart bold enough to speak with her; like a gauche simpleton you stood near her without uttering a word. You will think that you acted badly in not speaking to the beauty before she had gone. You are bound to become exceedingly vexed, for if you had been able to elicit from her nothing but a fair greeting it would have been worth a hundred marks to you.

"Then you will take to lamenting and will look for an occasion 2377 to go again along the street where you saw the one to whom you dared not speak. You would enter her house very gladly, if you had the opportunity. It is right that all your walks, all your comings and goings, should come back to that neighborhood, but hide yourself well from other people and seek out some pretext other than that which impels you to that area. It is very good sense to cover yourself.

2391   "If it happens that you find the beauty where you must speak to her or greet her, then your color will be bound to change, and all your blood will thrill. When you think to begin, your sense and powers of speech will fail you; and if you can get so far that you dare to begin your speech, then you will be so full of shame that when you should say three things you will not utter two of them. There never was a man so prudent in such a case that he did not forget a great deal, unless he were a trickster. But false lovers tell their streams of tales just as they wish, without fear. They are great liars; these cruel, wicked traitors say one thing and think another.

2411   "When you have finished your discussion—without saying a single word of villainy—you will think yourself tricked because you forgot something you should have said. Then again you will feel your martyrdom. This is the battle, the fire, this the struggle that lasts forever. A lover will never possess what he seeks; something is always missing, and he is never at peace. This war will never finish until I wish to seek the peace.

2423   "When night comes, then you will have more than a thousand torments. You will lie down in your bed with small delight, for when you think that you are about to sleep, you will begin to tremble, to shudder and shake. You will have to turn on one side, then on the other, then on your stomach, like someone with toothache. Then you will remember her incomparable manner and appearance. And I will tell you of a great wonder: there will be a time when you will think that you are holding her, with shining face, quite naked in your arms, just as if she had become wholly your sweetheart and your companion. Then you will build castles in Spain and will take joy in nothing as much as in going around deluding yourself with this delectable thought that contains only lies and fables. But you will not be able to dwell long on this thought. Then you will begin to weep and will say:

2449   " 'God! Have I been dreaming? What is this? Where was I lying? Where did this thought come from? Certainly I would wish that it might come back ten or twenty times a day, for it nourishes me completely and fills me with joy and good fortune. But it is death to me that it lasts for so little. God! Shall I ever see the day when I may actually be in the situation that I imagine? I would want it even with the condition that I should die straightway. Death would not trouble me if I might die in my sweetheart's arms. It is Love that troubles and torments me: I often complain and lament my state. But if Love arranges that I may have complete joy of my sweetheart, my woes will be well purchased.

" 'Alas! I ask for a possession too dear. I do not think myself   2468 wise in making such an outrageous request. It is right to refuse him who makes a stupid request. I don't know how I dared say it. Many a man worthier and more renowned than I would be highly honored by a considerably smaller recompense. But if the fair one deigned to ease my pain with no more than a single kiss I would have a rich reward for the pain that I have suffered. Still, that is a big thing to expect. I may indeed think myself a fool when I have set my heart where I shall have neither joy nor profit. Now I am speaking like a stupid wretch, for one look from her is worth more than the complete enjoyment of another. God help me, I should like very much to see her at this instant. He who saw her now would be cured. O God! When will the dawn come? I have stayed in this bed too long, for I can hardly bear to lie down without that which I desire. To lie without rest or sleep is a vexatious thing. Certainly it troubles me very much that the dawn does not spring up at this instant and that the entire night has not passed, for, if it were day I would get up. Ah, sun! For God's sake, hurry, and do not delay or stop; banish the dark night, with its troubles that weigh me down.'

"Thus, if I ever knew the sickness of love, you will carry on,   2505 with little sleep, throughout the night. And when you can't bear your suffering lying awake in your bed, you will have to dress, put on your shoes, and adorn yourself. Then, whether it is raining or freezing, you will go in secret directly to the house of your sweetheart, who will be sound asleep, with hardly a thought of you. One hour you will go to the back door to see if it were left unclosed, and there you will perch like a crane all alone, outside in the wind and rain. Afterward you will come to the front door, and if you find a chink, a window or lock, put your ear to it to hear if they are lying asleep. And if the fair one alone wakes up, I advise and counsel you to lament and sigh so that she hears you and knows that for love of her you cannot rest in your bed. A woman who is not hardhearted ought certainly to have pity on him who endures such pain for her sake.

2535   "Now I will tell you what you should do for the love of that high sanctuary whose comfort you cannot possess: on your return, kiss the door, and in order that no one sees you in front of the house or in the street, take care that you have left before the light of day. These comings and goings, these night watches and conversations make lovers waste away under their garments, as you know very well from your own experience. It is normal that you should waste away, for love, you understand, leaves no color or fat on pure lovers. Those who go around betraying women are readily recognizable by this test. In order to flatter they say that they have lost their taste for food and drink, but I see these tricksters fatter than an abbot or a prior.

2557   "Furthermore, I command and charge you to be generous toward the servant girl of the house. Give her something to adorn herself such that she will call you a worthy man. You should honor and hold dear both your sweetheart and all those who wish her well. Through them much good can come to you. When those close to her tell her that they have found you upright, courteous, and accomplished, she will value you half again as much for their praise.

2569   "Don't leave the country often; if some great necessity compels you to do so, take care that your heart remains, and plan to return quickly. You should delay very little; pretend that any delay keeps you from the sight of her who has your heart in her keeping.

2577   "Now I have told you how and in what manner a lover should perform my service. Do so if you wish to have your pleasure of the fair one."

2581   When Love had made these commands, I asked him: "Sir, how and in what way can these lovers endure the woes that you have told me about? I am greatly terrified by them. How can one keep on living when he is in burning pain and sorrow, weeping and sighing, weighed down by the care and attention that he must give to every detail and every condition? God help me; I marvel greatly how any man, even one of iron, can live for a year in such hell."

The God of Love then replied to my question with a good 2595 explanation: "Fair friend, no one has anything good unless he pays for it. Men love a possession more when they have bought it at a higher price, and the good things for which one has suffered are received with greater thanks. It is true that no woe measures up to that which colors lovers. No more than one can empty the sea could any man recount in a romance or a book the woes of love. And in any case, lovers must live, for life is their occupation. Everyone willingly flees death: he who is put into a dark prison, in a verminous, filthy place, with nothing to eat but barley or oat bread, does not die from his suffering. Hope brings him comfort, and he always thinks that some change will see him free. He whom Love keeps in his prison has exactly the same expectation: he hopes for a remedy; this hope comforts him, and his heart's desire brings him to offer his body in martyrdom. Hope makes him bear pains that no one can tell for the joy that is worth a hundred times as much. Hope triumphs through suffering and enables lovers to live. Blessed be Hope, who thus furthers the cause of lovers! Hope is very courteous: right up to the end, she will never leave any valiant man, in any peril or distress, by so much as one fathom. Even to the robber whom men want to hang she always brings the expectation of her grace. She will protect you and will never part from you without helping you in your need.

"Along with her I give you three other gifts that bring great 2640 comfort to those in my nets. The first to comfort those whom Love enmeshes is Sweet Thought, who recalls to them what Hope agrees to. When the lover sighs and complains and lies in sorrow and martyrdom, Sweet Thought comes after a certain time, disperses his wrath and sorrow, and, by his coming, makes the lover remember the joy that Hope had promised him. Afterward he presents him with images of laughing eyes, a well-formed nose, neither too large nor too small, and a red mouth whose breath is fragrant. Sweet Thought pleases the lover very much when he recalls to him the beauty of each member. He continues by doubling the lover's solace when he brings to his memory a smile, a lovely appearance, or a beautiful face that his sweetheart had turned upon him. Sweet Thought thus assuages the sorrow and torment of love. I very much want you to have this comfort.

2668   "And if you refused the second, which is no less sweet, you would be very resistant. This second is Sweet Talk. He has brought help to many young men and women, for everyone who holds conversation about his loves is diverted. I remember that in this connection a lady who loved well uttered a courteous word in her song: 'I am in a good school,' she said, 'whenever anyone discusses my lover with me. God help me, anyone who speaks to me of him, no matter what he says, has given me relief.' She knew whatever there was to know about Sweet Talk, for she had tested him in many ways.

2686   "Now I want you to seek out a wise and discreet companion, one to whom you can tell all your desires and reveal your whole heart. He will be a great help to you. When your troubles wring you with anguish, you will go to him for comfort, and the two of you will talk together about the beautiful lady who, with her beauty, her appearance, with her mere countenance, is stealing your heart. You will tell him your whole situation and will ask his advice on how you can do something which might be pleasing to your sweetheart. If he who is so much your friend has given his heart in good love, then the companionship will be worth more. It is quite right that he tell you in turn whether his sweetheart is a young girl or

2707 not, who she is and what her name is. And you will not fear that he will try to take your love away nor expose you. Rather will you keep good faith between you, you to him and he to you. Know that it is a very pleasant thing when one has a man to whom one dares to tell one's counsel and one's secrets. You will take this pleasure with great thanks and, when you have tried it, you will consider yourself well repaid.

2717   "The third benefit to come up for consideration is Sweet Looks, who usually comes late to those whose loves are far away. However, I advise you to stay close to yours for the sake of Sweet Looks, so that his comforts are not too long delayed. He is very delightful and delicious to lovers. The eyes have many a good fortune in the morning, when God shows them the precious sanctuary for which they have such longing. No misfortune should happen to them on the day when they can see it. They fear neither dust nor wind nor any other troublesome thing. And when the eyes live in delight, they are so taught and instructed that they cannot be joyful alone, but want the heart to enjoy itself too. The eyes alleviate the heart's woes, for, like true messengers, they send the heart immediate reports of what they see; and then the heart for joy must forget the sorrows and darkness in which it had dwelt. In just the same way as the light drives darkness before it, so Sweet Looks effaces the shadows where the heart lies night and day, languishing of love; for the heart suffers no pain when the eyes see what it wishes.

"Now, it seems to me, I have declared to you what I saw you   2751
were lacking, for I have told you, without lying, the benefits that can protect lovers and keep them from death. Now you know what will bring you comfort: at the least you will have Hope, and without doubt you will have Sweet Thought, Sweet Talk, and Sweet Looks. I want each of these to watch over you until you can expect something better, for in the future you will have other good things, not less but greater. For the moment, however, I give you this much."

As soon as Love had told me his pleasure, he vanished before I   2765
knew a word to say; I was completely stupefied when I saw no one near me. My wounds pained me sorely, and I knew that I could not be cured except through the rosebud where I had placed all my heart's yearning. And to obtain it, I had confidence in no one except the God of Love. Indeed, I knew for a truth that there was no hope of obtaining it if Love did not intervene for me.

The rosebushes were enclosed about with a hedge, as if forever,   2779
but I would very willingly have penetrated the enclosure for the sake of the rosebud, which was better than balm, if I had not feared to incur blame; as soon as I tried, it could appear that I wanted to steal the roses.

As I thus thought over the possibility of passing to the other   2787
side of the hedge, I saw, coming straight toward me, a handsome and personable youth in whom there was nothing to find fault with. He was called Fair Welcoming, and he was the son of Courtesy the wise. He very pleasantly left the passage through the hedge open to me and said in a friendly way:

"Dear fair friend, if it pleases you, pass without hindrance   2797
through the hedge to smell the perfume of the roses. I can well

assure you that you will experience no trouble or churlishness provided that you avoid folly. If I can help you in any way, never seek to plead with me, for I am ready at your service. I tell you all this without pretense."

2807 "Sir," I said to Fair Welcoming, "I accept this promise with thanks, and may you have grace and merit in return for the kindness that you have uttered, for it comes from your great generosity. And when it pleases you, I am ready to undertake your service willingly."

2814 Through thorns and briars, of which there were many in the hedge, I passed straightway to the other side. I went wandering toward the rosebud, which gave forth a better odor than the others, and Fair Welcoming directed me. I tell you that I was overjoyed at being able to remain so near that I might have attained to the rose.

2823 Fair Welcoming served me well when I saw the bud so close. But a base churl—shame come to him—was resting nearby. His name was Resistance, and he was keeper and guard of all the rosebushes. The wretch was off to one side, all covered with grass and leaves, in order to spy on and catch unaware those whom he saw reaching out their hands toward the roses. The evil dog was not alone but had as his companions Foul Mouth the tale-bearer and Shame and Fear along with him. The most worthy among them was Shame. If one tells her parentage and ancestry correctly, she was the daughter of Reason the wise, and her father's name was Misdeeds, a man so hideous and ugly that Reason never lay with

2845 him but conceived Shame just upon seeing him. When God had caused Shame to be born, Chastity, who should be the lady of roses and buds, was attacked by scoundrels of unbridled appetite so that she needed help, for it was Venus who had attacked her. Venus often steals from her, night and day, both roses and buds together. Chastity then asked Reason for her daughter. Since Chastity was the disheartened victim of Venus's persecution, Reason wanted to grant her her prayer and, in accordance with her request, loaned her her daughter Shame, a simple, honest girl. Then, the better to guard the rosebushes, Jealousy had Fear come, who strives mightily to do her bidding. Now there are four to guard the roses, and these four will let themselves be soundly beaten before anyone carries off a bud or a rose. I would have arrived at a fair harbor if they had not been watching me, for Fair Welcoming, open and well brought up, did whatever he knew that should have pleased me. He often urged me to approach the rosebud and touch the bush that bore it. He gave me permission for all this because he thought that I wanted it; he cut a green leaf near the bud and gave it to me because it had been born nearby.

I became very proud of the leaf, and when I felt myself ac-   2879
quainted and thus intimate with Fair Welcoming, I thought that I had indeed arrived. Then I took heart and boldly told him how Love had captured and wounded me.

"Sir," I said, "I shall never have any joy except through one   2886
thing, for I have enclosed within my heart a very heavy sickness that I don't know how to tell, for I fear greatly that I would anger you. It would be better for me to be cut up piece by piece with a steel knife than that you should be angered."

"Tell me your wish," he said, "since nothing that you want to   2895
say will ever cause me sorrow."

Then I said to him, "Know, fair sir, that Love torments me   2898
grievously. Do not think that I am lying to you; he has made five wounds in my heart, and their pain will never cease if you do not give me the rosebud that is more beautifully formed than the others. It is my death and my life; I have no desire for any other thing."

Then Fair Welcoming grew frightened and said to me: "Brother,   2907
you aspire to what cannot take place. What! Do you want to disgrace me? You would indeed have made a fool out of me if you had plucked the rosebud from its bush. It is not just to strip it of its nature, and you are base to ask it. Let it grow and improve; I love it so much that for no living man would I want it exiled from the bush that bore it."

At this point the scoundrel Resistance jumped out from where   2920
he was hidden. He was large and black, with bristly hair, and his eyes were as red as fire; his nose was flat, his face hideous, and he cried out in rage:

"Fair Welcoming, why have you brought this young man in   2926
among the roses? God save me, you have done wrong, since he hopes for your degradation. Cursed be he—except you only—who led him into this garden. He who serves a criminal is himself as much one. You plan his good and he seeks to shame and oppose

you. Flee, young man, flee from here, for it would take only a little to make me kill you. Fair Welcoming knew you very badly when he took such pains to serve you, while you seek only to trick him. Ask me no more to trust you, for the treason that you have hatched is now indeed proved."

2943　　Because of the hideous, black villain who threatened to attack me, I dared stay there no longer. He made me clear the hedge in great fear and haste; the villain shook his head and said that if I ever returned he would give me harsh treatment.

2951　　Then Fair Welcoming fled and I remained stupefied, overcome with shame, and I repented for ever saying what I thought. I remembered my folly, and I saw that my body was given over to suffering, pain, and martyrdom. And with all this I was most angry that I had dared to pass through the hedge. No one has suffered who has not tried Love. Do not believe that anyone, if he has not loved, has known what great anguish is. Love was acquitting himself very well toward me of all the suffering that he had told me about. No heart could think or mouth of man tell over the fourth part of my sorrow. My heart almost left me when I remembered the rose from which I had to be thus separated.

3

THE INVOLVEMENT OF REASON AND

THE CASTLE OF JEALOUSY

I was in this state for a long time, until the lady who looks down   2971
from her tower saw, from her observation-point, that I was thus
downcast. This lady's name was Reason. She then came down from
her tower and came straight to me. She was neither young nor
white with age, neither too tall nor too short, neither too thin nor
too fat; the eyes in her head shone like two stars, and she wore a
crown on her head. She looked like a person of high estate. By
her appearance and her face it seemed that she was made in
paradise, for Nature would not have known how to make a work
of such regularity. Know, if the letter does not lie, that God made
her personally in his likeness and in his image and gave her such
advantage that she has the power and the lordship to keep man
from folly, provided that he be such that he believe her.

While I was thus lamenting, Reason began thereupon: "Fair   2996
friend, folly and childishness have brought you this suffering and
dismay. It was an evil hour when you saw the beauty of May that
gladdened your heart so much. It was an evil hour when you went
to shelter in the cool shade of the garden where Idleness carries
the key with which she opened the gate for you. He who acquaints
himself with Idleness is a fool; acquaintance with her is very
dangerous, for she has betrayed and deceived you. Love would
never have seen you if Idleness had not led you into the fair garden
of Diversion. If you have behaved stupidly, now do what you can
to recover, and take good care not to believe any advice that would
make you act stupidly. He who corrects himself commits the best
kind of folly, and one should not wonder when a young man commits a folly. Now I want to tell and advise you to forget the love
by which I see that you are thus weakened, thus conquered and
tormented. I cannot otherwise envisage your health or cure, for
cruel Resistance hopes to wage a very violent war against you. You

do not have to test him. Moreover, Resistance is worth nothing in comparison with my daughter Shame, who guards and protects the roses like one who is no simpleton. Thus on her account you should have great fear, for I see no one worse for your desires.

3033 With these is Foul Mouth, who will allow no man to touch the rose. Before anything can be done, he will have reported it in a hundred places. You have very hard people to deal with. Now consider carefully which course is better, to abandon or to pursue what makes you live in sorrow, that sickness called love, in which there is nothing but madness. Madness, God help me, is the truth! A man who loves can do nothing well nor attend to any worldly gain: if he is a clerk, he loses his learning, and if he follows some other trade, he can hardly accomplish it. Moreover, he suffers more than a hermit or a white monk. The pain of love is immeasurable and its joy of short duration. If a man has any joy of love, it lasts but little, and he has it by chance, for I see that many strive for love who in the end miss it completely. You didn't heed any of my counsel when you gave yourself to the God of Love. It was your too-fickle heart that made you enter into such folly. Your folly was quickly undertaken, but to leave off requires great skill. Now don't set store by the love that makes you live without worth, for if one does not prevent it, madness increases constantly. Take the bit hard in your teeth; subdue and curb your heart. You must pit your strength and resistance against the thoughts of your heart. He who always believes his heart cannot keep from committing acts of folly."

3073 When I heard this rebuke I replied angrily: "Lady, I very much want to beg you to give over lecturing me. You tell me that I should curb my heart, so that Love may no longer subjugate it. Do you think then that Love would agree that I should curb and subdue the heart which is his in full and complete possession? What you say cannot be. Love has so subdued my heart that it is not subject to my will; he rules it so firmly that he has made a key to lock it. Now let me be immediately, for you could waste your French in idleness. I would rather die thus than that Love should have accused me of falsity or treason. I want to be praised or blamed, at the end, for having loved well. Anyone who lectures me annoys me."

Thereupon Reason left, since she saw that by speech she could   3096
not turn me from my purpose.

I remained, full of anger and sorrow, often weeping, often com-   3099
plaining, for I knew of no way of getting out of my plight by
myself, until it came to my memory that Love had told me that I
should seek out a companion to whom I might say quite openly
what I thought. This companion would take my torment from
me. Then I reflected that I had a companion whom I knew to be
a very loyal one: his name was Friend, and I have never had a
better companion.

I went off quickly to him and, just as Love had recommended,   3111
disclosed to him the obstacles by which I felt myself surrounded: I
complained to him of Resistance, who all but wanted to swallow
me whole, who made Fair Welcoming go away when he saw me
talking to him about the rosebud toward which I yearned, and
who told me that I would pay for it if he ever saw me enter the
enclosure for any reason.

When Friend knew the truth, he was not frightened, but said   3123
to me: "Now, companion, be reassured and undismayed. I have
known Resistance well for a long time. He has learned to maltreat,
injure, and menace those who are beginning to love. I found out
about him a long time ago. If you have found him cruel, he will
be quite otherwise at the end. I know him like a penny. He knows
well how to become mild when you use flattery or supplication.
Now I will tell you what to do. I recommend that you beg him
to pardon you and, through love and accord, to give over his ill
will; and put it to him as an agreement that never from now on
will you do anything to displease him. When anyone flatters him
with such blandishments, it is a thing that mollifies him very much."

Friend talked and spoke so much that he comforted me a little   3146
and gave me the hardihood and will to go forth and see if I might
placate Resistance.

I came contrite to Resistance, eager to make my peace, but I did   3151
not pass through the hedge because he had forbidden me the
passage. I found him standing upright, menacing and angry in
appearance, with a thorn club in his hand. With bent head I held
my course toward him and said:

"Sir, I have come here to beg for your mercy. I am weighed   3159 down with chagrin if I ever did anything that could have angered you, but now I am ready to make amends in any way that you can command. Unquestionably, it was Love, from whom I cannot withdraw my heart, who made me act so. But I shall never aspire to anything that would trouble you. I would rather endure my discomfort than do anything to displease you. Now I request that you have pity on me and soften your anger, which greatly frightens me, and I swear to you and promise that I shall behave toward you in such a way that I shall never commit any fault, provided that you might wish to accord me what you cannot forbid me. Please grant only that I may love; I ask no other thing. If you grant this request I shall perform all your other wishes. Although you cannot prevent me, I shall not seek to trick you in this matter, for, since it suits me, I shall love no matter whom it may please or harm. But I would not, for my weight in silver, want you to be burdened."

3189   I found Resistance very difficult and slow to give over his bad humor. Still, I had spoken so well to him that, in the end, he pardoned me and said in a brief speech:

3194   "Your request does not harm me in any way, and I don't want to refuse you. Understand that I am not at all angry at you, and if you love, what does that matter to me? It leaves me neither warm nor cold. Love forever, as long as you are always far from my roses. I shall have no mercy on you if you ever pass through the hedge."

3203   Thus he granted my request, and I went in haste to tell Friend, who, like a good companion, rejoiced when he heard the news. "Now," he said, "your affair is going well. Resistance will be friendly toward you. After he has shown his arrogance, he does what many people wish. If you were to catch him in a good humor he would take pity on your suffering. Now you should endure and wait until you can catch him in a good state. I have well proved that one conquers and curbs the wicked by enduring."

3217   Friend, who wanted my advancement as much as I did, comforted me very tenderly. Thereupon I took leave of him and returned to the hedge that Resistance guarded, for I could not wait at least to see the rosebud, since I might have no other joy of it. Resistance took care often to see if I were indeed keeping my agreement with him, but I feared him so much that I had no desire to do wrong to him. In fact, to get acquainted with him and win him over, I took pains for a long time to perform his command, but it hindered me greatly that he withheld his grace for such a long time. Many times he saw me weep, lament, and sigh because he left me too long to shiver beside the hedge, for I dared not pass through to go to the rose. Certainly he saw by my behavior that Love ruled harshly over me and that in me there was neither dissimulation nor disloyalty, but he was so cruel that, however much he might hear me lament or complain, he did not yet deign to unbend.

Just as I was in this distress, God led Openness to me, and Pity   3247
with her. Without any more delay, the two of them went straight to Resistance, for the one and the other wanted to help me willingly, if they might, since they saw that there was need. Lady Openness—my thanks to her—spoke first and said:

"Resistance, so help me God, you have wronged this lover,   3257
whom you have treated very badly. Know that you dishonor yourself, for I have never learned that he has wronged you in any way. If Love's power makes him love, should you therefore blame him? He loses more thereby than you do, for he has endured many pains of love. But Love will not allow him to repent of it; even if someone were to burn him alive, he could not keep from loving. But, fair sir, how does it help you to inflict pain and torment on him? Have you declared war on him in order that he fear and honor you and be your subject? If Love holds him captive in his nets and makes him obey you, ought you therefore to hate him? You should rather have spared him sooner than a boastful rogue. It is an act of courtesy to come to the aid of him to whom one is superior. He who does not relent when he finds someone who makes a supplication to him has a very hard heart."

Pity spoke in turn: "It is true that harshness conquers humility,   3285
but it is a wicked crime for harshness to last too long. Therefore, Resistance, I want to request you not to continue your war against this captive who languishes there and who has never beguiled love. It is my opinion that you give him much more trouble than you should. From the time that you withdrew Fair Welcoming's company from him he has done too harsh a penance, for that is the thing that he most desires. He was troubled enough before, but now his grief is doubled; now that he lacks Fair Welcoming his

lot is as bad as if he were dead. Why do you create any opposition
to him? Love made him endure a great deal of woe, so much that
even to please you, he wouldn't need anything worse. Do not continue to maltreat him, for you gain nothing by doing so. Allow
Fair Welcoming to perform some act of mercy from now on.
Have mercy on a sinner. Since Openness is of the same opinion
and begs and urges you to pity him, do not refuse her request.
He who will not do anything for the two of us is very cruel and
wicked."

3317   Then Resistance could hold out no longer; he had to moderate
his stand. "Ladies," he said, "I dare not refuse you this request,
for to do so would be too great a villainy. Since it pleases you, I
want him to have the company of Fair Welcoming; I will impose
no barrier."

3325   Openness, the eloquent one, went then to Fair Welcoming and
courteously said to him, "Fair Welcoming, you are too far separated from this lover, whom you do not deign to look upon. Ever
since you have not seen him, he has been pensive and sad. If you
want to enjoy my love, consider being friendly toward him and
doing what he wishes. Know that, between us, Pity and I have
subdued Resistance, who exiled you from the lover."

3339   "I shall do whatever you would like," said Fair Welcoming,
"for, since Resistance has granted it, it is right."

3342   Then Openness sent him to me. To begin with, Fair Welcoming
saluted me sweetly. If he had been angry toward me, he was none
the worse for having been so; rather he showed me an appearance
fairer than he had ever shown before. He took me by the hand
then to lead me within the enclosure that Resistance had forbidden
to me. Now I had leave to go everywhere; now I had fallen, as
I thought, from deepest hell to paradise, for Fair Welcoming,
troubling himself to do what pleased me, led me everywhere.

3357   As I approached the rose, I found it somewhat enlarged, and
I saw that it had grown since the time when I had seen it from
close up. It was a little enlarged at the top; and I was pleased
that it was not so open that the seed was revealed. It was still
enclosed within the rose leaves, which raised it straight up and
filled the space within, so that the seed, with which the rose was
full, could not appear. God bless it, it was much more beautifully
open and redder than it had been before. I was amazed at the

marvel, and to the extent that it had grown more beautiful Love bound me more and more, and he always tightened his net more when I experienced more solace.

I remained there for a long time, for in Fair Welcoming I found   3379
much love and companionship. When I saw that he forbade me neither his comfort nor his service, I requested of him a thing that it is good to mention:

"Sir," I said, "know for a truth that I yearn strongly to have a   3386
precious kiss of the rose that exhales this sweet perfume, and if it should not displease you, I would request it of you as a gift. For God's sake sir, tell me then if it please you that I kiss it, for I could never do so unless it was pleasing to you."

"Friend," he said, "God help me, if Chastity did not hate me, I   3395
would never forbid you; but because of Chastity, toward whom I do not want to misbehave, I dare not let you. It is her constant custom to forbid me to give permission for a kiss to any lover who begs me for one, for he who can attain to a kiss can hardly remain at that point. Know well that he to whom one grants a kiss has the best, most pleasing part of his prize, along with a pledge for the rest."

When I heard him reply thus, I no longer wanted to beg him   3409
for the kiss, for I feared to anger him. One should not pursue a man beyond his welcome nor trouble him too much. You know very well that one doesn't cut down an oak tree at the first blow, any more than one gets wine from the wine-grapes before the press is squeezed. The boon of the kiss that I always desired was always delayed, but Venus, who wages continual war on Chastity, came to my rescue. She is the mother of the God of Love, who has rescued many a lover. In her right hand she held a blazing torch, whose flame has warmed many a lady. She was so quaint and so beautifully adorned that she looked like a goddess or a fairy. Whoever saw her could recognize from her splendid adornment that she was not a religious. I shall not now mention her dress, her handkerchief, the gold lace on her hair, her buckle or her belt, for I should delay too long; but you may know that she was very elegant but without a trace of pride. Venus drew near to Fair Welcoming and then started speaking to him:

"Why, fair sir, do you make such resistance to this lover's having   3442
a sweet kiss? It should not be forbidden him, for you know well

and see that he serves and loves loyally and that he is beautiful enough to be worthy of being loved in return. See how graceful he is, how handsome, how pleasant, sweet, and open toward all men. Moreover, he is not old but rather a child, and therefore worth more. There is no lady, no châtelaine whom I should not consider base if she were to make any resistance to him. His heart will not change if you grant him the kiss. A kiss would be very well used on him, since, believe it, he has very sweet breath; his mouth is not ugly but seems to be made on purpose for solace and diversion, for the lips are red and the teeth white and so clean that there is neither tartar nor filth on them. In my opinion, it would be very reasonble to accord him a kiss. If you believe me, give it to him, for you know that the longer you wait the more time you will lose."

3473   Fair Welcoming, who felt the breath of Venus's torch, gave me a gift of a kiss with no more delay. Venus and her torch had done so much that I had no longer to wait, but straightway took a sweet and delicious kiss from the rose. No one need ask if I was joyful, for into my heart there entered an odor that drove out my sorrow and sweetened the woes of love that had long been so bitter. I had never been so comforted. He who kisses a flower so pleasant, so very fragrant, is quickly cured. I shall never be so sorrowful that I may not be filled with delight and joy if I remember it. Even so, I have suffered many troubles and many bad nights since I kissed the rose. The sea will never be so calm that it may not be a little troubled by the wind. Love changes often: one hour he soothes, another pierces; he is rarely in the same situation.

3499   From now on it is right for me to tell you how I struggled with Shame, who gave me a lot of trouble afterward, and how the walls were raised and how there rose the rich and powerful castle that Love seized later through his efforts. I want to pursue the whole history, and I shall never be idle in writing it down as long as I believe that it may please the beautiful lady—may God be her cure—who better than any other shall, when she wishes, give me the reward.

3511   Foul Mouth, who thinks out and divines the plans of many lovers and who recounts all the evil that he knows, watched out for the fair reception that Fair Welcoming deigned to give me. At length he could not keep silent, since he was the son of an angry old woman and had a tongue that was exceedingly sharp, piercing, and bitter. In this respect he resembled his mother very much. From that time he began to accuse me and said that he would wager his eye that there was an evil relationship between me and Fair Welcoming. The glutton spoke so wildly about me and Courtesy's son that he awoke Jealousy, who rose up in fright when she heard the scandalmonger. When she had arisen, she ran as if mad toward Fair Welcoming, who would have preferred to be at Etampes or Meaux, and then attacked him in this speech:

"Worthless wretch, why have you taken leave of your senses to   3536 become the friend of a boy of whom I suspect evil? It is very apparent that you easily believe the flatteries of strange young nobodies. I will no longer trust you. Indeed, I shall have you bound or shut up close in a tower, for I see no other solution. Shame is too far removed from you, and she has not exerted herself much in guarding you and in holding you up short. It is my opinion that she gave very bad help to Chastity; she allowed a misguided wretch to come into our enclosure in order to dishonor both me and Chastity."

Fair Welcoming did not know what to reply. He would rather   3553 have gone to hide if she had not found him there and caught him with me and with full proof. But when I saw this contentious woman come, who argued and struggled against us, I straightway turned and fled from the dispute, which vexed me.

Shame, who was very afraid that she had done wrong, then   3561 drew forward. She was humble and simple, and instead of a wimple she wore a cloth like that of a nun in an abbey. Because she was stupefied, she began to speak in a low voice:

"For God's sake, lady, do not believe Foul Mouth the scandal-   3568 bearer; he is a man who lies easily and who has tricked many a worthy man. Fair Welcoming is not the first that he has accused. Foul Mouth is indeed in the habit of telling false tales about young men and young ladies. Without fail, and it is no lie, Fair Welcoming has too long a tether and has been allowed to attract men of a kind he has no business with, but certainly I do not believe that he had any intention of wickedness or folly. But it is true that his mother Courtesy, since she never loved a stupid man, taught him not to hesitate to become acquainted with people. You may know that Fair Welcoming has no other fault, no other secret design than that he is full of enjoyment and that he plays and speaks with people. Without fail, I have been too soft in watching over him and punishing him, and I therefore want to beg your mercy. If I have been a little too slow to do good, I am sorry for it and I repent of my folly. But from now on I shall put my whole thought on guarding Fair Welcoming; I shall never seek to avoid this task."

3601 "Shame, Shame," said Jealousy, "I am very afraid of being betrayed, for Lechery has risen so high that all could be brought to shame. It is no wonder that I fear; for Lechery reigns everywhere: her powers never cease growing; Chastity is not safe even in abbey or cloister. Therefore I shall build a wall again to enclose the rosebushes and roses. I shall not leave them thus revealed; I put little trust in your guardianship, for I see very well and know for certain that one might lose out with even a better guard. I would never see a year pass when people would not consider me stupid if I were not to take care. I must look after this business. Certainly I shall close off the way of access to those who come to spy out my roses in order to trick me. I shall never be idle in making a fortress that will enclose the roses all around. In the middle it will have a tower where Fair Welcoming will be imprisoned, for I fear treason. I plan to guard his body so well that he will not have the power to go outside nor to keep company with rascal boys who, in order to bring him to shame, go around flattering him with pretty speeches. These vagrants have too much found him a fool, a stupid shepherd easy to deceive. But, as I live, he may know as truth that it was an unhappy day when he ever turned a pleasant face toward them."

3638 With this word, Fear came trembling; she was so thunderstruck when she heard Jealousy that, knowing Jealousy's anger, she never dared say a word. She drew off behind, to one side, and straightway Jealousy withdrew and left Fear and Shame together. The whole slack of their rumps trembled. Fear, her head bent, spoke to her cousin Shame:

3649 "Shame," she said, "it weighs on me that we must hear this contention over a matter in which we can do nothing. April and May have passed many times, and we have never been blamed; but now Jealousy, who mistrusts us, vilifies and despises us. Let us go now to Resistance; let us tell him and show him well that he committed a great wrong in not taking greater trouble to guard this enclosure well. He allowed Fair Welcoming too much to do openly what he liked, and now he will have to mend his ways or—may he know it well and truly—he will have to flee from the earth, since he would not last out a war or quarrel with Jealousy if she conceived a hatred for him."

They confirmed this counsel and then came to Resistance. They   3669
found the peasant lying beneath a hawthorn. Instead of a pillow, he had, at his head, a large heap of grass, and he was beginning to sleep, but Shame awoke him and, as she stood over him, ran on with her abuse:

"How can you sleep at a time like this," she said, "with all   3678
this misfortune? Anyone is a fool to trust you, any more than a sheep's tail, to guard a rose or a rosebud. You are too lazy and idle; you should have been fierce and treated everyone brutally. It was madness that made you allow Fair Welcoming to introduce within the enclosure a man who could bring blame upon us. When you sleep, we, who can do nothing about it, hear all the contention. Have you been lying down now? Get up immediately and stop up all the holes in this hedge; be kind to no man. It doesn't agree with your name for you to do anything but make trouble. If Fair Welcoming is open and sweet, you are to be cruel and violent, full of offensive words that wound. I have heard it said in a proverb that a courtly boor talks nonsense, and that one can in no way make a sparrow hawk out of a buzzard. All those whom you have found agreeable consider you a simpleton. Do you want then just to be agreeable to people, to do good and serve them? Such an attitude inspires you with laziness, and everywhere you will have the glorious reputation of one who is weak and soft and who believes in those who bring pretty speeches."

Then Fear spoke afterward: "Certainly, Resistance, I marvel   3712
greatly that you are not wide awake to guard what you should. You could soon suffer if Jealousy's wrath grew, for she is very proud, very cruel, and disposed to quarrel. Today she saw Shame attacked, and, by her threats, has driven Fair Welcoming out of this place and sworn that he cannot remain without being walled in alive. All this has happened because of your wickedness, since there

is not a trace of rigor in you; I believe that you lack heart. But, if ever Jealousy knew, you would be in a bad state of pain and torment."

3731 Then the knave lifted his hood, rubbed his eyes, shook himself, puckered his nose, and rolled his eyes; he was full of wrath and anger when he heard himself thus abused.

3736 "I could go mad with rage now," he said, "when you consider me overcome. Certainly I have now lived too long if I cannot guard this enclosure. Let me be grilled alive if any man living ever enters here. My heart is angered from my belly that any man ever put his feet there; I would rather have had two lances thrust through my body. I acted like a fool—I recall it well—but now, with the two of you, I shall amend my fault. I shall never be lazy in defending this enclosure, and if I can capture anyone there within, he would be better off at Pavia. I swear to you and promise that never, on any day of my life, will you consider me neglectful of duty."

3755 Then Resistance drew himself up on his feet and put on the appearance of being enraged. In his hand he took a stick and went looking around the enclosure to see if he would find a path, trace, or hole that required stopping up. From now on the situation is very much changed, for Resistance becomes more cruel than he was before. The one who thus enraged him has made me die, for I shall never have the chance to see what I want. My heart is angered from my belly that I have offended Fair Welcoming. Know well, too, that all my limbs tremble when I remember the rose that I used to see nearby when I wished; and when I recall this kiss that placed in my heart an odor sweeter than balm, I almost swoon, for I still have the sweet taste of the rose enclosed in my heart. And know that when I remember that I must be separated from it, I

3782 would rather be dead than alive. It was an evil hour when I touched the rose to my face, my eyes, and my mouth, if Love does not allow me to touch it again for another time. Now that I have tried its taste, the covetousness that inflames and excites my heart has grown much greater. Now weeping and sighing will return, with long, sleepless thoughts, shivers, pangs, and lamentations. I will have many such sorrows, for I have fallen into hell. Cursed be Foul Mouth! It was his disloyal and false tongue that bought me this sauce.

From now on it is time for me to tell you of the activities of   3797
Jealousy, with her foul suspicion. There remained no mason or
ditcher in the country that she had not sent for, and, for a beginning, she had them construct ditches around the rosebushes. They
would cost a great deal of silver, for they were very wide and
deep. Above this moat the masons built a wall of cut stone, not
seated on shifting soil but founded on hard rock. This foundation,
all in suitable dimensions, went down to the foot of the moat and
grew narrower as it rose, so that the construction was very strong.
The wall was so regularly made that it formed a perfect square;
each side extended a hundred fathoms, so that the whole was as
long as it was broad. The turrets, side by side, were richly crenel-
lated and made of squared stone. There were four at the four
corners, very difficult to knock down, and again at the four gates,
where the wall was thick and high. There was one gate before
the front, necessarily capable of easy defense, nor did the two at the
sides or the one behind need to fear any stones from a catapult.
There were fine doors that could slide up and down, to the sorrow
of those outside, for if they dared venture too close, they could be
captured and held by these doors.

Within, in the middle of the enclosure, the master-builders con-   3833
structed a tower with great skill. There could not be a more
beautiful one, for it was large and broad and tall. The walls should
not give way to any machine for throwing missiles, for the mortar
was made of quicklime soaked in strong vinegar. The stone from
which they made the foundation was the native rock, as hard as
diamond. The tower was completely round; in all the world was
none so rich or better arranged within. Outside, it was surrounded
by a bailey that went right around so that between this wall and
the tower the rosebushes, bearing quantities of roses, were planted
thick. Within the castle were catapults and machines of many
sorts. You could have seen the mangonels above the crenels, and
at the apertures all around were arbalests that were stretched by
means of a screw jack and that no armor could withstand. Anyone
who wanted to approach the walls could only commit a stupidity.
Outside of the moat there was an enclosure of good strong walls,
with low embrasures, so that horses could not, at the first onset,
reach the moat without a battle beforehand.

Jealousy had placed a garrison in the castle that I am describing   3867 to you. It seemed to me that Resistance carried the key of the first gate, which opened toward the east, and, to my knowledge, there was a total count of thirty followers with him. Shame guarded the second gate, the one opening to the south. She was very wise, and I tell you that she had a great plenty of followers ready to do her will. Fear also had a large troop and was stationed to guard the third gate, which was placed on the left hand, toward the north. Fear will never be secure unless she is locked in, and she seldom opens the door, for, when she hears the wind moan or sees two grasshoppers jump, she is seized by panic on such occasions. Foul Mouth—God curse him—had soldiers from Normandy and guarded the door behind. Know, too, that he came and went, when it suited him, at the other three gates, since he had to be on the look-out at night. In the evening he would mount up to the crenels and make his pipes, his trumpets, and his horns resound. At one time he would play lays and discords and improvisations on the Cornish pipes; at another he would sing, to a flute accompaniment, that he never found a true woman.

3903   "There is no woman who does not smile with delight when she hears talk of lechery. This one's a whore, that one paints herself, and another looks around as if she were crazy. One is vulgar, another mad, and a third talks too much." Foul Mouth, who spares nothing, found some fault in every woman.

3911   Jealousy (God confound her!) garrisoned the round tower, and you may know that she placed there her closest friends until there was a large troop. And Fair Welcoming was in prison, locked up above in the tower, with the door so well barred that he had no possibility of coming out. With him there was an old woman—God shame her—to watch him; she had no other occupation except solely to spy and see that he did not conduct himself outrageously. No one could have tricked her, by sign or appearance, for there was no fraud that she did not know. In her youth she had indeed had her share of the blessings and the griefs that Love dispenses to his servants. Fair Welcoming kept quiet and listened, for he feared the old woman and was not so bold as to make a move, so that she might not perceive any foolish look on his face; she knew the whole of the old dance.

3937   As soon as Jealousy had seized Fair Welcoming and walled him up, she considered herself secure. Her castle, which she saw was very strong, gave her great comfort. She had no reason to fear that gluttons might steal roses or buds: the bushes were too strongly enclosed, and, waking or sleeping, she could be very secure.

But I, outside the wall, was given over to sorrow and woe. If anyone knew the life I led, he would have to take great pity upon it. Love now knew how to sell me the benefits that he had loaned me. I thought that I had bought them, but now he sold them all to me again, for I was in greater trouble, on account of the joy that I had lost, than I had ever been. Why should I go on telling you? I was like the peasant who casts his seed on the earth and rejoices when it begins to be fair and thick when it is in the blade; but before he collects a sheaf of it, the weather worsens and an evil cloud arises at the time when the ears should sprout and damages it by making the seed die within and robs the wretch of the hope that he had had too soon. I too feared that I had lost my hope and my expectation, for Love had advanced me so far that I had already begun to tell my greatest intimacies to Fair Welcoming, who was prepared to accept my advances. But Love is so changeable that he robbed me of everything at once, when I thought that I had won. It is just as with Fortune, who puts discontent into the hearts of men but at other times caresses and flatters them. Her appearance changes in a short time: one hour she smiles, at another she is sad. She has a wheel that turns, and when she wishes she raises the lowest up to the summit, and with a turn plunges him who was on top of the wheel into the mud. And I am the one who is so turned. It was an evil time when I saw the walls and the moat that I neither dare nor can pass. Since Fair Welcoming has been put in prison, I have no blessings or joy whatever, for my joy and my remedy lies wholly in him and in the rose that is enclosed within the walls, and he must come forth from his prison if Love ever wants me to be cured, for I shall never seek elsewhere to have honors or blessings, health or joy. Ah, Fair Welcoming, fair sweet friend, even if you have been put into prison, keep me at least in your heart! Do not, at any price, allow Jealousy the Savage to put your heart in servitude as she has done your body. If she punishes you on the outside, keep a heart of adamant within to oppose her correction. If your body stays in prison, watch at least that your heart loves me. A free heart does not stop loving because of blows or mistreatment. If Jealousy is hard toward you

3948

3991

and causes you harm and injury, be just as hard toward her; and take revenge, at least in thought when you cannot do otherwise, for the opposition that she shows to you. If you were to do so, I should consider myself well repaid; but I am in very great anxiety that you may not do so, for perhaps, because you have been put in prison on my account, you will not feel grateful to me. However, this situation does not exist because of any wrong that I may have committed toward you, for I never mentioned anything that should have been kept hidden. Indeed, God help me, this misfortune weighs more heavily on me than on you, for I suffer penance greater than anyone could tell. I almost melt with anger when I remember my loss, which is very great and apparent. And I think that my fear and my pain will bring me my death. Should I not indeed be fearful when I know that slanderers and envious traitors are eager to injure me? Ah! Fair Welcoming, I know in truth that they hope to deceive you and to influence you with their fables so that they may take you in tow on their line; and perhaps they have done so. I do not know now how things are going, but I am terribly afraid that you may have forgotten me, and I am in sorrow and pain. If I lose your good will, there will never be any comfort for me, since I have no ties of faith elsewhere.

PART II

BY JEAN DE MEUN

The Overthrow of Reason

4

DISCOURSE OF REASON

AND perhaps I have lost it; I am ready to despair of it. Despair!   4059
Alas! I shall not do so. I shall never despair of it, for if Hope were
to fail me, I should lack valor. I ought to comfort myself with the
thought that Love has told me, in order that I might the better
bear my ills, that Hope would be my surety and would go with me
everywhere. But what about this situation? What shall I do about
it? Even though Hope is courteous and kindly disposed, she is
still not certain in anything. She puts lovers into great distress
and becomes their lady and mistress. With her promise, she deceives many of love, for she often makes promises which she will
never keep. Here is the danger, God help me, for she keeps and
will keep in torment many good lovers who will never arrive at
their goals. No one knows what to hold to since he doesn't know
what will happen, and thus he who draws too near to Hope is a
fool. For when she constructs a good syllogism, one must be in
great fear lest she draw the worse conclusion; it has often been
seen that many have been deceived by her. At the same time she   4089
would wish that he who takes her side would have the better conclusion to the disputation; and I am a fool if I dare blame her.
Moreover, what is her good will worth to me if she doesn't help
me out of my torment? Too little, since she can give no counsel
except a promise. A promise without a gift is worth little, and possession of her promise leaves me with so many contraries that no
one can know their number. Resistance, Shame, and Fear encumber
me, and Jealousy and Foul Mouth (he poisons and taints all those
with whom he has to do and by his tongue delivers them to
martyrdom). All these have Fair Welcoming in prison, whom I
take into all my thoughts; and I know that if I cannot have him,
in a short time I shall no longer be alive. Above all, that dirty,
stinking, foul old woman, who has to guard him so close that he
dares look on no one, is making me waste away.

From now on my sorrow will strengthen. Certainly it is true   4113 that the God of Love by his grace gave me three gifts, but I lose them here: Sweet Thought, who helps me not at all; Sweet Talk, whose aid has also failed me; the third, named Sweet Looks, I have, God keep me, lost as well. Certainly they are fine gifts, but they will never be worth anything if Fair Welcoming does not come forth from the prison where he is being held unjustly. In my opinion, I shall die for him, since, believe me, he will never escape from there alive.

4127   Escape? Certainly not. By what force could we ever break out of such a fortress? It will certainly never come about through my efforts. Nor, believe me, did I show a grain of sense, but rather folly and madness, when I gave homage to the God of Love. It was Lady Idleness who made me do so. Shame to her and to her busybodying for giving in to my plea for shelter in the lovely garden; if she had known anything good, she would never have believed me. One should not believe a foolish man to the value even of an apple; he should be condemned and reproved before one allows him to commit folly. I was just such a fool, and she believed me. But she never believed me for any good. She brought about my desires too well, and now I must lament and sorrow. Reason warned me well of this situation. I may count myself as bereft of reason when from that time I neither renounced love nor trusted Reason's advice.

4151   Reason was right to blame me for ever setting out to love. It is fitting that I should feel these burdensome woes, and, believe me, I want to repent. Repent? Alas! What would I be doing? I should be a false, shameful traitor. Bad faith would indeed have attacked me: I would have betrayed my lord, and Fair Welcoming as well. Should he have my hatred if, to do me a courtesy, he languishes in the tower of Jealousy? Has he done me a courtesy? Indeed, one so great that no one could have believed it when he wanted me to trespass beyond the hedge and kiss the rose. I should not give him ill thanks for that courtesy, nor truly shall I ever do so. Never, please God, shall I utter complaints or cries against the God of Love, nor against Fair Welcoming or Hope, or against Idleness, who has been so gracious toward me, for it would be wrong of me to complain of their beneficence.

4175   So there is nothing to do but suffer and offer my body to martyrdom and wait in good hope until Love sends me solace. I must wait for his mercy, for he said to me, I well remember: "I shall take your service in grace and exalt you to a high place, as long as evil does not put you down again. But perhaps your advancement will not come about quickly." This was his whole speech, word for word. It is very clear that he loved me tenderly. Therefore I have only to serve well if I wish to merit his grace; any fault could lie only in me, not in the God of Love, for indeed a god is never deficient in any respect. The fault then lies certainly in me, and I do not know where it comes from, nor, perhaps, shall I ever know.

So let things go as they can, let the God of Love do as he wishes, 4195 whether it be to let me escape, to go on farther, or, if he wishes, to let me die. I shall never come to the end of my task, and I shall die if either I or another for me do not finish it. But if Love, who grieves me sorely, wished to finish it for me, no trouble that I encountered in his service could daunt me. Now may all go according to his design. Let him turn his thought toward my affair if he wishes; I can no longer undertake it alone. But whatever happens, I pray that after my death he remember Fair Welcoming who, without doing harm to me, has killed me. In any case, to divert him, and since I cannot bear the burden of his misfortune, I make my confession to you before I die, O Love, as do all loyal lovers, and I wish to make my testament here: at my departure I leave my heart to Fair Welcoming; I have no other goods to bequeath.

While I raved thus about the great sorrows I was suffering, 4221 not knowing where to seek a remedy for my grief and wrath, I saw fair Reason coming straight back to me; as she descended from her tower she heard my complaints.

"Fair friend," said Reason the fair, "how does your dispute 4229 progress? Will you ever be tired of loving? Have you not had enough suffering? How do the woes of love seem to you now? Are they too sweet or too bitter? Do you know how to choose the mean among them, the mean which can give you aid and sufficiency? Have you chosen a good lord, this one who has thus captured and subjugated you and who torments you without respite? The day you ever swore homage to him was an unhappy one for you; you were a fool when you set out on this affair. But undoubtedly you do not know about the lord with whom you are dealing; for if you knew him well you would never have become his man, or if you had become, you would not have served him for a summer, nor for a day, nor for an hour, but without delay, I think, you would have renounced your homage to him and would never have loved *par amour*. Do you really know him at all?"

4253　"Yes, lady."

"You do not."

"Yes, I do."

"How? By your soul?"

"Because he said to me, 'You should be very joyful since you have such a good master and a lord of so great renown.'"

4258　"Do you know him any further?"

"No, except that he gave me his commandments, then flew away quicker than an eagle while I remained in peril."

4262　"Indeed that's a poor acquaintance; but now I want you to understand him. You have drunk so much bitterness that your outlook is distorted. No unhappy wretch can support a greater load. It is a good thing to know one's lord; if you knew this God of Love well, you could escape easily from the prison where you are thus wasting away."

4272　"Truly, lady, since he is my sire and I his liege man wholly, my heart would listen willingly and would learn more if there were someone who could teach it."

4277　"By my head, I want to teach you, since your heart wants to hear. Now I shall show you without fable what is not demonstrable. You shall know straightway without knowledge and understand without understanding what can never be better known, demonstrated, or understood by any man who fixes his heart on love; but one will not suffer the less on account of this knowledge unless he is the sort that may wish to flee from love. Then I will have untied for you the knot that you will always find tied. Now give me your attention; here is the description of love.

4293　"Love is hateful peace and loving hate. It is disloyal loyalty and loyal disloyalty, fear that is completely confident and despairing hope. It is reason gone mad and reasonable madness, the sweet danger of drowning, a heavy burden easily handled. It is the treacherous Charybdis, repellent but attractive. It is a healthful languor and diseased health, a hunger satiated in the midst of abundance, a sufficiency always covetous. It is the thirst that is always drunk, a drunkenness intoxicated by its own thirst. False delight, joyous sorrow, enraged happiness, sweet ill, malicious sweetness, and a foul-smelling sweet perfume, love is a sin touched by pardon but a pardon stained by sin. It is suffering which is too joyous, a piteous cruelty, a movement without any certainty, a state of rest both too fixed and too movable. It is a spineless force, a strong weakness that moves all by its efforts. It is foolish sense, wise folly, a prosperity both sad and pleasant. It is the laugh filled with tears and weeping, and the repose always occupied by labor. Sweet hell and heaven of sorrow, it is the prison which solaces captivity. It is the springtime full of cold winter, the moth that refuses nothing but consumes everything from purple robes to homespun, for lovers are found beneath coarse clothing as well as in fine.

"There is no one, however high his lineage nor however wise he   4335 may be found, of such proved strength, bravery, or other good qualities, who may not be subjugated by the God of Love. The whole world travels that road. He is the god who turns them all from their road, if they are not those of genuinely evil life whom Genius excommunicates because they commit wrongs against Nature. However, since I have nothing to do with these, I do not wish people to love with that love by which at the end they proclaim themselves unhappy and sorrowful wretches because the God of Love goes about making fools of them. But if indeed you wish to win through to the point where the God of Love will be unable to harm you, and to be cured of that madness, you can drink nothing better than the thought of fleeing from him. You can become happy in no other way. If you follow him, he will follow you; if you flee, he will flee."

But Reason argued in vain, for when I had heard her through   4359 I replied: "Lady, I flatter myself that I know no more than before of how I can extricate myself from love. There are so many contraries in this lesson that I can learn nothing from it; and yet I can repeat it well by heart, for my heart never forgot any of it; indeed, I can make a public lecture of the whole thing, but to me alone it means nothing. But since you have described love to me, and have praised and blamed it so much, I beg you to define it in such a way that I may better remember it, for I have never heard it defined."

"Willingly," she replied. "Now listen carefully. Love, if I think   4376 right, is a sickness of thought that takes place between two persons of different sex when they are in close proximity and open to each other. It arises among people from the burning desire, born of disordinate glances, to embrace and kiss each other and to have the solace of one another's body. A lover so burns and is so enraptured that he thinks of nothing else; he takes no account of bearing fruit, but strives only for delight.

4389   "There are those of a certain kind who do not hold this love dear, but who always pretend to be pure lovers and do not deign to love *par amour*; thus they deceive ladies by promising them their hearts and souls and by swearing lies and fables to those whom they find gullible, until they have taken their pleasure with them. But such people are less deceived than the others; for it is always better, good master, to deceive than to be deceived, particularly in this battle, when one never knows where to seek the mean.

4403   "But I know very well without divination that whoever lies with a woman ought to wish with all his might to continue his divine self and to maintain himself in his likeness in order that the succession of generations might never fail, since all such likenesses are subject to decay. Nature wills, since father and mother disappear, that children rise up to continue the work of generation, and that one's life may be regained by means of another. For this purpose Nature has implanted delight in man because she wants the workman to take pleasure in his task in order that he might neither flee from it nor hate it, for there are many who would never make a move toward it if there were no delight to attract them. Thus Nature uses this subtle means of gaining her end.

4422   "Now understand that no one who desires only his pleasure in love travels the right road or has a right intention. Do you know what they do who go seeking delight? They give themselves up, like serfs or foolish wretches, to the prince of all vices; to seek delight is the root of all evil, as Tully concludes in the book that he wrote *On Old Age*, which he praises and desires more than youth.

4433   "Youth pushes men and women into all sorts of danger to body and soul; it is too powerful a thing to pass through without dying or breaking a limb, or without bringing shame or harm to oneself or one's family. Man passes his youth in every dissolution, follows evil company and disordinate ways, and often changes his goal. He may go into some convent because he does not know how to keep the freedom which Nature has endowed him with; he thinks that he can pluck the crane from the sky when he mews himself up there and remains until he is professed. Or again, he may feel the burden too heavy. If so, he may repent of his vows and leave the convent, or perhaps he may finish out his life there because he dare not return, and, held by shame, he may remain against his heart's desire. He will live in great discomfort and bewail the liberty that he has lost and that cannot be returned to him unless God grant him the grace to relieve his discomfort and keep him in a state of obedience through the virtue of patience. Youth pushes men into folly, debauchery, ribaldry, lechery, excesses, and fickle changes of heart; it creates situations so complex that they are scarcely ever untangled. Into such perils does Youth put those who turn their hearts to Delight. Delight thus ensnares and directs both the body and the mind of man by means of his chambermaid, Youth, who habitually does evil and attracts men to delight; she seeks to do no other task.

"But Age takes men away from Delight. Let whoever does not   4477
know this either learn it here, or ask it of the old whom Youth has held in her grasp. They will still recall enough of the many great perils which they have passed through and the follies that they have committed. When Old Age, their good companion on their journey, has taken from them the forces which ruled them in youth and the willful follies by which they were habitually tempted, she leads them back to the right path and guides them right up to the end of their course. But her favors are badly employed, since no one loves her or values her, at least, I know, not to the extent where he would wish to have old age for himself. No one wants to grow old, nor does Youth want to finish her life. So the old are amazed and marvel when their memories awaken and, as they must, they remember their follies and how they did this or that without any shame or remorse. Or if they did feel any shame or hurt, they wonder how they may escape such perils without worse consequences for their souls, their bodies, or their property.

"Now do you know where Youth lives, so esteemed by many   4507
men and women? As soon as she arrives at the proper age, Delight takes her into his household and wants her to serve him. She would be his servant even for nothing and does so so willingly

that she follows all his paths, abandons her body to him, and would not wish to live without him.

4517   "And do you know where Age lives? I want to tell you without delay, for you must go there, if during your youth Death does not make you descend into his dark, sombre cave. Labor and Suffering give Age a dwelling place, but they chain her and put her in irons and so beat her and torment her, so make her feel their flails, that they present her with the prospect of approaching death and the desire for repentence. Then, with this long-delayed thought, when she sees herself feeble and white with age, it comes to her memory that Youth, who plunged her whole past into vanity, has deceived her badly and that she will have wasted her life if she is not saved by the future, which may sustain her in her penitence for the sins that she committed in her youth, and which, through its good influence in the midst of this suffering, may lead her back to the sovereign good from which Youth severed her when she was drowned in vanities. The present lasts so short a time for her that it cannot be counted or measured.

4545   "But however the matter may go, whoever wants to enjoy love, without fail, man or woman, whether lady or girl, should seek its fruit, although they should not deny their share of delight. But I know that there are a lot of these women who don't want to become pregnant, and, when they become so, they are very chagrined and utter no complaint nor show any sign of distress except something silly or stupid when Shame has no control whatever over them.

4557   "Briefly then, everyone who gives himself over to the work of love turns only to Delight, except for those worthless ones who, corrupted by their filthy lives, are not bound by any laws and basely give themselves for money. Certainly there would never be a good woman who would abandon herself to take gifts. No man should ever take to himself a woman who wants to sell her flesh. Does he think that any woman who wants to flay her living body will hold it dear? A man so vilely tricked is indeed a wretch led astray when he believes that such a woman loves him just because she calls him her lover, smiles at him, and makes much of him. Certainly no such animal ought to be called friend or lover, nor is she worth being loved. A woman who seeks to despoil a man should be valued at nothing. I do not say that she may not, for pleasure and solace, wear an ornament given or sent by her friend, but she must not ask for it, since she would then be taking it basely; in return she should give him something of hers if she wants to act blamelessly. In this way their hearts join together, they love each other and pledge themselves by their gifts. Don't 4589 think that I would separate them; I want them to unite and do whatever they ought that is courteous and well behaved, but I want them to keep themselves from that foolish love which inflames hearts and makes them burn with desire. I want their love to be free of that covetousness that excites false hearts to grasp. Good love should be born of a pure heart; love should not be mastered by gifts any more than by bodily pleasures.

"But the love which holds you in its bonds gives you the prospect 4600 of carnal delight so that your intention runs nowhere but upon wishing to have the rose; you dream of no other possession. But you are not within two fingers' length of having it, and that is what is making your skin waste away, what takes away all your strength. When you took in the God of Love you received a burdensome guest; you have an evil guest in your inn. Therefore I advise you to eject him lest he rob you of all the thoughts which should turn to your profit; don't let him dwell there any longer. Hearts drunk with love are too much given over to misguided acts. You will know this at the end when you have lost your time and wasted your youth in this sorry pleasure. If you can live long enough to see yourself delivered from love, you will bewail the time you have lost, but you will never be able to recover it, if indeed you escape that far, for, in that love where you are caught, many, I dare say, lose their sense, their time, possessions, bodies, souls, and reputations."

Thus Reason preached to me. But Love prevented anything from 4629 being put into practice, although I heard the whole matter word for word, for Love drew me strongly and hunted through all my thoughts like a hunter whose course lies everywhere. He kept my heart constantly under his wing, and when I was seated for the sermon, he kept watch over me, outside of my head, with a shovel. Whenever Reason cast a word into one ear, he threw one into the other, with the result that she wasted all her efforts and only filled me with anger and wrath. Then, filled with ire, I said to her:

"Lady, you wish to betray me. Should I now hate people? 4645

Shall I despise everyone? If love were not good, I would never love with refined love, but live always in hatred. Then I would be a mortal sinner, in fact worse, by God, than a sneak thief; I couldn't help sinning. I have to get out of this difficulty by one of two ways: either I love or I hate. But perhaps I should pay more in the end for hatred, even though love weren't worth a penny. You would have given me good advice, then, you who have kept on preaching to me that I should renounce Love. He who wants to believe you is a fool.

4663 "But you have recalled to me another, little-known love which people may feel for each other. I have not heard you decry it; if you would define it, I should consider myself a fool if I did not listen and find out at least if I might learn the nature of love, if it would please you to explain it."

4673 "Certainly, fair friend," she replied, "you are a fool when you don't consider the sermon I have given you for your own profit as worth a straw; I will give you another one, for I am ready with all my power to fulfill your good request, but I do not know if it will do you any good.

4680 "Love is of several sorts other than that which has transformed you and taken away your rightful sense. You encountered it in an evil hour; for God's sake, see that you know it no further. One kind of love is named Friendship. It consists of mutual good will among men, without any discord, in accordance with the benevolence of God. Through the power of charity, goods are held in common in such a way that there may be no exception by any intention. No friend is slow to help another, but all are dependable, wise, discreet, and loyal, for the mind where loyalty is lacking is worthless. Whatever a man dares to think, he may as safely recount it to his friend as to himself alone, without any fear of denunciation. Such are the manners that those who wish to love perfectly ought to have as habitual practices. No man may be truly friendly if he is not so reliable and dependable that he will not change because of changing Fortune, so that his friend, who has put his whole heart in him, always finds him, rich or poor, in the same state of mind. And if he sees his friend being pushed toward poverty, he should not wait until he has to ask for help, for a favor granted upon request is sold at a price too niggardly

to hearts of great value. A worthy man is very ashamed when he   4715
asks someone to give him something. He thinks about it and
worries about it a great deal and is extremely uncomfortable before
he will ask, because he is ashamed to say what he has to and fears a
refusal. But when a person has been found who has previously
proved trustworthy in his love, then every occasion that one dare
think of is one for rejoicing and gladness, with no shame about
anything. For how could a person be ashamed before anyone of this
sort I have described? When one has told a secret to him, no third
person will ever know it; nor will the teller fear any reproach, for a
wise man keeps watch over his tongue, a thing no fool could do,
for a fool doesn't know how to keep his tongue still. A friend
will do even more; he will help one with everything that he can,
and will be happier to do so, to tell the truth, than his friend will
be to receive his help. Moreover, so great is the mastery of love,
that if he does not fulfill the request for the friend, he will be
no less troubled by his failure than will he who asked him. He who
comforts a friend, in any way he can, bears half his sorrow and
partakes of his joy, as long as their love is rightly shared.

"Tully says, in one of his works, that as long as our request   4747
is honest, we should make it of our friends according to the law
of this friendship, and in the same way should perform the request,
if it is made with right and reason. Without such a just request,
one should act in only two cases, which he excepts. If anyone
wanted to send them to death, we should try to deliver them
from it; and if their reputation is assailed, we should take care
that they are not defamed. In these two cases it is possible to
defend them without waiting for right and reason. No man should
refuse to do so in so far as love can excuse the case.

"This love which I put forward to you is not contrary to my   4763
purpose. I certainly want you to follow it and to avoid the other
love. This love is connected with every virtue, but the other leads
men to death.

"I want to tell you now of another love, which in its turn is   4769
contrary to the good love and is also to be strongly condemned:
it is the simulated desire of loving in hearts sick with the disease
of coveting gain. This love vacillates in the following way: as
soon as it loses hope of the profit that it wants to get, it inevitably

flickers and dies away, for the heart which does not love people for themselves can never be a loving one. Instead, it pretends and goes about flattering for the gain it hopes to have.

4783   "This is the love which comes from Fortune. It is eclipsed as is the moon which, when it falls into the shadow of the earth, is obscured and darkened, and, losing sight of the sun, loses its clear light. Then when it has passed through the shadow it returns wholly illuminated by the rays which the sun showers upon it as it beams again from the other side. Such is the nature of this love, now clear, now dark. As soon as Poverty covers it with his hideous shadowy mantle and it no longer sees the brightness of wealth, it must darken and flee; but when wealth shines again, it is brought back bathed in light. When riches are absent, love is lacking; as soon as they appear, love springs up.

4803   "Nearly all rich men are loved with this love that I have just described, particularly the misers who do not wish to cleanse their hearts of the great ardor and vice of covetous Avarice. A rich man who thinks himself loved is more horned than an antlered stag. Now isn't this a great folly? It is certain that he doesn't love; and how can he believe that anyone loves him unless he calls himself a fool? In such a case he is no wise man, but a fine branched stag. By God, he who wants real friends must be a friend. I can prove that he doesn't love: when he has his wealth and thinks his friends poor, he keeps his wealth and guards it from them. He plans to keep it always, until his mouth is closed and wicked death has struck him down. For he would first let his body be carved up limb by limb before he allowed his wealth to leave him, so that none of it would be shared with his friends. Thus love has no part whatever in this situation, for how could there be any real friendship in a heart that knows no lawful pity? Certainly, the man who neither loves nor is loved is much to be blamed.

4837   "And now that we come to Fortune when we hold a discourse above love, I should like to tell you a great marvel of which I don't believe you have ever heard the like. I don't know if you'll be able to credit it, but it is true nevertheless, and one may find it written, that perverse, contrary Fortune is worth more and profits men more than does pleasant and agreeable Fortune. If this idea seems doubtful to you, it still can be proved by reasoning.

Pleasant, agreeable Fortune lies to men, tricks them, and makes fools of them. Like a mother, she suckles them, and does not seem to give bitter milk. She gives them the appearance of being loyal when she distributes among them her delights—riches and honor, dignities and authority—and promises them stability in a condition of mutability; and when she places them on her wheel, she feeds them all on vain glory in worldly prosperity. Then they believe themselves such great rulers and see their estates as so secure that they can never fall from them. Then, when she has 4865 placed them in such a situation, she makes them believe that they have so many friends that they don't know how to number them, and that they cannot rid themselves of these friends who come and go around them and consider them their lords, who promise their services up to the point of giving the shirts off their backs, indeed, to the point of shedding blood, ready to obey them and follow them all the days of their life. And those who hear such speeches glorify themselves and believe them as though they were the Gospel. But all is flattery and guile, as these dupes would discover if they had lost all their good fortune and had no means of recovery. Then they will see these 'friends' get busy; for if, out of a hundred apparent friends, whether companions or relatives, one could remain to them, they ought to praise God for him. When this Fortune of whom I speak dwells among men, she confuses their understanding and feeds them on ignorance.

"But when contrary, perverse Fortune turns them from their 4893 high estate and tumbles them around the wheel from the summit toward the mire; when, like a mother-in-law, she places on their hearts a painful plaster moistened, not with vinegar, but with unhappy, meager poverty; then she shows that she is sincere and that no one should trust himself to prosperous Fortune, in whom there is no security whatever. Contrary Fortune makes men understand and know, as soon as they have lost their possessions, the kind of love with which they were loved by those who were formerly their friends; for those friends whom good Fortune gives are so shocked by evil fortune that they all become enemies. Not one of them remains, not even a half one; instead, they run away from and renounce their friends as soon as they see that they are poor. They no longer have anything to do with them, but everywhere they go around blaming, defaming, and proclaiming them wretched fools. Even those to whom they gave more, when they saw themselves in their high estate, go around testifying in gleeful voice that their loss arrived through their folly. Nor do they find anyone who will help them out.

4924   "But true friends remain with them; they have such noble hearts that they do not love for riches nor for any profit that they expect from their friend. Friends of this sort come to the aid of the unfortunate one and protect him, for Fortune has put nothing in them. A friend loves forever. Whoever would draw his sword on a friend, would he not have cut their love? I except these cases that I wish to speak of: love may be lost through pride, wrath, and reproach; by revealing secrets which should be kept hidden; and by the woeful complaints of venomous detraction. In such cases a friend would flee; nothing else would offend him. But such friends prove themselves very well if a single one of them is found out of a thousand. And since no amount of riches can equal the value of a friend or attain such high status that the value of friends is not greater, so likewise a friend on the way is always better than money

4949 in the belt. And when adverse Fortune is in the process of falling upon men, she makes them, through the mishaps themselves, see so completely clearly that she causes them to discern their friends and prove by test that they are worth more than any possessions that they might have in this world. Thus adversity profits them more than prosperity, for the latter brings them ignorance, and adversity brings them knowledge. The poor fellow who, by such a test, distinguishes the pure friend from the false, understands them and separates them. Wouldn't he, when he was as rich as he wished and everyone always offered him heart, body, and everything he owned, wouldn't he have wanted to buy then the knowledge that he now has? He would have been less deceived had he then understood. Thus the misfortune that he receives brings him a better bargain than the riches which deceive him, since it has made a wise man out of a fool.

4975   "Riches do not enrich the man who locks them up in treasure, for only sufficiency makes men live richly. The man in easier circumstances and richer than one with a hundred barrels of grain still possesses nothing worth two crumbs, and I can tell you why: perhaps he is a merchant with a heart so evil that, until he has made his pile, he is in fearful torment and never stops worrying about

increasing and multiplying; as a result he will never have enough
nor ever know how to get so much. But the other, who trusts   4991
only in having enough to live for the day and is satisfied with what
he gains and keeps himself on it, thinks that he lacks nothing;
even though he hasn't a sou, he sees well enough that, when the
need arises, he will earn enough to eat, to buy shoes and suitable
clothing; or, if it happens that he falls sick and finds his meat
tasteless, he reflects, in order to thrust himself from the wrong
track and out of danger, that in any case he doesn't need food or
that a little food will do him, no matter how he feels. Or again,
he reflects that he will be carried off to the Hôtel-Dieu, where
he will be well taken care of. Or perhaps he never thinks at all that
he will ever come to such a pass; if he does think so, he believes
that, before the misfortune takes him, he will have saved up
enough by then to support himself when it happens. Or if saving
up against cold and heat, or against death by starvation, does not
matter to him, he thinks, perhaps, and comforts himself with the
thought that the sooner he finishes the sooner he will go to paradise, and he believes that God will grant it to him when he will
have left this present exile. Pythagoras himself tells you, if you   5025
have seen his book called the *Golden Verses*, esteemed for its sayings: 'When you depart from the body, you will move freely into
a holy atmosphere and will leave humanity to live in pure deity.'
He who believes that his country is here is very much a wretched
captive and a naïve fool. Your country is not on earth. You can
easily learn this from the clerks who explain Boethius's *Consolation*
and the meanings which lie in it. He who would translate it for
the laity would do them a great service.

"Again, if such a man knows how to keep himself on his income   5041
and doesn't covet the goods of another, he will not think himself
a victim of poverty; for, as your masters say, no man is a victim
who doesn't think himself one, whether he is king, knight, or
knave. Many carefree roustabouts, carrying sacks of charcoal in
La Grève, have hearts so light that difficulties don't bother them.
They work in patience, dancing, skipping, jumping, and go to Saint
Marcel for tripe. Since they consider treasures not worth three
pipes, they spend all their wages and savings in the tavern, then
go back to carry their burdens, but with joy, not misery. They
earn their bread lawfully, without stooping to robbery and theft,

and then go back to the cask and drink, living as they ought. All who think they have enough are abundantly rich, richer, the just God knows, than if they were usurers. For usurers, be well assured, could never be rich; instead, they are so miserly and covetous that they are all poor and tortured.

5071   "And it remains true, no matter whom the idea displeases, that no merchant lives at ease. He has put his heart into such a state of war that he burns alive to acquire more, nor will he ever have acquired enough. He fears to lose the wealth that he has gained, and he pursues the remainder that he will never see himself possess, for his strongest desire is to acquire another's property. He has undertaken a wondrous task: he aspires to drink up the whole Seine, but he will never be able to drink so much that there will not remain more. This is the distress, the fire, the anguish which lasts forever; it is the pain, the battle which tears his guts and torments him in his lack: the more he acquires, the more he needs.

5091   "Lawyers and physicians are all shackled by this bond. They sell knowledge for pennies; they all hang themselves by this rope. They find gain so sweet and pleasant that the physician wishes he had sixty patients for the one he has, and the lawyer thirty cases for one, indeed two hundred or two thousand, so much covetousness and guile burn in their hearts.

5101   "The same is true of the divines who walk the earth: when they preach in order to acquire honors, favors, or riches, they acquire, in addition, hearts torn by such anguish. They do not live lawfully. But, above all, those who pursue vainglory buy their souls' death. Such a deceiver is himself deceived, for you know that however much such a preacher profits others, he profits himself nothing; for good preaching that comes in fact from evil intention is worth nothing to the preacher, even though it may save others. The hearers take good example by it, but the preacher is filled with vain glory.

5119   "But let us leave such preachers and speak of those who heap up treasure. Certainly they neither love nor fear God when they purse up coins into treasure and save them beyond their need while they look upon the poor outside, trembling with cold and perishing of hunger. God will indeed know how to reward them. Three great misfortunes come to those who lead such lives: first, they acquire riches through great labor; then, as long as they do not cease guarding their treasures, fear keeps them in great distress; and, in the end, they grieve to leave their wealth. Those who pursue great riches die and live in this torment. Nor does this situation exist except through the lack of love, which is absent from the world; for, if those who heap up riches loved and were loved— if right love reigned everywhere, not seduced by wickedness, and if those who had more either gave more to those whom they knew to be needy, or loaned, not at usury, but out of charity pure and simple, as long as the recipients directed their efforts toward good and kept themselves from idleness—then there would be no poor man in the world, nor ought there to be any. But the world is so sick that they have made love a piece of merchandise; no one loves except for his profit, to obtain gifts or some service. Even women want to sell themselves. May such selling come to an evil end!

"Thus has Fraud dishonored everything by which the goods formerly common to everyone were appropriated to men. So bound by avarice are they that they have submitted their natural freedom to a base servitude; they are all slaves of the money which they lock up in their storehouses. Lock up! Indeed, they are the ones imprisoned when they have fallen into such error. These wretched earthly captives have made their possessions their masters. Wealth is profit only when spent; they do not know how to understand this proposition, but instead, when faced with it, they will all reply that wealth is profit only when hidden. Not so. But they hide it so well that they never spend it nor give it away. But no matter what happens it will be spent, even though they had all been hanged; for in the end, when they have died, they will leave it to the first chance passerby, who will spend it joyfully without returning any profit to them. They are not even sure that they will keep it that long, for there are those who could lay their hands on the treasure and carry it all off tomorrow. 5155

"They do great evil to riches when they pervert them from their nature. Their nature is that they should fly to the aid and comfort of poor men, without being loaned at usury. God has provided them for this end, and now men have hidden them in prison. But riches, which, according to their natural destiny, should be led, revenge themselves honorably on their hosts, for they drag them ignominiously behind, they rend them and stab them re- 5183

peatedly. They pierce their hearts with three blades. The first is
the labor of acquisition. The second that oppresses their hearts is
the fear that men may rob them and carry off their riches when
they have gathered them up; this fear torments them unceasingly.
The third blade is the pain of leaving the riches behind. As I have
told you before, these deceivers walk the earth spreading evil.

5205   "It is thus that Riches, like a free lady and queen, revenges
herself upon the slaves who keep her locked up. She holds her
peace, rests, and makes the wretches watch and care and toil. She
subjugates them and keeps them so close underfoot that she has the
honor while they have the shame, torment, and misery as they pine
away in her service. No profit is to be made in such servitude,
at least for him who keeps her. Without fail, after the death of
him who dared not attack her, nor make her run and jump, she will
dwell with just anyone. But valiant men assail her, bestride her
and make her gallop, and so spur her that with their generous
hearts, they take their pleasure and divert themselves with her.
5226   They take example from Daedalus, who made wings for Icarus,
when, by artifice rather than by natural custom, they took the common way through the air. These valiant men do the same with
Riches: they make wings for her so that she might fly and they
gain glory and esteem rather than let themselves be tormented.
They don't want to be reprimanded for the great ardor and vice
of covetous Avarice. Therefore they perform acts of great courtesy,
for which their good qualities are esteemed and celebrated throughout the world. Their virtues superabound from this practice; God
considers them very sympathetic on account of their charitable,
generous hearts. For as much as Avarice stinks to God, who nourished the world with His gifts when He had forged it—no one has
taught you this except me—by that much is Generosity, with her
courtesy and beneficence, pleasing to Him. God hates misers, these
bound wretches, and damns them as idolaters, these captive slaves
of immoderation, fearful and wretched. Of course they think, and
say it as true, that they do not bind themselves to riches except to
be secure and to live in happiness.

5257   "O, sweet mortal riches, say, are you then such that you gladden
men who have thus imprisoned you? The more they assemble
you, the more they will tremble with fear. How can the man be

happy who is not in a secure estate? Would blessings leap up at
him if he lacked security?

"But no one who heard me say this could oppose me, to con-   5267
demn and scorn my words, by bringing up the case of the kings
who, to glorify their nobility, as the lower classes think, pride-
fully put their care into building up armed bodyguards of five
hundred or five thousand sergeants. It is quite commonly said that
this situation exists because of their great courage; but God knows
quite the contrary. Fear, which constantly torments and troubles
them, makes them act in this way. But a roustabout of La Grève
could more easily go everywhere alone and secure, and dance
before robbers without fearing them or their activities, than could
the king in his squirrel cloak, even if he were to carry to his High
Mass his amassed treasure of gold and precious stones. Every robber would take his share; whatever he brought they would steal
from him, and perhaps they would want to kill him. And he would   5291
be killed, I think, before he had moved from the spot, for the
thieves would be afraid that if they let him escape alive he would
have them captured anywhere and have them led forcibly away
to be hanged. Forcibly! But, of course, through the force of his re-
tainers, for his own force isn't worth two apples beside that of a
workman who goes around with such a light heart. By *his* re-
tainers? In faith, I lie, or do not speak properly. Indeed they are
not his, even though he may have dominion over them. Dominion?
No, but service, in that he should keep them in freedom. Thus
they are their own, for, when they wish, they withdraw their support from the king, who will then dwell alone as soon as the
people wish. Their goodness, their good qualities, their bodies,
power, wisdom—none are his, nor anything they have. Nature
has indeed denied them to him.

"No matter how agreeable Fortune is to men, she cannot give   5315
them possession of things which Nature has made foreign to them,
no matter how these things have been acquired."

"Ah, lady, for the king of angels, teach me by all means what   5320
things can be mine, and if I can have anything of my own. I
would very much like to know this."

"Yes," replied Reason, "but do not expect fields or houses,   5325
clothing or such adornment, or any earthly dwelling, or furnishings

of any sort. You have a much better and more precious thing. All
the good things that you sense within, and which you so well understand in yourself, which will dwell in you constantly nor can ever
leave you to perform similar service for another—these good
things are yours in a right way. The other benefits which you
have, alien ones, are not worth an old bridle rein; neither you
nor any man living has anything worth a shallot; for know that
all your possessions are enclosed within yourself. Every other
good belongs to Fortune, who disperses and collects them, gives
and takes them away as she pleases and with them makes fools
laugh and weep. But nothing Fortune did would entrap a wise
man nor would the revolution of her turning wheel bind him or
make him sorrowful. All her deeds are too dangerous, because
5353   they are not stable. For this reason, love of her is neither profitable
nor in any way pleasing to a worthy man; nor is it just that it
should be pleasing when it falls into eclipse for so small reason.
Therefore I want you to know that your heart is not for anything
to be attached to it. You are not tainted by it, but it would be a very
great sin if, later on, you were infatuated and sinned against men
to the extent of proclaiming yourself their friend only in order to
collect their wealth or the esteem which would come to you from
them. No worthy man would consider this esteem a good thing.
Fly from this love that I have described as from a thing base and
despicable. Renounce loving *par amour*; be wise and believe me.
But I see that you are stupid about another thing in that you have
reproached me, saying that I have commanded you to hate. But I
ask 'When? In what place? How?' ''

5375   "You haven't stopped telling me today that I should despise
my lord, on account of some primitive love, I don't know what. If
a man were to search as far as Carthage, from east to west; if he
lived until his teeth fell out from old age; if he ran, without
stopping to idle, visiting south and north until he had seen everything; still he would not have attained the love you have told me
of. Indeed the world was washed clean of it from the time that
the gods fled, when the giants attacked them and when Right and
Chastity and Faith fled at the same time. That love was so con-
founded that it also fled and is lost. Justice, who was heavier,
fled last. They deserted all lands, since they couldn't endure wars,
and made their dwelling in the heavens; never since, except by a

miracle, have they dared descend to earth. Fraud, who has in-
herited control of the earth by his strength and insolence, has
made them all leave the earth.

"Even Tully, who took great pains to search out the secrets   5405
of ancient writings, could not so flog his ingenuity that he ever
found more than three or four pairs of such pure loves in all the
centuries since this earth was created. And I believe that he found
less of it among those who lived at his time and who were his
dinner-mates. I haven't yet read anywhere that he had ever had
any such. And am I wiser than Tully? I would be a stupid fool
indeed if I wanted to seek such loves, since there are no more of
them on earth. Where then would I seek such a love when I
wouldn't find it here below? Can I fly with the cranes, or indeed,
like Socrates' swan, leap beyond the clouds? I don't wish to speak
of it any longer; I'll be quiet. I have no such foolish hope. Perhaps
the gods thought that, like the giants of old, I would attack paradise, and that I could then be struck down by their thunder. I
don't know if that's what you want, but I shouldn't remain in
any doubt."

"Fair friend," she said, "now listen. If you cannot attain to this   5434
love—for it can just as well fail through your fault as through
that of another—I will now teach you of another. Another? No,
but the same kind that everyone can be capable of as long as he
grasps a somewhat more comprehensive understanding of love. He
must love generally and leave particular loves. Let him form there
a lasting union in which many participate. You can lawfully love
all those of the world in a general way: love them all as much
as one, at least with the love of what is common to all. Act in such
a way that you may be toward all as you would wish them all to
be toward you. Neither act nor pursue a course of action toward
any man except that course that you want men to take toward you.
If you want to love in this way, men should proclaim you free
from any blame for it. You are bound to pursue this love; no man
should live without it.

"Because those who strive to do evil neglect this kind of love,   5459
judges are established on earth as the defense and refuge of those
treated unjustly by the world, to see that the injustice is made up
to them, and to punish and chastise those who, to deny this love,
assassinate men or kill, rape, rob, or steal, or who harm by detrac-

tion, false accusation, or by whatever evildoing, either open or hidden. They must be brought to justice."

5474   "Lady, since we are speaking of Justice, formerly in such great renown, and you are troubling to teach me, teach me a little of this Justice."

5479   "Say what you want to know."

"Willingly. I ask you to make a reasoned statement about love and justice and their relationship. Which is worth more, as it seems to you?"

5483   "Which love are you talking about?"

"About the one you want me to devote myself to, for I don't aspire to submit to judgment the kind which has been implanted in me."

5487   "Certainly, fool, I believe that; but if you are seeking a true judgment, the good love is worth more."

5489   "Prove it."

"Willingly. When you find two things which are compatible, necessary, and profitable, the one which is more necessary is worth more."

5494   "Lady, that is true."

"Now take care then in this matter; consider the nature of both. These two things, wherever they exist, are necessary and useful."

5499   "True."

"Then I possess as much of each as is consistent with the value of the more profitable?"

"I certainly agree with that, lady."

5502   "Then I don't wish to say more about it. But Love which comes from charity possesses greater necessity by far than does Justice."

5506   "Prove it, lady, before you go on."

"Willingly. I tell you without feigning that the good which can suffice itself is more necessary and greater, therefore the better choice, than that which needs help. You will not contradict me."

5513   "Why not? Make yourself understood, and I can then know if there is any objection. I should like to hear an example before I can know if I might agree."

"My faith, when you bid me give examples and proofs, they become great burdens. Nevertheless you shall have your example, since by it you will know better. If a man can, without the necessity of any other help, drag a boat easily which already you were unable to drag by yourself, wouldn't he pull better than you?"

"Yes, lady, at least by cable."   5525

"Now take here your likeness. If Justice were always asleep, still Love would be enough to lead a good and pure life, without judging anyone. But Justice without Love? No. It is for this reason that I call Love the better."

"Prove this to me."   5533

"Willingly. Now keep quiet while I do so. If Justice, who reigned formerly at the time when Saturn held power—Saturn, whose testicles Jupiter, his hard and bitter son, cut off as though they were sausages and threw into the sea, thus giving birth to Venus, as the book tells—if Justice, I say, were to return to earth and were as well esteemed today as she was then, there would still be need for men to love each other, no matter how they maintained Justice; for, from the time that Love might wish to flee, Justice would cause great destruction. But if men loved, they would never harm each other; and since Transgression would leave, what end would Justice serve?"

"I don't know what end, lady."   5555

"I well believe you, for everyone in the world would then live peacefully and tranquilly, and they would never have a king or prince; there would be neither bailiff nor provost as long as people lived honestly. Judges would never hear any clamor. So I say that Love by itself is worth more than Justice, even though the latter works against Malice, the mother of lordships, by which freedom has perished; for if there had been no evil or sin to stain the world, man would never have seen a king nor known a judge on earth. Judges judge evily where they ought first to make themselves just, since men want to trust in them. In order to do right by the complainants, they should observe law, be diligent, not lazy and negligent, nor covetous, false, and feigning. But now they sell their decisions, and turn the elements of the legal process upside down; they tally, they count, they erase, and poor men all pay. Each strives to take from the other. Such a judge makes a robber hang when he himself ought rather to be hanged, if a judgment were rendered against him for the rapines and the wrongs that he has committed through his power.

5589   "Wouldn't Appius have done well to hang? According to Titus Livius, who knows well how to recount the case, Appius had his sergeant institute a trumped-up case with false witnesses against the maiden Virginia, daughter of Virginius. Because Appius couldn't intimidate the girl, who cared for neither him nor his lechery, his hireling said in audience: 'Sir judge, pronounce sentence for me, for the girl is mine. I will prove against anyone living that she is my slave, for, wherever she may have been nourished, she was stolen from my household almost at the time of her birth and given to Virginius. I demand, Sir Appius, that you deliver my slave to me, for it is just that she serve me, not the one who has brought her up. If Virginius refuses, I am ready to prove all that I have said, for I can find good witnesses to it.' Thus spoke the evil traitor, the minister of the false judge. Virginius was quite ready to reply and confound his adversaries, but, as the case went, Appius spoke before he did and made the hasty judgment that the

5624   girl was to be returned to the servant without delay. When the fine, worthy man, the good and widely renowned knight named before, that is, Virginius, saw well that he couldn't defend his daughter against Appius and that he had to give her up perforce and deliver her body to infamy, he exchanged shame for injury, in a marvelous process of reasoning, if Livy doesn't lie. For, through love and without any hatred, he immediately cut off the head of his beautiful daughter Virginia and then presented it to the judge before all, in open court. The judge, according to the story, commanded that he be seized immediately and led out to be killed or hanged. But he was neither killed nor hanged, for the citizens, all moved by pity, defended him as soon as this action was known. Then, for this injustice, they put Appius in prison, where he quickly killed himself before the day of his trial. And Claudius, who initiated the case against Virginia, would have been condemned to death as a thief if Virginius, through his pity, had not saved him. He begged the citizens to have him sent into exile. All the witnesses to Claudius's case were condemned to death.

5659   "In short, judges commit many wrongs. Lucan, a very wise man, has said also that no one could see virtue and great power together. But know that, even though these judges do not mend their ways and give back what they have wrongly taken, the powerful immortal judge will put them, with a rope around their necks, in hell with the devils. I do not except kings or prelates. No matter what kind of judges they are, temporal or ecclesiastical, they do not have their positions to act in this way. They should bring to a conclusion, without recompense, the cases that are brought to them; they should open the door to plaintiffs, and in their own persons hear the arguments, false ones and good ones. They don't have their honors for nothing, nor to go around giving themselves airs. They are the servants of the lower classes, who enrich and people the land, and they should give oath and swear to do right as long as they survive; the people should live in peace through them, and, since their duty is to do justice, the judges should pursue malefactors and arrest robbers with their own hands if there were no one who wished to undertake such a job personally. It is in this direction that they should turn their attention. It is for this that men gave them salaries, and it was this that they promised the people when they first took on these dignities.

"Now, if you have understood well, I have answered what you   5693
have asked, and you have seen the reasons which seem to me appropriate to this judgment."

"Lady, you have certainly repaid me well, and I consider my-   5697
self well recompensed; I thank you. But I heard you speak at one point, it seems to me, some words so shameless and excessive that I believe that if anyone wanted to waste time in undertaking to excuse you, he wouldn't be able to find any defense."

"I see well," she said, "what you are thinking about. At another   5706
time, whenever you wish, you will hear an explanation, if you will please remember."

"Indeed, I will remind you," I said, with a lively memory, "of   5710
the very word you used. My master has forbidden me—I heard him very clearly—ever to let fall from my mouth any word approaching ribaldry. But as long as I didn't use the word originally, I can easily repeat it; I will name it right out without restriction. He does well who reveals folly to him whom he sees commit folly. Now I can chastise you to that extent, and you who pretend to be so wise will see as well your own trespass."

"I will await that," she said, "but meanwhile I must answer   5725
what you have objected to me about hatred. I wonder how you dare say it. Don't you know that it doesn't follow at all that, if I wish to

leave off one folly, I must commit a similar or greater one? If I wish to destroy the mad love to which you aspire, do I order you to hate to that end? Don't you remember Horace, who had such good sense and grace? Horace, no fool, said that when madcaps flee from vices, they turn to the contraries, and their affairs go no better. I do not wish to forbid love which one ought to understand as good, only that which is harmful to men. If I forbid drunkenness, I do not wish to forbid drinking. Such a course would not be worth a grain of pepper. When I forbid senseless generosity, I would be counted mad were I to counsel avarice, for one is just as great a vice as the other. I do not make such arguments."

5752   "Yes, indeed you do."

"Certainly you lie; I'm not trying to flatter you. You have not, to overcome me, examined old books; you are not a good logician. I do not explain love in that way. Never, out of my mouth, has come the counsel that one ought to hate anything. One must find the right mean. It is the love which I love and esteem so much that I have taught you to love.

5763   "There is another love, a natural one, which Nature has created in beasts, by means of which they rear their young, suckle them, and nourish them. If you want me to tell you the definition of this love of which I speak, it is a natural inclination to wish to preserve one's likeness by a suitable intention, either by engendering or by caring for nourishment. Male and female of man as well as beast are prepared for this love. However much good it does, this love carries neither praise nor blame nor merit; it is to be neither praised nor blamed; Nature makes creatures give themselves to it; in truth, they are forced to it. Nor does this love bring any victory over vice. But, without fail, if men do not perform this duty, they should be blamed. When a man eats, what praise is due him? But if he foreswears food, he should certainly be shamed. But I know very well that you are not interested in this love, and I therefore pass on. You have undertaken, in this love of yours, a much more senseless enterprise. It would be better for you to leave it, if you wish to advance toward your own profit.

5795   "Nevertheless I don't want you to live without a friend. If it pleases you, turn your attention to me. Am I not a lady beautiful, noble, fit to serve a worthy man, even the emperor of Rome? I

want to become your friend, and if you wish to hold to me, do
you know what my love will be worth to you? So much that you
will never lack anything you need, no matter what misfortune
comes to you. You will then be a lord so great that no one ever
heard tell of a greater. I will do whatever you wish; you can never
make a wish too high provided only that you carry out my work.
You must never work in any other way. Furthermore, you will
have a lover of such noble family that there is none to compare
with her; I am the daughter of God, the sovereign father who
made and shaped me so. Look at my form and at yourself in my
clear face. No girl of such descent ever had such power of loving   5820
as have I, for I have leave of my father to take a friend and be
loved. I shall never be blamed for it, nor need you worry about
sin, since you will be in my father's keeping, and he will feed us
both together. Do I say well? Answer me: how does it seem to
you? Does the god who has made you mad know how to pay his
followers as well? Does he dress them at such cost, these fools
whose homage he demands? Before God, take care lest you refuse
me. Maidens unaccustomed to begging are thrown into great sorrow and turmoil when they are refused. You can prove this fact
yourself by the case of Echo, without seeking other proofs."

"Now tell me, not in Latin, but in French, what you want me   5839
to serve."

"Allow me to be your servant and you my loyal friend. You   5842
will leave the god who has put you in this plight and will not value
at one prune the whole wheel of Fortune. You will be like Socrates,
who was so strong and stable that he was neither happy in prosperity nor sad in adversity. He put everything in one balance,
good happenings and mishaps, and made them of equal weight,
neither enjoying luck nor being weighed down by misfortune.
Whatever might come to pass, he was neither joyous nor heavy because of things. He was the one, says Solinus, who, according to
Apollo's answer, was judged the wisest man in the world. He was
the one whose face always wore the same expression no matter
what happened. He was never found changed even by those who
killed him with hemlock because he denied the existence of many
gods and believed in a single god, and preached that others should
avoid swearing by many gods.

"Heraclitus and Diogenes were also of such heart that, even   5869

in poverty and distress, they never were saddened. Firmly fixed
in their resolutions, they underwent all the misfortunes which came
to them. Do you the same, nor ever serve me in any other way.
Do not let Fortune overcome you, however she torments or
strikes you. He is neither a good nor strong fighter who cannot
contend against Fortune when she makes her efforts and wishes
to discomfit and vanquish him. One must not let himself be taken
but must defend himself vigorously. She knows so little of fighting that everyone who fights against her, whether in palace or
dunghill, can overcome her in the first round. He who fears her
at all is not brave, for no man who knew all her strength, and
understood himself without doubt, could be tripped up by her
5894   as long as he didn't voluntarily throw himself to earth. It is still
a great pity to see men who can defend themselves let themselves
be led out to hang. He who wanted to complain of such a situation
would be wrong, since there is no greater laziness. Take care then
never to take anything from her, neither honors nor services. Let
her turn her wheel, which she turns constantly without stopping,
while, like a blind person, she remains at the center. Some she
blinds with riches, honors, and dignities, while she gives poverty
to others; and when it pleases her, she rakes everything back. He
who allows himself to be upset by events or who takes pleasure in
anything is a great fool, since he can protect himself; he can certainly do so, but only if he wishes to. Apart from this, there remains one thing certain: you are making a goddess of Fortune and
elevating her to the heavens. You should not do so, since it is
neither right nor reasonable that she have her dwelling in paradise. She is not so very fortunate; instead, she has a very perilous
house.

5921   "There is a rock placed in the depths of the sea, in its center,
projecting on high above it, against which the sea growls and
argues. The waves, continually struggling with it, beat against it,
worry it, and many times dash against it so strongly that it is entirely engulfed; again it sheds the water which has drenched it,
the waves draw back, and it rises again into the air and breathes.
It does not keep any one shape, but is always changing, always
re-forming, appearing in a new shape and transforming itself. It
is always clothed in a different manner: when it is open to the air
and Zephirus rides the sea, this breeze brings out flowers and

makes them flame like stars, and makes the grass spring up green. But when Bise, the north wind, blows in his turn, he cuts down the flowers and grass with the sword of his cold, so that the flower loses its being as soon as it begins to be born.

"There is a strange wood on the rock; the trees in it are won-   5947
drous. One is sterile and bears nothing; another delights in bearing fruit. One never stops producing leaves; another is bare of foliage. While one remains green, many are without leaves. When one begins to put forth blossom, the flowers are dying on others. One raises itself on high as its neighbors are bent toward the earth. While buds are appearing on one, the others are blighted. There the broom plants are giant, while pine and cedar, their growth arrested, are dwarf. Every tree is deformed in some way; one takes the shape of another. The laurel, which should be green, has tarnished leaves; the olive in its turn dries up when it should be fecund and living; the willows, which should be sterile, flower and bear fruit; the elm strives against the vine and steals the form of the grapevine. There the nightingale rarely sings, but the screech-owl with his great beard, the prophet of misfortune and hideous messenger of sorrow, cries out and raves.

"Two rivers, different in taste, form, and color, flow there sum-   5978
mer and winter: they issue from two different fountains which come in turn from very different springs. One of them pours out waters so sweet, so flavorful and honeyed that there is no man who drinks of it who does not drink more than he should; the drink is so sweet and so dear that he cannot satisfy his thirst with it, for those who go on drinking more burn with thirst more than before. No one drinks of it without getting drunk, but no one is freed from his thirst; the overpowering sweetness so deceives men that there is no one who swallows so much that he doesn't want to swallow more; that is how well the sweetness knows how to deceive them. Lechery so stimulates them that they become hydroptic.

"This river runs so pleasantly, with such a murmuring, that   5999
it thrums and strums and sounds sweeter than a drum or tambourine; there is no one who goes that way whose heart is not brightened. There are many who, hastening to enter there, are stopped at the entrance and have no power to go farther. They go on, hardly wetting their feet, and scarcely touch the sweet waters, no matter how close they come to the river. They drink no

more than a little of it, and, when they taste its sweetness, they wish so deeply to continue that they plunge themselves entirely therein. Others pass so far ahead that they go washing themselves in the depths of the gulf and congratulate themselves on the comfort that is theirs in thus bathing and swimming. Then there comes a light wave that pushes them to the shore behind and puts them back on dry land, where their hearts burn and dry up.

6023   "Now I shall tell you about the other river and its nature. Its waters are sulfurous, dark, and evil-tasting, like a smoking fireplace, and all scummy with its stench. It does not flow sweetly but descends so hideously that in its travels it disturbs the air more than any fearful thunder. At no time—and I do not lie—does Zephirus blow over this river or ripple its waves, which are very ugly and deep. But Bise, the sorrowful wind from the north, has taken up battle against it and constrains it by necessity to stir up all its waves. The wind makes the valleys and plains rise up and look like mountains and makes them battle each other, so strongly does the river want to struggle. Many men dwell on the bank and there sigh and weep so much, without putting bounds or limits to their weeping, that they plunge themselves entirely into their tears and never cease to fear that they may have to drown in the river. Many people enter that river, not just up to the belly, but they plunge into its torrents until they are completely swallowed up. There they are pushed to and fro by the hideous, fearful river. The water swallows and engulfs many of them, and many are thrown out by the waves; but the torrents absorb many who are thrown down so far into the depths that they do not know how to remember a track by which they might return. Instead, they have to dwell there without ever returning above.

6065   "This river winds so much as it flows, changing its course through so many branches, that it falls, with all its sorrowful poison, into the river of sweetness and, with its stench and filth, changes the other's nature, giving to it a share of its corruption, full of evil misfortune; it so poisons and agitates the sweet river that it makes it bitter and roily and, with its excessive heat, robs the other river of its moderate temperature. The dark river exhales such a stench at its host that it even carries off its pleasant odor.

"On high, at the top of the mountain, on the slope, not on the 6079
plateau, always threatening ruin and ready to accept a fall, the
house of Fortune stands aslant. There is not a single storm of the
winds nor any torment that they can offer that this house does
not have to endure. There it receives the attacks and the torments
of many tempests. Zephirus, the sweet wind without peer, rarely
comes there to moderate, with its soft, peaceful breezes, the terrible
attacks of the harsh winds.

"One part of the hall mounts upward; another descends. One 6093
can see the house inclined so much that it seems as though it must
fall. No one, believe me, ever saw so variegated a house. In one
part it shines brilliantly, for there the walls of gold and silver are
fine, and the entire roof as well is of the same workmanship, glowing with the clearest and most brilliant precious stones. Everyone
praises this part as a marvel. In another part, the walls are of mud
not as thick as the width of a palm, and the entire roof is made of
thatch. In one part the house remains proud of its marvelously
great beauty, and in another it feels so weak and gaping, so rent
with cracks in more than five hundred thousand places, that it
trembles with fright. And if anything unstable, vagabond, and
mutable has any definite habitation, Fortune has her mansion there.

"When she wants to be honored, she withdraws into the golden 6119
part of her house and dwells there. Then she apparels and adorns
her body and, like a queen, clothes herself in long dresses that trail
behind her, with many different perfumes and with highly varied
colors, dresses made of silks and woolens, with patterns of plants
and grains and many other things with which are colored the
cloths in which rich people dress when they prepare themselves to
receive honors. Fortune disguises herself in this way. But I tell
you indeed that she does not value all those of the world at a
straw when she sees her body thus dressed; she is so proud and
haughty that there is no pride to be compared with hers. For when
she sees her great riches, her great honors and glories, she is so
full of her overweening folly that she does not believe, no matter
how things may go afterward, that there is anywhere in the world
a man or woman worth as much as she. Then she goes along, with
her whole wheel flying, roaming through her hall until she comes
to the part that is dirty, weak, cracked, and shaking. She goes 6149

stumbling along and throws herself to the ground as if she had seen nothing there; and when she sees herself fallen there, she changes her countenance and her clothing; she bares and undresses herself until she is stripped of her clothing, and she is so lacking in every good thing that it seems that she has nothing worth anything. And when she sees her misfortune, she seeks a shameful way out and, full of sorrow and sighing, goes to stagnate in a whorehouse. There, with lavish tears, she weeps over the great honors that she has lost and the delights in which she lived when she was dressed in magnificent robes. And since she is so perverse that she overturns the good into the mire, dishonors and grieves them, and elevates the wicked on high and gives them dignities, honors, and powers in great abundance, then afterward, when she pleases, robs and steals from them—since she is thus perverse, she does not know, it seems, what she herself wants. For this reason the ancients, who knew her, thought of her with her eyes bandaged.

6175 "I can find many examples of how Fortune acts thus, of how she degrades and destroys the good and maintains the evil in honor, for I want you to remember all these examples. I have already told you before about Socrates, the valiant man whom I loved and who loved me so much that he referred to me in all his deeds. One can prove the nature of Fortune immediately by both Seneca and Nero, of whom we will speak quickly because of the length of our matter. I would use up too much time in telling the deeds of Nero, that cruel man, and about how he set fire to Rome and had the senators killed. Indeed, he had a heart harder than stone when he had his brother killed, when he had his mother dismembered so that he might see the place where he was conceived. After he saw her dismembered, according to the story that men remember, he judged the beauty of her limbs. Ah, God! What a criminal judge she had! According to the story no tear issued from his eyes, but, as he was judging the limbs he commanded that wine be brought from his rooms, and he drank for his body's pleasure. But he had known her before, and he had also possessed his sister. And he gave himself to other men, this disloyal one that I speak of.

6211 "He made a martyr of Seneca, his good master, and he made him choose the death by which he wanted to die. Seneca saw that the devil was so powerful that he could not escape. 'Then,' he said, 'since it is impossible to escape, let a bath be heated and have me bled therein so that I may die in warm water and that my joyous, happy soul may return to God, who formed it and who forbids it any further torments.'

"After these words, without delay, Nero had the bath brought and the good man put into it. Then, the text says, he had him bled until he was forced to give up his soul, so much blood was he made to pour out. Nero knew no other cause for this deed than that, by custom, he had from his infancy practiced showing respect to him, as a disciple does to his master.   6223

" 'But this should not be,' said Nero. 'It is not fitting that any man, after he is emperor, should show reverence to another man, whether he be his master or his father.'   6234

"Therefore it troubled him greatly when he saw his master coming and he arose in his presence, but he could not refrain from showing reverence from the force of habit, and he therefore had the worthy man destroyed. And it was this unlawful creature of whom I speak who held the empire of Rome; the east, the south, the west and north he held in his jurisdiction.   6239

"And if you know how to listen well to me, I can teach you, in our talks, that riches and reverences, dignities, honors, and powers, and all other gifts of Fortune—for I do not except even one—are not powerful enough to make good men of those who possess them or to make them worthy of having wealth, honors, or high station. But if they have inner qualities of harshness, pride, or some other evil, they show and reveal these qualities sooner in the grand estate to which they raise themselves than if they had occupied low stations, in which they could do no such harm; for, when they use their powers, their deeds reveal their wills and give a demonstration, an outward sign, that they are neither good nor worthy of riches, dignities, honors, or powers.   6251

"In this connection, men have a common saying that is very foolish, if their silly reasoning gets them off the track and they take it as entirely true. Honors, they say, change manners. But they reason badly, for honors work no change, but give a demonstration, an outward sign that those who have taken the roads by which they came to these honors had just such manners in themselves before, when they were in low estate. If they are cruel and   6273 proud, spiteful and malicious after they have come to receive honors, you may know that, if they had then had the power, they would formerly have been such as you can see them afterward.

6291   "However, I do not give the name of power to evil or unregulated power, for our text says, and says well, that all power comes from the good and that no man fails to do good except through weakness and omission; and he who understood clearly would see that evil is nothing, for so the text says. If you do not care for authority, for perhaps you do not believe that all authorities are true, I am ready to find reasons, for there is nothing that God cannot do. But if you want to extract the truth from this observation, it is that God cannot do evil; and if you understand well, and see that God, who has not the power to do evil, is all-powerful, then you can see clearly that no matter who numbers the being of things, evil contributes nothing to their number. Just as the shadow places nothing in the air that is darkened except a lack of light, so in an exactly similar way, in a creature in whom good is lacking, evil puts nothing except a simple lack of goodness and

6320   can put there nothing more. The text, which embraces the whole range of evil things, goes on to say that the wicked are not men, and it brings lively reasons to this conclusion; but I do not want to take the trouble now to prove all that I say when you can find it in writing. Nevertheless, if it does not disturb you, I can very well bring out some of the reasons in a short talk. The wicked are not men because they abandon the common goal toward which things that receive being aspire and must aspire. That goal, which we call the first, is the sovereign of all good things. I have another reason, fair master, why the evil have no existence, if you will listen carefully to the conclusion: since they are not in the order in which all things existing have placed their being, then it follows, for him who sees clearly, that the evil are nothing.

6343   "You see now how Fortune serves, here below in the desert of this world, how spitefully she works; she chose the worst among evil men and made him lord and master over all men of this world and thus brought about Seneca's destruction. One does well then to flee her favor when no one, however happy, can consider it secure. Therefore I want you to despise her and to give no value to her favors. Even Claudian used to be amazed at them and used to wish to blame the gods for allowing the wicked to rise to great honors, high stations, powers, and riches. But he himself gives the answer and explains the cause to us like a man who uses his reason well. He absolves and excuses the gods and says that they agree to this situation so that afterward they may torment the wicked to the same extent that they have grieved the gods. For they are raised on high in order that afterward men may see them fall from a greater height.

"And if you do me the service that I here enjoin and describe   6371 to you, you will never, at any time, find a man richer than you, nor will you ever be angered, no matter how much the condition of your body, your friends, or your possessions may decline, but instead you will want to have patience. And you will want to have it as soon as you wish to be my friend. Why then do you dwell in sorrow? Many times I see you crying as an alembic does into an aludel. You should be stirred into a mud-puddle like an old rag. Certainly I would consider anyone a big joke who said that you were a man, for no man at any time, provided that he used his understanding, ever encouraged sorrow or sadness. The living devils, the evil ones, have heated your furnace, which makes your eyes thus flow with tears; but if you had used your understanding you should never have been downcast by anything that happened to you. This is the work of the god who put you here, your good master, your good friend; it is Love who fans and inflames the coals that he has put in your heart, who makes the tears come back to your eyes. He wants to sell his company at a high price, for it might not be suitable for a man to make his intelligence and prowess widely known. Certainly you are badly defamed. Leave weeping to children and women, weak and inconstant animals; be strong and firm when you see Fortune coming. Do you want to hold back her wheel that cannot be held back by the great or the small?

"Nero, the great emperor himself, whose example we have   6414 brought up and whose empire stretched so far that he was lord of the world, could not stop her wheel, however many honors he might conquer. For, if history does not lie, he afterward received an evil death, hated by all his people and fearing that they would attack him. He sent for his close friends, but the messengers sent to them never found any of them, whatever they might say, who would open their doors to them. Then Nero came secretly, in great fear, and pounded with his own hands; they did no more, but less, for the more he called to each of them, the more each one shut himself up and hid, and no one wanted to reply a word to him. Then he had to go and hide, and for protection he installed himself, with two of his servants, in a garden, for already several people who sought him out to kill him were running about everywhere, crying 'Nero! Nero! Who has seen him? Where can we find him?' Even though Nero heard them clearly, he could give no advice. He was quite dumbfounded that he himself was hated; and when he saw himself in such a situation, with no hope whatever, he begged his servants to kill him or to help him kill himself. He then killed himself, but first he requested that no one should ever find his head so that if afterward his body were seen it would not be recognized. And he begged that they burn his body as soon as they could.

6455   "The old book called *The Twelve Caesars*, where we find the account of his death, as Suetonius wrote it—Suetonius, who calls the Christian law a false and wicked religion (he so names it; look up the words of the unlawful man)—the old book says that the line of the Caesars finished with Nero. By his deeds he secured the obliteration of his whole lineage. Nevertheless, he was so accustomed to doing good in the first five years that no prince that one could have sought ever governed the land so well, so valiant and merciful did this lawless and merciless man seem. In audience at Rome, when, to condemn a man, he was required to write out the death order, he said without shame at his words that he would rather not know how to write than put his hand to write such an order. According to the book, he held the empire about seventeen years, and his life lasted for thirty-two. But pride and his criminality had attacked him so powerfully that he fell from high to low degree, as you have heard me tell. It was Fortune who caused him to mount up so high and afterward to descend, as you may hear and understand.

6489   "Croesus could in no way hold back her wheel from turning both below and above. He was a king, of all Lydia. Afterward men put a bridle on his neck, and he was given over to the fire to be burned but was freed by a rain that extinguished the great fire. No man whatever dared remain there; all fled on account of the rain, and when Croesus saw that he was alone in that place, he immediately took flight without hindrance or pursuit. Afterward he again became lord of his land, stirred up a new war, was captured again, and then was hanged. Thus was fulfilled the dream about the two gods who belonged to him and who served him at the top of a tree. Jupiter, it was said, washed him, and Phoebus had the towel and took pains to wipe him. It was an evil hour when he wanted to depend on the dream; his trust in it grew so great that he became foolishly proud. His daughter Phania, who was very wise and subtle, told him indeed that she knew how to explain the dreams, and she wanted to reply to him without flattery:

" 'Fair father,' said the girl, 'there is sad news here. Your pride   6517
is not worth a shell. Understand that Fortune mocks you. By this dream you may understand that she wants you hanged on the gibbet. And when you are hanging in the wind, without cover or roof, then, fair lord king, it will rain on you and the fair sun will wipe your body and face with his rays. Fortune pursues you to this end. She steals honors and gives them; she often makes great men lowly and again elevates the lowly to greatness and exercises her lordship over lords. Why should I go about to flatter you? Fortune awaits you at the gibbet, and when you make your way there with the halter on your neck, she will take back the beautiful golden crown with which she has crowned your head. Then with it will be crowned another to whom you give no thought or care.

" 'To explain the matter more openly to you: Jupiter, who gives   6541
you water, is the atmosphere that rains and thunders, and Phoebus, who holds the towel, is, without fail, the sun. I gloss the tree to you as the gibbet; I can understand nothing else by it. You will have to walk that plank. Thus Fortune avenges the people for the haughty way in which, like one beside himself with pride, you have conducted yourself. Thus she destroys many a valiant man, since she considers neither treachery nor loyalty, low estate nor royalty worth an apple. Instead, she plays pelote with them, like a silly, stupid girl, and in a completely disordered way throws out wealth, honor, and reverence; she gives dignities and powers without regard for which person receives them, for when she spends her graces she so spreads them about that she throws them over dirty pools and prairies as though they were dust. She counts nothing worth a ball except her daughter Nobility, cousin and neighbor to Fall, and Fortune keeps her very much in suspense. But it is true

without fail that Fortune gives Nobility to no one, however he may go about to capture her, if he does not know how to polish his heart so that he may be courteous, valiant, and brave. For no man is so valiant in combat that Nobility does not desert him if he is beset by base cowardice.

6579   " 'I love Nobility because she is noble, for she never enters a base heart. Therefore I beg you, my dear father, that you show no such base feelings. Be neither proud nor miserly; in order to teach the wealthy, have a heart that is generous, courteous, noble, and compassionate toward the poor. Every king should act thus. If he seeks the people's friendship, let him keep a heart that is generous, courteous, sweet-tempered, and full of compassion, for without the love of his subjects, no king, at any time, can be anything more than a common man.'

6593   "Thus Phania scolded him. But a fool sees nothing in his folly, as it seems to him in his foolish heart, except sense and reason together. Croesus did not humble himself in any way; full of pride and folly, he thought all his deeds wise, no matter what great outrages he might commit.

6601   " 'Daughter,' he said, 'don't teach me about courtesy or good sense. I know more about them than do you, who have thus scolded me about them. In your foolish response, when you explain my dream to me in this way, you have served me with great lies; for know that this noble dream, to which you want to put a false gloss, should be understood according to the letter. I myself understand it in this way, just as we shall see it in time. No such noble dream ever had so base an explanation. You may know that each of the gods is so much my friend that together they will come to me and do me the service that they have indicated through this dream, for I have well deserved it for a long time.'

6620   "Now see how Fortune served him. He could in no way prevent her having him hanged on the gibbet. Is it not then a matter open to proof that her wheel cannot be delayed, since no man, no matter how exalted a station he may know how to reach, can hold it back. And if you know any logic, an authentic science indeed, you will know that after the great lords fail to stop it, the little ones will exert themselves in vain to the same end.

6631   "And if you give no value to these proofs taken from old stories, you have others from your own recent times, proofs from fresh, beautiful battles. The beauty, you should know, is such as there can be in a battle. This proof concerns Manfred, King of Sicily, who for a long time kept the whole country peaceful by force and by guile until the good Charles, Count of Anjou and Provence, made war on him. Now, through divine providence, Charles is King of Sicily, since the true God, who has always held with him, has wished it so. This good King Charles not only seized Manfred's lordship from him but also took the life from his body. When Charles attacked, with the sword that cuts well, and discomfited Manfred in the front ranks of his army, he advanced on his gray horse to say 'check' and 'mate' with the move of an errant pawn in the middle of the chessboard.

"I do not seek to speak of Manfred's nephew Conradin, a ready   6656
example, whose head King Charles took in spite of the German princes. As for Henry, brother to the King of Spain and filled with pride and treason, Charles put him in prison to die. These two, like foolish boys, lost rooks, fools, pawns, and knights in the game and scrambled off the board, such fear did they have of being captured in the game that they had undertaken. For if one considers the truth, one sees that they took no precaution against being mated; since they fought without a king they had no fear of check and mate. Nor could he who played against them at chess put them in check or mate, either on foot or upon his saddle-bows, for one does not check or mate pawns, fools, knights, queens, or rooks. If I dare tell the truth and do not seek to flatter anyone, according to what I remember of chess and the process of mating, if you know anything of it, it must be a king that one puts in check or mates; and this process occurs when all his men are taken, so that he sees himself alone in that place. Nor does he see there anything to please him; instead, he flees because of the enemies who have thus impoverished him. One cannot check or mate any other man. All follow this rule, whether they are generous or miserly, for Athalus, who invented the custom of chess when he was occupied with arithmetic, wished it so. You will see in the *Polycraticus* that he digressed from his matter, since he should have been writing of numbers, where he found this excellent, pretty game which he tested by demonstration.

"Therefore, Henry and Conradin took to flight for fear of   6699
being captured. What have I said? To avoid capture? Rather on

account of death, which could have troubled them more and was worth least. For the game was going badly, at least on the side of their party, which had departed from God and undertaken the battle against the faith of holy church; and if anyone had said 'check' to them, there was no one to protect against it, for the queen had been captured in the moves of the first attack, in which, like a fool, the king lost rooks, knights, pawns, and fools. She was not present there, but, as a sorrowing captive, she could neither flee nor defend herself after they had given her to understand that Manfred lay mated and dead, his head, his feet, and his hands all cold. Then after good King Charles heard that Henry and Conradin were thus fled, he captured both of the fugitives and did what he wanted with them and with many other prisoners who were accomplices in their folly.

6727   "This valiant king of whom I tell you, whom people had the custom of calling 'count'—may God protect and guide, night and day, morning and evening, his soul and body and all his heirs— this king, before he had been given the kingdom of Sicily, of which he is now the crowned king and vicar of the whole empire, subdued the pride of Marseilles and took the heads of the greatest in the city. But I don't want to say more of him now; I would have to make a large book of it.

6741   "Here you see men who held great honors, and now you know what end they came to. Fortune, then, is insecure. Isn't he who rests confident in her indeed a fool, when those whom she wants to anoint in front she is accustomed to stab behind? And you, who kissed the rose and, as a result, have so heavy a burden of sorrow that you do not know how to lighten it, do you think that you can always kiss, always have comfort and delights? By my head, you are foolish and stupid. But in order that this sorrow may hold you no longer, I want you to remember Manfred, Henry, and Conradin, who acted worse than Saracens when they started a bitter battle against their mother holy church, and to remember the deeds of the men of Marseilles and the great men of old like Nero, like Croesus, of whom I have told above. With all the great powers that they possessed they could not restrain Fortune. Thus a free man who values himself so highly that he prides himself on his freedom does not know the time that Croesus came into bondage; nor, to my knowledge, does he keep the memory of Hecuba, the wife of King Priam, or of the story of Sisigambis, the mother of Darius, King of Persia. Fortune was so perverse to these that they held freedom and kingdoms and then in the end became slaves.

"Besides, I consider it a great shame, since you know what the letter shows and that one must study, when you don't remember Homer after you have studied him; but it seems that you have forgotten him. Isn't this effort vain and empty? You give your attention to books, and then forget everything through negligence. What is the value of whatever you study when its sense fails you, through your fault alone, at the very time that you need it? Certainly you should always have its significance in your memory; so should all wise men, and they should so fix it in their hearts that it would never escape them until death captured them. For he who knew the significance, who always had it in his heart and knew how to weigh it well, could never be burdened by anything that happened to him, since he would hold fast against all happenings, good and bad, soft and hard. As for the operations of Fortune, it remains as true as it is common that everyone sees her every day if he has good understanding. It is a marvel that you do not understand it, for you have put your attention very much within; but you have turned it elsewhere, toward this disordinate love. Therefore I now want to recall it to you to make you perceive the better.

"Jupiter, in every season, says Homer, has two full casks on the threshold of his house. There is no old man or boy, no lady or girl, old or young, ugly or beautiful, who may receive life in this world and not drink from these two casks. It is a tavern full of people, where Fortune, the hostess, draws absinthe and sweetened wine in cups, to make sops for everybody; with her own hands she gives them all to drink from them, but some more, others less. There is no one who does not drink every day from these casks, either a quart or pint, a hogshead, a pail, or a cup, just as it pleases Maid Fortune to drip it into their beaks, either with open hand or a few drops at a time; for she pours out good and evil to everyone, just as she is both sweet and perverse. There will never be anyone so happy that, when he ponders thoroughly, he may not find something to displease him in his great ease; nor will he ever have so much misfortune but what, again when he knows how to ponder, he may not find something in his discomfort to comfort him, either something done or something to do. But he must

6777

6813

think well about his situation and not fall into despair, the obstacle of sinners; and no man, however deeply read in letters, may give any advice in this matter. What good does it do you then to get angry, to weep, or to grumble? Take good heart and go forward to receive in patience whatever Fortune may give you, beautiful or ugly, evil or good.

6855   "I could not count all the turns of wily Fortune and of her perilous wheel. It is the conjuror's strap-folding trick that Fortune knows how to arrange so that no one, at the beginning, can have any certain knowledge of whether he will gain or lose. But with this much I shall keep silent about her, except that I shall return again a little when I make three honest requests of you, for the mouth willingly utters what touches one near the heart. If you want to refuse them, there is nothing that can excuse you for doing what is much to be blamed. They are that you will love me, that you despise the God of Love, and that you put no value on Fortune. If you are too weak to sustain this triple feat, I am ready to lighten it so that it may be more lightly carried. Take the first alone; and if you understand me sensibly you will be relieved of the others, for if you are not crazy or drunk, you should know— and mark it well—that whoever accords with Reason will never love *par amour* nor value Fortune. For this reason Socrates was such that he was my true friend. He did not fear the God of Love in any way, nor did he budge on account of Fortune. Therefore I want you to be like him and bring your whole heart together with mine. If you have planted it in mine, you have satisfied me in great plenty. Now you see how the matter stands: I make only one request of you; take the first of those that I have told you and I will pronounce the others paid. Now keep your mouth closed no longer. Reply: Will you do this thing?"

6901   "Lady," I said, "I can be nothing other than I am. I must serve my master, who will make me a hundred thousand times more rich when it pleases him, for he should give me the rose if I know well how to exert myself for it. And if, through him, I can possess it, I would have no need of any other possession. I wouldn't give three chick-peas for Socrates, no matter how rich he were, and I don't seek to hear any more talk of him. I should go back to my master: I want to keep my covenant with him because it is right and pleasing. If it must lead me to hell, I cannot hold back my heart. My heart! It is never mine. I never impaired, nor do I hope to impair my testament in order to love another. I left it all to Fair Welcoming, for I know the whole of my legacy by heart, and through my great impatience, I had confession without repentance. Therefore I would not want to exchange the rose with you for anything. You must see my thought on that subject.

"Moreover, I do not consider you courteous when just now you named the testicles to me; they are not well thought of in the mouth of a courteous girl. I do not know how you, so wise and beautiful, dared name them, at least when you did not gloss the word with some courteous utterance, as an honest woman does in speaking of them. Often I see that even when these nurses, many of whom are bawdy and simple, hold and bathe their children, they use other names for them. Now you know well if I lie." 6928

Then Reason began to smile, and smiling began to say to me: "Fair friend, I can very well, without creating a bad reputation for myself, name openly and by its own name a thing which is nothing if not good. In truth, I can safely speak properly of evil, for I have no shame about anything if it is not such that it may be sinful. But a thing in which sin lay could make no difference to me, for I never sinned in my life; if I name noble things in plain text, without gloss, I still commit no sin, since my father in paradise made them formerly with his own hands, along with all the other instruments that are the pillars and arguments for sustaining human nature, which, without them, would now be destroyed and empty. For God put the force of generation into testicles and penis with marvelous intention—willingly, not in spite of himself—so that the species might be always alive through fresh renewal. Through birth that is susceptible to fall and through a fall that can be reborn, God makes humanity endure so long that it cannot suffer death. He did the same for dumb beasts, that are also sustained by this process; for when single beasts die, their forms dwell in other beasts." 6943

"Now this is worse," I said, "than before, for I see clearly now by your bawdy speech that you are a foolish ribald; even if God made the things that you have mentioned before here, at least he did not make the words, which are filled with villainy." 6979

"Fair friend," said Reason the wise, "folly is not courage; it never was and never will be. You will say whatever you please, 6987 for indeed you have time and space for it, and you do not have to fear me, who wish to have your love and favor, for I am ready to listen and endure and keep silent. But take care that you don't do worse, even though you may devote yourself to vilifying me. In faith it seems that you want me to give foolish replies, but I shall never do so. I scold you for the sake of your own good. I am not so much yours that I will begin any such base thing as to detract or quarrel. It is true—don't let it displease you—that a quarrel is a bad vindication; and you should know that detraction is a still worse form of vindication. If I wanted vindication, I would avenge myself very differently; for if, through what I do or say, you misspeak or misbehave, I can, without blaming or slandering you, correct you privately in order to chastise you and teach you. Or I can avenge myself in yet another way, if you do not want to believe my good and true utterance, by pleading, when the time comes to appear before the judge, who would give me a just decision. Or

7023   by any reasonable deed I can take an honorable revenge. I do not want to quarrel with anybody, nor, by what I say, to lessen or defame any person, whatever he may be like, bad or good. Everyone carries his own burden of responsibility for his deeds; let him confess them if he wishes, or never do so if he does not wish. I shall never press them about it. I have no desire to commit folly, provided that I may be able to withdraw from it; I shall never even utter folly. To keep silent remains a small virtue; but to speak the things to be kept silent is to commit a diabolical deed.

7037   "The tongue should be held in check. We read a very honest saying of Ptolemy at the beginning of the *Almagest*: he who takes trouble over what restrains his tongue is a wise man, except when he speaks of God and nothing more. On that subject one does not speak too much, for no man can praise God too much; too much acknowledge him as lord; fear, obey, love, or bless him too much; or too much call on him for grace or return thanks to him. No one can occupy himself too much with this subject, for all those who receive good things from him should always invoke his name. Cato himself agrees, if there is anyone who recalls his book, where you may find in writing that the first virtue is to put a bridle on one's tongue. Subdue yours then, and refrain from saying foolish and wild things; then you will do only what is worthy and wise. It is good to believe the pagans, for we may gain great benefit from their sayings.

"But there is one thing that I can tell you, with no hatred   7063
or anger whatever, without blaming or vexing you, for he who
vexes people is a fool. It is that, saving your grace and your peace,
you commit a great fault against me, who love you and bring you
peace, when you rebel and call me a foolish ribald and vilify me
without cause. God my father, the king of the angels, courteous
without villainy, from whom proceeds all courtesy, both nourished
me and taught me. Nor does he consider me badly taught; rather
he taught me this behavior. With his permission it is my custom to
speak properly of things when I please, without using any gloss.

"And when, in turn, you want to oppose me, you require me to   7081
gloss. Want to oppose! Rather you do oppose to me that, although
God made things, at least he did not make their names. Here I
reply to you: perhaps not, at least the names that things have
now; however, he could indeed name them then when he first
created the whole world and whatever exists in it, but he wanted
me to find names at my pleasure and to name things, individually
and collectively, in order to increase our understanding. He gave
me speech, in which there lies a very precious gift. You can find
what I have here recounted to you in an authority, for Plato read
in his school that speech was given us to make our desires known,
for teaching, and for learning. This sentence, rhymed here, you
will find written in the *Timaeus* of Plato, who was not stupid.
When, in addition, you object that the words are ugly and base,
I say to you before God who hears me: if, when I put names to
things that you dare to criticize thus and blame, I had called
testicles relics and had declared relics to be testicles, then you, who
here criticize me and goad me on account of them, would reply
that 'relics' was an ugly, base word. 'Testicles' is a good name and
I like it, and so, in faith, are 'testes' and 'penis.' I have hardly ever
seen any more beautiful. I made the words and I am certain that
I never made anything base. God, who is wise and sure, considers
whatever I made well done. By the body of Saint Omer, how
would I dare not to name the works of my father properly? Must
I compare with him? The works had to have names by which men
might know how to name them, and withal such names that one

might name the things themselves by their very names. If women
in France do not name these things, it is only that they are not
accustomed to, for the right names would have been pleasing to
those who were accustomed to them; and if they named them
correctly, they would commit no sin in doing so.

7137   "Custom is very powerful, and, if I know it well, many a thing
is displeasing when new that becomes beautiful by custom. Every
woman who goes around naming them calls them I don't know
what: purses, harness, things, or prickles, as if they were thorns.
But when they are well joined to them and feel them, they do
not consider them piercing; then they name them as they are
accustomed to do. When they don't want to name them correctly,
I shall never make an issue of it; but I do not go out of my way
for anyone when I want to say anything openly to the extent of
speaking correctly.

7153   "In our schools indeed they say many things in parables that
are very beautiful to hear; however, one should not take whatever
one hears according to the letter. In my speech there is another
sense, at least when I was speaking of testicles, which I wanted
to speak of briefly here, than that which you want to give to the
word. He who understood the letter would see in the writing the
sense which clarifies the obscure fable. The truth hidden within
would be clear if it were explained. You will understand it well
if you review the integuments on the poets. There you will see a
large part of the secrets of philosophy. There you will want to
take your great delight, and you will thus be able to profit a great
deal. You will profit in delight and delight in profit, for in the
playful fables of the poets lie very profitable delights beneath
which they cover their thoughts when they clothe the truth in
fables. If you want to understand my saying well, you would have
to stretch your mind in this direction.

7181   "But afterward I pronounced these two words—and you understood them well—which should be taken quite strictly according
to the letter, without gloss."

7185   "Lady, I can indeed understand them; they are so easy to perceive that no one who knows French ought not to perceive them.
They have no need of other clarifications. But as for the sentences,
fables, and metaphors of the poets, I do not now hope to gloss
them. If I can be cured and if my service, for which I expect so

great a reward, is meritorious, I shall gloss them all in time—at least as much as is fitting—so that everyone will see into them clearly. I consider you well excused for the speech that you used before and for the two words named above, for you named them so correctly that I do not need to waste any more effort on them or use up my time in glossing. But I do beg your grace for the sake of God: do not blame me any more for loving here. If I am a fool, it is my misfortune. At least—and I think that I am quite certain of it—I am doing what is wise when I pay homage to my master. It makes no difference to you if I am a fool. However it goes, I want to love the rose to which I am pledged; no other will ever fill my heart. If I promised my love to you, I would never keep my promise; and then if I did not keep my word, I would either deceive you or rob my master. But I have told you often that I do not want to think elsewhere than on the rose, where my thoughts are turned. When you make me think elsewhere, by means of the speeches that you repeat here, until I am constantly tired of hearing them, you will see me flee away from here if you do not immediately keep quiet, for my heart's attention is turned elsewhere."

7220

When Reason heard me, she turned back and again left me pensive and sad.

7229

5

THE ADVICE OF FRIEND

7231   Straightway then I remembered Friend and had to bestir myself. At all costs I wanted to go to him. And there he was; God led him to me. When he saw me in that state, with such sorrow piercing my heart, he said:

7237   "What is the matter, fair sweet friend? Who has put you into such torment? Since I have seen you so downcast, I know that some unhappiness has come to you. Now tell me what your news is."

7242   "God help me, neither good nor fair."

"Tell me all."

And I told him just as you have heard; I will never record it again.

7246   "You see—" he said, "for God's sweet body!—you have calmed Resistance and kissed the bud. You are in no way hindered if Fair Welcoming has been captured. After he has conceded so much that you were given the kiss, prison will never hold him. But without fail, you will have to carry on a little more discreetly if you want to arrive at a good result. Comfort yourself, for you know well that he will be taken out of the prison where he has been put on your account."

7260   "Oh! The enemy is too strong, even if there were no one except Foul Mouth. It is he who wounds my heart most, who has incited the others. I would never have been found out if the glutton had not trumpeted the fact. Fear and Shame hid me most willingly; even Resistance had given over vilifying me. All three were staying competely quiet when the devils arrived that the glutton assembled there. Whoever had seen Fair Welcoming trembling when Jealousy cried out on him—for the old woman cried out a great deal of wickedness—could have taken great pity on him. I fled without waiting, and then the masons built the castle where the sweet one is imprisoned. That is why, Friend, I turn to you for counsel; I am dead if you do not give it."

Then Friend said, like one well taught, for he had learned a 7281
great deal about love:

"Do not be without comfort, my companion. Take pleasure in
loving well, serve the God of Love loyally night and day without
ceasing. Do not be disloyal to him. Such disloyalty, if he found
you recreant, would be too great; he would consider himself too
cruelly deceived after he has received you as his man. No loyal
heart ever deceived him. Do whatever he charges you with and
keep all his commandments, for no man who keeps them well will
ever fail of his intent, however late he may be, provided that some
misfortune from elsewhere, as when Fortune absents herself, does
not come to him. Think of serving the God of Love; let all your
thought be on him, for such thought is sweet and lovely. Therefore it would be a very great folly to leave him, since he does
not leave you. Nevertheless he holds you on leash, and you must
submit to him when you cannot leave him.

"Now I will tell you what to do. For a time you will delay 7307
going to see the strong castle. Do not go to play or to sit still;
let no one hear or see you near the walls or in front of the gate—
at least no more than usual—until this storm has completely sub-
sided, even though you don't wish it so. And if circumstance
brings you there, pretend, however things go, that Fair Welcoming
means nothing to you. But if you see him from a distance at a
crenel or a window, look on him with pity, but do so very covertly.
If he also sees you, he will be glad of it; but on account of the
guard he will never leave, nor show any sign on his face, except,
perhaps, by stealth. Or perhaps, when he hears you talking to
people, he will close his window and spy through the crack as long
as you are in that area, until you are turned from it, if he is not
turned away by another.

"But take care in any case that Foul Mouth does not see you. 7333
If he does, salute him, but take care not to change or to show any
sign of hatred or rancor. And if you encounter him elsewhere, do
not show any ill feeling toward him. A wise man covers his bad
humor. Know, too, that those who deceive deceivers do a good deed
and that all lovers, at least the wise ones, should do so. I counsel
you to serve and honor Foul Mouth and his followers, even
though their duty is to destroy you. Pretend to offer them every-

thing, heart and body, possessions and service. Men are accustomed
to say, and, believe me, it is true: a cunning man against a crafty
one. It is no sin to trick those who are tainted by trickery, and
Foul Mouth is a trickster. Take away the tricks, and he remains a
thief. You know that it's true that he is a thief; you can easily see
that he should have no other name, for he robs men of their good
name, and he never has the power to give it back. One ought rather
to lead him out to be hanged than all these other petty thieves who
steal piles of money. If a thief steals money, clothing by the perch,
or storehouses of grain, he is requited for at least four times as
much, according to the laws that are written, if he be caught in
the act. But Foul Mouth commits too great a crime with his filthy,
vile, spiteful tongue: once he has spoken slander with his mouth
he cannot repair it, nor destroy a single word that he has produced
with his chatter.

7377   "It is good to appease Foul Mouth, for at any time men are
accustomed to kiss the hand that they would wish burned. Would
that the glutton were now in Tarsus, where he could slander all
that he wanted, as long as he stole nothing from lovers! It is
good to stop up Foul Mouth so that he may utter no blame or reproach. One has to trick Foul Mouth and his kin—may God never
be their surety!—with fraud: one must serve them, caress, blandish
and flatter them with ruse, adulation, and false simulation; one
must bow to them and salute them. It is a very good idea to stroke
a dog until one has passed by. His chatter would indeed be destroyed if he could be led to believe no more than that you had
no desire to steal the bud that he has made safe from you. By this
means you could triumph over him.

7399   "Serve also the old woman—may bitter flames burn her!—who
guards Fair Welcoming. Do the same with Jealousy—may our
lord curse her—the suffering, wild woman whom the joy of others
always enrages. She is so cruel and greedy that if she left something for everyone to take a share, she would want to have the
whole of it so that she would never find her portion smaller.
Whoever monopolizes such a thing is a fool. It is the candle in the
lantern: whoever brought light with it to a thousand would never
find its flame smaller. Everyone whose understanding is not bar-
barous knows this similitude.

7415   "If the old woman and Jealousy need you, serve them with your skill. You should be courteous to them, for courtesy is a thing that is highly valued, but they must not be able to recognize that you are intending to deceive them. You must proceed in this way: one should lead one's enemy to be hanged or drowned with arms around his neck, with caresses and flattery, if one can reach one's goal in no other way. In this case I can swear and guarantee that there is no other issue, for they are so powerful that, believe me, whoever attacked them openly would fail of his intention.

"Afterward, when you come to the other gatekeepers—if you   7431
can ever get that far—you will proceed thus: If it is possible without ruining yourself, lull them by giving them such gifts as you hear me tell of: flower chaplets made on forms, purses or head ornaments or other little jewels that are fine and beautiful and well made. Afterward you will complain of your woes and of the toil and torment that Love, who brought you there, has made for you. Now if you can give nothing you must promise something by oath; however the payment goes, make a strong promise without delaying. Swear vehemently and pledge your faith rather than go away beaten; beg them to save you. And if your eyes weep in front of them it will be a very great advantage for you. Weep; you will do a very wise thing. Kneel down before them with joined hands and, right on the spot, moisten your eyes with hot tears that run down your face so that they can easily see them falling; it is a very pitiable sight to see. Tears are not despicable, especially to men of pity.

"And if you cannot weep, without delay take your saliva, or   7463
squeeze the juice of onions, or garlic, or take many other juices with which you may anoint your eyelids; if you do so, you will weep as many times as you want. Many tricksters have done so who afterward were pure lovers whom the ladies let hang in the snare that the men wanted to stretch for them, until, through their compassion, the ladies removed the rope from their necks. By such fraud wept many who never loved *par amour*; and thus, with such tears and stories, they deceived young girls. Tears attract the hearts of such people, provided only that they do not recognize fraud in them. But if they knew your fraud, they would never have any pity on you. It would be useless to beg for mercy; you would never enter within.

"If you cannot go to them, send word, by voice, letter, or   7487 tablet, through someone who is a suitable messenger. Never set down your own name. In this way, a man may be called a lady, a lady in turn a man, and the fact will be much better hidden from them. They may think a man a lady, a lady a gentleman. Write whatever you write in this way, for many thieves have deceived many lovers who read their messages. The lovers are accused by them, and the delights of love betrayed. Never, however, trust children, for you would be duped; they are not good messengers. Children always want to play, to chatter, or to show, to the traitors that coax them, whatever they are carrying, or, because they are not wise, they convey their messages stupidly. Unless they were not tricked, everything would be made public immediately.

7511   "These gatekeepers, it is certain, are of such compassionate nature that if they deign to receive your gifts, they will not want to deceive you. Know that, after your gifts, you will be received. Once they take them, the thing is done, for just as the decoy teaches the noble hawk to come to hand in the evening and in the morning, so are the gatekeepers taught by gifts to give favors and pardons to pure lovers. For gifts they all surrender conquered.

7525   "If it happens that you find them so proud that you cannot bend them with gifts or prayers, with tears or in other ways, and that instead they all repulse you with harsh deeds and haughty speeches and vilify you cruelly, take leave of them courteously and leave them in their grease. No autumn cheese ever cooked better than they will cook. Through your flight they will become used to pursuing you many times, and this process can advance you a great deal. Base hearts are so haughty toward those who love them that the more they beg the less they value them, and the more they serve the more they despise them. But when people leave them, their pride immediately falls. Those whom they used to despise now please them. They become subdued and pacified; when one leaves, it is not pleasant for them, but very harsh and unpleasant.

7549   "Although the sailor who navigates the sea, looking for many a savage land, keeps sight of one star, he does not always run under one sail, but changes it very often to avoid a tempest or wind. So the heart that does not cease to love does not always run in a single stage; he who wants to enjoy good love must pursue at one time, flee at another.

"Besides, it is very clear (I will not give you any gloss; you 7559
can trust in the text) that to beg of these three gatekeepers is a
good act, for, however arrogant they may be, he who wishes to
commit himself to beseeching them can lose nothing by it and
can indeed advance himself. He can safely plead with them, for he
certainly will be either refused or received; he can hardly be
deceived. Those who are refused lose nothing except what they
sought to obtain; and the gatekeepers will never be ungrateful
to those who have begged them, but rather will even be grateful
to them when they have forced their way there, since there is no
one so cruel who, on hearing them, may not feel great joy in his
heart. Keeping quite silent, they think that, when they are loved
by such people, they are now valiant, fair, and pleasing, and that
they have all good qualities, in spite of their refusal, either excused
or conceded. If the petitioners are received, they are fortunate, for
then they have what they sought. And if they have so much
misfortune that they do not succeed, then they may go away quite
free, without any obligation. If envy is possible to those who do
not succeed, so is some new and pleasing delight.

"But don't let them get into the habit of saying at once to the 7591
gatekeepers that they want to join them in order to pluck the
flower from the rosebush; but let them say that they come through
lawful and pure love, entirely with clean thought. Know that the
porters can without doubt be subdued. Provided that it be someone
who asks them well, he will never be repulsed. No man should be
refused there. If you use my advice, never take the trouble to
ask if you don't carry your project through to the end, for perhaps
if they were not overcome, they would have plumed themselves at
being asked. But they will never plume themselves after they are
accomplices in the deed.

"Whatever face they put on, they are of the sort that, if they 7609
had not been asked before, they would certainly do the asking,
and would give for nothing, whoever came asking them. But im-
petuous talkers and those who foolishly give overgenerous gifts make
them so overweening that their roses become much dearer to them;
the petitioners think that they will create advantages for themselves, but they work cruel hardships, for they would have had
everything for nothing if they had never put forward a request
for it, provided that everyone had acted in such a way that no one

made a request of them before another. And if they had wanted to hire themselves out, they would have had a good return for it if all had set themselves to agree that no one should ever make a speech to the gatekeepers nor give himself away for nothing; instead, the better to subdue the gatekeepers, he would have let the roses wither on their hands. But he who offered his body for sale, at least in order to do such a job, would not and should not please me the least bit. But do not hesitate on this account: ask them and stretch the snare for them, in order to capture your prey, for you could wait so long that one, two, three, four, indeed fifty-

7645   two dozen could push their way in quickly in fifty-two weeks. If you waited too long, the gatekeepers would suddenly have turned elsewhere. Because you wait too long, you will hardly come to it in time. I advise that no man wait until a woman asks him for his love, for he who does so puts too much trust in his beauty. And whoever wants to begin and to further his task quickly, let him not fear that she will strike him, however proud and haughty she may be, nor that his ship may not come to port, provided that he conducts himself sensibly. You will exploit the gatekeepers in this way, companion, when you come to them. But never request anything of them when you see them angry. Spy out when they are happy; never ask them when they are sad, unless their sadness is born of the anger that might have arisen when Jealousy, maddened by the rage into which she was thrown, had beaten them because of you.

7669   "And if you can come to the point where you might keep them apart, so that the place may be so convenient that you need not fear that anyone will come up unexpectedly, and if Fair Welcoming, who is now imprisoned for your sake, may escape, then, when he has turned on you the fair appearance that he can—and he knows very well how to receive handsome people—then you should cut the rose, even though you see Resistance himself, who receives you only to abuse you, or even though Shame and Fear grumble at your deed. They only pretend to get angry, and they defend themselves lazily, since in their very defense they give themselves up conquered, as it will then seem to you. Although you see Fear and Shame blush, and Resistance become agitated, or all three lament and groan, count the whole thing as not worth a husk. When place and time and season occur, cut the rose by force and show that you are a man, for, as long as someone knows how to exercise it, nothing could please them so much as such force. Many men customarily have such diverse ways that they want to be forced to give what they do not dare abandon, and they pretend that they have been robbed of what they allowed and wanted to be taken. Know too that they would be sorrowful, however happy they pretended to be, if they were to escape by such a defense; I fear that, no matter how much they had grumbled, they would be so angry at escaping that they would hate you for it. But if you feel, as a result of what they say openly, that they are in fact angered and defending themselves vigorously, you should not reach out your hand but in all cases should give yourself up a captive, begging their mercy, and wait until these three gate-keepers, who grieve and vex you, go away, and Fair Welcoming, who deigns to abandon everything for you, remains alone. Conduct yourself toward them in this way, like a worthy, valiant, and intelligent man.

"Another thing: pay attention to the way that Fair Welcoming looks at you. No matter how he may be nor what appearance he may have, adapt yourself to his manner. If he is old and serious, put all your attention on conducting yourself in a serious way; and if he acts stupidly, you act stupidly. Take trouble to follow his lead: if he is happy, put on a happy face; if he is angry, an angry one. If he laughs, you laugh, and weep if he does. Maintain your conduct in this way at every hour. Love what he loves, blame what he wants to blame, and give praise to whatever he does. He will then have much more confidence in you.

"Do you think that a lady with a worthy heart loves a foolish and flighty boy who will go dreaming off at night, as if he had to go mad, and who will sing from midnight on, no matter whom he pleases or annoys? She would be afraid of being blamed and considered cheap and degraded. Such love affairs, since they are fluted about the streets, are known immediately. It doesn't matter to these people who knows them. He who links his heart with them is a fool.

"And if a man wise in the ways of love speaks to a foolish girl and puts on the appearance of being wise, he will never turn her heart. Never think that he may succeed because he conducts himself well. Let him make his manners like hers; otherwise he would

7695

7719

7737

7749

be shamed, since she may think him a trickster, a fox, a sorcerer; the wretched girl will leave him immediately and take another, to whom she lowers herself a great deal. She repulses the worthy man and takes the worst of the lot. She feeds her loves there and broods over them just as the she-wolf does, whose madness makes her so much worse that she always takes the worst of the wolves.

7767   "If you can find Fair Welcoming and play chess, dice, back-gammon, or other delightful games with him, always get the worst of the games; always be the low man. Lose the game that you undertake whenever you play it. Let him win the games and make fun of your losses. Praise all his expressions, the ways he is turned out, his appearances, and serve him with your might. Even bring him a seat or a stool when he has to sit down. Your suit will prosper by such acts. If you can see dust fall somewhere on him, remove it from him immediately, even if there was none; or if his clothing is dusty, dust it off for him. In short, on any occasion do whatever you think may please him. If you do so, never fear, for you will never be repulsed. In this way you will come to your goal just as I propose it."

7795   "Sweet friend, what are you saying? No man who was not a false hypocrite would commit such deviltry. No greater wicked-ness was ever started. Do you want me to honor and serve people who are false and servile? Truly they are so, except Fair Wel-coming alone. Is such your advice now? I would be a deadly traitor if I were to serve in order to deceive, for I can indeed say truly that where I want to spy on people, I am in the habit of defying them in advance. At least allow me to defy Foul Mouth, who spies on me so much, before I go deceiving him in this way, or beg him to abate the storm that he has raised against me; if not, I shall have to beat him. Or, if he pleases, let him make amends to me for this tempest or I shall exact payment for myself. At least let me make a complaint to the judge, who may take ven-geance on him."

7819   "Companion, companion, those who are at open war should seek these solutions. But Foul Mouth is too covert. He is no open enemy, for when he hates a man, or woman, he blames and defames him behind his back. God shame him, he is a traitor, and it re-mains just to betray him. I say fie upon a man who is a traitor. Since he is not trustworthy, I have no faith whatever in him.

Within his heart he hates people and laughs at them with his mouth and teeth. No such man ever pleased me; he keeps away from me and I from him. It is right that he who gives himself over to treason should get his own death in turn through treason, if one cannot revenge oneself in any more honorable way.

"And if you want to complain of him, do you hope to stop his 7837 scandalmongering? Perhaps you could not prove it or find enough witnesses. And even if you had proof now, he would not keep his silence. The more you prove, the more scandal he will spread, and you will lose more thereby than he will. The whole affair will become more widely known and your shame more believed in, for he who thinks to lessen his shame through revenge increases and multiplies it. Indeed he would never suppress his scandal on account of any plea that it be suppressed or beaten down—no, by God, no matter who beat it down. So help me God, it would be useless to expect that he might make amends to you for it. In fact I would never accept reparation from him, even if he offered it, but I would pardon him. And if you show any defiance, I swear to you by the saints that truly Fair Welcoming will be put in irons, burnt in fire, or drowned in water, or he will be locked in so tightly that perhaps you will never see him. Then you will have a heart more sorrowful than ever Charles had for Roland, when he received his death at Roncesvalles through the treachery of Ganelon."

"Oh! I'm not going to look for that result. Let Foul Mouth 7867 go now; I give him back to the devil. I would like to have him hanged for having thus wasted my pepper."

"Companion, hanging him would mean nothing to you; you 7871 must take another form of revenge. That office belongs not to you but indeed to the judges. However, if you want to believe my advice you can trick him by treachery."

"Companion, I agree to this advice, and I shall never desert 7877 my agreement. Nevertheless, if you knew any art that showed you a route to find any means for taking the castle more easily, I would listen to it carefully if you wanted to teach it to me."

"Yes, there is a lovely and pleasant road; but it is not useful 7885 for a poor man. To conquer the castle, companion, one may choose a shorter way, without my art or my teaching, and break through right to the root of the fortress at the first onset. The gate would never hold, and all would let themselves be captured; nothing could be defended because no man would dare to utter a word. The road has the name of Give-Too-Much. It was laid down by Foolish Generosity, who has engulfed many lovers. I know this path very well, for I came out of it the day before yesterday, and I have been a pilgrim on it for more than a winter and a summer. You leave Generosity on the right and take the turn on the left. You will never have traveled the beaten path for more than a bow-shot, without using your shoes up at all, before you will see the walls shake and the towers waver, however strong or fine they are, and the gates will open by themselves. It would have made no difference if all the people had been dead. At that point the castle is so weak that a toasted cake is harder to divide into four than the walls are to break down. There it would be captured immediately. One would need no more of an army than Charlemagne would if he wanted to conquer Maine.

7921   "No poor man, in my opinion, enters on this road at any time. No one can lead a poor man to it, nor can he reach it by himself. But whoever had led him into it, he would know the road as well as I, no matter how well I had been taught. And you shall know it, if it please you, for you could learn it just as quickly if, with nothing more, you had great possessions to spend wildly. However, I shall not lead you there, for Poverty has prevented that step; she forbid it to me when I left that road. I spent whatever I had and whatever I received from others. I deceived all those who trusted me so that I can repay none of them if they had to hang me or drown me. 'Never come here,' said Poverty, 'for you have nothing to spend.'

7943   "You will enter upon that road with very great difficulty, if Wealth does not lead you to it. Moreover, she refuses to show the way back to those whom she conducts upon the road. She will stay with you on the outward journey, but you may be sure that she will never lead you back. No matter when you enter the road, you will never leave it, night or morning, if Poverty does not put out her hand to you; and she has caused distress to many. Foolish Generosity remains within the road; she thinks of nothing except playing and spending wildly, for she spends her money as if she drew it from granaries, without counting or measuring, no matter how long it has to last.

7961   "Poverty stays at the other end, full of shame and misfortune.

She makes so many humiliating requests and gets so many harsh refusals that she suffers great agitation of heart. She receives neither good deeds nor good words, nothing delightful or pleasant. She will never do anything so well that everyone will not blame her deeds. Everyone treats her with scorn and contempt. But Poverty does not concern you, except that you should think, in any event, how you can avoid her. Nothing can give a man so much trouble as to fall into poverty. Debtors who have spent all they had know this truth very well. Many have been hanged by her. Those who beg against their will also know it well and tell of it; they have to suffer great anguish before people may give them anything of what they have. Those who want to have joy of love should also know this, for as Ovid admits, the poor man has nothing with which to feed his love.

"Poverty makes men despise and hate and live in martyrdom;   7987
it even robs people of their sense. For God's sake, companion, protect yourself against it, and make a good effort to believe that what I say is proved and true, for you may know that I have proved and discovered by experiment, even in my own person, all of what I am preaching to you. And I know better than you do, fair companion, who have not endured it very much, that poverty mounts up with my discomfort and shame. Therefore you should have confidence in me, for I tell you this to correct you; the man who is corrected by another leads a very blessed life.

"I was accustomed to being called a valiant man and loved by   8005
all my companions. I spent gladly in all places, more than generously, so much that I was considered a rich man. Now I have become a poor man through the expenditures of Foolish Generosity, who has put me into this distress, so that, except with great hardship, I have nothing to drink, to eat, to put on my feet, or to wear. To this extent has Poverty, who steals away all friends, subdued and mastered me. And know, companion, that as soon as Fortune put me in this plight, I lost all my friends except one— this I believe truly—who alone remained with me. Fortune robbed me of them thus through Poverty, who came with her. Robbed! In faith, no, I lie; rather she took rightly the things that were her own, for I know for a truth that, if they had been mine, they would never have left me for her. She did not then wrong me in any way when she took her own friends. Hers, indeed, but I

knew nothing about them, for I thought that I could possess them all, and I had bought them so much with my heart, my body, and my possessions, that when it came to the end, I had nothing worth a penny; and when they sensed that I was in such a state, all these friends fled. They all made fun of me when they saw me at the bottom of Fortune's wheel, struck down to the opposite position, overcome by Poverty. Still, I should not complain, for Fortune did me a courtesy greater than I ever deserved of her; I saw so clearly round about me and so well did she anoint my eyes with a pure ointment, which she compounded for me as soon as Poverty came, that if a lynx had put his eyes to it he would not have seen what I saw. Poverty robbed me of more than twenty—it is certainly true, for I do not lie—more than four hundred and fifty friends, and Fortune immediately showed me, on the spot and in full detail, the good love of my true friend. He met me through Poverty, for I should never have known him if he had not seen my need. When he knew it he rushed to me, helped me as much as he could, and offered me all that he had because he knew my need.

" 'Friend,' he said, 'I assure you that here is my body, here are my possessions, to which you have as much right as I. Take them without asking leave. How much? If you don't know, take everything, if your need is that great, for in comparison with a friend, the gifts of Fortune are not worth a prune to a friend. We have searched each other until we know each other well; we have joined our hearts together, have tried each other and found ourselves true friends (for no one knows without trial if he can find a loyal friend); and therefore, so powerful are the bonds of love, I keep even my natural goods engaged to you. If it will cure you,' he went on, 'you can put me in prison as a guarantee or hostage and sell my goods and give them as pledge.' He still did not stop at that; he did not go along flattering me, but forced me to take from him, for I was so downcast and ashamed that I did not want to stretch out my hand. I was like the needy poor man whose mouth is so tightly closed from shame that he dares not tell his discomfort, but suffers, shuts himself up and hides so that no one may know his poverty, and shows his best appearance outside. This was the way I acted at that time.

8043

8065

"I recall well that beggars who are sound of body do not do so; they go around forcing themselves in everywhere with sweet speeches of flattery, and they show the ugliest exterior to all those who meet them, while they hide the fairest interior in order to deceive those who give to them. They go around saying that they are poor when they have fat doles and a lot of money stored away. But I shall keep silent about them right from now on, for I could say so much about them that things would go from bad to worse with me; hypocrites always hate the truth which is told against them.

"Thus, you see, my foolish heart put forth its effort upon those whom I had called friends, and, for no other reason than the loss that I spoke of, I am betrayed by my stupid sense and despised, defamed, and hated by all men together, except for you alone. You do not lose your love; you are attached to my heart, and, as I believe—and I shall not cease loving you—if it please God, you will always be attached to it. It is true that you will lose me, as far as bodily companionship in this earthly life is concerned, when the last day comes and Death exercises his rights over the body. (That day, I remember well, robs us only of the body and those things that go with bodily substances; and both of us, I know, will die, sooner, perhaps, than we wish, for Death separates all companions, but not, perhaps, at the same time.) But still I know for certain that, if loyal love does not lie I shall always live in your heart if you live and I die; and if you die before me, you will always live again through memory in mine, after your death, just as, according to the story, Pirithous, whom Theseus loved so much, lived on after his death. For he lived within Theseus's heart, and Theseus had loved him so much while he was alive on the earth that after his death he sought him and followed him until he went alive to seek him in hell. Poverty acts worse than Death, for she torments and gnaws at soul and body, not just for a single hour but as long as the one dwells with the other; and in addition to damnation she adds larceny and perjury to their account, along with all other difficulties by which everyone is sorely struck down, every thing, in fact, that Death does not want to do. Instead, Death takes all these things away from them and, by her coming, brings all their temporal torments to an end; to say no more, she

8099

8115

8155

troubles them, however sorely, for a single hour. Therefore, fair companion, I urge you to remember Solomon, who was king of Jerusalem, for we have gained much good from him. He says— and pay careful attention to it—'Fair son, keep from poverty all the days of your life.' And in his book he gives the reason: 'In this terrestrial life, it is better to die than to be poor.' As for shameful poverty, he speaks of her, the needy one, whom we call indigence. She works such harms upon her guests that one never saw people so despicable as those poor creatures. Everyone who uses the right text refuses them even as witnesses, because in law they are called equivalent to those who are dishonored.

8189   "Poverty is a very ugly thing, but in any case I dare say that if you had amassed enough money and jewels and wanted to give as much as you could promise of it, then you could cut buds and roses, no matter how enclosed they were. But you are neither that rich nor that miserly. Therefore give pretty little presents in a pleasant and reasonable way, so that you don't fall into poverty, for in poverty you would suffer harm and loss. Many would mock you and would not help you for anything if you had paid more for a piece of merchandise than it was worth.

8207   "It is very suitable to give a lovely present of fresh fruit in cloths or in baskets. Never be lazy about doing so. Send them apples, pears, nuts, or cherries, sorb-apples, plums, strawberries, wild cherries, chestnuts, quinces, figs, barberries, peaches, large pears, or service-berries, grafted medlars or raspberries, bullaces, yellow or other sorts of plums, and fresh grapes, and have some fresh mulberries. And if you have bought them, even if you buy them in the streets, say that they were given to you by a friend who came from a long way off. Or give red roses, primroses, or violets in pretty wicker baskets during the season. Don't go beyond reason in such gifts. Know that gifts fool people and rob the scandalmongers of their gossip. Even if they knew evil of the donors, they would speak all the good in the world of them. Fair gifts sustain many bailiffs who were formerly in poor circumstances; fair gifts of wine and food have been the source of many prebends; and fair gifts, without doubt, bear witness to a good life. Everywhere gifts give strong support to a fair place, and he who gives them is a worthy man. Gifts give praise to the givers and put those who take in a worse light, for gifts put their natural freedom under the obligation to serve another. What should I say? In sum, both gods and men are captured by gifts.

"Companion, listen to my observation and admonition: know 8245 that if you wish to do what you have here heard me tell, the God of Love will never fail, when he attacks the strong castle, to give you what he promised. Both he and the goddess Venus will fight so fiercely with the gatekeepers that they will subdue the fortress, and then you will be able to cut the rose no matter how strongly they have enclosed it.

"But when one has acquired something, he must exercise great 8257 mastery in keeping it well and wisely if he wants to enjoy it for long, for to keep and protect things after they are acquired is no less a virtue than to acquire them in various ways. When a young man loses what he loves, provided that the loss is his fault, it is just that he be called a wretch. For it is a very high and worthy thing to know well how to guard one's sweetheart so that one does not lose her, particularly when God gives her as one who is wise, simple, courteous, and good, who gives her love and in no way sells it. No commercial love was ever invented by a woman unless she was a proven ribald; nor, without fail, is there any love whatever in a woman who gives herself for a gift. May evil fire burn up such a feigned love! One should not keep watch on her.

"Truly, however, women are nearly all eager to take and greedy 8281 to ravish and devour until nothing can remain to those who most proclaim themselves theirs and who love them most loyally. Juvenal tells us as much when he relates of Hiberina that she would rather lose one of her eyes than be attached to one man, for she was of such hot matter that no one man could satisfy her. No woman will ever be so ardent nor her love so secure that she may not wish to torment and despoil her sweetheart. But see what the others do, who give themselves to men in return for gifts: one cannot find a single one of them who does not want to act in this way, so that she may have a man in subjection to her; they all have this intention. This is the rule that Juvenal gives, but there is no infallible rule, for when he handed down this judgment he had heard of the wicked women.

"But if she is such as I describe, loyal of heart, pure of face, 8307 I will tell you what to do. A courteous, well-poised young man who wants to give attention to this matter should take care not to put all his trust in his beauty or his figure. It is right for him to train his intelligence with manners, arts, and sciences, for beauty, if one could consider its ends and its ways of working, can last a very short time. Like the flowers in the meadow, it declines quickly, for the stuff of beauty is such that the more it lives the more it fades.

8323   "But good sense, if one wants to acquire it, keeps its master company as long as he can live on earth, and it is worth more at the end of his life than it ever was at the beginning. It always goes forward and will never be diminished by time. A young man of noble understanding, when he uses it wisely, should be greatly loved and valued highly. And a woman should be happy when she has used her love on a fair young man who is courteous and wise, and who gives such evidence of good sense.

8337   "Nevertheless, if he were to ask my advice in order to find out if it would be a good idea for him to make pretty rhymes, motets, little stories and songs that he may want to send to his sweetheart to hold her and make her happy, I must answer that, alas, it can make no difference. Pretty songs can be worth very little in this case. Perhaps the songs will be praised, but they will bring in little other profit.

8347   "But if she saw a great heavy purse, all stuffed with bezants, rise up all at once, she would run to it with open arms; women are not so maddened that they would run after anything except purses. Although formerly they had other customs, now everything is going into decline.

8355   "Of old, in the time of our first fathers and mothers, according to the testimony of the writings through which we know this field, loves were loyal and pure, without greed or rapine, and the world was a very precious place. Dress and food were not so luxurious. For bread, meat, and fish, they gathered acorns in the woods, and they searched through groves, valleys, plains, and mountains for apples, pears, nuts, and chestnuts, rose hips and mulberries and sloes, raspberries, strawberries, and haws, broad beans, peas, and such things as fruits, roots, and plants. They ground ears of grain and gathered grapes in the fields without putting them in presses or vats. They extracted honey from oak trees and lived abundantly on it, and they drank clear water without seeking sweetened wine or clary. They never drank wine that was specially prepared.

"The earth was not plowed at all then, but, just as God had prepared it, bore by itself the things by which each person was made comfortable. They did not seek salmon or pike, but dressed in shaggy skins and made garments of fleeces just as they came from the animals, without dyeing them by means of plants or seeds. Their huts and villages were covered with broom plants, with leaves and branches, and they made trenches in the earth. When the stormy sky threatened the approach of some tempest, they sheltered among the rocks or in the huge trunks of grown oaks, where they fled for safety; and when they wanted to sleep at night, they did not use featherbeds, but, instead, carried piles or bundles of leaves or moss or grass into their huts. 8381

"And when the sky was calm, the weather sweet and pleasant, the wind soft and delightful as in an eternal springtime, and every morning the birds strove in their warbling to salute the dawn of the day, which makes all their hearts stir, then Zephirus and his wife Flora, the goddess and lady of flowers, spread out for men the counterpanes of little flowers. (These two make flowers spring up. Flowers know no other master, for he and she go together throughout the whole world sowing flowers; they shape them and color them with those colors that the flowers use to bring honor, in gay and beautiful chaplets, to young girls and men who, with the love of pure lovers, value each other because of their great love.) The little flowers that they spread out reflected such splendor among the grass, the meadows, and the woods that you would have thought that the earth was grown so haughty on account of its flowers that it wanted to take up war with heaven over the question of which had the better field of stars. Upon such couches as I describe, those who were pleased by Love's games would embrace and kiss each other without rapine or covetousness. The groves of green trees stretched out their pavilions and curtains over them with their branches and protected them from the sun. There these simple, secure people led their carols, their games and their idle, pleasant activities, free of all cares except to lead a life of gaiety in lawful companionship. No king or prince had yet committed any crime by robbing and seizing from another. All were accustomed to being equal, and no one wanted any possessions 8403 8431 of his own. They knew well the saying, neither lying nor foolish, that love and lordship never kept each other company nor dwelt together. The one that dominates separates them.

8455   "It is the same in marriages, where we see that the husband thinks himself wise and scolds his wife, beats her, and makes her live a life of strife. He tells her that she is stupid and foolish for staying out dancing and keeping company so often with handsome young men. They undergo so much suffering when the husband wants to have control over the body and possessions of his wife that good love cannot endure.

8467   " 'You are too giddy,' he says, 'and your behavior is too silly. As soon as I go to my work, you go off dancing and live a life so riotous that it seems ribald, and you sing like a siren. And when I go off to Rome or Friesland with our merchandise, then immediately you become very coquettish—for word of your conduct goes around everywhere, and I know through one who tells me of it—and when anyone speaks about the reason that you conduct yourself so demurely in all the places where you go, you reply, "Alas! It is on account of my love for my husband." For me, sorrowful wretch that I am? Who knows whether I forge or weave, whether I am dead or alive? I should have a sheep's bladder shoved in my face. Certainly I am not worth a button if I don't scold you. You have created a great reputation for me when you boast of such a thing. Everyone knows very well that you lie. For me, sorrowful wretch! For me! I formed evil gauntlets with my own hands and deceived myself cruelly when I ever accepted your faith, the day of our marriage. For me you lead this life of riot! For me you lead this life of luxury! Who do you think you go

8503   around fooling? I never have the possibility of seeing these quaint little games, when these libertines, who go around spying out whores, greedy for pleasure and hot with desire, gaze and look upon you from top to bottom when they accompany you through the streets. For whom are you peeling these chestnuts? Who can trick me more than you? The instant I approach near you, you make a rain-cape out of me. I see that, in this coat and that wimple, you seem simpler than a turtledove or dove. It doesn't matter to you if it is short or long when I am all alone near you. No matter how good-tempered I am, I would not hold back, if someone gave me four bezants or if I did not refuse them out of shame, from beating you in order to subdue your great pride. Understand that it does not please me for you to wear any quaint adornment at a carol or dance, except in my presence.

" 'Furthermore—I can hide it no longer—do you have any 8527 lands to divide up between you and this young bachelor, Robichonnet of the green hat, who comes so quickly when you call? You cannot leave him alone; you are always joking together. I don't know what you want of each other that you can always talk with one another. Your silly conduct makes me mad with anger. By that God that doesn't lie, if you ever speak to him, your face will grow pale, in fact more livid than mulberry; God help me, before I get you away from this life of dissipation I will give you some blows in that face that is so pleasing to the libertines, and you will then stay meek and quiet. You will be held in good iron rings; you will never go out without me, and you will serve me in the house. The devils make you very secret with those rascals, full of lies, toward whom you should be distant. Didn't I take you to serve me? Do you think that you deserve my love in order to consort with these dirty rascals just because they have such gay hearts and find you so gay in turn? You are a wicked harlot, and I can have no confidence in you. The devils made me marry.

" 'Ah! If I had believed Theophrastus, I would never have 8561 married a wife. He considers no man wise who takes a wife in marriage, whether she is beautiful or ugly, poor or rich, for he says, and affirms it as true in his noble book, *Aureolus* (a good one to study in school), that married life is very disagreeable, full of toil and trouble, of quarrels and fights that result from the pride of foolish women, full, too, of their opposition and the reproaches that they make and utter with their mouths, full of the demands and the complaints that they find on many occasions. One has great trouble keeping them in line and restraining their silly desires. He who wants to take a poor wife must undertake to feed her, 8579 clothe her, and put shoes on her feet. And if he thinks that he can improve his situation by taking a very rich wife, he will find her so proud and haughty, so overweening and arrogant, that he will again have great torment to endure her. And if, in addition, she is beautiful, everybody will run after her, pursue her and do her honor; they will come to blows, will work, struggle, battle, and exert themselves to serve her; and they all will surround her, beg her, try to get her favor, covet her, and carry on until in the end they will have her, for a tower beseiged on all sides can hardly escape being taken.

8597   " 'If, on the other hand, she is ugly, she wants to please everybody; and how could anyone guard something that everyone makes war against or who wants all those who see her? If he takes up war against the whole world, he cannot live on earth. No one would keep them from being captured, provided that they had been well-solicited. He who understood how to take a prize well would capture even Penelope, and there was no better woman in Greece.

8608   " 'In faith, he would do the same with Lucrece, even though she killed herself because King Tarquin's son took her by force. According to Titus Livius, no husband or father or relative could prevent her, in spite of all the trouble that they took, from killing herself in front of them. They urged her strongly to let go her sorrow; they gave her persuasive reasons; and her husband particularly comforted her with compassion and pardoned her with generous heart for the entire deed, and lectured her and studied to find lively arguments to prove to her that her body had not sinned when her heart did not wish the sin (for the body cannot be a sinner if the heart does not consent to it). But she, in her sorrow, held a knife hidden in her breast, so that no one might see it when she took it to strike herself; and she answered them without shame:

8634   " ' "Fair lords, no matter who may pardon me for the filthy sin that weighs on me so heavily, no matter how I am pardoned, I do not pardon myself of the penance for that sin."

8638   " 'Then, full of great anguish, she struck and rent her heart and fell to the ground dead, in front of them. But first she begged them to work to avenge her death. She wanted to establish this example in order to assure women that any man who took them by force would have to die. As a result, the king and his son were sent into exile and died there. After that disturbance, the Romans never wanted to make anyone king.

8651   " 'And if one knows how to beseech women, there is no Lucrece, no Penelope in Greece, nor any worthy woman on earth. If a man knew how to take her, no woman ever defended herself. The stories of the pagans tell us so, and no one ever found an exception. Many women even give themselves away when they lack suitors.

" 'Again, those who marry have a very dangerous custom, one   8661 so ill-arranged that it occurs to me as a very great wonder. I don't know where this folly comes from, except from raging lunacy. I see that a man who buys a horse is never so foolish as to put up any money if he does not see the horse unclothed, no matter how well it may have been covered. He looks the horse over everywhere and tries it out. But he takes a wife without trying her out, and she is never unclothed, not on account of gain or loss, solace or discomfort, but for no other reason than that she may not be displeasing before she is married. Then, when she sees things accomplished, she shows her malice for the first time; then appears every vice that she has; and then, when it will do him no good to repent, she makes the fool aware of her ways. I know quite certainly that, no matter how prudently his wife acts, there is no man, unless he is a fool, who does not repent when he feels himself married.

" 'By Saint Denis! Worthy women, as Valerius bears witness,   8687 are fewer than phoenixes. No man can love one but what she will pierce his heart with great fears and cares and other bitter misfortunes. Fewer than phoenixes? By my head, a more honest comparison would say fewer than white crows, however beautiful their bodies may be. Nevertheless, whatever I say, and in order that those who are alive may not say that I attack all women with too great impunity, a worthy woman, if one wants to recognize her, either in the world or in the cloister, and if he wants to put in some toil in seeking her, is a rare bird on earth, so easily recognized that it is like the black swan. Even Juvenal confirms this idea when he reiterates it in a positive statement: "If you find a chaste wife, go kneel down in the temple, bow down to worship Jupiter, and put forth your effort to sacrifice a gilded cow to Juno, the honored lady, for nothing more wonderful ever happened to any creature."

" 'And if a man wants to love the wicked women—of whom,   8717 according to Valerius, who is not ashamed to tell the truth, there are swarms, here and overseas, greater than those of the bees that gather in their hives—if he wants to love them, what end does he expect to come to? He brings harm to himself by clinging to such a branch; he who clings to it, I well recall, will lose both soul and body.

8727   " 'Valerius, who sorrowed because his companion Rufinus wanted to marry, made a stern speech to him: "My friend," he said, "may omnipotent God keep you from ever being put into the snare of an all-powerful woman who smashes all things through cunning."

8735   " 'Juvenal himself writes to Postumus on his marriage: "Do you want to take a wife, Postumus? Can't you find ropes, cords, or halters for sale? Can't you jump out of one of the high windows that we can see? Or can't you let yourself fall from the bridge? What Fury leads you to this torment and pain?"

8745   " 'King Phoroneus himself, who, as we have learned, gave the Greek people their laws, spoke from his deathbed and said to his brother Leonce: "Brother, I reveal to you that I would have died happy if I had never married a wife." And Leonce straightway asked him the cause of that statement. "All husbands," said Phoroneus, "test it and find it by experiment; and when you have taken a wife, you will know it well in every detail."

8759   " 'Pierre Abelard, in turn, admits that Sister Heloise, abbess of the Paraclete and his former sweetheart, did not want to agree for anything that he take her as his wife. Instead, the young lady of good understanding, well educated, loving and well loved in return, brought up arguments to convince him not to marry; and she proved to him with texts and reasons that the conditions of marriage are very hard, no matter how wise the wife may be. For she had seen, studied, and known the books, and she knew the feminine ways, for she had them all in herself. She asked him to love her but not to claim any right of her except those of grace and freedom, without lordship or mastery, so that he might study, entirely his own man, quite free, without tying himself down, and that she might also devote herself to study, for she was not
8785   empty of knowledge. She told him also that in any case their joys were more pleasing and their comfort grew greater when they saw each other more rarely. But, as he has written for us, he loved her so much that he afterward married her in spite of her admonition, and unhappiness resulted. After she had taken the habit of a nun at Argenteuil—by agreement of both of them together, as it seems to me—Pierre's testicles were removed, in his bed in

Paris, at night; on this account he endured great suffering and torment. After this misfortune, he was a monk of Saint Denis in France, then abbot of another abbey; then, it says in his *Life*, he founded a widely known abbey that he named the Abbey of the Paraclete, where Heloise, who was a professed nun before, was abbess. She herself, without shame, in a letter to her lover, whom   8807
she loved so much that she called him father and lord, tells a wondrous thing that many consider demented. It is written in the letters, if you search the chapters well, that she sent to him by express, even after she was abbess: "If the emperor of Rome, to whom all men should be subject, deigned to wish to take me as his wife and make me mistress of the world, I still would rather," she said, "and I call God to witness, be called your whore than be crowned empress." But, by my soul, I do not believe that any such woman ever existed afterward; and I think that her learning put her in such a position that she knew better how to overcome and subdue her nature, with its feminine ways. If Pierre had believed her, he would never have married her.

" 'Marriage is an evil bond, so help me Saint Julian, who harbors   8833
wandering pilgrims, and Saint Leonard, who unshackles prisoners who are truly repentant, when he sees them lamenting. It would have been better for me to go hang, the day I had to take a wife, when I became acquainted with so quaint a woman. With such a coquette I am dead. For Saint Mary's son, what is that quaintness worth to me, that costly, expensive dress that makes you turn your nose up, that is so long and trails behind you, that irks and vexes me so much, that makes you act so overbearing that I become mad with rage? What profit does it give me? No matter how much it profits others, it does me only harm; for when I want to divert myself with you, I find it so encumbering, so annoying and troublesome that I can come to no result. You make me so many turns and parries with your arms, legs, and hips, and you go twisting so much that I cannot hold you properly. I don't know how all this   8862
comes about, but I see very well that my love-making and my comforts are not pleasing to you. Even at night, when I lie down, before I receive you in my bed, as any worthy man does his wife, you have to undress yourself. On your head, your body, or your haunches you have only a head-covering of white cloth, with perhaps lace ornaments of blue or green, covered up underneath the

head-covering. The dresses and the fur linings are then put on the pole to hang all night in the air. What can all that be worth to me then, except to sell or pawn? You will see me burn up and die with evil rage if I do not sell and pledge everything; for, since they give me such trouble by day and no diversion at night, what other profit can I expect of them except by selling or pawning them? And if you were to admit the truth, you are worth no more because of them, neither in intelligence, nor in loyalty, nor even, by God, in beauty.

8889   " 'And if any man, to confound me, wanted to oppose me by replying that the bounties of good things go well with many different kinds of people and that beautiful apparel creates beauty in ladies and girls, then, no matter who said so in fact, I would reply that he lied. For the beauties of fair things, violets or roses, silk cloths or *fleurs de lys*, as I find it written in a book, are in themselves and not in ladies. All women should know that no woman will ever, as long as she lives, have anything except her natural beauty. And I say the same about goodness as I have told you about beauty. Thus, to begin my speech, I say that if one wanted to cover a dung-heap with silken cloths or little flowers, well-arranged and beautifully colored, it would certainly still be a dung-heap, whose custom it is to stink just as it did before. Someone might want to say, "If the dung-heap is ugly within it appears more lovely without; and in just the same way the ladies apparel themselves in order to appear more beautiful or to hide their ugliness." If someone were to say thus, I do not know, by my faith, how to reply, except to say that such deception comes from the maddened vision of eyes that see them in all their fine apparel. As a result, their hearts are led astray because of the pleasing impression of their imaginations, and they do not know how to recognize a lie or the truth, or how, for lack of clear vision, to explicate

8931   the sophism. But if they had the eyes of a lynx, they would never, for any sable mantles, surcoats, or skirts, any head ornaments, kerchiefs, undergarments, or pelisses, for any jewels or objects of value, for any covert, smirking coquetries, if one considered them well, for any gleaming exteriors, which make them look artificial, and never for any chaplets of fresh flowers, would they seem to them to be beautiful. However well Nature had formed Alcibiades, whose body was always beautiful in color and molding, anyone

who could see within him would want to consider him very ugly.
So Boethius tells us, a man wise and full of worth, and he draws
upon the testimony of Aristotle, who observes that the lynx has a
gaze so strong, piercing, and clear that he sees all that one shows
him, quite open both without and within.

" 'Thus I say that in no epoch were Beauty and Chastity ever   8957
at peace. Always there was such great strife that I have never
heard it said or recounted in fable or song that anything could
reconcile them. So mortal is the war between them that the one
will never let the other hold a full foot of ground, provided that
she might come out ahead. But things are very badly divided,
since, with what Chastity received as her share, she knows so little
of combat and parry when she attacks or defends herself that she
has to surrender her arms; she has not the power to defend herself
against Beauty, who is very cruel. Even Ugliness, Chastity's chambermaid, who owes her honor and service, does not love or value
her enough not to chase her from her mansion; she runs after her,
on her neck the club that is so huge and weighs so much that it
vexes her exceedingly as long as her mistress remains active for the
total of a single hour. Chastity is in a very bad situation, since she
is attacked from two directions and has no help from anywhere.
She has to flee the field, for she sees that she is alone in the combat.
Even if she had sworn it by her throat, she would have her fill of   8988
struggle, and when everyone does battle against her, so that she
cannot win, she would not dare to resist. Now cursed be Ugliness
when she runs thus after Chastity, whom she should have defended
and protected. If she could even have hidden her between her
flesh and her shirt, she should have put her there. Beauty, also, is
certainly very much to blame. She should have loved Chastity
and, if it had pleased her, striven for peace between them. She
should at least have done all she could to put herself in Chastity's
good graces, since, if she had been worthy, courteous, and wise,
she should have indeed done homage to her, not brought shame
and disgrace; for even the letter bears witness, in the sixth book of
Virgil, by the authority of the Sibyl, that no man who lives a
chaste life can come to damnation.

" 'Therefore I swear by God, the celestial king, that a woman   9013
who wants to be beautiful, or who exerts herself to appear beautiful,
examines herself and takes great trouble to deck herself out and

look attractive, because she wants to wage war on Chastity, who
certainly has many enemies. In cloisters and abbeys all the women
are sworn against her. They will never be so walled in that they
do not hate Chastity so strongly that they all aspire to shame her.
They all do homage to Venus, with no consideration for worth
or harm; they primp and paint in order to fool those who look
at them, and they go searching along through the streets in order
to see, to be seen, and to arouse desire in people, so that they will
9033   want to lie with them. Therefore they wear their finery to carols
and churches, for not one of them would ever do so if she did not
think that she would be seen and that she would thus more quickly
give pleasure to those whom she could deceive. Certainly, if the
truth be told, women give great shame to God. Misguided fools,
they do not consider themselves rewarded with the beauty that
God gives them. Each one has on her head a crown of flowers,
of gold, or of silk. She preens herself and primps as she goes
through the town showing herself off, and thus the unhappy
wretch abases herself in a very wicked way when, to increase or
perfect her beauty, she wants to draw onto her head an object lower
and more base than she. Thus she goes around despising God
because she considers him inadequate, and in her foolish heart she
thinks to herself that God did her a great outrage in that, when he
proportioned the beauty in her, he acquitted himself very negli-
gently. Therefore she searches for beauty in creations that God
made with much worse appearance, things like metals or flowers or
other strange things.

9063   " 'As for men, it is the same, without fail. If, to be more beautiful, we make chaplets and adornments for the beauties that God
has put in us, we misbehave toward him when we do not consider
ourselves rewarded by the beauty that he has given us above all
creatures that are born. But I have no interest in such tricks. I
want only enough clothing to protect myself from cold and heat.
This homespun of mine, lined with lamb, protects my body and
head against wind, rain, and storm just as well—may God protect
me as truly—as would fine sky-blue cloth lined with squirrel. It
seems to me that I lose my money when I buy you a dress of blue,
of camelot, of brown or scarlet material and line it with squirrel
or costly gray fur. To do so makes you run wild, simpering and
posturing as you go through dust and mud, while you value neither

God nor me. Even at night when you lie all naked beside me in   9088
my bed, you can't be held, for when I want to embrace you to
kiss you and comfort you, and when I am thoroughly warmed up,
you sulk like a devil and do not want to turn your face toward
me for anything that I may do. You pretend to be so sick, you
sigh and complain so much and make so much resistance that I become so fearful that I don't dare attack you again, when I wake
up after I have slept, so great is my fear of failing. It strikes me as
a very great wonder how those ribalds attain anything when, by
day, they hold you with your clothes on, if you twist about in
the same way when you play with them and if you give them as
much trouble as you do to me, both day and night. But I believe
that you have no desire, that instead you go along singing and
dancing through the gardens and meadows with these unlawful
rogues. They drag this married woman through the green grass
with the dew on it and there they go along despising me and saying to each other, "It's in spite of that dirty, jealous villain!"
Now may the flesh and bones that have brought me such shame be
given over to wolves and mad dogs! It is through you, lady slut,   9123
and through your wild ways, that I am given over to shame, you
riotous, filthy, vile, stinking bitch. May your body never see the
end of this year when you give it over to such curs! Through you
and your lechery I am placed in the confraternity of Saint Ernoul,
the patron of cuckolds, from whom no man with a wife, to my
knowledge, can be safe, no matter how much he may go about to
guard her and spy on her, even though he may have a thousand
eyes. All women get themselves attacked, and there is no guard
worth anything. If it happens that they omit the deed, they never
are without the wish, by which, if they can, they will jump to the
deed, for they always carry their desire with them. But Juvenal
gives one great comfort for this situation when he says, of the need
that is called a woman's carnal need to be made happy, that it is
the least of the sins by which the heart of a woman is stained, for
their nature commands each of them to give her attention to doing
worse. Do we not see how the mothers-in-law cook up poisons for
their sons-in-law, how they work charms and sorceries and so many
other diabolical things that, no matter how stout his powers of
thought, no man could count them?

" 'All you women are, will be, and have been whores, in fact or   9155 in desire, for, whoever could eliminate the deed, no man can constrain desire. All women have the advantage of being mistresses of their desires. For no amount of beating or upbraiding can one change your hearts, but the man who could change them would have lordship over your bodies.

9165   " 'Now let us leave what cannot be. But O! fair sweet God, fair celestial king, what can I do with the rascals who thus shame me and oppose me? If I happen to threaten them, how seriously will they take my threat? If I go to fighting with them, they can kill me or beat me straightway, so cruel and unprincipled, so eager to do all sorts of wickedness, so young and handsome, wild and headstrong are they. They will think me not worth a straw, for youth so enflames them, filling their hearts with fire and flame and inciting them, by necessity, to foolish, light, and giddy deeds, that each one thinks himself Roland, indeed Hercules or Samson.

9184   " 'These latter two, as men think—it is written and I recall it— had strong bodily resemblances. According to the author Solinus, this Hercules was seven feet tall, and no man, as he said, could ever attain a greater height. Hercules had many struggles: he conquered twelve horrible monsters, and when he had overcome the twelfth he could never finish with the thirteenth, his sweetheart Deïaneira, who, with her poisonous shirt, lacerated his flesh, all enflamed by the poison. His heart had already been made mad with love for Iole. Thus Hercules, who had so many virtues, was subdued by woman.

9203   " 'In the same way Samson, who, if he had had his hair, would have feared ten men no more than ten apples, was deceived by Dalila. I commit nothing but folly in saying these things, for I know very well that when you leave me you will recount, one after the other, all the things that I say. You will go crying to those wretches, and, if you ever can go to them, you can have my head laid open, my thighs smashed, or my shoulders gashed. But if I can hear word of it before it happens and if my arms are not held or my pestle removed, I will break your ribs. Neither friends, neighbors, nor relatives will ever be protection for you, nor your lechers themselves. Alas! Why did we ever see each other? Alas! in what an hour was I born, when you consider me so vile that these wretched stinking curs, who go around flattering and caressing you, are thus your lords and masters! I should have been their lord, since I support you, buy your shoes and clothes, and feed you, while you make me share with these dirty scoundrels, these rascals who bring you nothing but shame. They have robbed you of your reputation, of which you take no care when you hold them in your arms. In front of you they say that they love you, but behind your back they call you a whore. When they are again together, they tell what seems worse to them, how each of them serves you. I know their tales very well, and, without fail, it is true that when you lie in their power they indeed know how to put you to it, for there is no resistance whatever in you when you are entered into the crowd where each one stabs you repeatedly and tramples on you. My faith, I am overcome with envy of their comfortable life. But know, and remember well, that all this is not on account of your body or the pleasure they get from you; instead, they do so only to have the delight of the jewels, the golden buckles and buttons, the robes and pelisses that I, like a foolish simpleton, allow you. For when you go off to the carols or to your silly gatherings and I remain like a drunken fool, you carry a hundred pounds worth of gold and silver on your head; and you order people to dress you in camelot, squirrel, and gray fur so that I quite pine away with anger and anxiety, so chagrined and tormented am I.

9236

" 'What are they worth to me, these head ornaments, these coifs with golden bands, these decorated head-laces, the ivory mirrors, these well-formed circlets of gold with precious enameling, and these crowns of fine gold, all these things that give you such a bawdy appearance? These crowns are so fine, so well-polished, with so many beautiful gems, sapphires, rubies, and emeralds, that I cannot cease raging. These golden buckles with fine stones, at your sides and on your bosom, these precious materials, and these belts whose mountings are so expensive, as much for gold as for seed pearls—what are such baubles worth to me? Besides, you wear your shoes so tight that you often raise your dress to show your feet to those knaves. So may Saint Thibaut comfort me, I shall sell everything within three days, and I shall consider you dirt beneath my feet. By God's body, no matter who moans and complains, you shall have nothing from me but a coat and surcoat and a hempen kerchief, not fine but coarse and badly woven, torn and mended. And by my head, you will be well belted, but I will

9271

9289

tell you with what kind of belt: one of plain leather without a buckle. You will also have big shoes made out of my old boots, wide enough to stuff with large rags. You will take off those baubles that give you the occasion for committing fornication, and you will no longer go out to display yourself in order to get yourself thrown to the ground underneath those rascals.

9313 " 'But now tell me without making up any lies. Where, for the sake of love, did you get that other rich new dress in which you fixed yourself up here the other day when you went to the carols, for I know very well that I am right to think that I never gave it to you. You swore to me by Saint Denis, Saint Philibert, and Saint Peter that it came to you through your mother, who sent you the cloth for it because, as you gave me to understand, her love for me is so great that she wants to spend her money in order to make me keep mine. May she be grilled alive, that dirty old whore, that priest's concubine, that mackerel, that pimping whore, and may you, for your merits, fry along with her, if the case is not exactly as you say. I would certainly ask her, but I would exert myself in vain; the whole thing would not be worth a ball to

9337 me: like mother, like daughter. I know that you have talked together, and it is obvious that you both have hearts touched by the same wand. I know which foot you jump with, and that dirty painted old whore agrees with your attitude; she used to act in the same way. She has followed so many roads that she has been bitten by many curs. But now, I know, her looks are so bad that she can make nothing by herself, and so now she sells you. Three or four times a week she comes in here and leads you out on the pretext of new pilgrimages according to her old customs—for I know the whole plan—and then she doesn't stop parading you, as one does with a horse for sale, while she grabs and teaches you to grab. Do you think that I don't know you well? Somebody hold me so that I don't break your bones with this pestle or this spit until you are like a pâté of baby chicks.'

9361 "Then the jealous husband, sweating with anger, may seize her straightway by the hair and pull and tug her, break and tear her hair and grow mad with rage over her. A lion's rage at a bear would be nothing in comparison. In anger and rage, he drags her through the whole house and vilifies her foully. His intent is so evil that he doesn't want to hear excuses on any oath. Instead he hits her, beats her, thumps her, and knocks her about while she gives out howls and cries and sends her voice flying on the winds past windows and roofs. She reproaches him in every way she knows how, just as it comes into her mouth, in front of the neighbors who come there. The neighbors think them both crazy; with great difficulty they take her away from him while he is out of breath.

"When the lady feels this torment and takes account of this 9383 riot and this diverting viol on which our jongleur plays to her, do you think that she will ever love him more? She would want him to be at Meaux, indeed in Romagna. I will say more; I don't think that she might ever want to love him. She might pretend, but if he could fly up to the clouds or raise his view so high that from there, without falling, he could see all the deeds of men, and if he reflected upon all at leisure, he still would have to choose into which peril he fell, and he has not seen all the frauds that a woman knows how to meditate in order to protect and defend herself. Afterward, if he sleeps in her company, he puts his life in very great peril. Indeed, sleeping and waking, he must fear most strongly that, in order to avenge herself, she may have him poisoned or hacked into pieces, or make him languish in a life of desperate ruses. Or he must fear that, if she cannot play any other way, she may take it into her head to flee. A woman values neither honor nor shame when anything rises up in her head; this is the truth without doubt. A woman has no reason whatever. Valerius even claims that, toward whatever she hates and whatever she loves, a woman is bold, cunning, and studious of bringing injury to others.

"My friend, consider this mad jealous boor—may his flesh be 9421 fed to the wolves—so filled with his jealousy, as I have described him for you here in this story. He makes himself lord over his wife, who, in turn, should not be his lady but his equal and his companion, as the law joins them together; and, for his part, he should be her companion without making himself her lord or master. Do you think that, when he arranges such torments for her and does not consider her his equal but rather makes her live in such distress, he will not be displeasing to her and that the love between them will not fail? Yes indeed, without fail, whatever she says, he will not be loved by his wife if he wants to be called 'lord,' for love must die when lovers want lordship. Love cannot endure or live if it is not free and active in the heart.

9443   "For this same reason we see that those who at first are accustomed to love each other *par amour* may, after they want to marry each other, find that love can hardly ever hold them together; for when the man loved *par amour* he would proclaim himself his sweetheart's sergeant, and she grew used to being his mistress. Now he calls himself lord and master over her whom he called his lady when she was loved *par amour*."

    "Loved?" I said.

9455   "Truly," he replied.

    "In what way?" I asked.

9456   "In such that if, without entreaty, she were to command him, 'Jump, lover,' or 'Give me that thing,' he would immediately give it and jump when she ordered him to. In fact, whatever she might say, he would jump so that she might see him, for he had placed his whole desire in doing all her pleasure. But then after they have married each other, as I have told you, the wheel is turned, so that he who was in the habit of serving her now commands her to serve him, just as if she were his slave, and he holds her with a short rein and orders her to give an account of her doings. And he used to call her his lady! He who has not learned this truth is hardly dying. Then she considers herself ill-used when she sees herself thus attacked by the best, most trusted man that she found in the world, the man who thus wants to oppose her. When she sees her master on her neck, the man against whom she never took any precaution, she does not know whom to trust. The verse is changed for the worse. Now that he has changed the dice on her, the throws are so different, so cruel and strange, that she cannot and dare not play. How can she be happy? If she does not obey, he gets angry and berates her, and she grumbles. There they are, fallen into anger and straightway through anger become enemies.

9493   "It was for this reason, my friend, that the ancients maintained their friendship for each other without bonds of servitude, peaceably, and without boorishness, and they did not give away their freedom for the gold of Araby or Friesland, for he who wanted to take all gold for it could not very well sell it. At that time there was no pilgrimage: no man went out from his own shores to search for a foreign country. Jason had not yet passed over the sea, and he was the first to do so when he organized the ships for the journey to seek the Golden Fleece. When Neptune saw the ships sailing along, he thought for certain that he was captured in war. Triton, too, had to puff his cheeks with rage; and Doris and all her daughters, because of the marvelous tricks, thought that they were all betrayed, so greatly were they dumbfounded by the ships that flew over the sea just as the sailors wished them to.

"But the first of which I tell you did not know the value of navigation. In their own country they found everything that seemed good to seek. All were equally rich, and they loved each other lawfully. Thus they lived peacefully together, for these simple people of good life loved each other naturally. At that time there was no simony in love; one did not demand something from another. Then Fraud came, with his lance at rest, and Sin and Misfortune, who take no heed of Sufficiency, and along with them came Pride, equally disdainful in her grand array, Covetousness, Avarice, Envy, and all the other vices. Then they all made Poverty spring up from hell, where she had been so long that no man knew anything of her, for she had never been on earth. Coming so quickly, she came at a bad time, for her arrival was a thing of great evil. 9517

"Poverty, who has no comfort whatever, led her son Larceny, who beats out his path to the gibbet in order to bring help to his mother; and sometimes he gets himself hanged, for his mother cannot protect him, any more than his father Faint Heart, who from sorrow remains in a very bad situation. Not even Mademoiselle Laverne, the goddess of thieves, who guides and rules robbers, who shrouds night's sins in darkness and covers deceit with clouds so that its workings do not appear without until in the end they are found out and captured with complete proof—even Laverne has not so much pity, when these thieves stand with ropes on their necks, that she ever wants to protect them, no matter how well they know how to repent. 9541

"Immediately these wretched devils, excited by fury, sorrow, anger, and envy when they saw men leading such a life, rushed off through all countries, sowing discord, contention and war, slander, rancor, and hatred through anger and quarreling. Because they held gold dear, they had the earth flayed for it, and they 9561 drew out its bowels for its old deposits of metals and precious stones that make men grow envious. For Avarice and Covetousness established in the hearts of men the burning desire to acquire possessions. The latter acquires them and the former locks them up, and the wretched slave will never spend them as long as she lives, but instead will make her heirs and executors the principal guardians of her possessions, if some misfortune does not happen. And if she goes off to her damnation, no one of them, I think, will ever mourn for her; but if she has done well they may take these possessions.

9587   "As soon as this troop had played its evil trick, men abandoned their first life, and after that they did not cease doing evil, for they became false and treacherous. Then they held properties, and they even divided up the earth and made boundaries to show the divisions. They fought each other many times when they set up their boundaries, and they carried off what they could. The strongest held the largest portions, and when they ran about seeking more possessions, the idle ones who remained behind would enter their caves and steal what they had amassed. Then they had to seek out someone who would guard their dwellings, catch wrongdoers, and give justice to complainants without anyone daring to contradict him. Therefore they assembled to elect some one.

9609   "They elected a great scoundrel among them, the one who was largest, with the strongest back and limbs, and made him their prince and lord. He swore that he would maintain justice for them and would protect their dwellings if each one individually were to hand over to him enough goods to enable him to support himself. They agreed thus among themselves as he suggested, and he held this office for a long time. When the robbers, full of malice, saw him alone, they got together and beat him on many occasions when they came to steal. Then the people had to assemble again and urge, each one for himself, that the prince be given sergeants. Then, collectively, they taxed themselves and gave him tribute, revenues, and large holdings of land. From this source, according to the writings of the ancients, arose the first kings and earthly princes; for we know the deeds of the ancients by the writings that we have, and we should give them thanks and praise for what they have left.

9637   "Then the people amassed treasures of silver, gold, and gems.

Out of gold and silver, because they were both precious and workable, they made vessels, money, clasps, rings, buttons, and belts. To fight battles with their neighbors, they forged iron weapons, knives, swords, halberds, glaives, and armor. They made towers, entrenchments, and walls of squared stone. Those who assembled their treasures enclosed castles and cities and built large decorated palaces, for they all trembled with fear on account of the treasures that they had amassed, because they might be stolen from them or carried off by some force. The sorrows of the captives of misfortune increased so that they were never afterward secure. When they bound themselves to riches, they appropriated what had been common property before, like the sun and the moon, until now one person has more than twenty others. Such a situation never came from a good heart.

"Without question, I would not give two buttons for such greedy scoundrels. No matter how much they lacked good hearts, such a fault would mean nothing to me. Indeed, they could love each other, hate each other, or sell their love to one another. But it is a great sorrow and shame when these ladies with bright faces, these pretty, joyous women, who should value lawful love and defend it, are sold into such great filth. That a noble heart could sell itself is too ugly a thing to understand. 9665

"But, however that may be, the young man should see that he doesn't neglect his study of arts and sciences, in order that, if need arises, he may have security and protection for himself and his sweetheart, so that she would not abandon him. Such a course can advance a young man, and, in any case, it cannot do him harm. 9679

"Next, he must also remember to hold to this counsel of mine: if he has a sweetheart, young or old, and knows and thinks that she wants to find another lover, or has already looked for one, he should not blame her or criticize her for seeking or acquiring them, but should recapture her by being friendly, without reproaching or vilifying her. Moreover, the less to estrange her, if he finds her even in the act, he should take care not to open his eyes in that direction. He should pretend to be blind, or more stupid than a buffalo, so that she may think it entirely true that he could detect nothing. And if anyone sends her a letter he should not interpose by reading it or looking it over or trying to find out their secrets. 9687

"His heart should never desire to go against her will. Instead, 9707 he should make her very welcome when she comes from any street. And she should be allowed to go wherever she wants, just as her desires turn her, for she doesn't want to be tied down.

9714   "Now I want you to know thoroughly what I want to tell you next. One ought to study it in a book: anyone who wants to have a woman's grace must always give her space, must never hold her to a rule, but rather let her go and come according to her wish. For he who wants to hold her back so that she may neither go nor come, whether she is his wife or his mistress, has immediately lost her love.

9725   "He must never believe anything against her, no matter how certain he may be of it, but he should tell the men or women who bring him the news that what they said was foolish, that they never saw so worthy a woman, always doing good without ceasing, and that therefore no man should mistrust her.

9733   "He should not reproach her with her vices, nor beat nor touch her; for he who wants to beat his wife in order the better to entrench himself in her love when, afterward, he wants to pacify her, is the same man who, in order to tame his cat, beats it and then calls it back to tie it up. But if the cat can jump away, he may fail to capture it.

9743   "If the woman beats the man or vilifies him, he should take care that his heart does not change. If he sees himself beaten or reviled, even if she should pull out his nails alive, he must not take revenge, but rather thank her and say that he would like to live in such martyrdom all the time, as long as he knew that his service was pleasing to her, indeed that he would rather even quite freely die at that moment than live without her. And if it happens that he may strike her because she seems to him too haughty and has made him very angry by grumbling at him so much or, perhaps, by wishing to threaten him, then immediately, to purchase peace, he must take care to play the game of Love before she leaves the place. The poor man must particularly do so, for she could leave a poor man immediately, for the slightest cause, if she didn't see him bow down toward her. A poor man must love wisely and must suffer very humbly, without a sign of anger or ire, whatever he sees her either do or say; he must do so especially more than the rich man, who perhaps would not give two chick-peas for her hauteur or resistance if he could indeed revile her.

"And if he is such that he doesn't want to maintain his fidelity 9775
to his sweetheart but, while he would not wish to lose her, wants
to form an attachment with another, and if he wants to give his
new mistress a kerchief or head-cloth, chaplet, ring, clasp, belt, or a
jewel of any shape, then he must take care that his first sweetheart
does not recognize these things, for her heart would be full of
anguish when she saw the other wearing them; nothing could
comfort her. Let him take care also that he does not have the
second come to the same place where the first one met him and
where she is accustomed to come, for if she comes—provided that
she discovers the second—there is nothing which can provide any
counsel. There is no old wild boar, with his bristles erect when
he is excited by dogs, that is so cruel, nor any lioness as sullen or
cruel when the hunter who is attacking her presses his attack at
the moment when she is feeding her cubs, nor is there any serpent
as malicious, when one steps on its tail (the serpent does not enjoy
being stepped on), as a woman when she finds his new mistress
with her lover. She spouts fire and flame everywhere, and she is
ready to lose both body and soul.

"And if she hasn't captured the two of them together in their 9807
nest, but falls into jealousy over it, because she knows or thinks
that she is deceived, then, however it may be, whether she knows or
believes, let him take care never to cease denying quite openly
what she knows for certain, and let him not be slow to swear his
innocence. Immediately, on the spot, he must again make her
endure the game of Love. Then he will be free of her clamors.

"And if she attacks him and vexes him so much that he has 9819
to confess to her and does not, perhaps, know how to protect
himself, he should then, if possible, bend his efforts toward forcing
her to believe that he did so in self-defense. For (he will say)
the other woman held him so close and led him such a difficult
time that he could never escape until he had performed the act;
moreover (he will go on), it never happened except that once.
Then he swears and pledges and promises that it will never happen
again, and that he will conduct himself so faithfully that if she
ever hears a word of that kind of thing, he wants her to kill him
or beat him to death. She would prefer that the other woman,
that unlawful perverter of vows, should be harmed so that he
would never come to the place where she held him in such an

embrace, for if it then happened that she ordered him, he would not go at her bidding nor, if possible, allow her to come to a place where she might hold him. Then he must embrace her close, kiss her, flatter her, and comfort her; he must beg her mercy for his misdeed and promise never to do it again. He must say that he is truly repentant, ready to perform any penance that she can prescribe, after she has pardoned him. Then, if she wants to pardon him, let him do love's duty.

9853   "Let him not boast about her so that she might become downcast. Many men have thus boasted with false and feigned words about women whose bodies they could not possess; they blackened their names most wrongfully. But indeed, they lack hearts; they are neither courteous nor valiant. Boasting is a very base vice; he who boasts commits great folly, for, even though he had done something, he should in any case have hidden it. Love wants to hide his treasures, except from loyal companions who also want to keep them quiet and hide them; there one may indeed reveal them.

9869   "Now if she falls sick it is right, if possible, for him to study how to be of greatest service to her so that afterward he will be better received. He should take care not to harbor any grudge over the drawn-out illness. He should stay near her, watching, kiss her with tears in his eyes, and, if he is wise, vow many distant pilgrimages—as long as she hears his vows. He must not forbid food to her, nor offer her something bitter or anything that is not sweet and tender.

9883   "He must pretend to have unusual dreams, all stuffed with pleasing falsehoods. Let him say that when night comes and he lies all alone on his bed in his room, it seems to him, when he sleeps—for he sleeps but little and is often awake—that she was completely healthy and cured, and that all night long and through the day, in delightful places, he held her all naked in his arms in the solace of love-making. He should tell her such fables or similar ones.

9895   "Now, up to this point, I have sung to you of how he who wants to merit the favor of women and prolong their love, but who wants to be free to change his mind and would not wish to give great attention to doing whatever pleases them, should serve them in sickness and in health. For no woman will ever know so much or be so firm of heart, so loyal or serious, that one could ever be certain of holding her, no matter how much trouble one took, any more than if one held an eel by the tail in the Seine; for he hasn't the power to prevent her saving herself, so that immediately she will have escaped, however strongly he might seize her. There is no animal so well trained that is always ready to flee; she has so many different changes that no man should have confidence in her.

"I do not say these things on account of good women, who establish restraints through their virtues; but I have not yet found any, however many I may have tested. Not even Solomon could find them, no matter how well he knew how to test them, for he himself affirms that he never found a stable woman. And if you take the trouble to seek one and find her, take her; you will have the pick of sweethearts, one who will be wholly yours. If she doesn't have the possibility of running about looking, so that she might provide for herself elsewhere, or if she does not find someone who will solicit her, such a woman will give herself up to Chastity. 9917

"Now I want to say another brief word before I leave this subject. In short, a man who wants to keep the love of any girl, whatever she may be, ugly or beautiful, must observe this commandment of mine, and he should remember it always and consider it very precious: let him give any girl to understand that he cannot protect himself against her, so dumbfounded and amazed is he by her beauty and worth, for there is no woman, however good she may be, old, young, worldly or cloistered, no lady so religious, however chaste of body or soul, who does not take delight in hearing someone go about praising her beauty. No matter how ugly she may be called, one should swear that she is more beautiful than a fairy; one may do so securely, since she will easily believe him, for every woman, I know well, thinks of herself as one so beautiful, however ugly she may be proven, that she is indeed worthy to be loved. 9933

"Thus should all handsome, worthy, and noble young men be diligent in keeping their sweethearts, without criticizing them for their follies. Women do not care for correction; instead, they have minds so constructed that it seems to them that they do not need to be taught their trade. And no man who doesn't want to 9959

displease them should dissuade them from anything that they want
to do. Just as the cat knows by nature the science of catching, and
cannot be diverted from it, because he is always born with such
a faculty and was never put to school to learn it, just so a woman,
however foolish she is, knows by her natural judgment that, whatever excess she commits, good or bad, wrong or right, or whatever
you wish, she does nothing that she should not, and she hates
whoever corrects her. She does not get this faculty from a teacher,
but has had it from the time that she could be born, and she cannot
be dissuaded from it. She is always born with such a faculty so
that anyone who wished to correct her would never enjoy her love.

9987   "So it is, companion, with your rose, which is such a precious
thing that you would not take any possession for it if you could
have it. When you are in possession of it, as your hope foretells, and
your joy overflows, then take care of it in the way that one should
take care of such a little flower. Then you will enjoy the little
love with which no other compares; you will not find its equal in
perhaps fourteen cities."

10000   "Indeed," I said, "that's true; not in the world, I am sure, so
good was, and is, its power to bring happiness."

6

THE ASSAULT ON THE CASTLE.

FALSE SEEMING'S CONTRIBUTION

Thus Friend comforted me. I took great comfort from his counsel, and it seemed to me, indeed, that he knew at least more than Reason did. But before he had finished his argument, which agreed strongly with me, Sweet Thought and Sweet Talk came back, and from then on they stayed close to me and hardly ever left me afterward. But they did not bring Sweet Looks; I did not blame them for having left him, for I knew well that they couldn't bring him. 10003

I took leave and left, and at length I went off all alone across the meadow, bright with grass and flowers, enjoying myself and listening to those sweet birds singing those new songs. Their sweet songs, which so pleased me, filled my heart with all good things. But Friend had burdened me with one thing when he ordered me to turn and flee from the castle and not to go and play around it. I did not know if I could keep myself away, for I always wanted to go there. 10015

After my departure then, I made my way to the left, avoiding the right hand, to seek the shortest road. I would willingly seek such a road, and if it were found, I would throw myself onto it completely unreined, with no denial, unless someone stronger opposed me, to draw Fair Welcoming, the open, sweet, good-natured one, from prison. As soon as I saw the castle weaker than a toasted cake, and the gate open, no one would stop me; indeed I would certainly have the devil in my stomach if I did not capture it and enter therein. Then Fair Welcoming would be liberated. I would not take a hundred thousand pounds for it—I can truly declare it to you—if I could establish myself on that road. In any case, I drew away from the castle, but not very far. 10029

As I was thinking of the new rose in a beautiful, very delightful place near a clear fountain, I saw an honorable lady of high 10051 rank, pleasant of body, with a beautiful figure, standing beneath the shade of an elm tree with her lover beside her. I do not know his name, but hers was Wealth, and she was a lady of great nobility. She guarded the entry to a little path, but she had not entered it. As soon as I saw them, I bowed toward them and saluted them with bent head. They returned my greeting immediately, but that did me little good. In any case, I asked them the right way to Give-Too-Much. Wealth, who spoke first, told me in a speech that was somewhat haughty:

"Here is the road. I am guarding it."

10072   "Ah! Lady, may God protect you. Then I pray you, as long as it does not burden you, to allow me to go by this way to the newly built castle that Jealousy established."

10077   "Vassal," she said, "that will not take place now, for I still know nothing of you. You are not well-arrived, since you are not one of my close friends. I will not set you within that way before perhaps ten years. No man, even though he is from Paris or Amiens, enters there if he is not close to me. I let my friends go there indeed, to carol and dance in balls, and they have a little gay life, but no wise man envies them for it. There they are served with gay times, with farandoles and *espingueries*, tabors and viols, new *rotruenges*, with games of dice, chess, and backgammon, and with

10095 all my immoderate delights. Young men and girls go there, brought together by old mackerel-procuresses, and explore the meadows, gardens, and groves, gayer than parrots. Then, with chaplets of flowers on their heads, they go back together to the stews and bathe together in tubs all prepared in the rooms of the house of Foolish Generosity. She makes them poor and wounds them so that afterward they can hardly be cured. She knows how to sell to them at a high price and make them pay for her service and her hospitality; she takes from them so cruel a tribute that they have to sell their lands before they can turn the whole fee over to her. When I take them there they are full of great joy, but when Poverty brings them back they are cold, trembling, and quite bare. I keep the entry and she the exit. I can never interfere with them, no matter how wise or learned they may be. They can go to the devil, thousands of them in the end.

10119   "I do not say that, if they did so much as to reconcile themselves with me afterward—but that would be a very difficult thing

—I would never be so tired that I would not lead them back to the path again every time that it pleased them, but you know that the more they frequent it the more they repent in the end; because of their shame they dare not look at me. They are so angry and so full of chagrin that each of them is just short of killing himself, and I abandon them because they abandon me. I promise you for certain, without lying, that you will come to repent too late if you ever put your feet there. No bear, when he is thoroughly baited, is so wretched, so prostrated, as you will be if you go there. If Poverty can get you in her power, she will make you give so much that she will let you die of hunger on a little stubble or hay. Hunger was formerly Poverty's chambermaid and served her in such a way that for her service, in which Hunger was eager and ardent, Poverty taught her all sorts of malice and made her the mistress and nurse of Larceny, the ugly young fellow. She nursed him with her own milk and had no other pap to feed him. Her situation, if you want to know it, is neither soft nor on good earth; Hunger lives in a stony field where neither grain, grove, nor thicket grows. This field lies at the end of Scotland, so cold that a little more and it would be marble. Hunger, who sees neither grain nor trees, tears out the very grass with cutting nails, with hard teeth, but, because of the thickly scattered rocks, she finds the grass very sparse. And if I wanted to describe her, I could be quickly free of that task. 10148

"She is long and lean, weak and hollow, and in great want from a diet of oat-bread. Her hair is all bristly, her eyes hard and hollow, her face pale and her lips dry, her cheeks soiled with dirt. Whoever wanted to could see her entrails through her hard skin. Along her flanks, where all humors are lacking, her bones stick out, and she has no stomach whatever, only the place for it, which goes in so deep that the girl's whole chest hangs on her backbone. Her leanness has elongated her fingers and made her knees lose their roundness. Her heels are tall, sharp, and prominent; it looks as though there is no flesh on them, so closely does the lean skin hold to them. The goddess of the harvest, Ceres, who makes the grain grow, does not know how to keep to that road; nor does he who guides her dragons, Triptolemus, know that way. The Fates, who do not want the goddess of fertility and the exhausted sufferer, Hunger, to join themselves together, keep them apart 10163

10187

from each other. But when Poverty takes hold of you she will lead you there soon enough if you want to go in that direction and be idle, as is your habit. In any case one can certainly turn toward Poverty by other ways than by that which I guard here; one can come to Poverty through an idle, lazy life. If it pleased you to stick to the way I have told you about here, the one toward exhausted, hateful Poverty, in order to attack the strong castle, you could indeed fail to capture it.

10205   "But I think it certain that Hunger will be your close neighbor, for Poverty knows the road better by heart than by parchment instructions. Furthermore, you should know that Hunger the wretched is always so attentive and courteous toward her mistress— whom she neither loves nor values, even though she is supported by her, however exhausted and naked she may be—that she comes to see her every day and sit with her. She takes her by the beak and, uncomfortable and uneasy, kisses her. Then, when she sees Larceny asleep, she takes him by the ear and wakens him. In her distress she leans toward him and counsels and teaches him how he must get things for them, however much he may have to endure for them. And Faint Heart agrees with them, although he dreams in any case of the rope, and the thought makes his hair stand straight out on end for fear that he may see them hang his son Larceny, the trembler, if they can catch him stealing.

10231   "But you will never enter here. Seek your road elsewhere, for you have not served me so well that you have deserved my love."

10235   "Lady," I said, "before God, if I could I would willingly have your grace. As soon as I entered upon that path, I would release Fair Welcoming from the prison within which he is held. If it please you, give me this gift."

10241   "I have understood you well," she said, "and I know that you have not sold all your woods, the great and the small; you have held out a beech, and no man can live without folly as long as he may want to follow Love. As long as men live in such madness, they think that they are very wise. Live! Indeed, they do not do so; rather they die while they dwell in such torment, for one should not give the name life to such madness and folly. Indeed Reason knew what to tell you, but she could not cure you of your stupidity. You know that when you did not believe her you deceived yourself cruelly; in fact, before Reason came to you there was nothing that held you back, and never afterward, from the time that you loved *par amour*, did you consider me worth anything. Lovers do not want to value me; instead they strain themselves to disparage my goods when I take them away from them, and they reject them elsewhere. Where the devil could one get whatever a lover wanted to spend? Flee from here, and leave me in peace."

Since I could conquer nothing there, I left without delay. The beautiful lady remained with her lover, who was well dressed and adorned. With my thoughts in a turmoil, I went off through the delicious garden, as beautiful and precious as you have heard before; but I took very little delight in this beauty, for I had put all my thought elsewhere. In all times and in all places I thought in what way, without pretense, I would best perform my duty of service, for I would very willingly have done it without fault in anything; if I had committed any fault whatever, my value would not have grown in any way as a result. 10268

My heart held close to and watched over what Friend had advised me. I constantly showed honor to Foul Mouth in all the places where I found him, and I set myself to showing great honor to all my other enemies, and I served them with my might. I don't know if I deserved their thanks, but to gain their esteem I restrained myself from daring to approach the enclosure as I was accustomed to do, for I always wanted to go there. Thus for a long time I performed my penance with such a conscience as God knows, for I did one thing and thought another. In this way I had a double intention, but it was never I, on any occasion, who made it double. I had to pursue treason to gain my end. I had never been a traitor, never yet incriminated myself to anyone. 10285

When Love had tested me thoroughly and saw that he had found me loyal, as loyal in every way as I ought to be toward him, he appeared and, smiling at my discomfort, put his hand on my head and asked if I had done whatever he commanded, how it was with me and how it seemed to me with the rose that had stolen my heart. He knew very well, of course, all that I had done, for God knows the whole of whatever man does. 10307

"Have you performed all the commandments," he asked, "that I give to pure lovers? I do not want to distribute them elsewhere, and pure lovers should never depart from them." 10319

10323   "I do not know, sir, but I have done them as loyally as I know how."

10325   "True, but you are too changeable. Your heart is not very steadfast, but unfortunately full of doubt; indeed I know the whole truth about it. The other day you wanted to leave me. You were just a little short of robbing me of the homage due me, and you made a sorrowful complaint about Idleness and me. Moreover, you said of Hope that she was not certain in her knowledge, and you even considered yourself a fool for coming into my service, and you agreed with Reason. Weren't you indeed a wicked man?"

10339   "Mercy, sir, I have confessed it. You know that I did not flee, and I made my bequest, I well remember, just as one must make it, to those who are bound to you in homage. When Reason came to me she did not consider me unfailingly wise, but reprimanded very severely and preached to me for a long time; indeed she thought that by preaching she could prevent me from serving you. However, no matter how much she knew how to put her mind to it, I did not believe her; without fail—may I not lie—she made me fear, nothing more. But, if it please God, whatever may happen to me, as long as my heart stays with you, and that will be as long as it is not torn out of my body, Reason will never move me to anything which may go against you, or even against any other, 10361 of smaller worth. In fact I know for certain that I showed bad grace in ever thinking as I did and in listening to her, and I beg that I may be pardoned, for I wish, in order to amend my life as it pleased you to command, to die and live in your law, without ever following Reason. There is nothing that may erase this law from my heart. Nor may Atropos ever, for anything that I may do, bring death to me except in the performance of your work; instead may she take me in the very task in which Venus operates most willingly. For I do not doubt in any way that no man has so much delight as in this particular. And those who should weep for me, when they see me thus dead, can say: 'Fair sweet friend, you who are placed there in that situation, now it is true, without any fable whatever, that this death is indeed suitable to the life that you led when you kept your soul together with this body.'"

10385   "By my head, now you speak wisely. Now I see that in you my homage is well-used. You are not among the false renegades, the thieves who renounce me when they have done what they sought. Your heart is very loyal; when you navigate so well, your ship will come to a good harbor, and I pardon you more because of your entreaty than because of any gift, for I wish neither silver nor gold. But in place of the confessional, I want you, before you reconcile yourself with me, to recall all my commandments, for your romance will contain ten of them, counting prohibitions and commandments. If you have remembered them well, you have not thrown a double ace. Say them."

"Willingly. I should flee villainy. I am not to utter slander. 10403 I should give and return greetings immediately. I should have no tendency to say anything vile. I must labor at all times to honor all women. I am to flee from pride, to maintain an elegant appearance, to become gay and lively, to abandon myself to being generous, and to give my whole heart in a single place."

"In faith, you know your lesson well; I am in no doubt of it. 10413 How is it with you?"

"I am in lively sorrow; my heart is hardly alive."

"Don't you have three comforts?" 10417

"Not at all. I lack Sweet Looks, who used to take away the poison of my sorrow with his most sweet perfume. All three have fled, but of them, the other two came back to me."

"Don't you have Hope?" 10423

"Yes, sir; she does not let me be conquered, for Hope once believed is held to for a long time afterward."

"Fair Welcoming, what has happened to him?" 10427

"He is held in prison, the sweet, open fellow who loved me so much."

"It doesn't matter now; don't be dismayed. By my eyes, you 10430 shall yet have more of your will than you are used to having. Since you serve so loyally, I will order my men immediately to lay siege to the strong castle. The barons are strong and active. Before we leave our siege, Fair Welcoming will be brought out from his trap."

The God of Love, without making any specification of time or 10439 place in his message, ordered his entire barony to come to his parliament. He begged some; others he commanded. They all came without making any excuse, ready to carry out his wish, each one according to his ability. I shall name them briefly, without rank, in order to gnaw away at my rhymes more quickly.

10449   Lady Idleness, the keeper of the garden, came with the largest banner. Nobility of Heart came, Wealth, Openness, Pity, and Generosity; Boldness, Honor, Courtesy, Delight, Simplicity, and Company; Security, Diversion, and Joy; Gaiety, Beauty, Youth, Humility, and Patience; Skillful Concealment; and Constrained Abstinence, who led False Seeming with her—without him she could hardly come; all these came with all their followers. Each one of them had a very noble heart, but not Constrained Abstinence and False Seeming with his face of pretense. Whatever appearance they put on outside, they embrace Fraud in their thought.

10467   Fraud engendered False Seeming, who goes around stealing men's hearts. His mother's name is Hypocrisy, the dishonored thief who suckled and nursed the filthy hypocrite with a rotten heart who has betrayed many a region with his religious habit.

10475   When the God of Love saw him, his whole heart was disturbed within him. "What is this?" he asked. "Am I dreaming? Tell me, False Seeming, by whose leave have you come into my presence?"

10480   Constrained Abstinence jumped up and took False Seeming by the hand: "Sir," she said, "I brought him with me, and I beg you not to be displeased. He has brought me many honors and comforts; he sustains and consoles me, and if it weren't for him I would be dead from hunger. Therefore you should blame me the less. Although he does not want to love people, still it is important for me that he be loved and called a good man and a saint. He is my friend and I his sweetheart, and he comes with me for companionship."

10493   "So be it," said the God of Love. Thereupon he made a short speech to everyone.

10495   "I have had you come here," he said, "to vanquish Jealousy, who makes martyrs of our lovers and who aspires to hold against me this strong castle that she has erected and that has caused my heart a grievous wound. She has had it so strongly fortified that before we can capture it it will be necessary to fight a great deal. Thus I am full of sorrow and vexation over Fair Welcoming, whom she has imprisoned there and who used to advance our friends' causes so well. If he does not come out from there, I am undone, for I lack Tibullus, who knew my characteristics so well. For his death I shattered my arrows, broke my bow, and dragged my quiver in shreds. His death gave me so much and such anguish that at his tomb I trailed my poor wings, all torn because I had beaten them so much in my sorrow. My mother wept for his death so much that she nearly died. No man who saw us weeping for him would not have felt pity. There was neither rein nor bridle on our tears. We would have needed Gallus, Catullus, and Ovid, who knew well how to treat of love; but each of them is dead and decayed. Here is Guillaume de Lorris, whose opponent, Jealousy,   10526 brings him so much anguish and sorrow that he is in danger of dying if I do not think about saving him. He took counsel with me willingly, like one who is wholly mine; and he was right, for it is for him that we put ourselves to the trouble of assembling all our barons to carry off Fair Welcoming or steal him. But he is not, let it be said, very wise. Still, it would be a very great pity if I lost so loyal a sergeant, when I both can and should help him; he has served me so loyally that he has deserved well of me. I should sally forth and gird myself to burst the walls and tower and to lay siege to the castle with all the power that I have. He should serve me still more, for, to merit my grace, he is to begin the romance in which all my commandments will be set down, and he will finish it up to the point where he will say to Fair Welcoming, who now languishes, unjustly and in sorrow, in the prison: 'I am terribly afraid that you may have forgotten me, and I am in sorrow and pain. If I lose your good will, there will never be any comfort for me, since I have no confidence elsewhere.' Here Guillaume shall rest. May his tomb be full of balm, of incense, myrrh, and aloes, so well has he served me, so well did he praise me!

"Then will come Jean Chopinel with gay heart and lively body.   10565 He will be born at Meung-sur-Loire; he will serve me his whole life, feasting and fasting, without avarice or envy, and he will be such a very wise man that he will have no concern for Reason, who hates and blames my unguents, which exhale a perfume sweeter than balm. And if it happens, however things go, that he fails in any respect—for there is no man who does not sin, and each person always has some blemish—he will have so pure a heart toward me that he will always, at least in the end, repent of his misdeed when he feels himself at fault, and then he will not want to betray me. He will be so fond of the romance that he will want to finish it right to the end, if time and place can be

10587 found. For when Guillaume shall cease, more than forty years after his death—may I not lie—Jean will continue it, and because of Fair Welcoming's misfortune, and through the despairing fear that he may have lost the good will that Fair Welcoming had shown him before, he will say, 'And perhaps I have lost it. At least I do not despair of it.' And he will set down all the other speeches, whatever they may be, wise or foolish, up to the time when he will have cut the most beautiful red rose on its green, leafy branch, to the time when it is day and he awakes. Then he will want to explicate the affair in such a way that nothing can remain hidden. If they could have given their counsel in this matter, they would have given it to me immediately; but that cannot now take place through Guillaume nor through Jean, who is yet to be born, for he is not here present. Thus the situation remains so grievous that certainly, after he is born, if I do not come to him, all furnished with wings, to read your sentence to him as soon as he emerges from infancy, I dare swear and guarantee you that he could never finish it.

10617   "And since it could happen that this Jean who is yet to be born might, perhaps, be hindered, and since such a situation would be a sin and sorrow, a detriment to lovers, for he will do them much good, I pray to Lucina, the goddess of infancy, to grant that he be born without pain and difficulty so that he may live for a long time. And then afterward, when he comes to the point where Jupiter will take him alive and he will have to be made to drink, even from before the time when he is weaned, from the double casks that he always has, the one clear, the other roiled, the one sweet and the other bitterer than soot or the sea, and when he is put in his cradle, I shall cover him with my wings because he will be so much my friend. I shall sing to him such airs that, after he is out of his infancy, he will, indoctrinated with my knowledge, so flute our words through crossroads and through schools, in the language of France, before audiences throughout the kingdom, that those who hear these words will never die from the sweet pains of love, provided that they believe only him. For he will read so fittingly that all those alive should call this book *The Mirror for Lovers*, so much good will they see there for them, provided that Reason, that wretched coward, be not believed.

10655   "Therefore, I wish to be counseled here, for you are all my counselors. And I beg your grace with joined palms that this poor wretched Guillaume, who has borne himself so well toward me, may be helped and comforted. And if I did not beg you for him, I should certainly beg you at least that you give Jean the advantage of lightening his burden so that he may write more easily, for I prophesy that he will be born. I beg you also on behalf of the others who will come and who will try with devotion to follow my commandments, which they will find written in the book, that they may overcome Jealousy's envious machinations and destroy all the castles that she will dare erect. Advise me what we shall do, how we shall deploy our host, in which part we can best injure them in order to destroy their castle soonest."

Thus Love spoke to them, and they received his speech well. When he had finished his reasoning, the barons consulted among themselves. They supported several opinions, and different ones said different things, but after several of them composed their disagreements, they announced their consensus to the God of Love.   10679

"Sir," they said, "we are agreed through the consent of all our people except Wealth alone. She has sworn her oath never to lay siege to that castle nor ever, she says, to strike a blow with dart, lance, or ax, or with any other arm that may exist, no matter what any man may say about it. She holds this young man in such despite that she scorns our undertaking and has left our band, at least for this operation. She blames him and despises him and turns such an unfavorable countenance upon him because, she says, he never held her dear; therefore she hates him and will hate him from now on because he doesn't want to lay up treasure. He never gave her other tribute; whatever he has given her is here. Indeed, she says, without fail, that the day before yesterday he asked her if he could enter the path that is called Give-Too-Much, and he flattered her in addition, but he was poor when he made his plea to her, and therefore she denied him the entry. As Wealth tells us, he has since then not worked enough to recover a single penny that might be lodged with her as her very own. When she told us all this, we came to an agreement without her.   10687

"We find then in our agreement that False Seeming and Abstinence, along with all those under their banners, will attack the rear gate, which Foul Mouth guards with his Normans (may the fires of evil burn them!). Along with them, Courtesy and   10719

Generosity will exhibit their prowess against the Old Woman, who rules Fair Welcoming with a harsh hand. Next, Delight and Skillful Concealment will go to kill Shame. They will assemble their host against her and lay siege to that gate. Boldness and Security are opposed against Fear; they will besiege her with all their followers, who never knew anything of flight. Openness and Pity will present themselves against Resistance and attack him. Thus the host will be well deployed. They will break down the castle if each one puts his attention to it, and to that end may your mother Venus be present; she is very wise, for she knows a great deal about this kind of operation. It will never be completed, by word or by deed, without her. It would have been good to send for her, for she would have made the job easier."

10749   "My lords," said Love, "my mother the goddess, who is my lady and my mistress, is in no way subject to my desire, and she does not do whatever I wish. But she is very much accustomed to running to my aid, when it pleases her, to finish my tasks, but I do not want to trouble her now. She is my mother, and I have feared her since my infancy. I have a very great reverence for her, for a child who does not fear his father and mother can never become their equal. Nevertheless we shall know well how to send for her when we need her. If she were near here she would come straightway, since nothing, I believe, would hold her back. My mother has very great prowess. She has taken many a fortress that cost more than a thousand bezants, when I was never present. Of course people imputed the victory to me, but I never entered in at any time, nor was I ever pleased by such a capture of a fortress without me; for it seems to me that, whatever one says, it is nothing but merchandising. If a man buys a war horse for a hundred pounds, he pays them and will be free of obligation; he owes noth-

10779   ing more to the merchant, and the merchant owes him nothing. I do not call a sale a gift. A sale owes no reward; it involves neither grace nor merit. One person leaves the other completely clear of debt. This situation is not like a sale, for when the buyer has put his horse in the stable, he can sell it again and recover his property or profit. At least he cannot lose everything. If he had to hang on to the hide, the hide at least would remain with him, and he would be able to realize something from it. Or, if he holds the horse so dear that he keeps it for his riding horse, he will always be the lord of the horse. But the market in which Venus is accustomed to intervene is far worse, for no man will ever know how to traffic there without losing all that he owns and all that he has bought. The seller has both the thing sold and the price for 10799 it, so that the buyer loses everything, for he will never hand over so much money that he may have lordship over it. And in spite of his own gifts, he could never, for any amount of gift or preaching, prevent a strange newcomer—whether Breton, English, or Roman —from getting as much by giving either the same amount, or more, or less. Perhaps, indeed, he can go around telling so many stories that he can get everything for nothing. Are such merchants then wise? They are but foolish, unhappy wretches when they buy a thing knowingly or lose everything that they put out; no matter how much they can work, it cannot dwell with them.

"Nevertheless—I do not seek to deny it—my mother is not in 10817 the habit of paying anything for it. She is not so foolish or stupid as to meddle with such a vice. But you know very well that such a person pays her and afterward, when Poverty holds him in distress, repents of the price, no matter how much a disciple of Wealth he had been. Wealth remains wide awake for me when she wants what I want.

"But by Saint Venus my mother and by Saturn her old father 10827 who engendered her as one who was already a young girl—but not on his espoused wife—by these I want to swear to you once more, the better to make the matter secure. By the faith that I owe to all my brothers, whose fathers no one knows how to name, so diverse, so many are they, all of whom my mother binds to herself —by these I swear to you again, and take the swamp of hell, the Styx, as witness. If I lie here, I shall not drink sweetened wine before a year has passed, for you know the custom of the gods: the one who forswears the Styx is not to drink until a year has passed. Now I have sworn enough; I am in a bad situation if I forswear 10844 myself, but you will never see me forsworn. Since Wealth fails me here, I think that I will sell that failure dearly to her. She shall pay for it if she does not arm herself at least with sword or halberd. Since she does not hold me dear today, she will have seen today's dawning in an evil hour from the moment that she knows that the fortress and its two towers are to tumble. If I can get a rich man in my power, you will see me so incite him that he will

never have so many marks or pounds that he may not be freed
of them in a short time. I shall have all his money stolen unless
it gushes out of granaries for him. Our girls will pluck him until
he lacks even pinfeathers, and they will set him to selling his land
if he does not know well enough how to protect himself.

10865   "Poor men have made me their master. Although they may not
have anything to eat, I do not despise them; no worthy man does.
Wealth is very greedy and gluttonous, and she treats them harshly,
harries and spurns them. They love better than the rich, the misers
and greedy hoarders, and, by the faith that I owe my grandfather,
they are more eager to serve and more loyal; their good heart
and willingness satisfy me in large measure. They have placed their
entire thought in me, and I must necessarily think of them. Their
outcries move me to such pity that if I were god of riches as I am
of love, I would set them immediately in stations of great splendor.
Moreover, I must protect those who labor so hard to serve my
interests, for if they died from the ills of love, it would appear
that there was no love whatever in me."

10887   "Sir," they said, "everything that you recount is the truth. The
judgment that you have made about rich men remains indeed a
tenable one, good, well-distilled, and appropriate, and thus it shall
be, we are certain. If rich men do you homage, they will not act
wisely, for you will never perjure yourself, never endure the pain
of leaving off drinking sweetened wine. If they can fall into the
traps of ladies, those ladies will grind such pepper for them that
they should have all kinds of misery. The ladies will be so courteous that they will collect your debt handsomely. You need never
seek other vicars, for they will tell them so much black and white,

10907   be not dismayed, that you will consider yourself paid. Never interfere with them. They will tell their victims such news and so incite
them with requests, through dishonest flatteries, and will give them
such volleys of kisses and embraces, that, if the men believe them,
certainly there will not remain to them a single holding that will
not follow after the movable goods of which they will be relieved
first. Now command whatever you want, and we will do it, be it
wrong or right. But False Seeming does not dare interpose in this
matter, for he says that you hate him, and he doesn't know if you
intend to put him to shame. Therefore we all beg you, fair sir, that
you give over your anger toward him, and we beg that, with his

friend Abstinence, he may be part of our barony. That is our agreement, our compact."

"By my faith," said Love, "I grant this permission. From now   10928
on I want him to be in my court. Here, come forward." And False
Seeming ran forward.

"False Seeming, by such an agreement you are now mine. You   10931
will aid our friends and never give them any trouble; rather you
will think of how to raise them and to give trouble to our enemies.
Let yours be the power of surveillance. You will be my king of
the camp followers, since our chapter wishes it thus. Without
fail, you are a wicked traitor and unrestrained thief. You have
perjured yourself a hundred thousand times. But in any case, to
relieve our people of their uncertainty, I command you in their
hearing to teach them, at least with general indications, in what
place they would best find you if they needed to, and how you
will be recognized, for one needs good wits to recognize you. Tell
us what places you frequent."

"Sir, I have various mansions that I would never try to tell   10952
you about, if it please you to relieve me of doing so, for if I tell
you the truth about them, I can bring harm and shame to them.
If my companions knew it, they would certainly harass me and
make trouble for me, if I ever knew their cruelty. In all places
they want to silence the truth which runs contrary to them; they
would never seek to hear it. If I said a word about them that was
not pleasing and friendly to them, I could enjoy it in a very unpleasant way. The words that sting them never please them at
all, even if they were words from the gospel that reprimanded
them for their treachery, for they are very cruel in an evil way.
Indeed I know for certain that, if I say anything to you about
them, they know about it sooner or later, no matter how enclosed
is your court. I give no attention to worthy men, for when they
hear me, they never apply what I say to themselves. But the
man who does take what I say as applying to him falls under the
suspicion of wishing to lead the life of Fraud and Hypocrisy, who
engendered and nourished me."

"They made a very good engendering of it," said Love, "and   10984
a very profitable one, since they engendered the devil. But in any
case," he went on, "it is necessary, without fail, that you name
your mansions for us immediately, in the hearing of all our men,

and that you explain your life to us. It is not good to hide it any more; you must reveal everything: how you serve and by what means, since you have thrown yourself in among us. And if you are beaten for telling the truth—something you are not accustomed to do—you will not be the first."

10999   "Sir, when it occurs to you as your pleasure, even if I should lie dead as a result, I shall do your will, for I have a great desire to do so." Then, without waiting any longer, False Seeming began his lecture and said to all in hearing:

11006   "Barons, hear my theme: he who wants to become acquainted with False Seeming must seek him in the world or in the cloister. I dwell in no place except these two, but more in one and less in the other. Briefly, I am lodged where I think that I am better hidden. The safest hiding place is under the most humble garment. The religious are very covert, the worldly more open. I do not want to blame or defame the religious calling, in whatever habit one may find it. I shall not, as I may, blame the humble and loyal religious life, although I do not love it.

11023   "I have in mind the false religious, the malicious criminals who want to wear the habit but do not want to subdue their hearts. The religious are all compassionate; you will never see a spiteful one. They do not care to follow pride, and they all want to live humbly. I never dwell with such people, and if I do, I pretend. I can indeed assume their habit, but I would rather let myself be hanged than desert my main business, whatever face I put on it.

11037   "I dwell with the proud, the crafty, the guileful, who covet worldly honors and who carry out large dealings, who go around tracking down large handouts and cultivating the acquaintance of powerful men and becoming their followers. They pretend to be poor, and they live on good, delicious morsels of food and drink costly wines. They preach poverty to you while they fish for riches with seines and trammel nets. By my head, evil will come of them. They are neither religious nor worldly. To the world they present an argument in which there is a shameful conclusion: this man has the robe of religion; therefore he is a religious. This argument is specious, not worth a knife of privet; the habit does not make

11059   the monk. Nevertheless no one knows how to reply to the argument, no matter how high he tonsures his head, even if he shaves with the razor of the *Elenchis*, that cuts up fraud into thirteen branches. No man knows so well how to set up distinctions that he dare utter a single word about it. But whatever place I come to, no matter how I conduct myself, I pursue nothing except fraud. No more than Tibert the cat has his mind on anything but mice and rats do I think of anything except fraud. Certainly by my habit you would never know with what people I dwell, any more than you would from my words, no matter how simple and gentle they were. You should look at actions if your eyes have not been put out; for if people do something other than what they say, they are certainly tricking you, whatever robes they have or whatever estate they occupy, clerical or lay, man or woman, lord, sergeant, servant, or lady."

When False Seeming had preached in this way, Love again   11083
spoke to him and said, interrupting his talk as if it were false or foolish, "What is this, you devil, are you shameless? What people have you told us about here? Can one find religion in a secular mansion?"

"Yes, sir. It does not follow that those who are attached to the   11091
clothing of the world lead a wicked life or that they therefore lose their souls, for that would be a very great sorrow. Holy religion can indeed flower in colorful robes. We have seen many holy men die, and many saintly women, devout and religious, who always wore ordinary clothing, but were none the less sainted. I might   11103
name many of them for you. But nearly all the holy women who are prayed to in the churches, whether chaste virgins or married women who bore many beautiful children, wore the robes of the world and died in those very clothes; and these women were, are, and will be saints. Even the eleven thousand virgins who held their candles before God, and whose feast is celebrated in the churches, were taken in worldly clothing when they received their martyrdom; but they are still none the worse on that account. A good heart makes the thought good; the robe neither takes away nor gives. And it is good thought that inspires the man who reveals the religious life. In such a life lies religion based upon a right intention. If you were to put the fleece of Dame Belin, instead of a sable mantle, on Sir Isengrin the wolf, so that he looked like a sheep, do you think that if he lived with the ewes he would not

devour them? He would never drink their blood the less, but he would deceive them sooner, for as long as they did not recognize him they would follow him if he wanted to flee.

11133   "If there are even a few such wolves among your new apostles, O Church, you are in a bad situation. If your city is attacked by the knights of your table, your lordship is very weak. If those to whom you have given its defense attack the city, who can protect it against them? It will be captured without feeling a shot from a mangonel or a catapult, without displaying a banner to the wind. And if you don't want to rescue it from them, then you let them run everywhere. Let them! But if you command them, then there is nothing for you to do except to surrender or become their tributary by making peace with them and keeping it, as long as no greater misfortune comes to you than that they become lords of the entire church. In fact they know now how to mock you. By day they run around strengthening the walls, and by night they don't stop undermining them. Think about setting out elsewhere the grafts from which you want to gather fruit; you should not wait to do so. But peace! I shall come back from that subject. I want to say no more now about it, if I may pass along, for I could tire you too much.

11163   "But indeed I want to promise you to further the causes of all your friends, provided that they want my companionship. They are dead if they don't receive me, and they will serve my friend, or, by God, they will never succeed! Without fail, I am a traitor, and God has judged me a thief. I am perjured, but one hardly knows before the end what I am bringing to an end, for several who never recognized my fraud have received their deaths through me, and many are receiving them and will receive them without ever recognizing it. The man who does so, if he is wise, protects himself from it, or it will be his great misfortune. But the deception is so strong that it is very difficult to recognize it. For Proteus, who was accustomed to change into whatever form he wished, never knew as much fraud or guile as I practice; I never entered a town where I was recognized, no matter how much I was heard

11187 or seen. I know very well how to change my garment, to take one and then another foreign to it. Now I am a knight, now a monk; at one time I am a prelate, at another a canon; at one hour a clerk, at another a priest; now disciple, now master, now lord of the manor, now forester. Briefly I am in all occupations. Again I may be prince or page, and I know all languages by heart. At one hour I am old and white, and then I have become young again. Now I am Robert, now Robin, now Cordelier, now Jacobin. And in order to follow my companion, Lady Constrained Abstinence, who comforts me and goes along with me, I take on many another disguise, just as it strikes her pleasure, to fulfill her desire. At one time I wear a woman's robe; now I am a girl, now a lady. At another time I become a religious: now I am a devotee, now a prioress, nun, or abbess; now a novice, now a professed nun. I go through every locality seeking all religions. But, without fail, I leave the kernel of religion and take the husk. I dwell in religion in order to trick people; I seek only its habit, no more. What should I tell you? I disguise myself in the way that pleases me. The time is very much changed in me; my deeds are very different from my words."

At this point False Seeming wanted to stay silent, but Love   11223
did not pretend that he was annoyed at what he heard; instead, to delight the company, he said to him:

"Tell us more especially in what way you serve disloyally.   11227
Don't be ashamed to speak of it, for, as you tell us of your habits, you seem to be a holy hermit."

"It is true, but I am a hypocrite."

"You go around preaching abstinence."

"True, indeed, but I fill my paunch with very good morsels   11234
and with wines such as are suitable for theologians."

"You go around preaching poverty."

"True, abundantly richly. But however much I pretend to be   11238
poor, I pay no attention to any poor person. I would a hundred thousand times prefer the acquaintance of the King of France to that of a poor man, by our lady, even though he had as good a soul. When I see those poor devils all naked, shivering with cold on those stinking dunghills, crying and howling with hunger, I don't meddle in their business. If they were carried to the Hôtel-Dieu, they wouldn't get any comfort from me, for they wouldn't feed my maw with a single gift, since they have nothing worth a cuttlefish. What will a man give who licks his knife? But a

visit to a rich usurer who is sick is a good and pleasant thing. I go to comfort him, for I expect to bring away money from him. And if wicked death stifles him, I will carry him right up to his grave. And if anyone comes to reprove me for avoiding the poor, do you know how I escape from him? I give out behind my cloak that the rich man is more stained with sin than the poor, and has greater need of counsel, and that that is the reason that I see him and advise him.

11269   "All the same, the soul in very great poverty may undergo as great a loss as it does in very great wealth. The one and the other are equally wounding to the soul, for they are two extremities, wealth and beggary. The name of the mean is sufficiency. There lies the abundance of virtues. Solomon has written it all, withholding nothing, in one of his books, entitled Proverbs, right in the thirteenth chapter: 'Keep me, O God, by your power, from wealth and from beggary.' For a rich man, when he applies himself to thinking too much about his wealth, so turns his heart toward folly that he forgets his creator. How can I save anyone from sin when he is attacked by beggary? He can hardly help being a thief and perjurer, or God is a liar, if Solomon said about him the very words that I spoke of to you just now. I can swear to you without delay that it is not written in any law, at least not in ours, that Jesus Christ or his apostles, while they went about on earth, were

11300   ever seen seeking their bread, for they did not wish to beg. The masters of divinity in the city of Paris were formerly accustomed to preach thus. Moreover, the apostles could ask in full power without begging, for they were pastors in the name of God and they held the cure of souls. In fact, after their Master's death, they again began to be manual laborers, and they again maintained themselves by their own labor, neither more nor less, and lived in patience. If they had anything left over, they gave it to other poor people. They did not establish palaces or halls, but lay in dirty houses.

11317   "I well remember that a capable man, if he doesn't have the means by which he may live, should seek his living by laboring with his own hands, his own body, no matter how religious or eager to serve God he may be. He must do thus except in the cases, as I remember them, that I can tell you about very well when I have time to do so. And Scripture has told me that, even if he is quite perfect in goodness, he should still sell everything and make his living by laboring. The idler who haunts another's table is a thief who serves him with fables.

"You know too that there is no reasoning by which he might   11333
excuse himself on account of prayers, since, in one way or another, he must leave the service of God from time to time for his other needs. It is true that he must eat and sleep and do other things; our prayer then takes its rest. Thus he must withdraw from prayer to do his work. Scripture, which records truth for us, is consistent on this point.

"Moreover, Justinian, who wrote our old books, forbids any   11345
man who is capable of body to ask for his bread in any way as long as he can find a place to earn it. One would do better to cripple him or punish him openly than to sustain him in such a malicious practice. Those who receive such alms, unless perhaps they have a privilege that lessens the penalty for them, are not doing what they should. But I don't think that they would have this privilege if the prince had not been deceived; nor do I believe that they may rightfully possess it. However, I do not make any limitation on the prince or his power, nor do I wish by my remarks to include the question of whether or not his power may extend to such a case. I should not meddle in this question. But I believe that, according to the letter, he who eats the alms that are due to the unfortunate who are poor, naked, weak, old, and crippled, who do not earn their bread because they haven't the strength—such a man, when he eats their alms to their detriment, eats his own damnation, if He who made Adam does not lie.

"Know too, that where God commands the man of substance to   11375
sell whatever he has, give it to the poor, and follow Him, He did not wish him to live in beggary in order to serve Him. That was not His meaning. Instead, He meant that he should work with his hands and follow Him with good works. Saint Paul ordered the apostles to work in order to recover what they needed to live on, and he forbade them to beg, saying, 'Work with your hands; never acquire anything through another.' He did not want them to ask for anything from any of the people to whom they preached, nor to sell the gospel. He feared that, if they asked, they might

be extorting what they asked for, for there are on earth many people who give because, to tell the truth, they are ashamed to refuse, or because the person who asks annoys them and they give so that he will go away. And do you know what this practice gains them? They lose the gift and the merit of giving it. When the good men who heard Saint Paul's sermon begged him for the sake of God that he might wish to accept what they had, he never wanted to stretch out his hand; but with the labor of his hands he took that with which he maintained his life."

11407   "Tell me then," said the God of Love, "how can a man live who is strong of body and wants to follow God after he has sold everything that is his and distributed his money to the poor? Suppose that he wants only to pray, without ever working with his hands. Can he do so?"

"Yes."

"How?"

11414   "If," replied False Seeming, "he entered, according to the commandment of Scripture, into an abbey that had been furnished with its own property, as nowadays are those of the white monks, those of the black, the canons regular, the Hospitalers, and the Templars—for I can indeed take these as examples—and if he took his livelihood there, for there is no beggary whatever there. Nevertheless many monks labor and afterward run to God's service.

11425   "And because there was great discord, at a time that I remember, about the estate of mendicancy, I will tell you briefly here how a man who has nothing with which he might feed himself may be a mendicant. You will hear the cases one after the other, so that there will be no need to tell them again, in spite of any wicked cackle, for Truth doesn't care for corners, and I could reward her well whenever I dared plow such a field.

11437   "Here are the special cases: If the man is such an animal that he has no knowledge of any trade and doesn't want to remain ignorant, he can take to begging until he knows how to perform some trade by which he may legitimately earn his living without begging.

11445   "Or if he cannot work because of a sickness that he has, or because of old age or dotage, he may turn to begging.

11449   "Or if by chance he has been accustomed by his upbringing to live very delicately, good men commonly should then have pity

on him and, through friendship, allow him to beg for his bread
rather than let him perish of hunger.

"Or if he has the knowledge, the wish, and the ability to work,   11457
and is ready to work well, but does not immediately find someone
who may want to give him work at anything that he can do or is
accustomed to do, then he may certainly obtain his needs by begging.

"Or if he has the wages of his labor, but cannot live on them   11465
adequately on this earth, then he may indeed set out to ask for his
bread and from day to day go about everywhere, obtaining what
he lacks.

"Or if he wants to undertake some knightly deed to defend   11471
the faith, either with arms, or by cultivation of his mind, or by
some other suitable concern, and if he is weighed down by poverty,
he may certainly, as I have said before, beg until he can work
to obtain his needs. But he should work with hands of this sort,

Manus corporalis

not with spiritual hands,

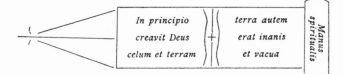

but with the actual bodily hands, without putting any double
meaning on them.

"In all these and similar cases, if you find any further cases that   11483
are reasonable, in addition to those that I have given you here,
the man who wants to live by beggary may do so, and in no other
cases, if the man from Saint-Amour does not lie. He was accustomed to argue and lecture and preach on this subject with the
theologians at Paris. May bread and wine never help me if in his
truth he did not have the support of the University and the gen-
erality of the people who heard his preaching. No worthy man
can excuse himself before God for denying this idea. Whoever

wants to grumble about it let him grumble, or if he wants to get angry, let him get angry, for I would not keep silent about it if I had to lose my life, or, like Saint Paul, be put unjustly into a dark prison, or be wrongfully banished from the kingdom, as was Master William of Saint-Amour, whom Hypocrisy, out of her great envy, caused to be exiled.

11509   "My mother plotted against him so much, on account of the truth that he supported, that she chased him into exile. He committed a great fault against my mother in writing a new book in which he exposed her entire life, and he wanted me to deny mendicancy and go to work, if I had nothing to live on. In fact he wanted to consider me a drunkard. Working can give me no pleasure: I have nothing to do with it, for there is too great difficulty in working. I prefer to pray in front of people and cover my foxlike nature under a cloak of pope-holiness."

11525   "What's this?" said Love. "The devil! What are your words? What have you said here?"

"What?"

"Great and open disloyalty. Don't you fear God then?"

11528   "Certainly not. The man who wants to fear God can hardly attain anything great in this world, for the good, who avoid evil, live legitimately on what they have, and keep themselves according to God, scarcely get from one loaf to the next. Such people drink too much discomfort; there is no life that displeases me so much.

11537   "But consider how usurers, counterfeiters, and loan sharks have money in their storehouses. Bailiffs, beadles, provosts, mayors, all live practically by rapine. The common people bow to them, while they, like wolves, devour the commoners. Everybody runs over the poor; there isn't anyone who does not want to despoil them, and all cover themselves with their spoil. They all snuff up their substance and pluck them alive without scalding. The strongest robs the weakest. But I, wearing my simple robe and duping both dupers and duped, rob both the robbed and the robbers.

11553   "By my trickery I pile up and amass great treasure in heaps and mounds, treasure that cannot be destroyed by anything. For if I build a palace with it and achieve all my pleasures with company, the bed, with tables full of sweets—for I want no other life—my money and my gold increases. Before my treasure can be emptied, money comes to me again in abundance. Don't I make my bears tumble? My whole attention is on getting. My acquisitions are worth more than my revenues. Even if I were to be beaten or killed, I still want to penetrate everywhere. I would never try to stop confessing emperors, kings, dukes, barons, or counts. But with poor men it is shameful; I don't like such confession. If not for some other purpose, I have no interest in poor people; their estate is neither fair nor noble.

"These empresses, duchesses, queens, and countesses; their high-ranking palace ladies, these abbesses, beguines, and wives of bailiffs and knights; these coy, proud bourgeois wives, these nuns and young girls; provided that they are rich or beautiful, whether they are bare or well turned out, they do not go away without good advice.   11577

"For the salvation of souls, I inquire of lords and ladies and their entire households about their characteristics and their way of life; and I put into their heads the belief that their parish priests are animals in comparison with me and my companions. I have many wicked dogs among them, to whom I am accustomed to reveal people's secrets, without hiding anything; and in the same way they reveal everything to me, so that they hide nothing in the world from me.   11587

"In order that you may recognize the criminals who do not stop deceiving people, I will now tell you here the words that we read of Saint Matthew, that is to say, the evangelist, in the twenty-third chapter: 'Upon the chair of Moses' (the gloss explains that this is the Old Testament), 'the scribes and pharisees have sat.' These are the accursed false people that the letter calls hypocrites. 'Do what they say, but not what they do. They are not slow to speak well, but they have no desire to do so. To gullible people they attach heavy loads that cannot be carried; they place them on their shoulders, but they dare not move them with their finger.' "   11599

"Why not?" asked Love.   11619

"In faith," replied False Seeming, "they don't want to, for porters' shoulders are often accustomed to suffer from their burdens, and these hypocrites flee from wanting to do such a thing. If they do jobs that may be good, it is because people see them. They enlarge their phylacteries and increase their fringes; since they are haughty, proud, and overbearing, they like the highest and most honorable seats at tables and the first in the synagogues. They like people to greet them when they pass along the street, and they want to be called 'master,' which they shouldn't be called, for the gospel goes against this practice and shows its unlawfulness.

11637 "We have another custom toward those that we know are against us. We want to hate them very strongly and attack them all by agreement among ourselves. He whom one hates, the others hate, and all are bent on ruining him. If we see that he may, through certain people, win honor in the land, income, or possessions, we study to find out by what ladder he may mount up, and the better to capture and subdue him, we treacherously defame him to those people, for we do not love him. We cut the rungs from his ladder, and we strip him of his friends in such a way that he will never know by a word that he has lost them. If we troubled him openly, we would perhaps be blamed for it and thus miss out in our calculation; if he knew our worst intention, he would protect himself against it so that we would be reprimanded for it.

11661 "If one of us has done something very good, we consider that we have all done it. Indeed, by God, if he was pretending it, or if he no more than condescends to brag that he has advanced certain men, we make ourselves partners in the deed and, as you should well know, we say that these people have been helped on by us. In order to win people's praise we tell lies to rich men and get them to give us letters bearing witness to our goodness, so that throughout the world people will think that every virtue abounds in us. We always pretend to be poor, but no matter how we complain, we are the ones, let me tell you, who have everything without having anything.

11679 "I also undertake brokerage commissions, I draw up agreements, I arrange marriages, I take on executor's duties, and I go around doing procurations. I am a messenger and I make investigations, dishonest ones, moreover. To occupy myself with someone else's business is to me a very pleasant occupation. And if you have any business to do with those whom I frequent, tell me, and the thing is done as soon as you have told me. Provided that you have served me well, you have deserved my service. But anyone who wanted to punish me would rob himself of my favor. I neither love nor value the man by whom I am reproved for anything.

I want to reprove all the others, but I don't want to hear their reproof, for I, who correct others, have no need of another's correction.

"I have no care either for hermitages. I have left the deserts   11701
and woods, and I leave desert manors and lodgings to Saint John the Baptist, for there I was lodged much too far away. I make my halls and palaces in towns, castles, and cities, where one can run with a free rein. I say that I am out of the world, but I plunge into it and immerse myself in it; I take my ease and bathe and swim better than any fish with his fin.

"I am one of Antichrist's boys, one of the thieves of whom it is   11713
written that they have the garment of saintliness and live in pretense; we seem pitiful sheep without, but within we are ravening wolves. And we inhabit sea and land. We have taken up war against the whole world, and we want to prescribe in every detail the life that one should lead. If there is a castle or city where heretics may be mentioned, even if they were from Milan (for men give the Milanese that reputation); or if anyone exacts unreasonable terms in selling on time or lending at usury, no matter how eager he is for gain; or if he is very lecherous, or a robber or simoniac, whether a provost, an official, a jolly-living prelate, a priest who keeps a mistress, an old whore with a house, a pimp, a brothel-keeper, or an old offender at whatever vice to which one should do justice; then—by all the saints to whom one may pray!— if he doesn't protect himself with lampreys, pike, salmon, or eels, as long as one can find them in town; or with tarts or pies or cheeses in wicker baskets—a very fine gem with a *caillou* pear—or with fat young geese or capons, with which we tickle our palates; or if he doesn't make haste to bring kids and rabbits, roasted on spits, or at least a loin of pork, he will have a leading rope by which he will be led off to be burned, so that one would hear him yell indeed for a good league all around; or he will be taken and put in a tower to be walled in forever if he hasn't done well by us; or he will be punished for his crimes, more, perhaps, than he has committed.

"But if he had ingenuity enough and knew how to build a large   11761
tower, it doesn't matter of what stone, even if it were unmeasured or unsquared, of earth or wood, or of anything else whatever, provided that he had amassed enough temporal goods inside it

and mounted on top of it a catapult that would launch, in front, behind, and to the two sides as well, a heavy fire against us of such pebbles as you have heard me name, so that he might get a good name for himself, and provided that he charged large mangonels with wine in barrels or casks, or with large bags of a hundred pounds—then he could see himself quickly freed. And if he does not find such pittances, let him study up on equivalent arguments and abandon commonplaces and fallacies if he hopes to gain our favor through them. Otherwise we will bear such witness against him that we will have him burned alive, or we will give him a penance more costly than the pittance.

11787   "You will never recognize them by their garments, these false traitors full of trickery; you must look at their deeds if you really want to protect yourself from them.

11791   "And if it had not been for the good protection of the University, which keeps the key of Christianity, everything would have been overturned when, in the year of the Incarnation 1255, there was released, through evil intent—no man living can give me the lie; it is a true case, to take a common example—a book from the devil, *The Eternal Gospel*, that, as it appears in the title, brings the Holy Spirit, for it is thus named. It is indeed worthy to be burned. There is not a man or woman in Paris, in the parvis in front of Notre Dame, who could not have had it to transcribe if he had pleased. In this book he would have found many such grossly erroneous comparisons as these: as much as by its great worth, in brightness or in heat, the sun surpasses the moon, which is much more dark and obscure, and as much as the nut surpasses its shell—don't think that I am making fun of you; on my soul I am speaking to you without guile—so much this gospel surpasses those which the four evangelists of Jesus Christ wrote under their names. One would have found there a great mass of such comparisons, which I pass over.

11825   "The University, which at that time was asleep, raised up its face. As a result of the noise the book made, it awoke and hardly ever slept afterward, but instead armed itself to go out, all ready to do battle and hand the book over to the judges when it saw this horrible monster. But those who had issued the book rose up and withdrew it and made haste to conceal it, for they did not know how to reply, by explication or glossing, to what the opposers wanted to say against the accursed things that are written in that book. Now I do not know what will come of it nor what result the book will bring about, but they still have to wait until they can defend it better.

"Thus we are awaiting Antichrist, and we are headed toward   11845
him all together. Those who don't want to join him will have to lose their lives. We will incite people against them by the frauds that we hide, and we will make them perish by the sword or by some other death if they don't want to follow us. For it is written in the book, where it expresses this idea: as long as Peter has lordship, John cannot show his power. Now that I have told you the rind of the sense, which hides the intent, I want to explain its marrow. By Peter it wants to signify the Pope and to include the secular clergy, who will keep, guard, and defend the law of Jesus Christ against all those who would impede it. By John, it means the preachers, who will say that there is no tenable law except the Eternal Gospel, sent by the Holy Spirit to put people on the good way. By the force of John is meant the favor by which he goes around vaunting himself because he wants to convert sinners to make them turn back to God. There are many other deviltries   11875
ordered and set down in this book that I have named for you, deviltries that are against the law of Rome and belong to Antichrist, as I find written in the book. Those of John's party will order all those of Peter's party to be killed, but they will never have the power to overcome the law of Peter, either to kill or to punish, I guarantee you this, since there will not be enough of them remaining alive to maintain it forever so that in the end everybody will come to it, and the law that is signified by John will be overthrown. But I don't want to say any more of it to you now, for it would be a very long subject here. But if this book had been passed, my estate would have been much greater. I already have very great friends who have always put me into high positions.

"My sire and father Fraud is emperor of the whole world, and   11897
my mother is its empress. In spite of the fact that men may have the Holy Spirit, our powerful line reigns. We reign now in every kingdom, and it is quite just that we do so, for we seduce the whole world, and we know how to deceive people so that no one can recognize the deception. Or if anyone can recognize it he does not dare reveal the truth. But he who fears my brothers more

than God places himself under God's wrath. He who fears such simulation is no good champion of the faith, any more than is he who wants to avoid trouble when he might come bringing accusations against us. Such a man does not want to listen to the truth nor have God before his eyes; and God will punish him for it, without fail.

11918   "But it doesn't matter to me how things go, once we have honor among men. We are considered such good men that we have the prize of being able to punish without being reproved by any man. What men should be honored except us, who do not cease praying openly before people, although it may be otherwise behind their backs? Is it a greater folly than to encourage chivalry and to love noble and splendid people who have pretty, elegant clothing? If they are such people as they appear to be, as fine as their fine apparel, so that what they say agrees with what they do, isn't such a situation a great sorrow and outrage? If they don't want to be hypocrites, may such people be cursed!

11937   "Certainly we shall never love such, but Beguines with large coifs and faces that are pale and sweet, who have these wide gray robes all spotted with filth, knitted leggings, and broad boots that look like a quail-hunter's pouch. Princes should give over to them the job of governing them and their lands, in peace or war; a prince should cleave to those who want to come to great honor. And if they are other than they seem, and by that means steal the world's favor, it is there that I want to fix my position, in order to deceive and trick.

11953   "Now I do not on that account want to say that one should despise a humble habit, as long as pride does not dwell underneath it. No man should hate a poor man on account of the habit he is dressed in, but God doesn't value him at two straws if he says that he has left the world and then abounds in worldly glory and wants to use its delights. Who can excuse such Beguines? When such a pope-holy gives himself up and then goes seeking worldly delights, and says that he has abandoned them all when afterwards he wants to grow fat on them, he is the cur that greedily returns to his own vomit.

11969   "But to you I dare not lie. However, if I could feel that you would not recognize it, you would have a lie in hand. Certainly I would have tricked you, and I would never have held back on account of any sin. And I would indeed desert you if you were to treat me poorly."

The god smiled at this wonder, and everyone laughed with   11977
amazement and said, "Here is a fine sergeant, of whom people should indeed be proud!"

"False Seeming," said Love, "tell me: since I have brought   11981
you so near to me that your power in my court is so great that you will be king of camp followers here, will you keep your agreement with me?"

"Yes, I swear it and promise you; neither your father nor your   11986
forefathers ever had sergeants more loyal."

"How! It is against your nature."

"Take your chances on it, for if you demand pledges, you will   11990
never be more sure, in fact, not even if I gave hostages, letters, witnesses, or security. I call on you as witness of the fact that one can't take the wolf out of his hide until he is skinned, no matter how much he is beaten or curried. Do you think that I do not deceive and play tricks because I wear a simple robe, under which I have worked many a great evil? By God! I shall never turn my heart from this kind of life. And if I have a simple, demure face, do you think that I may cease doing evil? My sweetheart Constrained Abstinence has need of my providence. She would long ago have been dead and in a bad plight if she hadn't had me in her power. Grant that we two, she and I, may carry out the task."

"So be it," said Love, "I believe you without guarantee."   12010

And the thief with the face of treachery, white without and black within, knelt down on the spot and thanked him.

Then there was nothing but to take up their positions. "Now to   12015
the assault without delay," said Love aloud, and they all armed themselves together with such arms as would endure. When they were thus armed and ready, they all sallied out, full of ardor, and came to the strong castle, which they would never try to leave until they were all martyred or captured there. They divided their forces into four parts and went off in four groups, as soon as their people were divided up, to attack the four gates. The guards on the gates were not dead, sick, or lazy, but strong and vigorous.

Now I will tell you about the conduct of False Seeming and   12033
Abstinence, who went against Foul Mouth. The two of them held a council between them on how they should act, whether they

should make themselves known or go disguised. By agreement, they worked out a plan of going stealthily as though they were on a pilgrimage, like good, pious, and holy people. Constrained Abstinence straightway put on a robe of cameline and fixed herself up as a Beguine; she covered her head with a large kerchief and a white cloth, and she did not forget her psalter. She had paternosters hanging on a white thread-lace. They had not been sold to her; a friar had given them to her. She told him that he was her father and visited him very often, more than any other in the convent; he also visited her often, and gave her many a fine sermon. He never omitted, on account of False Seeming, to confess her often, and they made their confession with such great devotion that it seemed to me that they had two heads together under a single headpiece.

12065   I would describe her as a woman of fine stature, but a little pale of face. She resembled, the dirty bitch, the horse in the Apocalypse that signified the wicked people, pale and stained with hypocrisy; for that horse bore no color upon himself except a pale, dead one. Abstinence had such a sickly color. According to her face, she was repentant about her estate. She had a stick of larceny, darkened with the brown smoke of sadness, that she had received as a gift from Fraud, and a bag full of cares. When she was ready, she went off.

12082   False Seeming, who was also equipping himself well, had dressed, as though to try it out, in the clothing of brother Seier. He had a very simple, compassionate face without any appearance of pride, a sweet, peaceful look. At his neck he carried a Bible. Afterward, he went off without a squire, and, to support his limbs, as though he had no power, he used a crutch of treason. Up his sleeve he slipped a very sharp steel razor, that he had made in a forge and that was called Cut-Throat.

12097   Each one went along and approached until they came to Foul Mouth, who sat at his gate, where he saw all the passersby. He picked out the pilgrims who were coming along, behaving themselves very humbly. They bowed toward him with great humility. Abstinence saluted him first and went near him, and False Seeming saluted him afterward. He saluted them in return, but never moved, since he neither suspected nor feared them. When he had seen them he recognized them well enough by their faces, it seemed to him, since he knew Abstinence well, but he knew nothing whatever about constraint in her. He did not know that her life of thievery and pretense was a constrained one, but thought instead that she came out of good faith. But she came from another level, and if she began with good faith, it was lacking from that point on.

Foul Mouth had certainly seen Seeming also, but he did not   12119
recognize him as false. He was false, but he had never been convicted of falsity, for he worked so hard on his appearance that he covered up his falsity. But if you had known him before you had seen him in these clothes, you would have indeed sworn by the king of heaven that he who before had been used to being handsome Robin in the dance was now become a Jacobin. But without fail, and this is the sum of it, the Jacobins are all worthy men—they would maintain their order badly if they were such minstrels— and so are the Cordeliers and the barred friars, no matter how large and fat they may be, and the friars of the sack and all others. There is not one who does not appear a worthy man. But you will never see a good consequence result from appearance in any argument that one may make, if a deficiency annuls any existence. You will always find a sophism that poisons the consequence, as long as you have the subtlety to understand the deception.

When the pilgrims had come to Foul Mouth, where they were   12147
supposed to come, they put down all their equipment very close to them and sat down next to Foul Mouth, who said to them:

"Now then, come on; teach me your news, and tell me what business leads you to this house."

"Sir," said Constrained Abstinence, "we have come here as pilgrims to perform our penance with pure hearts, clean and whole. We nearly always go by foot, and our heels are very dusty. We are sent, both of us, through this misguided world to give an example and to preach in order to fish for sinners, since we want no other catch; and we come to ask you for shelter in God's name, as we are accustomed to do. To better your life, we want to go over a good sermon in a few brief words, as long as you should not be displeased."

Foul Mouth spoke straightway: "Take such shelter as you see—   12172 it shall never be forbidden you—and say whatever you please. I shall listen to whatever it is."

12177

"Many thanks, sir."

Then Lady Abstinence began first: "Sir, the chief virtue, the greatest and most sovereign that any mortal man may have, through knowledge or possession, is to bridle his tongue. Everyone should take trouble to do so, since it is always better to keep silent than to utter a wicked thing, while he who listens to it willingly is neither worthy nor God-fearing. Sir, you are stained with this sin above all others. For a long time you have told a falsehood, for which you have been badly to blame, about a young man who came here. You said that he was only seeking to deceive Fair Welcoming. You did not tell the truth, but lied about it, perhaps. He neither goes nor comes here now, and perhaps you will never see him. On that account Fair Welcoming remains locked up, when he used to play with you here the loveliest games that he could, most

12205

of the days of the week, without any base thought. Now he does not dare solace himself here. You have had the young man chased away who used to come here to divert himself. Who incited you to harm him so much, outside of your evil mind, that has thought up many a lie? It was your foolish talk that brought this situation on. It howls and cries and chatters and quarrels; it foists blame on people and dishonors and brings trouble to them on account of a thing that has no proof whatever outside of appearance or a lying invention. I dare you to say openly that whatever appears is not true. It remains a sin to contrive something which brings reproof. Even you know that very well, and your wrong is greater for that reason. Nevertheless the young man doesn't make anything of it; he wouldn't give the bark of an oak for it, however it may be. You may know that he was not thinking of any evil, for he would

12229

have gone and come; no excuse would have held him back. Now he does not come here and has no concern to do so, except by some chance, just in passing by, and he does so less than others. And you, with your lance ready to attack, watch over this gate, without stopping. The simpleton wastes his time the whole day long. Night and day you watch. In truth, you do no real work there. Jealousy, who expects something of you, will never count you worth much. And it remains a shame that Fair Welcoming is kept as a pledge when no loan brings in interest, and that he dwells in prison without any forfeit being made. There the captive weeps and languishes. If you had committed no more wrong in the whole world than this one misdeed, one should, without troubling you further, shove you out of this job and put you in prison or in iron chains. If you don't repent, you will go to the pit of hell."

"You lie for certain," said Foul Mouth. "Now may you be unwelcome. Have I entertained you for this, that you should speak shame and vilification about me? To your great misfortune you took me for a shepherd. Go now and lodge somewhere else, you who call me a liar. You are a pair of tricksters who have come here to accuse me and mistreat me because I speak the truth. Is that what you come trying to do? I'll hand myself over to all the devils, or you, good God, may destroy me, if, not more than ten days before the castle was built, I was not told—and I tell you in turn—that that fellow kissed the rose. I don't know if he took any further comfort of it. Why should I be led to believe such a thing unless it were true? By God, I say it and say it again, and I believe that I was not lied to; and I will trumpet it to all the men and women in the neighborhood, how he came here and there."

Then False Seeming spoke: "Sir, all that they say around the town is not gospel. Now you don't have deaf ears, and I will prove to you that these reports are false. You certainly know that no one loves wholeheartedly a man who speaks ill of him. For all the other knows, he may know very little about him. And it remains true—I have always read it—that all lovers willingly visit the places where their sweethearts live. This young man honors you; he loves you and calls you his very dear friend. Everywhere that he meets you he shows you a gay and friendly face and never stops greeting you. At the same time, he does not press you too much or tire you; others come here much more. Know too that if his heart were tormented by the rose, he would have approached it, and you would have seen him here often. In fact you could have caught him red-handed, since he could not have kept away from it if he should have been grilled alive, and he would not now be in the situation that he is. You can understand then that he isn't thinking at all in that direction. Truly, neither does Fair

12250

12276

12305

Welcoming, even though he is being sorely rewarded for it. By God! If the two of them really wished it, they would cut the rose in spite of you. Now that you have slandered the young man who loves you, you know very well, and never doubt it, that if his intention had been such, he would never have loved you at any time, never have called you friend. If it were so, he would plan and watch for a chance to attack the castle and break in, for he would know; either someone would have told him or he could have known by himself that he could not have access to it as he had had before. He would have noticed it immediately. But now he acts in quite another way. Thus in subduing such people you have indeed completely deserved the death of hell."

12327   False Seeming proved the case to him thus, and Foul Mouth did not know how to reply to his argument, since he saw the appearance of logic in every case. He was about to fall into repentance and said to them, "By God! It may indeed be so, Seeming; I consider you a good master, and Abstinence a very wise woman. You seem indeed to have spirit. What do you recommend me to do?"

12336   "You will be confessed on this spot. Without anything more, you will tell this sin and repent of it. For I am from an order and thus am a priest, the highest master of confessing that may be, as long as the world lasts. The whole world is my charge; no priest-curé, sworn entirely to his church, ever had any such right. By the high lady, I have a hundred times more pity on your soul than your parish priest, no matter how much he were your special one. Moreover I have one very great advantage. There are no prelates so wise or learned as I. I have a license in divinity, and in fact, by God, I have lectured for a long time. The best people that one may know have chosen me as confessor on account of my sense and my knowledge. If you want to confess here and abandon this sin without further ado, without making any further mention of it, you will have my absolution."

12361   Straightway Foul Mouth got down, knelt, and confessed, for he was already truly repentant; False Seeming seized him by the throat, squeezed with his two hands, strangled him, and then took away his chatter by removing his tongue with his razor. Thus they finished with their host; they did nothing else to kill him, but tumbled him into a moat. They broke down the undefended gate, passed through it, and found all the Norman soldiers sleeping within, so much had they vied with each other in drinking wine that I had not poured. They themselves had poured out so much that they all lay sleeping on their backs. False Seeming and Constrained Abstinence strangled them, drunk and sleeping as they were. They will never again be capable of chattering.

12380

7

THE OLD WOMAN'S INTERCESSION

12381 And then Courtesy and Generosity passed through the gate without idling, and all four assembled there furtively and in secret. The Old Woman, who had been guarding Fair Welcoming for a long time, was not watching, and all four saw her together. She had descended from the tower and was having a good time in the bailey. She had covered her head with a coif, instead of a cloth, over her wimple. They ran up to her in haste and all four attacked her immediately. She didn't want to get beaten, and when she saw all four of them together, she said:

12396 "By my faith, you seem fine people, brave and courteous. Tell me now, without any noise, should I count myself the prize that you seek in this enterprise?"

12401 "The prize! Sweet tender mother! We don't come to capture you, but only to see you and, if it may please and suit you, to offer our bodies, wholly and completely, along with whatever we possess that is worthy, never to fail you, all at your sweet command, and, O sweet mother who have never been bitter, if it please you, we have come to beg you, with no evil intention, that it might please you that Fair Welcoming should no longer languish inside there, and to beg further that he might come outside to play with us a little bit, without getting his feet dirty. Or— please—at least let him speak a word with this young man and let the one comfort the other. It will be a very great comfort to them and will cost you scarcely anything. Then this young man will be your liege man, even your servant, and you will be able to do whatever you wish with him, sell him, hang him, mutilate him. It is good to win a friend. And look at these jewels; he gives you this clasp and these buttons, and truly he will soon give you

12431 a garment. He has a very free heart, courteous and generous, and he will not be a burden to you. You are greatly loved by him, and you will never be blamed, for he is very sensible and discreet. We beg that you will hide him, so that he may proceed with no

suspicion of bad conduct. In this way you will restore him to life.
And now take this chaplet of fresh little flowers, if you please,
from him to Fair Welcoming; comfort him for this young man
and make him a present of a warm salute. That will be worth
a hundred marks to him."

"God help me," said the Old Woman, "if it could be that   12445
Jealousy did not know and that I never heard any blame for it,
I would indeed do so, but Foul Mouth the scandalmonger is too
malicious a slanderer. Jealousy has made him her sentinel, and
he keeps watch on all of us. Without hindrance he shouts and
cries out whatever he knows, indeed, whatever he thinks; he even
makes up his matter when he doesn't know whom to slander. If he
had to be hanged for it, he would not be hindered. So you see,
if the thief were to tell Jealousy, I would be brought to shame."

"About that," they said, "you don't have to fear. He can never   12461
overhear or see anything in any way. He lies dead outside, in the
moat rather than on a bier, with his throat open. Understand
that, unless there is an enchantment, he will never tattle to the
gods, for he will never revive. If the devils don't perform miracles
with poisons and medicines, he can never make any accusation."

"Then I shall never seek to refuse your request," said the   12472
Old Woman, "but tell him to hurry. I shall find a passage for
him, but he must not talk too freely nor delay very long. When
I let him know, he must come quickly and keep his person and his
belongings hidden so that no one may see him, and he must not do
anything he ought not to, even if he might speak his whole will."

"Lady, without doubt he will be as you say," they said, and   12484
everyone thanked her. Thus did they fabricate their plan.

But, however things might be, False Seeming, who thought   12487
otherwise, said to himself in a low voice:

"He for whom we undertook this job would not cease loving,   12490
and he therefore trusted me to some extent; if so, then if you,
Old Woman, do not come to an agreement with him, you will
hardly succeed in going so far but what he might enter there
secretly, if he had either time or place. One doesn't always see the
wolf before he has stolen the ewes from the stable, no matter how
one guards the flock in the pasture. You might have gone for an
hour to the convent, where you stayed so long yesterday. Jealousy,
who now plays him this trick, might perhaps have gone elsewhere

out of town, or wherever she might need to go, and he would then come, in secret or by night, from the garden, alone, without candle or torches, if not with Friend, who watches over him, if the Lover had invited him. Friend would guide the Lover quickly and easily unless the moon was shining, for the moon's clear light has many times been an annoyance to lovers. Or, since the Lover knows the situation of the house well, he would enter by the windows and get down again with a rope. Thus he would come and

12519   go. Perhaps Fair Welcoming would descend into the garden where the Lover was waiting for him, or he might flee out of the enclosure where you have held him prisoner for many days and come to speak to the young man if the Lover could not go to him. Or when he knew that you were asleep and he could see the right time and place, he might leave the doors ajar for the young man. In this way the pure lover, if he succeeds in any way in getting the better of the other guards, might approach the rosebud on which his thought is fixed and then pluck it unforbidden."

12533   For my part—I was not far away—I thought that I would do exactly as he said. If the Old Woman wanted to guide me, I should have no trouble or difficulty; if she didn't, I would enter, just as False Seeming thought, by the route where I saw the best opportunity. I agreed with his idea in every way.

12541   The Old Woman stayed there no longer, but returned at a trot to Fair Welcoming, who kept to the tower against his will, for he suffered indeed from such captivity. She went until she came to the entry of the tower, where she passed through quickly. Blithely she mounted the steps as fast as she could with her trembling limbs. She looked for Fair Welcoming from room to room and found him, dejected by his prison, leaning over the battlements. Since he was pensive, sad, and mournful, she set herself to comfort him.

12555   "Fair son," she said, "I am very distressed when I find you so greatly dismayed. Tell me your thoughts, for if I know how to counsel you, you will never see me hesitate to do so at any time."

12560   Since Fair Welcoming did not know whether she spoke the truth or lied, he did not dare to complain nor to say "What?" nor "How?" to her. He denied her his thoughts, for he felt no security in her at all. He confided nothing to her; even his trembling and fearful heart mistrusted her, but he dared show no sign of his mistrust, so great had his fear always been of the senile old whore. Since he feared that she would betray him, he wanted to avoid the least hint of wrongdoing. Therefore he did not reveal his uneasiness to her, but calmed himself within and put on an outward show of gaiety:

"Certainly, my dear lady," he said, "however much you suspect, 12576 I am not in the least downcast, except because you stay away from me, no more. Without you, it is difficult to live in this place, so great a love do I have for you. Where have you dwelt for so long?"

"Where? By my head! You shall know immediately and you 12583 shall take great joy in your knowledge if you are at all valiant or wise, for instead of greetings from a stranger, I bring more than a thousand salutes from the most courteous young man in the world, who abounds in every grace. I saw him just now in the street as he was going along, and he sent you this chaplet by me. He said that he would gladly see you and that, if it were not through your desire as well, he would never afterward seek to live nor have a single day of health. God and Saint Foy keep him, he said, unless he could speak to you freely just one single time, provided that you were pleased. To say no more, he loves his life on your account. He would gladly be naked at Pavia on condition that he knew how to do one thing that could give you pleasure. It wouldn't matter what happened to him as long as he could keep you near him."

Before he would accept the present, Fair Welcoming asked in 12607 any case who had sent it to him; he felt fearful that it could have come from a source such that he would not wish to keep it at all. The Old Woman, without any other tales, told him the whole truth.

"It's the young man you know and have heard so much talk 12615 of, the one on whose account the late Foul Mouth made you suffer so greatly when he placed all the blame on you. May his soul never go to paradise! For he has brought woe to many a good man. Now that he is dead and the devils have carried him off, we have escaped, and I wouldn't give you two apples for all his chatter. We are free forever. Even if he could revive now, he could not harm us, however skillful he might be at putting blame on you, for I know more about that game than he ever did. Believe me now and take this chaplet and wear it, and comfort the young man at least as much in return, since he loves you, never doubt, with good love, not base. And if he intends any other thing, he did not disclose much of it to me. But we can indeed have confidence in him: for your part, you know very well how to deny him if he asks anything that he ought not to. If he commits folly, let him drink it; and if he is no fool, then he is wise. Since he has never committed any outrageous acts, I prize him more highly and love him myself. He will never be so base as to demand anything of you, who would do nothing on demand. He is more loyal than any living person: those who keep company with him have always so testified, and so do I. In his manners he is very well regulated; there is no man born of a mother who ever heard any evil of him, except as much as Foul Mouth told of him. But all that has been forgotten. I myself have forgotten it little by little; I don't even remember the statements, except that they were false and wild and that the thief invented them and proved none of them. Indeed, I know well that the young man, since he is valiant and brave without fail, would have killed him if he had known anything of it. His heart is so filled with nobility that there is no one in this country worth as much as he is. In largesse, he would surpass King Arthur, indeed, Alexander, if he had had as much gold and silver to spend as they had. They did not know how to give so much of anything that he would not have given one hundred times more. So good a heart is planted in him that his gifts would have astonished the whole world if he had had such plenty of possessions. No one can teach him about largesse. Now I advise you to take this chaplet, whose flowers smell sweeter than balm."

"Faith, I would be afraid of being blamed," said Fair Welcoming. He was very agitated: he trembled, started, and sighed; he blushed, then grew pale and lost countenance. The Old Woman thrust the chaplet into his hands and wanted to force him to take it, for he dared not stretch out his hand for it, but said, the better to excuse himself, that it would be better for him to refuse it. However, he wanted to take it, whatever might happen.

"The chaplet is very beautiful," he said, "but it would be better that all my clothes were burned to ashes than that I dared take it

12637

12661

12678

12689

from him. Now suppose that I took it: what could we then say to Jealousy the quarrelsome? I know well that she will be filled with rage and will tear it to pieces on my head and then kill me if she knows that it may have come from there; or I will be taken and held prisoner worse than I ever was in my life; or, if I escape from her and flee, where could I flee? You will see me buried alive if I am ever taken after my flight. I believe that, if I were caught in the act of fleeing, action would be brought against me. I will not accept the chaplet."

"Yes you will, certainly. You will have neither blame nor loss."   12709

"And what if she asks me where it came from?"

"You have more than twenty replies."

"All the same, if she asks me, what answer can I make? If   12713
I am blamed or reprimanded for it, where shall I say that I got it? For I shall have to hide or tell some lie. If she knew, I guarantee you that I would be better off dead than alive."

"What shall you say? If you don't know what, if you have   12721
no better reply, say that I gave it to you. You know well that my reputation is such that you will reap no blame or shame for taking anything that I might give you."

Without saying anything else, Fair Welcoming took the chaplet,   12727
put it on his blond hair, and reassured himself. The Old Woman laughed and swore by her soul, her body, her bones and skin, that no chaplet was ever so becoming on him. Fair Welcoming, admiring himself in his mirror, looked at it often to see how becoming it was.

When the Old Woman saw that there was no one there within   12736
except for the two of them, she sat down quite properly next to him and began to preach to him:

"Ah, Fair Welcoming, how very dear you are to me! How   12740
beautiful you are, and how worthy! My happy time is all gone, and yours is still to come. I shall hardly be able to hold myself up except with a stick or crutch, but you are still in your infancy. You do not know what you will be doing, but I know very well that, sooner or later, whenever it may be, you will pass through the flame that burns everyone, and that you will bathe in the same steam-room where Venus stews the ladies. I know that you will feel her burning brand. I advise you that, before you go to bathe,

you prepare yourself as you shall hear me teach you, for a young man who has no one to teach him goes there to bathe at his peril. Then, if you follow my advice, you will come to a good harbor.

12761　　"Know then, that if only, when I was your age, I had been as wise about the games of Love as I am now! For then I was a very great beauty, but now I must complain and moan when I look at my face, which has lost its charms; and I see the inevitable wrinkles whenever I remember how my beauty made the young men skip. I made them so struggle that it was nothing if not a marvel. I was very famous then; word of my highly renowned beauty ran everywhere. At my house there was a crowd so big that no man ever saw the like. At night they knocked on my door: I was really very hard on them when I failed to keep my promises to them, and that happened very often, for I had other company. They did many a crazy thing at which I got very angry. Often my door was broken down, and many of them got into such battles as a result of their hatred and envy that before they were separated they lost their members and their lives. If master Algus, the great calculator, had wanted to take the trouble and had come with his ten figures, by which he certifies and numbers everything, he could not, however well he knew how to calculate, have ascertained the number of these great quarrels. Those were the days when my body was strong and active! As I say, if I had been as wise then as I am now, I would possess the value of a thousand pounds of sterling silver more than I do now, but I acted too foolishly.

12801　　"I was young and beautiful, foolish and wild, and had never been to a school of love where they read in the theory, but I know everything by practice. Experiments, which I have followed my whole life, have made me wise in love. Now that I know everything about love, right up to the struggle, it would not be right if I were to fail to teach you the delights that I know and have often tested. He who gives advice to a young man does well. Without fail, it is no wonder that you know nothing, for your beak is too yellow. But, in the end, I have so much knowledge upon which I can lecture from a chair that I could never finish. One should not avoid or despise everything that is very old; there one 12821　finds both good sense and good custom. Men have proved many times that, however much they have acquired, there will remain to them, in the end, at least their sense and their customs. And since I had good sense and manners, not without great harm to me, I have deceived many a worthy man when he fell captive in my nets. But I was deceived by many before I noticed. Then it was too late, and I was miserably unhappy. I was already past my youth. My door, which formerly was often open, both night and day, stayed constantly near its sill.

"'No one is coming today, no one came yesterday,' I thought, 'unhappy wretch! I must live in sorrow.' My woeful heart should have left me. Then, when I saw my door, and even myself, at such repose, I wanted to leave the country, for I couldn't endure the shame. How could I stand it when those handsome young men came along, those who formerly had held me so dear that they could not tire themselves, and I saw them look at me sideways as they passed by, they who had once been my dear guests? They went by near me, bounding along without counting me worth an egg, even those who had loved me most; they called me a wrinkled old woman and worse before they had passed on by. `12836`

"Besides, my pretty child, no one, unless he were very attentive or had experienced great sorrows, would think or know what grief gripped my heart when in my thought I remembered the lovely speeches, the sweet caresses and pleasures, the kisses and the deeply delightful embraces that were so soon stolen away. Stolen? Indeed, and without return. It would have been better for me to be imprisoned forever in a tower than to have been born so soon. God! Into what torment was I put by the fair gifts which had failed me, and how wretched their remnants had made me! Alas! Why was I born so soon? To whom can I complain, to whom except you, my son, whom I hold so dear? I have no other way to avenge myself than by teaching my doctrine. Therefore, fair son, I indoctrinate you so that, when instructed, you will avenge me on those good-for-nothings; for if God pleases, he will remind you of this sermon when he comes. You know that, because of your age, you have a very great advantage in retaining the sermon so that it will remind you. Plato said: 'It is true of any knowledge that one can keep better the memory of what one learns in one's infancy.' `12857`

"Certainly, dear son, my tender young one, if my youth were present, as yours is now, the vengeance that I would take on them `12893` could not rightly be written. Everywhere I came I would work such wonders with those scoundrels, who valued me so lightly and who vilified and despised me when they so basely passed by near me, that one would never have heard the like. They and others would pay for their pride and spite; I would have no pity on them. For with the intelligence that God has given me—just as I have preached to you—do you know what condition I would put them in? I would so pluck them and seize their possessions, even wrongly and perversely, that I would make them dine on worms and lie naked on dunghills, especially and first of all those who loved me with more loyal heart and who more willingly took trouble to serve and honor me. If I could, I wouldn't leave them anything worth one bud of garlic until I had everything in my purse and had put them all into poverty; I would make them stamp their feet in living rage behind me. But to regret it is worth nothing;

12926   what has gone cannot come. I would never be able to hold any man, for my face is so wrinkled that they don't even protect themselves against my threat. A long time ago the scoundrels who despised me told me so, and from that time on I took to weeping. O God! But it still pleases me when I think back on it. I rejoice in my thought and my limbs become lively again when I remember the good times and the gay life for which my heart so strongly yearns. Just to think of it and to remember it all makes my body young again. Remembering all that happened gives me all the blessings of the world, so that however they may have deceived me, at least I have had my fun. A young lady is not idle when she leads a gay life, especially she who thinks about acquiring enough to take care of her expenses.

12949   "Then I came to this country, where I met your lady, who has put me into her service to guard you in her enclosure. May God, the lord and guardian of all, grant that I may make a good job of it! With your fair conduct, I shall certainly do so. But to guard you would have been perilous because of the wondrously great beauty that Nature has given you, if she had not taught you so many abilities, so much good sense, worth, and grace. Now time and occasion have come to the point where, without disturbance, we can say whatever we want, a little more than usual. I must advise you completely, and you should not wonder if I interrupt my talk a little. I must tell you that, before the attack, I didn't want to put you in the way of love, but if you want to get involved with it, I will gladly show the roads and the paths by which I should have traveled before my beauty had gone."

Then the Old Woman grew quiet and sighed, to hear what he   12977
wanted to say, but she delayed hardly at all; for, when she saw that he was being careful to listen to her and remain quiet, she took up her subject again, thinking, "Whoever says nothing agrees to everything. Since he is pleased to hear all that I say, I can say everything without fear."

Then she began her babbling again and spoke like a false old   12987
woman, a serf. She thought by her doctrine to make me lick honey from thorns, when she wanted me to be called friend without being loved *par amour*. Thus Fair Welcoming, who remembered the whole story, told me afterward. For, if he had been such that he believed her, he would certainly have betrayed me; but he committed no treason toward me for anything that she said. He so guaranteed to me by oath; he assured me in no other way.

"O fair, most sweet son," said the Old Woman, "O beautiful   13001
tender flesh, I want to teach you of the games of Love so that when you have learned them you will not be deceived. Shape yourself according to my art, for no one who is not well informed can pass through this course of games without selling his livestock to get enough money. Now give your attention to hearing and understanding, and to remembering everything that I say, for I know the whole story.

"Fair son, whoever wants to enjoy loving and its sweet ills   13011
which are so bitter must know the commandments of Love but must beware that he does not know love itself. I would tell you all the commandments here if I did not certainly see that, by nature, you have an overflowing measure of those that you should have. Well numbered, there are ten of them that you ought to know. But he who encumbers himself with the last two is a great fool; they are not worth a false penny. I allow you eight of them, but whoever follows Love in the other two wastes his study and becomes mad. One should not study them in a school. He who wants a lover to have a generous heart and to put love in only one place has given too evil a burden to lovers. It is a false text, false in

the letter. In it, Love, the son of Venus, lies, and no man should believe him; whoever does will pay dearly, as you will see by the end of my sermon.

13037   "Fair son, never be generous; and keep your heart in several places, never in one. Don't give it, and don't lend it, but sell it very dearly and always to the highest bidder. See that he who buys it can never get a bargain: no matter how much he may give, never let him have anything in return; it were better if he were to burn or hang or maim himself. In all cases keep to these points: have your hands closed to giving and open to taking. Certainly, giving is great folly, except giving a little for attracting men when one plans to make them one's prey or when one expects such a return for the gift that one could not have sold it for more. I certainly allow you such giving. The gift is good where he who gives multiplies his gift and gains; he who is certain of his profit cannot repent of his gift. I can indeed consent to such a gift.

13061   "Next, about the bow and the five arrows which are very full of good qualities and which wound so readily, know how to fire them so wisely that Love, the good archer, never drew a better bow, fair son, than do you, who have many times launched your arrows. But you have not always known where the blow has fallen, for when one fires into the pack, the shot may hit someone for whom the archer does not care. But, whoever considers your manner, you know so well how to draw a bow and how to stretch nets that I can teach you nothing about it. With your ability, you can wound such a person that, if it please God, your prize will be magnificent.

13079   "Moreover, it is unnecessary for me to bother teaching you about decorating your garments or about the baubles of which you will make your ornaments, so that you will seem worth more to men. Such tutelage can never be important to you when you know by heart the song that you have heard me sing so much, as we went out to play, about Pygmalion's image. Take care to ornament yourself and you will know more than an ox about how to work. There is no need for you to learn these trades. And if all this will not suffice you, you will hear me say something later, if you want to hear me out, from which you will be able to take

13097   an example. But I can tell you this much: if you want to choose a lover, I advise you to give your love, but not too firmly, to that fair young man who so prizes you. Love others wisely, and I will seek out for you enough of them so that you can amass great wealth from them. It is good to become acquainted with rich men if their hearts are not mean and miserly and if one knows how to pluck them well. Fair Welcoming may know whomever he wishes, provided that he gives each one to understand that he would not want to take another lover for a thousand marks of fine milled gold. He should swear that if he had wanted to allow his rose, which was in great demand, to be taken by another, he would have been weighed down with gold and jewels. But, he should go on, his pure heart was so loyal that no man would ever stretch out his hand for it except that man alone who was offering his hand at that moment.

"If there are a thousand, he should say to each: 'Fair lord, you   13119
alone will have the rose; no one else will ever have a part. May God fail me if I ever divide it.' He may so swear and pledge his faith to them. If he perjures himself, it doesn't matter; God laughs at such an oath and pardons it gladly.

"Jupiter and the gods laughed when lovers perjured themselves;   13127
and many times the gods who loved *par amour* perjured themselves. When Jupiter reassured his wife Juno, he swore by the Styx to her in a loud voice and falsely perjured himself. Since the gods give them, such examples should assure pure lovers that they too may swear falsely by all the saints, convents, and temples. But he is a great fool, so help me God, who believes in the oaths of lovers, for their hearts are too fickle. Young men are in no way stable—nor, often times, are the old—and therefore they belie the oaths and faith that they have given.

"Know also another truth: he who is lord of the fair should   13145
collect his market-toll everywhere; and he who cannot at one mill —Hey! to another for his whole round! The mouse who has but one hole for retreat has a very poor refuge and makes a very dangerous provision for himself. It is just so with a woman: she is the mistress of all the markets, since everyone works to have her. She should take possessions everywhere. If, after she had reflected well, she wanted only one lover, she would have a very foolish idea. For, by Saint Lifard of Meun, whoever gives her love in a single place has a heart neither free nor unencumbered, but basely enslaved. Such a woman, who takes trouble to love one

man alone, has indeed deserved to have a full measure of pain and woe. If she lacks comfort from him, she has no one to comfort her, and those who give their hearts in a single place are those who most lack comfort. In the end, when they are bored or irritated, all these men fly from their women.

13173   "No woman can come to a good end. Dido, the queen of Carthage, could not hold Aeneas, no matter how much she had done for him; she had received him poor, a wretched fugitive from the fair land of Troy, his birthplace, and had reclothed and fed him. Because of her great love for him, she honored his companions and, to serve and please him, had his ships rebuilt. To obtain his love, she gave him her city, her body, her possessions; and he so reassured her in turn that he promised and swore to her that he was and would forever be hers and would never leave

13191   her. She, however, had no joy of him, for the betrayer, without permission, fled by sea in his ships. As a result, the beautiful Dido lost her life. Before the second day, she killed herself in her chamber with the sword that he had given her in her own hand. Remembering her lover and seeing that she had lost her love, she took the sword, quite naked, raised it point upward and placed it under her two breasts, then let herself fall on it. It was a great pity to see, whoever saw her do such a deed. He would have been a hard man who was not touched by pity when he thus saw the beautiful Dido on the point of the blade. Her sorrow over him who tricked her was so great that she fixed the blade within her body.

13211   "Phyllis was another. She waited so long for Demophoön that she hanged herself because he overstayed the time when he was to return and thus broke both his oath and his faith.

13215   "What did Paris do with Oenone? She had given him her heart and her body, and he gave his love in return. But straightway he took back his gift. For on a tree by the river, instead of on paper, he had carved with his knife tiny letters that were not worth a tart. They were cut in the bark of a poplar and said that the Xanthus would turn back on itself as soon as he left her. Now the Xanthus may return to its source, for afterward he left her for Helen.

13229   "Again, what did Jason do with Medea? He deceived her shamefully, the false one, when he belied his faith to her after she had saved him from death. By means of her spells she delivered Jason from the bulls who shot fire from their mouths and who came to burn him or smash him to bits; he felt no fire and was not even wounded. She made the serpent drunk so that it could not waken, so soundly did she make it sleep. As for the knights born of the earth, warlike and enraged, who wanted to kill Jason, she worked a spell so that when he threw the stone among them they attacked and killed each other. And it was through her art and her potion that she enabled him to get the Golden Fleece. Later, in order 13249 the better to bind Jason to herself, she renewed the youth of Aeson. She wanted nothing from him but that he love her as he had before and that he might look upon her merits so that he might the better keep his faith to her. Then he left her, the evil trickster, the false, disloyal thief, and when she discovered his desertion, she took her children and, because she had had them by Jason, strangled them in her grief and rage. In doing so she did not bear herself wisely; she abandoned a mother's pity and acted worse than an embittered stepmother. I could tell you a thousand examples of the same sort, but I would have too long a story to tell.

"Briefly, all men betray and deceive women; all are sensualists, 13265 taking their pleasure anywhere. Therefore we should deceive them in return, not fix our hearts on one. Any woman who does so is a fool; she should have several friends and, if possible, act so as to delight them to the point where they are driven to distraction. If she has no graces, let her learn them. Let her be haughtier to-ward those who, because of her hauteur, will take more trouble to serve her in order to deserve her love, but let her scheme to take from those who make light of her love. She should know games and songs and flee from quarrels and disputes. If she is not beautiful, she should pretty herself; the ugliest should wear the most coquettish adornments.

"Now if, to her great sorrow, she should see her beautiful blond 13283 curls falling, or if, because of a serious illness, she has to have it cut off and her beauty spoiled, or if it happens that some roisterer has torn it out in anger so that she can do nothing with him to recover her long locks, she should have someone bring her a dead woman's hair, or pads of light silk, stuffed into shapes. Over her ears she should wear such horns that they could not be surpassed by stag, billy goat, or unicorn, even if he had to burst his forehead; if they need color, she should tint them with plant extracts, for fruits, woods, leaves, bark, and roots have strong medicinal properties. Lest she should suffer loss of complexion, a heartrending experience, she must make sure always to have pots of moistening skin creams in her rooms, so that she may hide away to put on her paint; but she must be very careful not to let any of her guests notice or see her or she would be in trouble.

13313   "If she has a lovely neck and white chest, she should see that her dressmaker lower her neckline, so that it reveals a half foot, in front and back, of her fine white flesh; thus she may deceive more easily. And if her shoulders are too large to be pleasing at dances and balls, she should wear a dress of fine cloth and thus appear less ungainly. And if, because of insect bites or pimples, she doesn't have beautiful, well-kept hands, she should be careful not to neglect them but should remove the spots with a needle or wear gloves so that the pimples and scabs will not show.

13329   "If her breasts are too heavy she should take a scarf or towel to bind them against her chest and wrap it right around her ribs, securing it with needle and thread or by a knot; thus she can be active at her play.

13335   "And like a good little girl she should keep her chamber of Venus tidy. If she is intelligent and well brought up, she will leave no cobwebs around but will burn or destroy them, tear them down and sweep them up, so that no grime can collect anywhere.

13341   "If her feet are ugly, she should keep them covered and wear fine stockings if her legs are large. In short, unless she's very stupid she should hide any defect she knows of.

13345   "For example, if she knows that her breath is foul she should spare no amount of trouble never to fast, never to speak to others on an empty stomach, and, if possible, to keep her mouth away from people's noses.

13351   "When she has the impulse to laugh, she should laugh discreetly and prettily, so that she shows little dimples at the corners of her mouth. She should avoid puffing her cheeks and screwing her face up in grimaces. Her lips should be kept closed and her teeth covered; a woman should always laugh with her mouth closed, for the sight of a mouth stretched like a gash across the face is not a pretty one. If her teeth are not even, but ugly and quite crooked, she will be thought little of if she shows them when she laughs.

"There is also a proper way to cry. But every woman is adept enough to cry well on any occasion, for, even though the tears are not caused by grief or shame or hurt, they are always ready. All women cry; they are used to crying in whatever way they want. But no man should be disturbed when he sees such tears flowing as fast as rain, for these tears, these sorrows and lamentations flow only to trick him. A woman's weeping is nothing but a ruse; she will overlook no source of grief. But she must be careful not to reveal, in word or deed, what she is thinking of.

"It is also proper to behave suitably at the table. Before sitting down, she should look around the house and let everyone understand that she herself knows how to run a house. Let her come and go, in the front rooms and in back, and be the last to sit down, being sure to wait a little before she finally takes her seat. Then, when she is seated at table, she should serve everyone as well as possible. She should carve in front of the others and pass the bread to those around her. To deserve praise, she should serve food in front of the one who shares her plate. She should put a thigh or wing before him, or, in his presence, carve the beef or pork, meat or fish, depending upon what food there happens to be. She should never be niggardly in her servings as long as there is anyone unsatisfied. Let her guard against getting her fingers wet up to the joint in the sauce, against smearing her lips with soup, garlic, or fat meat, against piling up too large morsels and stuffing her mouth. When she has to moisten a piece in any sauce, either *sauce verte*, *cameline*, or *jauce*, she should hold the bit with her fingertips and bring it carefully up to her mouth, so that no drop of soup, sauce, or pepper falls on her breast. She must drink so neatly that she doesn't spill anything on herself, for anyone who happened to see her spill would think her either very clumsy or very greedy. Again, she must take care not to touch her drinking cup while she has food in her mouth. She should wipe her mouth so clean that grease will not stick to the cup, and should be particularly careful about her upper lip, for, when there is grease on it, untidy drops of it will show in her wine. She should drink only a little at a time, however great her appetite, and never empty

13367

13385

13408

13420

a cup, large or small, in one breath, but rather drink little and often, so that she doesn't go around causing others to say that she gorges or drinks too much while her mouth is full. She should avoid swallowing the rim of her cup, as do many greedy nurses who are so foolish that they pour wine down their hollow throats as if they were casks, who pour it down in such huge gulps that they become completely fuddled and dazed. Now a lady must be careful not to get drunk, for a drunk, man or woman, cannot keep anything secret; and when a woman gets drunk, she has no defenses at all in her, but blurts out whatever she thinks and abandons herself to anyone when she gives herself over to such bad conduct.

13457   "She must also beware of falling asleep at the table, for she would be much less pleasant; many disagreeable things can happen to those who take such naps. There is no sense in napping in places where one should remain awake, and many have been deceived in this way, have many times fallen, either forward or backward or sideways, and broken an arm or head or ribs. Let a woman beware lest such a nap overtake her; let her recall Palinurus, the helmsman of Aeneas's ship. While awake, he steered it well, but when sleep conquered him, he fell from the rudder into the sea and drowned within sight of his companions, who afterward mourned greatly for him.

13475   "Further, a lady must be careful not to be too reluctant to play, for she might wait around so long that no one would want to offer her his hand. She should seek the diversion of love as long as youth deflects her in that direction, for, when old age assails a woman, she loses both the joy and the assault of Love. A wise woman will gather the fruit of love in the flower of her age. The unhappy woman loses her time who passes it without enjoying love. And if she disbelieves this advice of mine, which I give for the profit of all, be sure that she will be sorry when age withers her. But I know that women will believe me, particularly those who are sensible, and will stick to our rules and will say many paternosters for my soul, when I am dead who now teach and comfort them. I know that this lesson will be read in many schools.

13499   "O fair sweet son, if you live—for I see well that you are writing down in the book of your heart the whole of my teaching, and that, when you depart from me, you will study more, if it please God, and will become a master like me—if you live I confer on you the license to teach, in spite of all chancellors, in chambers or in cellars, in meadow, garden, or thicket, under a tent or behind the tapestries, and to inform the students in wardrobes, attics, pantries, and stables, if you find no more pleasant places. And may my lesson be well taught when you have learned it well!

"A woman should be careful not to stay shut up too much, for while she remains in the house, she is less seen by everybody, her beauty is less well-known, less desired, and in demand less. She should go often to the principal church and go visiting, to weddings, on trips, at games, feasts, and round dances, for in such places the God and Goddess of Love keep their schools and sing mass to their disciples. 13517

"But of course, if she is to be admired above others, she has to be well-dressed. When she is well turned out and goes through the streets, she should carry herself well, neither too stiffly nor too loosely, not too upright nor too bent over, but easily and graciously in any crowd. She should move her shoulders and sides so elegantly that no one might find anyone with more beautiful movements. And she should walk daintily in her pretty little shoes, so well made that they fit her feet without any wrinkles whatever. 13529

"If her dress drags or hangs down near the pavement, she should raise it on the sides or in front as if to have a little ventilation or as if she were in the habit of tucking up her gown in order to step more freely. Then she should be careful to let all the passersby see the fine shape of her exposed foot. And if she is the sort to wear a coat she should wear it so that it will not too much hinder the view of her lovely body which it covers. Now she will want to show off her body and the cloth in which she is dressed, which should be neither too heavy nor too light, with threads of silver and small pearls, and particularly to show off her purse, which should be right out for everyone to see; therefore she should take the coat in both hands and widen and extend her arms, whether on clean streets or on muddy ones. Remembering the wheel which the peacock makes with his tail, she should do the same with her coat, so that she displays openly both her body and the fur linings of her clothing, squirrel or whatever costly fur she has used, to anybody she might see staring at her. 13545

13575 "Now if her face is not handsome, she must be clever and show people her beautiful priceless blond tresses and her well-coifed neck. A beautiful head of hair is a very pleasant thing.

13582 "A woman must always take care to imitate the she-wolf when she wants to steal ewes, for, in order not to fail completely, the wolf must attack a thousand to capture one; she doesn't know which she will take before she has taken it. So a woman ought to spread her nets everywhere to catch all men; since she cannot know which of them she may have the grace to catch, at least she ought to hook onto all of them in order to be sure of having one for herself. If she does so, it should never happen that she will have no catch at all from among the thousands of fools who will rub up against her flanks. Indeed she may catch several, for art is a great aid to nature.

13601 "And if she does hook several of those who want to put her on the spit, let her be careful, however events run, not to make appointments at the same hour with two of them. If several were to appear together they would think themselves deceived and they might even leave her. An event like this could set her back a long way, for at the least she would lose what each had brought her. She should never leave them anything on which they might grow fat, but plunge them into poverty so great that they may die miserable and in debt; in this way she will be rich, for what remains theirs is lost to her.

13617 "She should not love a poor man, for a poor man is good for nothing; even if he were Ovid or Homer, he wouldn't be worth two drinking mugs. Nor should she love a foreign traveler, for his heart is as flighty as his body, which lodges in many places; no, I advise her not to love a foreigner. However, if during his stay he offers her money or jewels she should take them all and put them in her coffer; then he may do as he pleases in haste or at his leisure.

13631 "She must be very careful not to love or value any man who is too elegant or who is haughty about his beauty, for it is pride which tempts him. The man who pleases himself, never doubt it, incurs the wrath of God; so says Ptolemy, the great lover of knowledge. Such a man has so evil and bitter a heart that he cannot love well. What he says to one woman he says to all. He tricks many to despoil and rob them. I have seen many complaints of maidens thus deceived.

"And if any man, either an honest man or a swindler, should   13647
make promises, hoping to beg for her love and bind her to him by
vows, she may exchange vows, but she must be careful not to put
herself at his mercy unless she gets hold of the money also. If he
makes any promise in writing, she must see if there is any deception
or if his good intentions are those of a true heart. She may
then soon write a reply, but not without some delay. Delay excites
lovers as long as it is not too great.   13663

"Now when she hears a lover's request, she should be reluctant
to grant all her love, nor should she refuse everything, but try
to keep him in a state of balance between fear and hope. When he
makes his demands more pressing and she does not yield him her
love, which has bound him so strongly, she must arrange things,
through her strength and her craft, so that hope constantly grows
little by little as fear diminishes until peace and concord bring
the two together. In giving in to him, she, who knows so many
wily ruses, should swear by God and by the saints that she has
never wished to give herself to anyone, no matter how well he
may have pleaded; then she should say, 'My lord, this is my
all; by the faith which I owe to Saint Peter of Rome, I give myself
to you out of pure love, not because of your gifts. The man isn't
born for whom I would do this for any gift, no matter how greatly
he desired it. I have refused many a worthy man, for many have
gazed adoringly at me. I think you must have cast a spell over
me; you have sung me a wicked song.' Then she should embrace
him closely and kiss him so that he will be even better deluded.

"But if she wants my advice, she should think only of what   13695
she can get. She is a fool who does not pluck her lover down to
the last feather, for the better she can pluck the more she will
have, and she will be more highly valued when she sells herself
more dearly. Men scorn what they can get for nothing; they don't
value it at a single husk. If they lose it, they care little, certainly
not as much as does one who has bought it at a high price.

"Here then are the proper ways to pluck men: get your servants,   13709
the chambermaid, the nurse, your sister, even your mother, if she
is not too particular, to help in the task and do all they can to get

the lover to give them coats, jackets, gloves, or mittens; like kites, they will plunder whatever they can seize from him, so that he may in no way escape from their hands before he has spent his last penny. Let him give them money and jewels as though he were playing with buttons instead of money. The prey is captured much sooner when it is taken by several hands.

13725   "On occasion let them say to him, 'Sir, since we must tell you so, don't you see that my lady needs a dress? How can you allow her to go without? By Saint Gile! If she wanted to be with a certain one in this town, she would be dressed like a queen and ride out in fine trappings. My lady, why do you wait so long before asking him for it? You are too shy toward him when he leaves you thus in your destitution.' Then, however pleased she is, she should order them to keep quiet, she, who has perhaps relieved him of so much that she has harmed him seriously.

13741   "And if she sees that he recognizes that he may be giving her more than he ought and that he may think himself seriously harmed by the large gifts on which he is in the habit of feeding her, and if she feels that she does not dare urge him to give anything, then she should ask him to lend to her, swearing that she is quite ready to pay him back on any day that he will name. But I certainly forbid that anything ever be given back.

13753   "If another of her friends comes back—she has several of them, perhaps, but has not given her heart to any one of them, although she calls them all her sweethearts—she should complain, like a wise person, that her best clothes and her money are running out every day for usury, and that as a result she is in such great anguish and torment of heart that she will do nothing to please him unless he gets back her pledges. If the young man is not very wise and is blessed with money, he will put his hand to his purse immediately or in some way bring about the release of those pledges that don't need to be bought back but are, perhaps, all locked up on his account within some iron-bound coffer, since it may be necessary to hide them in order to be the better believed, if he searches her closet or clothes pole, until she gets the money. She should reserve a third friend for a similar trick; I advise her to ask him for a silver belt, a dress, or a wimple, and then for money which she can spend.

13781   "And if he has nothing to bring her and swears, in order to comfort her, and promises by his foot and his hand that he will bring her something the next day, she should turn deaf ears to him. Let her believe nothing; all his tales are tricks. All men are very expert liars. These wastrels have told me more lies, made me more vows and oaths in past times than there are saints in paradise. When he has nothing to pay with, at least let him pledge at the wine merchant's for two, three, or four pennies, or let him go have a good time somewhere else outside.

"A woman who is not a simpleton should pretend to be a 13795
coward, to tremble, be fearful, distraught, and anxious when she must receive her lover; she should let him understand as true that she is receiving him in very great peril when she deceives her husband for him, or her guardians or her parents, and that if the thing that she wants to do in secret were open, she would be dead without fail. She should swear that he cannot stay if his presence is to bring about her instant death. Afterward, when she has enchanted him well, he will remain at her will.

"She should also remember well, when her sweetheart is to 13811
come, to receive him through the window, if she sees that no one will notice him, even though she might better do so through the door. She must swear that she would be destroyed and dead, and he no more, if it were known that he was within. He could not be protected with sharp weapons, with helm, halberd, pike, or club, with hutches, cabinets, or chambers, from being cut to pieces, limb by limb.

"Next, a lady must sigh and pretend to get angry, to attack 13823
him and run at him and say that he hasn't been late without some reason, and that some other woman was keeping him at home, someone whose solaces were more pleasing to him, and that now she is indeed betrayed when he hates her on account of another. She should certainly be called a miserable creature, when she loves without being loved. When the man, with his silly ideas, hears this speech, he will believe, quite incorrectly, that she loves him very loyally and that she may be more jealous of him than Vulcan ever was of his wife Venus, when he found her taken in the act with Mars. The fool had so spied upon them that he captured the two of them in strong bonds, as they were joined and linked in the game of love, in the nets that he had forged of brass.

"As soon as Vulcan knew that he had caught the two of them 13847 in the act with the net that he had put around the bed—he was a great fool when he dared to do so, for he who thinks that he can keep his wife to himself has very little knowledge—he had the gods come quickly. They laughed a lot and made fun when they saw them in this situation. Nearly all of the gods were amazed by the beauty of Venus, who made many complaints and laments, shamed and angered as she was at having been thus captured; never had she experienced such shame. But it was no great wonder if Venus gave herself to Mars, for Vulcan was so ugly and so blackened from his forge, on his hands, his face, and his neck, that Venus would not have loved him for anything, even though she called him her husband. No, by God, not even if he had been Absalom, with his blond locks, or Paris, son of the king of Troy, would she ever have been compliant with him, since she, the fair one, knew very well what all women know how to do.

13875   "Moreover, women are born free. The law, which takes away the freedom in which Nature placed them, has put them under conditions. Nature is not so stupid that she has Marotte born only for Robichon, if we put our wits to work, nor Robichon only for Marietta or Agnes or Perette. Instead, fair son, never doubt that she has made all us women for all men and all men for all women, each woman common to every man and every man common to each woman. Thus, when they are engaged, captured by law, and married, in order to prevent quarreling, contention, and murder and to help in the rearing of children, who are their joint responsibility, they still exert themselves in every way, these ladies and girls, ugly or beautiful, to return to their freedoms. They maintain their freedom as best they can; as a result, many evils will come, do come, and have come many times in the past. In fact, I would count over ten of them straightway, but I pass on, since I would be worn out and you overburdened with listening before I had numbered them.

13907   "In former times, when a man saw the woman who suited him best, he wanted to carry her off immediately, if someone stronger did not take her away from him; and he left her, if he pleased, when he had done his will with her. In former times, too, they killed one another and abandoned the care and feeding of their offspring. This was the time before men made marriages, through the counsel of wise men. On this subject Horace has said something good and true, if anyone wants to believe him. He knew very well how to instruct and teach, and I would like to repeat his statement here, for a wise woman is not ashamed when she recounts a good authority.

"Formerly, before the time of Helen, there were battles spurred by *con*, in which those who fought for it perished with great suffering; but the dead are not known when we do not read about them in written records. For these were not the first nor will they be the last through whom wars will come and have come between those who will keep and have kept their hearts set on the love of woman. As a result, many have lost body and soul, and they will do so if the world endures.

13923

"But pay good attention to Nature, for in order that you may see more clearly what wondrous power she has I can give you many examples which will show this power in detail. When the bird from the green wood is captured and put in a cage, very attentively and delicately cared for there within, you think that he sings with a gay heart as long as he lives; but he longs for the branching woods that he loved naturally, and he would want to be on the trees, no matter how well one could feed him. He always plans and studies how to regain his free life. He tramples his food under his feet with the ardor that his heart fills him with, and he goes trailing around his cage, searching in great anguish for a way to find a window or hole through which he might fly away to the woods. In the same way, you know, all women of every condition, whether girls or ladies, have a natural inclination to seek out voluntarily the roads and paths by which they might come to freedom, for they always want to gain it.

13936

"It is the same, I tell you, with the man who goes into a religious order and comes to repent of it afterward. He needs only a little more grief to hang himself. He complains and goes frantic until he is completely tormented by the great desires that come to him. He wants to find out how he can regain the freedom that he has lost. The will is not moved on account of any habit that one may take, no matter what place one goes to give oneself up to religion.

13967

"He is like the foolish fish who passed through the mouth of the trap-net and then, when he wanted to get back out, had to remain, in spite of himself, within his prison forever, for there

13979

was no chance to go back. The others who remained outside rushed together when they saw him. When they saw how he was turning and appearing to enjoy himself they thought that he really was having a good time, one of great diversion and joy. They thought so especially when they saw very clearly that there was plenty of food within, as much as each of them might ask for, and they would willingly enter there. They went all around the trap, twisted and bumped and examined it so much that they found the hole and threw themselves through it. But when they had come inside, they were captured and held forever; and afterward they could not keep from wanting to go back, but it was not possible to do so, since they were captured more securely than in a hoop-net. They had to live there in great sorrow until death delivered them from it.

14007　　　"That is just the sort of life that a young man goes in search of when he gives himself up, for he will never have shoes or hood or cowl so large that Nature may be hidden in his heart. Then when his state of freedom is gone he is dead and in a miserable situation if, through great humility, he does not make a virtue of necessity. But Nature, who makes him feel freedom, cannot lie. Even Horace, who knows well the meaning of such a thing, tells us that if anyone wanted to take up a pitchfork to protect himself against Nature and shove her out of himself, she would come back, and I agree. Nature will always run back, and she will not remain away on account of any habit. What good does it do to insist? Every creature wants to return to its nature; it will never leave it because of the violence of force or necessity. This fact must give a good deal of excuse to Venus, since she wanted to use her freedom, and to all ladies who play around, no matter how much they are bound in marriage, for Nature makes them act thus because she wants to draw them to freedom. Nature is a very strong thing; she surpasses even training.

14039　　　"Fair son, take a kitten that had never seen a rat, large or small. If it had been fed for a long time, with the most careful attention, on delicate fare, without ever seeing a rat or a mouse, and then saw a mouse come, there is nothing that could hold it back, if one let it escape, from going immediately to seize the mouse. He would leave all his other food for it, no matter how hungry he was; and no matter what trouble one went to, nothing could make peace between them.

"If anyone could raise a colt that had never seen a mare right to the time that it was a great charger bearing saddles and stirrups, and then afterward a mare came, you would hear him neigh immediately, and he would want to run against her if there were no one to rescue her. A black horse will mate not only with a black mare, but with a sorrel or dapple or gray, if the rein or bridle doesn't hold him back, since he doesn't examine any of them as long as he may find them untied or can jump on them. He would want to attack them all. And if he didn't stick to the black mare, she would come all the way to a black horse, indeed to a sorrel or a gray, just as her will urges her. The first that she saw would be her husband, since she in turn doesn't examine any of them as long as she may find them untied.

"And what I say about the black mare, about the sorrel horse and mare and the gray and black horses, I say about the cow and bull and the ewe and ram; for we do not doubt that these males want all females as their wives. Never doubt, fair son, that in the same way all females want all males. All women willingly receive them. By my soul, fair son, it is thus with every man and every woman as far as natural appetite goes. The law restrains them little from exercising it. A little! but too much, it seems to me, for when the law has put them together, it wants either of them, the boy or the girl, to be able to have only the other, at least as long as he or she lives. But at the same time they are tempted to use their free will. I know very well that such a thing does rise up, only some keep themselves from it because of shame, others because they fear trouble; but Nature controls them to that end just as she does the animals that we were just speaking of. I know it from my own experience, for I always took trouble to be loved by all men. And if I had not feared shame, which holds back and subdues many hearts, when I went along the streets where I always wanted to go—so dressed up in adornments that a dressed-up doll would have been nothing in comparison—I would have received all or at least many of those young boys, if I had been able and if it had pleased them, who pleased me so much when they threw me those sweet glances. (Sweet God! What pity for them

14053

14077

14104

seized me when those looks came toward me!) I wanted them all one after the other, if I could have satisfied them all. And it seemed to me that, if they could have, they would willingly have received me. I do not except prelates or monks, knights, burgers, or canons, clerical or lay, foolish or wise, as long as they were at the height of their powers. They would have jumped out of their orders if they had not thought that they might fail when they asked for my love; but if they had known my thought and the whole of our situations they would not have been in such

14133   doubt. And I think that several, if they had dared, would have broken their marriages. If one of them had had me in private he would not have remembered to be faithful. No man would have kept his situation, his faith, vows, or religion unless he were some demented fool who was smitten by love and loved his sweetheart loyally. Such a man, perhaps, would have called me paid and thought about his own possessions, which he would not have given up at any price. But there are very few such lovers, so help me God and Saint Amand; I certainly think so. If he spoke to me for a long time, no matter what he said, lies or truth, I could have made him move everything. Whatever he was, secular, or in an order, with a belt of red leather or of cord, no matter what head-dress he wore, I think that he would have carried on with me if he thought that I wanted him or even if I had allowed him. Thus Nature regulates us by inciting our hearts to pleasure. For this reason Venus deserves less blame for loving Mars.

14161   "Just as Mars and Venus, who loved each other, were in such a situation, there were many of the gods who would have wished while they were making fun of Mars, that the others had been making fun of them in the same situation. Afterward, Dan Vulcan would rather have lost two thousand marks than that anyone should ever have known about that business, for when the two who had such shame saw that everyone knew it, they then did in front of people's faces what they had done before in secret. Never afterward were they ashamed of the deed; the gods told the story about them and published it until it was well known through-out the heaven. The worse the deed was, the angrier Vulcan got, and could never afterward take any counsel. As the letter bears witness, it would have been better for him to suffer than to have stretched his nets near the bed; it would have been better not to

show emotion, but instead to pretend that he knew nothing, if
he wanted to have the good graces of Venus, whom he held so dear.

"Thus a man who watches over his wife or his sweetheart should   14187
take care when his silly spying works so well that he catches her
in the act. For you may be sure that she will do worse when she
is caught. And he who burns with that cruel sickness, jealousy,
and captures her with his ingenuity will never, after the capture,
have from her either a fair look or good service. Jealousy is a
very foolish disease. It makes the jealous husband burn with worry.
But the woman should pretend to be jealous and make a pretense
of suffering from this disease. Thus she amuses the simpleton, and
the more she amuses him the more he will burn.

"And if he does not deign to deny his fault but says, in order   14203
to make her angry, that he really has another sweetheart, he should
be careful that she does not fall into a rage. No matter what appearance she may make of it, if he takes another sweetheart, his
greedy promiscuity should never bother her as much as a button.
She should give him to believe, so that he won't stop loving, that
she wants to get another friend and that she does so only to get
rid of the one whom she wants to estrange, for it is quite right
that she separate from him. And she should say:

" 'You have misbehaved very much with me, and I must avenge   14217
myself for this wrong. Since you have tricked me, I will deal
you a similar trick.'

"Then, if he loves her at all, he will be in a worse situation   14221
than he ever was, and he will not know how to act. No man has
the ability to carry a great love in his breast if he is not afraid of
being tricked.

"Then let the chambermaid rush back, make a face of terror,   14227
and say: 'Unfortunate creatures, we are dead. My lord, or I don't
know what man, has entered our court.' Then the lady must run
and interrupt all business at hand. But she should hide the young
man under the roof, in the stable, or in a closet until she may call
him back when she returns there. Perhaps, out of fear and despair,
the man who desires her return would then want to be elsewhere.

"Then if it is another friend with whom the lady has fixed a   14241
time—and she was not very wise to do so, since the first will not
endure her stupidity at all, even though she may keep him in
mind—she can lead him into some room. He may then do his

will, but he will be unable to stay. As a result he will be very
aggrieved and angry, for the lady can say to him, 'There's no
hope of your staying, since my lord is within, and four of my
first cousins. So help me God and Saint Germain, some other time
when you can come, I will do whatever you want. But you will
have to wait that long. Now I must go back, for they are waiting
for me.' But she should put him out thus, since from that time
on she can suspect him of nothing.

14261   "Then the lady should return, since she may not keep the other
one waiting too long in his discomfort or he will be very displeased.
Then she may give him his ease again when it is all right for him
to come forth from his prison and go to lie in her arms, within
her bed, making sure that he does not lie there without fear. She
should say and give him to understand that she is too foolish and
bold, and even though she may be safer than those who follow
their own desires, dancing through fields and vineyards, she should
swear by her father's soul that she is paying too much for his love
when she takes such a chance. For delight taken in security is less
pleasant and has less value.

14281   "And when they are to come together, let her take care that
he never unites with her, however he may hold her in repose, if
she sees daylight, unless she half-closes the windows so that the
place may be in shadow; then, if she has a blemish or spot on her
skin, he will never know of it. Let her take care that he see no
filth on her or he would set off on his way immediately and flee
with his tail in the air; then she would be ashamed and grieved.

14293   "And when they set about their labor, each of them should
work so carefully and so exactly that the pleasure must come together for the one person and the other before they leave off the
task; and between them, they should wait for each other so that
they can direct their desires toward their good. One should not
leave the other behind; they should not stop navigating until they
come together into port. Then their pleasure will be complete.

14305   "And if she has no pleasure whatever, she should pretend that
she has a great deal; she must simulate all the signs that she knows
to be appropriate to pleasure so that he will think that she is taking
with gratitude what she doesn't think worth a chestnut.

14311   "And if, in order that they may be safer, he gets the lady to come to his own dwelling, then she must have the intention, the day that she is to undertake the trip, of making herself delay a little so that he may desire her very much before he takes her at his own pleasure. The longer the games of love are delayed, the pleasanter they are by reason of the delay; and those who enjoy them at their will are less desirous of them.

"When she comes to the house where she will be held so dear, 14323 then she should swear and give her lover to understand that she is all shivering and trembling in apprehension of her jealous husband, and that she is terribly afraid of being vilified or beaten when she goes back again. But, however distracted she acts and whether she tells the truth or lies, let him take her securely in fear, fearfully in security, and let them play their games out in their privacy.

"And if she has not the leisure to go to his dwelling to speak with 14337 him, nor dares receive him at her own because her jealous husband keeps her shut up so much, then, if she can, she should get her husband drunk if she knows no better way to set herself free. And if she cannot make him drunk on wine, she can take a pound of herbs more or less, which, at no danger to herself, she can get him to eat or drink. Then he will sleep so deeply that while he is sleeping he will leave her free for whatever she wants, for he will be unable to deflect her from anything.

"If she has a staff of servants, she can send one here and another 14351 there, or deceive them with trifling gifts and receive her lover with their help; or she can make them all drunk as well if she wants to keep them out of the secret.

"Or, if she pleases, she may say to the jealous husband, 'Sir, 14357 I don't know what disease, what fever or gout or boil, has seized and is firing my whole body. I have to go to the stews, even though we have two tubs here at home; a bath without a sweat would be worth nothing, and so I must go out to sweat myself.'

"When the wretch has thought, perhaps he will give her per- 14365 mission, even though he makes a nasty face. But she should take her chambermaid along, or some neighbor of hers who knows all about her affair and will, perhaps, have her own lover about whom the lady will know at the same time. Then off she will go to the bathhouse, but by no chance will she ever seek out a bath or tub;

she will go only to lie with her lover, unless they should bathe together because it seems good to them. He can wait for her there if he knows that she is to come that way.

14381 "No man can keep watch over a woman if she does not watch over herself. If it were Argus who guarded her and looked at her with his hundred eyes, of which one half watched while the other half slept, his watchkeeping would be worth nothing. (To revenge Io, whom Argus had changed into a cow and stripped of her human form, Jupiter had his head cut off. Mercury cut it off and thus revenged her against Juno.) Argus's watch would be worth nothing in this case; the man who guards such an object is a fool.

14395 "But she should take care never to be so stupid, for anything that anyone, clerical or lay, may tell her, as to believe at all that enchantment, sorcery, or incantation, that Balenus and his science, or that magic or necromancy can move a man by compulsion to love her or to hate someone else. Medea could never hold Jason with any enchantment, any more than Circe could keep Ulysses from fleeing, no matter what fate she could create.

14409 "A woman must be careful, no matter how much she claims a man as her lover, not to give him a gift that is worth very much. She may indeed give a pillow, a towel, a kerchief, or a purse, as long as they are not too expensive, a needle-case, a lace, a belt with metalwork that is worth little, a fine little knife, or a ball of thread of the kind that nuns usually make.

14420 ("He who frequents nuns is a fool; it is better to love women of the world, for one does not get blamed as much, and they can follow their desires better. They know how to feed their husbands and families with words. Moreover, even though either kind of woman is costly, the nuns are much more expensive.)

14429 "But a man who would indeed be wise should suspect all gifts from a woman, for truly, women's gifts are nothing but deceptive traps; and a woman with any trace of generosity sins against her nature. We should leave generosity to men, for when we women are generous, it is a great misfortune, a great vice. Devils have made us thus stupid. But it doesn't matter to me; there is scarcely one that is accustomed to giving gifts.

14441 "Fair son, you can very well use such gifts as I have told you about before to amuse these simpletons, as long as you do so to deceive them. Keep whatever people give you and let it remind you of the end toward which all youth is directed, if everyone can live that long: it is old age. It does not stop; it approaches us every day. Do not be considered a fool when you have arrived there. Be so furnished with possessions that no one will make fun of you for being old; for acquisitions that are not kept are not worth a grain of mustard.

"Alas! I have not done so. Now, through my own wretched act, 14457 I am a poor woman. I abandoned to men I loved better the large gifts that were given me by those who abandoned themselves to me. They gave to me, and I gave away; I have kept back nothing. Giving has reduced me to indigence. I did not remember old age, that has put me in such distress. I never thought of poverty. I let time go by just as it came, taking no care to spend moderately.

"By my soul, if I had been wise, I would have been a very 14471 rich lady, for I was acquainted with very great people when I was already a coy darling, and I certainly was held in considerable value by them, but when I got something of value from one of them, then, by the faith that I owe God or Saint Thibaut, I would give it all to a rascal who brought me great shame but pleased me more. I called all the others lover, but it was he alone that I loved. Understand, he didn't value me at one pea, and in fact told me so. He was bad—I never saw anyone worse—and he never ceased despising me. This scoundrel, who didn't love me at all, would call me a common whore. A woman has very poor judgment, and I was truly a woman. I never loved a man who loved me, but, do you know, if that scoundrel had laid open my shoulder or broken my head, I would have thanked him for it. He wouldn't have known how to beat me so much that I would not have had him throw himself upon me, for he knew very well how to make his peace, however much he had done against me. He would never 14499 have treated me so badly, beaten me or dragged me or wounded my face or bruised it black, that he would not have begged my favor before he moved from the place. He would never have said so many shameful things to me that he would not have counseled peace to me and then made me happy in bed, so that we had peace and concord again. Thus he had me caught in his snare, for this false, treacherous thief was a very hard rider in bed. I couldn't live without him; I wanted to follow him always. If he had fled,

I would certainly have gone as far as London in England to seek him, so much did he please me and make me happy. He put me to shame and I him, for he led a life of great gaiety with the lovely gifts that he had received from me. He put none of them into saving, but played everything at dice in the taverns. He never learned any other trade, and there was no need then for him to do so, for I gave him a great deal to spend, and I certainly had it for the taking. Everybody was my source of income, while he spent it willingly and always on ribaldry; he burned everything in his lechery. He had his mouth stretched so wide that he did not want to hear anything good. Living never pleased him except

14533 when it was passed in idleness and pleasure. In the end I saw him in a bad situation as a result, when gifts were lacking for us. He became poor and begged his bread, while I had nothing worth two carding combs and had never married a lord. Then, as I have told you, I came through these woods, scratching my temples. May this situation of mine be an example to you, fair sweet son; remember it. Act so wisely that it may be better with you because of my instruction. For when your rose is withered and white hairs assail you, gifts will certainly fail."

14547   Thus preached the Old Woman. Fair Welcoming, who had not spoken a word, listened very willingly to everything. He feared the Old Woman less than he had ever done before, and indeed he was beginning to recognize that, if it were not for Jealousy and her gatekeepers, in whom she trusted so much, at least the three that remained to her, who always ran about the castle in a complete frenzy to defend it, the castle would have been easy to capture. But it would never be taken, he thought, no matter how much attention the attackers gave to it. None of the porters made an unhappy face over Foul Mouth, who was dead, for he was not loved

14564 at all in that circle. He had always defamed and betrayed them all to Jealousy, so that he was so vehemently hated that no one who dwelt therein would have given so much as a bunch of garlic to free him, no one except Jealousy, perhaps. She liked his babble very much; she willingly lent him her ear, and was also wondrously sad when the thief made some scandalous accusation. He hid nothing from her that he could remember as long as ill was to come of it. But his very great fault was to tell more than he knew, and by his exaggerations he added to the things that he heard. He always increased news that was neither good nor fair, and he made little of good news. Thus, like one who was accustomed to envious slander in his whole life, he titillated Jealousy. The others never sang any Mass for him, so glad they were when they saw him dead. It seemed to them that they had lost nothing, for when they had collected together, they thought that they could guard the enclosure so that there would be no fear of its being taken if five hundred thousand men attacked it.

"Certainly," they said, "we are not very powerful, if, without   14594
this thief, we cannot guard everything that we have. May this false traitor, this miserable wretch, have his soul stinking in hell-fire, that can burn and destroy it! He never did anything in here except harm."

The three porters went around saying these things, but whatever they were planning, they were powerfully weakened.

When the Old Woman had told her story in this way, Fair Wel-   14604
coming took up the conversation. He began after a long time and spoke little; like one who was well taught, he said:

"My lady, when you teach me your art with such good grace,   14608
I thank you kindly for it; but when you spoke to me of love, the sweet sickness with so much bitterness, it was a subject strange to me. I know nothing of it but what I have heard, and I shall never seek to know more. And again you spoke to me about possessions and how I should amass many of them; but what I have is enough for me. I want to put all my attention on having a lovely, gentle manner. I have no belief in magic, the devil's art, whether it is true or false.

"But about the young man of whom you spoke to me, in whom   14623
there is so much goodness and merit that in him all graces mingle— if he has these graces, let them dwell with him. I do not hope for them to be mine, but leave them to him. In any case, I certainly do not hate him, nor do I love him so purely, even though I have accepted his chaplet, that I call him my friend except in the ordinary way, as every man says to every woman: 'You are welcome, my friend.' And she replies, 'My friend, and God bless you.' Nor do I love him or honor him except well and honorably. But since he has given me this gift and I have received it, it should please me and suit me for him to come to see me if he can and has any desire to do so. He will never find me slow to receive him

willingly, but it must be while Jealousy is out of town. She hates
him and reviles him so that I am afraid, however it may happen,
that if she were now away she might come upon us, for after she
has packed up all her gear to go out and we have leave to stay,
then often, when she has imagined something on her road, she
returns in mid-journey and storms at us and upsets us all. She is so
cruel and harsh toward me that if she comes by chance and can
find him in here, even though she may never be able to prove
anything further, I will, if you remember her cruelty, be completely dismembered alive."

14663   The Old Woman assured him very much. "Let me do the worrying," she said. "There is no question of finding him here. Even
if Jealousy were here, I know so many hiding places that, so help
me God and Saint Remi, she would sooner find an ant's egg in a
straw pile than she would find him after I have hidden him, so
well would I know how to hide him."

14673   "Then," said Fair Welcoming, "I would indeed like him to
come, provided that he conducts himself discreetly so that he avoids
anything offensive."

14676   "By God's flesh, you speak wisely, my son, like a worthy and
thoughtful person of knowledge and judgment."

14679   Then their conversation was over, and they departed from that
place. Fair Welcoming went into his room, and the Old Woman
also got up to do her tasks in the houses. When the place, time, and
occasion came that the Old Woman could select to find Fair Welcoming alone, so that one might indeed speak to him at leisure,
she began to descend the steps until she came forth from the
tower. She never stopped trotting right from the exit up to the
place where I was staying, and came to me tired and panting to
tell me about the affair. "Do I come," she said, "in time for the
gloves, if I tell you good news, completely fresh and new?"

14697   "For the gloves!" I said. "Lady, I tell you without joking that
instead you will have a coat and dress, a headdress of gray feathers,
and shoes of your design if you tell me something of value."

14702   Then the old lady told me that I might go up to the castle,
where someone waited for me. She did not want to leave immediately but taught me the way to enter:

14706   "You will enter by the rear door," she said, "and, the better
to conceal the matter, I will go to open it for you. The passage

is very well hidden. This door, you know, has not been open for more than two and a half months."

"Lady," I said, "by Saint Remi, even though it costs ten or twenty pounds a yard"—for I remembered very well that Friend had told me that I should make good promises, even if I could not fulfill them—"you will have good cloth, either blue or green, if I can find the door open." 14712

The Old Woman left me immediately. I went back in the other direction, by the rear door where she had told me to go, praying God to direct me to the right harbor. Without saying a word, I came to the rear door that the Old Woman had unlocked for me and still kept half closed. When I had entered, I closed it, so that we were in greater safety; I was especially so because I knew that Foul Mouth was dead. I was never so happy over a death. There I saw his gate broken. I had no sooner passed it than I found Love inside the gate, along with his host, who brought me comfort. God! What an advantage the vassals who overcame that gate had given me! May they have the benediction of God and Saint Benedict! There was the traitor False Seeming, son of Fraud and false minister of Hypocrisy, his mother, who is so bitter toward the virtues; there too was lady Constrained Abstinence, pregnant by False Seeming and ready to give birth to Antichrist, as I find it written in a book. Without fail, these were they who overcame the gate. Therefore I pray for them, for whatever that is worth. My lords, he who wants to be a traitor should make False Seeming his master and take Constrained Abstinence. He may then practice duplicity and pretend simplicity. 14719

When I saw this gate, of which I told you, thus taken and overcome, and found the armed host within, ready to attack, let no man ask if I was full of joy when I saw with my own eyes. Then I thought very deeply on how I might have Sweet Looks, and there he was, God keep him, for Love sent him for my comfort. I had lost him for a very long time. When I saw him, I was so full of joy that I almost fainted; and Sweet Looks was also very glad of my coming when he saw me. He directed me straightway to Fair Welcoming, who jumped up and came toward me like a courteous and well-brought-up person; his mother had taught him. Bowing, I saluted him on my coming, and he also saluted me in return and thanked me for his chaplet. 14753

14774   "Sir," I said, "don't trouble yourself; you should not thank me, but I should thank you a hundred thousand times for doing me so much honor as to take it. You know that if you pleased there is nothing of mine that is not yours to do with as you wish, no matter who were to laugh or grieve over it. I wish to put myself at your disposal in every way, to honor and serve you. If you want to order me to do anything, or send for me without any order, or if I may know about it in any other way, I shall put my body, my possessions, indeed my soul as well, without any remorse of conscience, into its execution. And in order that you may be more certain, I beg you to try it; if I fail, may I never enjoy my body or anything that I possess."

14795   "Thank you, fair sir," he said. "In turn, I want to tell you that if I have anything that may please you, I certainly want you to have its comfort. Take it even without permission, as if you were I, for your well-being and your honor."

14801   "Sir," I said, "I thank you a hundred thousand times for your favor. When I can thus take anything of yours, then I seek never to wait any longer, for here you have ready the thing on which my heart will make a greater feast than on all the gold of Alexander."

8

ATTACK AND REPULSE

Then I advanced to stretch out my hands toward the rose that   14808
I longed for so greatly, in order to fulfill my whole desire. I believed very much in the speeches that we had made, so sweet and
agreeable, and in our pleasant acquaintance, full of fair faces that
were very easily made, but what happened was quite different. A
great deal of what a fool plans is left undone. I found a very cruel
defense, for as I started in that direction, Resistance, the villain—
may the wicked wolf strangle him—forbade me to take a step. He
was hidden in a corner, behind, where he spied on us and set
down our entire conversation, word for word, in writing. Without
waiting he cried out at me.

"Fly, vassal," he said. "Fly, fly, fly. You give me too much   14827
trouble. The accursed devils, demented with fury, have led you
back; they participate in this fine ceremony where everyone takes
all he can before he goes away. May no holy man or woman ever
come to it! Vassal, vassal, may God save me, for just a little I
would break your head!"

Then Fear jumped up, and Shame ran in, when they heard the   14836
peasant saying "Fly, fly, fly"; but he still did not keep quiet, but
called upon the devils and turned back the saints. Ah! God!
What a cruel band he had! They ran out in a rage and all three
together took me and pushed my hands back.

"Never," they said, "will you have less or more than you have   14846
had. You understand poorly what Fair Welcoming offered you
when he allowed you to speak to him. He gladly offered you his
goods, but only in an honest way. You had no concern over
honesty, but took the offer simply, not in the sense that one ought
to take it, for it must be understood without saying that when a
worthy person offers his service, it is only in a good way, and he
who makes the promise so understands it. Now tell us, Dan
Trickster, when you heard what he said, why didn't you take it in

the right sense? Either it was your rude understanding that encouraged you to take it so basely, or you have learned to play the fool with skill. He never offered you the rose, because to do so is not honest, and you should neither ask for it nor have it without asking. And when you offered things to him, how did you intend this offer? Was it to come here and trick him in order to rob him of his rose? In fact, you do betray and trick him when you want to serve him in this way, by being a bosom enemy. There is nothing put in a book that can bring so much harm or trouble. If you should burst with grief, we should not believe it. You must vacate this enclosure. Devils have made you come back here, for you should remember very well that you were chased out of here once before. Now get out; get what you want somewhere else. You know, the old lady who sought passage for such a dolt was not very wise, but she didn't know your intention or the treason that you planned, for she would never have sought it for you if she had known about such disloyalty. Furthermore, Fair Welcoming, who is quite defenseless, was certainly deceived when he received you in his enclosure. He thought to do you a service, and you intended only trouble for him. My faith! He gains as much as one who transports a dog in a boat. As soon as he arrives, the dog barks at him. Now seek your prey elsewhere, and get out of this enclosure. You may ascend our steps in good health and with our thanks, or you will never count a single one, for someone could come here quickly who, if he got you in his power or held you, would make you miscount them if he had to break your head.

14909   "Sir Fool, Sir Presumption, empty of all loyalty, how has Fair Welcoming done you any wrong? For what sin, what misdeed have you taken so soon to hating him? You want to betray him here, and now you offer him every thing that you have? Is it because he received you, because he deceived us and himself for you and straightway offered you his dogs and his birds? He should know that he acted foolishly; and in view of what he has done here, both now and at other times, so keep us God and Saint Foy, he will be put forever in a prison stronger than any captive ever entered. He will be riveted in such strong bands that you will never, any day that you live, see him going along a way. He has troubled and disturbed us too much. It was an unhappy hour when you saw so much of him. We are all deceived by him!"

Then they seized him and beat him so much that they made   14933
him flee into the tower. There, after many shameful injuries,
they locked him with three pairs of locks under three pairs of
keys, without putting him behind bars or in a cell. They troubled
him no further at this time, but only because they were in a hurry;
but they promised to do worse when they returned.

They did not keep their promise. All three of them returned   14943
to me where I was waiting outside, sad, sorrowing, overcome, and
in tears. Again they attacked me and tormented me. Now may
God grant that they may yet repent! My heart almost melted
away from sorrow over the great outrage that they had done me.
I wanted to give myself up, but they did not want to take me
alive. I tried very hard to make peace with them and I would
have wished very much to be put in prison with Fair Welcoming.

"Resistance," I said, "fair noble fellow, open of heart and valiant   14956
of body, more compassionate than I can say, and you, O beautiful
Shame and Fear, wise, free, and noble girls, well regulated in
deeds and words and born of Reason's race, allow me to become
your servant with the agreement that I may stay within the prison
with Fair Welcoming, without ever being ransomed, and I will
promise to serve you loyally if you will put me in prison, where I
will serve you and do your pleasure. In faith, if I were now a
thief, traitor, or robber, or accused of some murder and wanted
to be imprisoned and made such a request, I do not think that
I would fail. In fact, by God, one could put me there in any country without any request; for that crime they should have me in
their power, and should cut me up completely and never let me
escape if they could catch me. For God's sake, I ask of you prison
with him forever, and if it can ever be found, either without proof
or in the very act, that I fail to serve well, may I go out of the
prison forever. Now there is no man who does not fail; but if I   14989
commit any fault, have me pack up my belongings and clear me
out of your bonds, for if I ever anger you, I want to be punished
for doing so. You yourselves may be the judges, as long as no one
except you may judge me. From head to toe, I submit myself
entirely to you as long as you are only three and as long as Fair
Welcoming may be with you, for I accept him as the fourth. We
can recount the deed to him and if you cannot agree to allow me,
let him bring you to an agreement; then you will hold to his de-

cision. For I would not want to move away from here, even if I were beaten or killed."

15007   Resistance cried out immediately: "Ah! God! What a request we have here! To put you in prison with him when you have such a playful heart and he such a well-disposed one would be to do nothing other than with the most exquisite love to put Renard with the hens. We know full well that whatever service you do you are only working out how to do us shame and villainy, and we have no care for such service. You are certainly still void of sense when you think that you can judge the case. Judge! For the beautiful King of heaven! How can a person already captured and judged ever be a judge or take any arbitration upon himself? Fair Welcoming has been captured and judged and you judge him to have so much dignity that he may be arbiter or judge! The deluge will come before he ever comes out of our tower and he will be destroyed when we return, for he has well deserved destruction because, outside of anything else, he did the service of offering you his things. We lose all the roses through him. Every dolt wants to gather them when he sees himself well received; but if one kept Fair Welcoming well encaged, no one would do them any harm, and no man living would carry off as much of the rose as the wind does if there were not the sort that misbehaves to the extent of using brute force. Indeed he might misbehave so much that he would be banished or hanged."

15045   "Certainly," I said, "anyone who destroys a man who has done nothing and who imprisons him without reason does a great wrong; and when you hold captive so worthy a person as Fair Welcoming, one so honest that he is the praise of everybody, and hold him on no other charge than that he turned a friendly face toward me and valued my acquaintance, you act very badly toward him. By reason he should be out of prison, if it pleased you; therefore I pray you that he may come forth and have done with his punishment. You have already done him too much wrong; take care that he may never be captured."

15061   "My faith," they said, "this fool is trying to trick us; in fact he is going around now feeding us his truffles when he wants Fair Welcoming released from prison and when he tries to trick us with his sermons. He asks for what cannot be. Fair Welcoming will never put even his head outside of the door or window."

Then they all attacked me again. Each one tried to thrust me
outside, but they didn't trouble me at all because I wanted to
crucify myself. I began to cry, not too loudly, for mercy from
them, and in a low voice I called on those who were to come to my
aid to attack. When the sentinels who were to guard the host saw
me and heard me being so badly treated, they cried out, "Now,
barons, upon them, upon them! If we do not appear straightway,
armed to help this pure lover, he is lost, God help us. The gatekeepers will kill him or put him in chains, beat him with sticks
or crucify him. He is crying out before their attack in a clear voice,
and calling for mercy from them in so low a voice that you can
scarcely hear the cry; for he cried and called so low that you
would think, to hear him, either that he was hoarse from yelling
or that they were squeezing his throat to strangle him or kill him.
They have already shut his voice so that he cannot or dares not
cry out. We don't know what they hope to do with him, but it is
something very much against him. He will be dead if he doesn't
get help immediately. Fair Welcoming, who used to comfort
him, has fled away very quickly, and now our lover must have
some other comfort until he can recover Fair Welcoming. From
now on we must labor with arms."

The porters would have killed me without fail if the men of
the host had not come. These barons leaped to their weapons
when they heard, knew, and saw that I had lost my joy and solace.
Without moving from the spot, I, who was captured in the net
where Love binds others, watched the tournament that began very
fiercely. As soon as the porters knew that they had so large an
army against them, all three of them allied themselves and swore
and promised that they would help each other and that never, on
any day of their life, in any extremity, would they abandon one
another. I didn't stop watching their appearance and bearing, and
I was very sad over their alliance. When those of the host saw that
the porters had made such an alliance, they got together and joined
forces. They had no desire to part company, but instead swore
that they would go so far as to lie dead on the spot, be overcome
and captured, or gain the victory in the fight, so ardent were they
to fight and beat down the porters' pride.

From now on we will come to the battle, and you will hear
how each one fights. Listen now, loyal lovers, so that the God

of Love may help you and grant that you may enjoy your loves! Here in this wood you may hear, if you listen to me, the dogs barking in chase of the rabbit that you are after and the ferret that must surely make him leap into the nets. Remember what I am saying here. You will have an adequate art of love, and if you have any difficulty, I will clarify what confuses you when you have heard me explain the dream. Then, if someone creates opposition, you will know how to reply about love, when you have heard me gloss the text. And then, by this text, you will understand whatever I have written before and whatever I intend to write. But before you hear me say anything more, I want to move aside a little to defend myself against wicked people, not so much to delay you as to excuse myself to them.

15159   Therefore I beg you, amorous lords, by the delicious games of love, if you find here any speeches that are too bawdy or silly and that might make slanderous critics who go around speaking ill of us rise up over things that I have said or will say, that you will courteously oppose them. Then when you have reproved, prevented, or opposed these speeches, if what I say is of such a nature that I may justly ask pardon for them, I beg you to pardon me and to reply to them through me that my subject matter demanded these things; it draws me toward such things by its own properties, and therefore I have such speeches. This procedure is just and right according to the authority of Sallust, who tells us in a true judgment:

15180   "Although there may not be the same glory for him who performs a certain deed and for him who wants to set down the deed accurately in a book, the better to describe the truth, still it is not an easy thing to set down deeds in writing; it requires great strength of technique, for if anyone writes something without wishing to rob you of its truth, then what he says must resemble the deed. Words that are neighbors with things must be cousins to their deeds." Therefore I have to speak thus if I want to proceed in the right way.

15195   And I pray all you worthy women, whether girls or ladies, in love or without lovers, that if you ever find set down here any words that seem critical and abusive of feminine ways, then please do not blame me for them nor abuse my writing, which is all for our instruction. I certainly never said anything, nor ever had the

wish to say anything, either through drunkenness or anger, in hate
or envy, against any woman alive. For no one should despise a
woman unless he has the worst heart among all the wicked ones.
But we have set these things down in writing so that we can gain
knowledge, and that you too may do so by yourselves. It is good
to know everything. Besides, honorable ladies, if it seems to you
that I tell fables, don't consider me a liar, but apply to the authors
who in their works have written the things that I have said and will
say. I shall never lie in anything as long as the worthy men who
wrote the old books did not lie. And in my judgment they all   15225
agreed when they told about feminine ways; they were neither
foolish nor drunk when they set down these customs in their
books. They knew about the ways of women, for they had tested
them all and had found such ways in women by testing at various
times. For this reason you should the sooner absolve me; I do
nothing but retell just what the poets have written between them,
when each of them treats the subject matter that he is pleased
to undertake, except that my treatment, which costs you little,
may add a few speeches. For, as the text witnesses, the whole
intent of the poets is profit and delight.

And if people grumble about me and get upset and angry   15243
because they feel that I reprove them in the chapter where I
record False Seeming's words, and therefore get together because
they want to blame or punish me because what I say gives them
pain, I certainly protest that it was never my intention to speak
against any living man who follows holy religion or who spends
his life in good works, no matter what robe he covers himself
with. Instead, I take my bow and bend it, sinner that I may be,
and let fly my arrow to wound at random. To wound, yes; but to
recognize, in the world or in the cloister, the unlawful people, the
cursed ones whom Jesus calls hypocrites. Many of them, to seem
more honest, give up eating the flesh of animals at all times,
and not for penance; they thus perform their act of abstinence, as
we do during Lent, but only to eat men alive, through venomous
intent, with the teeth of detraction. I never aimed to hit any other   15273
target; it is there that I wanted, and want, to place my arrows.
Therefore, I fire on them in the pack, and if it happens that any
man is pleased to put himself in the way of an arrow and receive
a shot, if he so deceives himself with his pride that he gets shot,

and then complains because I have wounded him, it is not my fault and never will be, even if he should perish as a result, for I can strike no one who wants to protect himself as long as he knows how to see where he stands. Even he who feels himself wounded by my arrow may take care to be a hypocrite no longer and will be rid of his wound. Nevertheless, in my opinion, no matter who complains, no matter how important he pretends to be, and no matter how he disputes me, I have never said anything that may not be found in writing, either proved by experience or at least capable of being proved by reason, no matter whom it may displease. And if I make any utterance that Holy Church may consider foolish, I am ready at her wish to change it if I am capable of making the change.

15303   Very humbly, Openness first encountered Resistance, who was very proud and courageous, cruel and wild in appearance. He held a mace in his hand, and brandished it so proudly and aimed such dangerous blows all around him that no shield could have held together without being smashed to bits unless it had been a wondrous one; he aimed blows so dangerous that anyone who stood up against him within range of the mace would have surrendered vanquished or, unless he was the sort that was very skillful at arms, been destroyed and obliterated. The ugly villain, repulsive to me, had taken his mace from the wood of Refusal. His targe was made from brutality, bordered with outrageous treatment.

15321   Openness was also well armed. She could hardly be scratched because she knew how to cover herself well. She threw herself against Resistance to get the gate open. In her hand she carried a strong lance, fair and polished, that she had brought from the forest of Cajolery. Nothing of the sort grows in the forest of Biere. Its tip was made of sweet prayer. She also held, with great devotion, a shield of every supplication, no less strong, bordered with handclasps, promises, agreements, oaths, and engagements, all colored very daintily. You would have said certainly that Generosity had given it to her, painted and shaped it, so much did it seem to be of her workmanship.

15342   Then Openness, covering herself well with her shield, brandished the haft of her lance and threw it toward the villain. He did not have a cowardly heart, but seemed rather to be Renouart de la Pole, if he had lived again. His shield would have been com-

pletely shattered, but it was so immeasurably strong that it feared
no arms, and he protected himself from the blow so that his
belly was not laid open. The point of the lance broke, and as a
result Resistance heeded the blow less. Furthermore, the cruel and
raging villain was well furnished with arms. He took the lance
and destroyed it, piece by piece, with his mace, and then aimed a
great fierce blow.

"Who is going to keep me from hitting you," he asked, "you   15360
filthy slut of a harlot? How have you dared to be so forward as
to attack a man of prowess?"

Then he struck the shield of the beautiful, courteous, and worthy   15364
lady, made her jump a good fathom with pain, and struck her to
her knees. He cursed and beat her vilely, and I think that at that
stroke she would have died if she had had a shield of wood.

"I believed you before," he said, "you filthy lady, you false   15371
slut, but it will certainly never happen again. Your lying betrayed
me, and because of you I allowed the kiss to give comfort to the
wanton young man. He found me foolishly agreeable; devils made
me do so. By God's flesh, it was a bad day for you when you
came here to attack our castle, for here you must lose your life."

When the fair one could go no further, she begged his mercy   15382
for God's sake, so that he would not destroy her. The scoundrel
shook his head, became furious, and swore by the saints that he
would kill her without delay.

Pity held him in great contempt and hastened to run toward   15388
him and rescue her companion. Pity, who is in accord with everything good, held, instead of a sword, a misericord that was flowing all over with weeping and tears. If my author doesn't lie, this
weapon would pierce a rock of diamond—if indeed it were so
directed—because it had a very sharp point. Her shield was made
of comfort and bordered with lamentation, full of sighs and complaints. Pity, weeping many tears, pierced the scoundrel on all sides
while he defended himself like a leopard, but when she had
bathed the dirty, unkempt scoundrel in tears he had to soften.
It seemed to him that he was to drown in a river, completely
dazed. He had never, by deeds or words, been struck so hard.
His force failed him completely; weak and drained, he staggered
and faltered and wanted to flee. Shame called out to him:

"Resistance, you have turned out a scoundrel. If you are found   15415 faithless, and Fair Welcoming is able to escape, you will get us all caught; then he will straightway give away the rose that we are keeping enclosed here. And I can tell you this much without fail, that if he gives the rose to gluttons, then you may know that as a result it will be blemished or pale, or flabby or withered. And so I can certainly claim again that such a wind could blow in here, if he found the entry open, that we would suffer harm and loss. Or the wind could move the seed or shower another seed there to burden the rose. God grant that such a seed may not fall here! It would be a great misfortune for us, for, before it could fall from the rose, our flower could immediately have died from it, without any help. Or if it escaped death and the wind struck such blows that the seeds intermingled, then the flowers would suffer; for the mingling of the seeds would weigh down the flower until, in its descent, it might tear away some of the leaves. The loss of the leaves—may God never wish such a thing—would reveal the green bud beneath; and then people would say everywhere that gluttonous knaves had held it in their clutches. We would have the hatred of Jealousy, who would know of it and sorrow so deeply from her knowledge that we would be given over to death. Devils must have made you raving drunk."

15453   Resistance cried, "Help, help!" and immediately Shame was there. She came at Pity and threatened her, and Pity was very much afraid of her threat.

15457   "You have lived too long," said Shame. "I will break that shield of yours, and today you shall lie on the ground; it was a bad day for you when you took up this war."

15461   Shame carried a large sword, beautiful, well made, and well tempered, one that she had forged in fear from the concern over being found out. She had a strong targe, named Fear-of-a-Bad-Reputation, for she had made it of that sort of wood. On the borders there was many a tongue portrayed. She struck Pity and made her fall back; she almost finished her off. Immediately Delight came up, a handsome bachelor, exceptionally strong, and made an attack on Shame. He had a sword of pleasant life, a shield of ease—something I had none of whatever—that was bordered with solace and joy. He struck at Shame, but she covered herself so judiciously with her shield that the blow never troubled her. Shame in turn went out seeking him and struck him with such force that she broke her shield over his head and beat him down until he was stretched out on the ground. She would have smashed him right up to his teeth, but God brought up a bachelor called Skillful Concealment.

Skillful Concealment was a very good warrior, a wise and wily earthly lord. In his hand he held a quiet sword, one like a tongue cut out. He brandished it without making any noise, so that one did not hear it a fathom off. No matter how strongly it was brandished, it gave off neither sound nor echo. His shield was made of a hidden place where no chicken ever laid an egg; it was bordered with safe outings and secret returns. He raised his sword and struck Shame such a blow that he almost killed her. Shame was completely dazed from it.

15487

"Shame," he said, "never will Jealousy, that sorrowful captive, know it any day of her life. I would assure you of that, give you my hand on it, and swear a hundred oaths. Isn't that a great assurance? Now that Foul Mouth is killed, you are captured; do not move."

15502

Shame did not know what to say. Fear, usually a coward, jumped up, full of anger. Shame looked at her cousin, who, when she felt that Shame was in such danger, put her hand to her sword, one that was terribly cutting. Its name was Suspicion-of-Ostentation, for it had been made of that material. When she had drawn it from its scabbard, it was clearer than any beryl. Fear had a shield made of the fear of danger, bordered with labor and suffering, and she exerted herself strongly to cut down Skillful Concealment. In order to avenge her cousin, she went to strike him such a blow on his shield that he could not save himself. Completely dazed, he faltered and then called on Boldness, who jumped in, for if Fear had got in a second blow, she would have worked great harm. Skillful Concealment would have been dead beyond recall if she had given him the second.

15511

Boldness was brave, hardy, and expert in deeds and in words. He had a good, well-burnished sword, made of the steel of fury. His shield had a great reputation; its name was Contempt-of-Death, and it was bordered with wild abandon to all dangers. He came at Fear and aimed to strike her down with a great and wicked blow. She let the blow come and covered herself, for she was skillful enough in the moves of that kind of fencing, and

15535

was well protected from his blow. Then she struck him so heavy
a blow that she beat him down until he was lying on the ground
and unprotected by any shield. When Boldness felt himself struck
low, he begged with joined hands and pleaded with her for the
mercy of God not to kill him, and Fear said that she would do as
he wished.

15556   Security said, "What will become of us? By God, Fear, you
will die here. Do the worst that you can. You have the habit
of the shakes, and you are a hundred times more cowardly than
a hare. Now that you have lost your cowardice, the devils have
made you so bold that you have set upon Boldness, who so loves
tourneying and knows so much about it, if he thought of it, that
no one ever knew more than he. Except in this instance, you have
never jousted since you walked upon the earth; otherwise you
have known nothing of the moves in fighting. Elsewhere, in all
other combats, you have fled or given up, you, who just now defended yourself here. You fled with Cacus when you saw Hercules
come running, with his club at his neck. You were quite completely
distracted then, and you put wings on his heels, wings such as he
had never had before. Cacus had stolen Hercules's cattle and
brought them together into his cave, a very deep one, by leading
them backward by the tail, so that no trace of them was found.
There your force was tested, and there you showed without doubt
that you were worth nothing in battle; and since you have not
frequented battle, you know little or nothing of it. So you must
not put up resistance but flee or give up those arms; otherwise you
must pay dearly, since you have dared match yourself with him."

15593   Security had a hard sword made of flight from every care, and
a shield of peace, unquestionably good, bordered all around with
agreement. She struck at Fear, thinking to kill her; Fear took
care to cover herself and interposed her shield, which met the
blow safely so that she was not hurt in any way. The blow
glanced and fell to the ground, and Fear returned her such a
blow on her shield that she was quite stunned, very close, in fact,
to being killed. So strongly was she struck that her sword and
shield flew from her hands. Do you know what Security did
then? To give an example to the others, she seized Fear around
the temples; Fear did the same to her, and thus they held each
other. All the others intervened. One seized another and joined

battle. I never saw such coupling in battle. The fight grew stronger, and the struggle was so fierce that there was never such an exchange of blows in any tournament. They came from here and they came from there; everyone called up his followers, and all ran up pell mell. I never saw snow or hail fall thicker than the blows flew. They all tore and smashed each other. You never saw such a fight with so many people thus engaged.

However—and I will not lie to you about it—the forces that were attacking the castle were constantly getting the worst of it. The God of Love was very much afraid that all of his people would be killed. He sent word by Openness and Sweet Looks for his mother to come and not to hold back for any reason. Meanwhile he took a truce of between ten and twelve whole days, or more or less; it could never be told for certain. Indeed he could have had truces forever if he had continued to ask for them, no matter how many wings were broken or who should violate it. But if he had known that he had the upper hand, he would never have taken a truce. And if the gatekeepers had not thought that the others would not break through them after they were left to themselves, they would never, perhaps, have given a truce in good faith, but instead would have become angry, no matter what appearance they showed. Nor would a truce have been made if Venus had interfered. However, it was necessary to make it in any case. One has to withdraw a little, either by truce or by some retreat, every time that one struggles in such a way that one cannot win, until one can more easily subdue his foe. 15627

The messengers left the army and traveled wisely until they came to Cytherea, where they were held in great honor. Cytherea is a mountain, within a wood on a plain, so high that no arbalest, no matter how strong or ready to fire, would fire an arrow or bolt up to it. There Venus, the inspiration of ladies, made her principal manor, and there she wished mainly to dwell. But if I described the entire situation I would perhaps bore you too much. Moreover, I could wear myself out, and therefore I want to pass over it briefly. 15659

Venus had gone down into the wood to go hunting in a valley, and the fair Adonis, her sweet friend with the lively heart, was with her. He was somewhat of a child, and was interested in hunting in the woods. A child he was, young and still growing, but 15675 very handsome and pleasing. Midday had passed a long time before, and each was tired from the hunt. They were enjoying the shade on the grass under a poplar, near a fishpond. Their dogs, tired out and panting from running, drank at the brook of the fishpond. They had leaned their bows, arrows, and quivers near them, and they diverted themselves pleasantly, listening to the birds in the branches all around them. After their sport, Venus held him embraced in her lap, and as she kissed him she taught him the way to hunt in the woods, as she was accustomed to practice it.

15699   "Friend," she said, "when your pack of dogs is ready and you go seeking the beast, if you find a beast that flees, chase it when it turns to flee; run after it boldly. But never let your horn be sounded against those that fiercely set their bodies to defend themselves. Against the bold be a lazy coward; for no bravery is safe against those in whom brave hearts are fixed. When a brave man fights another bold man, he wages a perilous battle.

15713   "Harts and hinds, he- and she-goats, reindeer and fallow deer, rabbits and hares—these are the ones I want you to chase; in such a hunt you will find comfort. But I forbid bears, wolves, lions, and wild boars. On my interdiction, do not hunt them. Such beasts defend themselves; they kill the dogs and cut them up, and very often make the hunters themselves fail of their designs. They have killed and wounded many of them. I will never have joy of you, but will be heavily burdened, if you do otherwise."

15727   Thus Venus lectured him, and in her scolding she begged him very much to remember her advice whenever he went hunting. Adonis, who cared little for what his sweetheart was saying, whether it was false or true, agreed to everything in order to have peace, since he cared nothing for her scolding. Whatever she did was worth little. Let her lecture as much as usual; if she goes away, she will never see him again. He did not believe her, and afterward he died; Venus never came to his help, since she was not present. Then the sorrowing girl wept for him, for afterward he hunted a wild boar that he thought to capture and strangle; but he neither captured nor tore him to pieces, for the boar defended himself like a fierce, proud beast. He shook his head at Adonis, sank his tusks into his groin, twisted his snout, and struck Adonis dead.

Fair lords, whatever happens to you, remember this example.   15751
You who do not believe your sweethearts, know that you commit
great folly; you should believe them all, for their sayings are as
true as history. If they swear, "We are all yours," believe what
they say as if it were the *paternoster*. Never go back on your belief
in them. If Reason comes, do not believe her at all. Even if she
brought a crucifix, believe her not one bit more than I do. If
Adonis had believed his sweetheart, his life would have grown
much longer.

Venus and Adonis played with one another and diverted them-   15765
selves when they pleased, and after their diversion returned to
Cytherea. The messengers, who had not delayed, told Venus point
by point, before she took off her clothes, everything of whatever
they had to say.

"By my faith," said Venus then, "it was a bad day for Jealousy   15772
when she held a castle or even a small house against my son. If I
don't set fire to the gatekeepers and their followers, or if they
don't give up the keys to the tower, I shouldn't value myself or
my bow or my torch as much as a block of wood."

Then she had her household called. She ordered them to harness   15779
her chariot, since she did not want to walk through the mud. The
chariot was beautiful; it was a four-wheeled one, starred with gold
and pearls. Instead of horses, there were six doves hitched in the
shafts; she kept them in her beautiful dovecote. Everything was
made ready, and Venus, who makes war on Chastity, mounted
into her chariot. None of the birds flew out of place; they beat
their wings and flew off. The air in front of them broke and parted,
and they came to the army. Having arrived, Venus got down from
her chariot immediately, and they ran toward her with great joy,
her son first. In his haste, he had already broken the truce before
it had expired; he never kept the code of an oath or a promise.

They set out to fight fiercely. One side attacked, the others de-   15801
fended themselves. The attackers set up catapults against the castle
and shot large pebbles of weighty supplications in order to break
down the walls, while the gatekeepers provided the walls with
defenses made of strong wattles full of denials, interlaced with
flexible wands that they had with great brutality cut from Resistance's hedge. The attackers fired at them barbed arrows feathered
with large promises, either of services or gifts, made in order to

get quick rewards, for no wood will ever go into them that is not made entirely of promises; the arrows were tipped firmly with points made of oaths and assurances. The defenders were not slow to protect themselves, but covered themselves with shields that were strong and hard, neither too heavy nor too light, of wood like that of the wattles that Resistance gathered in his hedges, so that it was no good shooting at them.

15826 As the matter was going thus, Love drew toward his mother, reported his entire situation to her, and begged her to help him.

15830 "May I perish in a miserable death," she said, "that may take me straightway, if I ever let Chastity dwell in any woman alive, and much good may Jealousy get from her efforts! We are often put to great trouble on her account. Fair son, swear likewise that all the men will leap along by your paths."

15838 "Certainly, my lady," he replied, "willingly. Not one of them will be relieved of doing so. Never, at least in truth, will men be called worthy unless they love or have loved. It is a great sorrow when there live men who avoid the diversions of love, provided that they can maintain them. May they come to a bad end! I hate them so much that if I could I would destroy them all. I complain of them and I always shall, nor shall I dissimulate my complaint. I shall complain like one who wants to harm them in every case as much as I can until I am so revenged that an end is put to their pride or they are all condemned. It was an evil hour in which they were ever born of Adam when they thought to trouble me thus. May their hearts break in their bodies for wishing to destroy my diversions. Certainly anyone who indeed wanted to beat me, let alone break in my head with four pikes, could not do worse to me, and I am not mortal. But I now feel such anger that if I could have been mortal I would have died of my suffering. If my games go begging, I have lost whatever I have that is worth anything except my body, my clothing, my chaplet, and my arms and armor. If these men don't have the power, at least they should have enough chagrin to bend their hearts to sorrow if they have to abandon my games. Where can one seek a life better than being in the arms of his sweetheart?"

15877 Then Venus and Love made their oath to the army and, to keep it more firmly, they pledged, instead of relics, their quivers and arrows, their bows, darts, and torches, and they said, "We do not ask for better relics for this purpose, no matter how much some could please us. If we forswear these, we shall never again be believed."

They swore by no other thing, and the barons believed them as much as if they had sworn by the Trinity, because they swore the truth.

15887

9

NATURE'S CONFESSION

15891 When they had made this oath so that all could hear it, Nature, who thinks on the things that are enclosed beneath the heavens, was entered within her forge, where she would put all her attention on forging individual creatures to continue the species. For individuals make the species live so that Death cannot catch up with them, no matter how much she runs after them. Nature goes so close to Death that when Death with her mace kills those among the individual creatures that she finds due her (there are some things corruptible that do not fear death at all, but that perish away in any case, that use themselves up in time and decay, and nourish other things)—when Death thinks to exterminate them all, she cannot bind them all down together. When she seizes one here, another escapes there; when she has killed the father, the son remains, or the daughter or mother, for they flee before Death when they see the one already dead. Then in turn these must die, no matter how well they can run, and no medicine or religious vow

15922 is worth anything. Then up jump nieces and nephews to flee away as fast as their feet can carry them, one of them to the carol, another to the church, another to a school, others to their businesses, to crafts that they have learned, or to the delights of wine, food, and bed. Others, to flee more quickly before Death forces them, mount great chargers with all their gilded stirrups. One trusts his life to wood and flees by sea in a boat; he guides his ship, oars, and sails by the sight of the stars. Another, humbling himself with a vow, assumes a cloak of hypocrisy with which he covers his thoughts as he flees until his thoughts appear in his outward deeds.

15943 All who live flee in this way; all would willingly escape death. Death, who has colored her face black, runs after them until she catches up with them. This is a very cruel hunt. Everyone flees and Death hunts them down, for ten or twenty, thirty or forty, fifty, sixty, or seventy years, indeed eighty, ninety, or a hundred; then she goes along destroying whatever she is holding. If they can pass along beyond this age, she runs after them without getting tired until she holds them in her bonds, in spite of all the physicians. And we have not seen any of the physicians themselves escape from her, not Hippocrates or Galen, no matter how good physicians they were. Rhases, Constantine, and Avicenna have left her their skins. And again, nothing can rescue those who cannot run so fast. Thus Death, never satisfied, greedily swallows up individuals. By land and sea she follows them until in the end she buries them all. But since she cannot keep them all together, she cannot finish by destroying the species entirely, so well can the individuals flee from her. For if only one remained, the form common to the entire species would live on. And in the case of the phoenix it seems that there cannot be two of them together.

There is always a single phoenix that lives, up until its end, for 15977 five hundred years. At the last it makes a large, full fire of spices where it sits down and is burned. Thus it brings about the destruction of its body; but because it keeps its form, another phoenix returns from its ashes, no matter how it was burned. It may possibly be the very same phoenix that Nature thus brings back to life. Nature is so fecund for her species that she would lose her entire being if she did not cause the phoenix to be reborn. Thus, if Death devours the phoenix, the phoenix still remains alive; if she had devoured a thousand, the phoenix would remain. It is the phoenix in its ideal common form that Nature reshapes into individuals; and this common form would be entirely lost if the next phoenix were not left alive. All things under the circle of the moon have this very same mode of being, so that if one of them can remain, its species so lives in it that Death can never catch up with it.

But when Nature, sweet and compassionate, sees that envious 16005 Death and Corruption come together to put to destruction whatever they find within her forge, she continues always to hammer and forge and always to renew the individuals by means of new generation. When she can bring no other counsel to her work, she cuts copies in such letters that she gives them true forms in coins of different monies. From these, Art makes her models, but she does not make her forms as true. However, with very attentive care, she kneels before Nature and like a truant beggar, poor in knowledge and force, she begs and requests and asks of her. She struggles to follow her so that Nature may wish to teach her how with her ability she may properly subsume all creatures in her figures. She also watches how Nature works, for she would like very much to perform such a work, and she imitates her like a monkey. But her sense is so bare and feeble that she cannot make

16035   living things, no matter how newborn they seem. For Art, no matter how hard she tries, with great study and great effort, to make anything whatever, no matter what shapes they have—whether she paints, dyes, forges, or shapes armed knights in battle, on handsome chargers all covered with arms, and worked in blue, yellow, or green or variegated with other colors if you want to mix them; or beautiful birds in green groves; or the fishes of all waters; all the wild beasts that feed in their woods; all plants, all the flowers that little boys and girls go to gather in the spring woods when they see them in bloom and leaf; tame birds and domestic animals; balls, dances, and farandoles with beautiful and elegantly dressed ladies, well portrayed and well represented, either in metal, wood, wax, or any other material, in pictures or on walls, with the ladies holding handsome bachelors, also well represented and portrayed, in their nets—even so, Art, for all her representations and skillful touches, will never make them go by themselves,

16065   love, move, feel, and talk. She may learn so much about alchemy that she may dye all the metals in color—for she could kill herself before she could transmute the species, even if she didn't go to the extent of taking them back to their prime matter—but she may work as long as she lives and never catch up with Nature. And if she did want to exert herself until she knew how to take them back to it, she would still perhaps lack the knowledge of how, when she made her elixir, to arrive at that suitable proportion of elements that should result in the form, a proportion that distinguishes their substances among themselves by their individual differences, just as, if one knows how to arrive at a result, it appears in the definition.

16083   Nevertheless, it is a notable thing that alchemy is a true art. Whoever worked wisely in it would find great miracles; for, however it goes with species, the individuals, at least, when they undergo intelligent operations, are changeable into many forms. They can so alter their appearances by various transformations that this change puts them into entirely different species and robs them of the original species. Do we not see how those who are masters of glass-blowing create from fern, by means of a simple process of purification, both ash and glass? And neither is the glass fern, nor does the fern remain glass. Again, when lightning and thunder come, one can see stones fall from the clouds, stones which did not ascend as stones. Those who understand can know the cause which brings such matter into the strange species. These are transmuted species, those whose individuals are alienated from them in both substance and shape, through Art in the case of the fern, ash, and glass, through Nature in the case of the stones.

One could do the same thing with metals if one knew how to carry the operation through to its conclusion, to take away the impurities from the impure metals and put them into pure forms according to their affinities, one resembling another. They are all of one matter, however Nature may attire them, for all are born, in various ways beneath their earthly appearances, from sulfur and from quicksilver. Thus the book avows. He then who knew how to make himself subtle enough to prepare the spirits so that they had the force to enter into bodies and not fly out again once they had entered, as long as they found the bodies cleansed and the sulfur, for white or red color, not burning—such a man, when he knew how to work in this way, would have his will with metals. For those who are masters of alchemy cause pure gold to be born from pure silver. They add weight and color to it with things that cost scarcely anything. They also make precious stones, shining and desirable, from pure gold; and they deprive other metals of their forms, to change them into pure silver, by means of white liquids, penetrating and pure. But those who work with sophistry would never do this. They work just as they will live; they will never catch up with Nature.

Nature, who is highly ingenious, claimed that, however attentive she was to the works that she loved so much, she was tired and sorrowful, and she was weeping so profoundly that no heart with any love or pity at all could look at her and hold back from weeping; for she felt such sorrow in her heart over a deed of which she repented that she wanted to abandon her works and cease all her thought, provided only that she might know that she had permission from her master. Her heart impelled and pressed her to go and make this request of him.

I would willingly describe her to you, but my sense is not equal

16113

16149

16165

to it. My sense! What have I said? That's the least one could say.
No human sense would show her, either vocally or in writing. Even
if it were Plato or Aristotle, Algus, Euclid, or Ptolemy, who now
have such great reputations for having been good writers, their
wits would be so useless, if they dared undertake the task, that they
could not do so. Nor could Pygmalion fashion her; Parrasius could
work at the job in vain; indeed Apelles, whom I call a very good
painter, could never describe her beauty, no matter how long he
had to live; and neither Miro nor Polycletus could ever attain
the skill to do so. Even Zeuxis could not achieve such a form
with his beautiful painting; it was he who, in order to make an
image in the temple, used as models five of the most beautiful
girls that one could seek and find in the whole land. They remained standing quite naked before him so that he could use each
one as a model if he found any defect in another, either in body
16196   or in limb. Tully recalls the story to us in this way in the book
of his *Rhetoric*, a very authentic body of knowledge. But Nature
is of such great beauty that Zeuxis could do nothing in this connection, no matter how well he could represent or color his likeness.
Zeuxis! Not all the masters that Nature ever caused to be born
could do so, for supposing that they grasped the whole of her
beauty and that they all wanted to waste their time in such a repre-
sentation, they could sooner wear out their hands than represent
such very great beauty. No one except God could do so. Therefore
I would willingly at least have tried if I had been able; indeed
I would have described her to you if I could have and had known
how; I have even wasted my time over it until, like a presumptuous fool, I have used up all of my sense, a hundred times more
than you suspect. I made too great a presumption when I ever set
my intent on achieving so very high a task. I found that the great
beauty that I value so highly was so noble and of such great worth
that I could break my heart before I might embrace it with my
thought, no matter how much work I might devote to it, or before
I even dared say a word about it, no matter how much I thought.
16229   I am tired out from thinking, and therefore I will now say no more
about it since, when I have thought on her more, she is so beautiful
that I know no more to say of her. For when God, the immeasurably beautiful, put beauty into Nature, he made of her a fountain

always flowing and always full, from which all beauty proceeds; but no one knows any bottom or bound to it. It is therefore right that I make no tale either about her body or her face, so pleasing and beautiful that no lily at the beginning of May, no rose on its twig nor snow on a branch is so red nor so white. Thus should I pay homage when I dare compare her to anything, since her beauty and worth cannot be understood by men.

When Nature heard the oath of Venus and Love, there was a very great lightening of the deep sorrow that she suffered. She considered herself deceived and said: "Alas! What have I done? I do not repent of the things that have happened to me since the time when this fair world began, except for one thing alone, in which I misbehaved most wickedly and for which I consider myself a stupid fool. And when I look at my stupidity, it is very right that I repent of it. Wretched fool! Sorrowful wretch! A hundred thousand times wretched! Where will faith now be found? Have I used my labors well? Am I indeed out of my mind? I always thought to serve my friends, to deserve their gratitude, and I have given all my labor to the advancement of my enemies. My good nature has ruined me."

Then she addressed her priest, who was celebrating a service in her chapel. It was not a new Mass, for he had always done this service from the time when he was a priest of the church. In a loud voice, instead of any other Mass, before the goddess Nature, the priest, who was in full agreement, recited in audience the representative shapes of all corruptible things that he had written in his book, just as Nature had given them to him.

"Genius," she said, "fair priest, the god and master of places, who set all things at work according to their properties and who achieve your task well just as is appropriate to each place, I want to confess to you of a folly that I have committed and from which I am not withdrawn, but repentance constrains me very much."

"My lady, queen of the world, toward whom every worldly thing bows, if there is anything that troubles you so much that as a result you go around repentant, or which it even pleases you to tell, whatever the subject may be, of joy or sorrow, you can indeed confess to me entirely at your leisure whatever you want; and at your pleasure," said Genius, "I wish to give to it all the advice that

16249

16272

16285

16295

I can. And if there is anything to keep silent, I shall certainly keep your affair secret. And if you need absolution I should not deprive you of it. But cease your weeping."

16312   "Certainly," she said, "it is no wonder, fair Genius, if I weep."

16314   "In any case, lady," he said, "I advise you to wish to abandon this weeping, if you indeed want to confess, and to be very attentive to the subject that you have undertaken to tell me. I believe that the misdeed is a great one, for I well know that a noble heart is not moved for a small thing. He who dares trouble you is a great fool.

16323   "But it is also true, without fail, that a woman is easily inflamed with wrath. Virgil himself bears witness—and he knew a great deal about their difficulties—that no woman was ever so stable that she might not be varied and changeable. And thus she remains a very irritable animal. Solomon says that there was never a head more cruel than the head of a serpent and nothing more wrathful than a woman, and that nothing, he says, has so much malice. Briefly, there is so much vice in woman that no one can recount her perverse ways in rhyme or in verse. Titus Livius, who knew well what the habits and ways of women are, says that women are so easily deceived, so silly and of such pliable natures that with their ways entreaties are not worth as much as blandishments. Again, Scripture says elsewhere that the basis of all feminine vice is avarice.

16347   "Whoever tells his secrets to his wife makes of her his mistress. No man born of woman, unless he is drunk or demented, should reveal anything to a woman that should be kept hidden, if he doesn't want to hear it from someone else. No matter how loyal or good-natured she is, it would be better to flee the country than tell a woman something that should be kept silent. He should never do any secret deed if he sees a woman come, for even if there is bodily danger, you may be sure that she will tell it, no matter how long she may wait. Even if no one asks her anything about it, she will certainly tell it without any unusual coaxing;

16366   for nothing would she keep silent. To her thinking she would be dead if the secret did not jump out of her mouth, even if she is in danger or reproached. And if the one who told her is such a person that, after she knows, dares strike her or beat her just once, not three or four times, then no sooner than he touches her will she reproach him with his secret, and she will do so right out in the open. He who confides in a woman loses her. And do you know

what the wretch who confides in her does to himself? He binds his
hands and cuts his throat; for if, just one single time he ever dares
grouch at her or scold her or get angry, he puts his life in such
danger—if he deserved death for his deed—that she will have
him hanged by the neck, if the judges can catch him, or secretly
murdered by friends. Such is the unfortunate harbor at which he
has arrived.

"But when the fool goes to bed at night and lies near his wife 16389
in his bed, he neither can nor dare be at rest. Perhaps he has done
something or wishes to commit some murder or some other unlawful act as a result of which he is afraid for his life if he is caught;
so he turns and complains and sighs. His wife, who sees very well
that he is uneasy, draws him toward her, caresses him, embraces him
and kisses him, and nestles herself between his breasts.

" 'Sir,' she says, 'what news? Who makes you sigh thus and 16402
jump and turn? Here we two are now alone by ourselves, the
only people in this whole world, you the first and I the second,
who should love each other best with hearts that are loyal, pure,
and without bitterness. I well remember that I closed our chamber
door with my own hand; the walls are a half-fathom thick, and I
value them more for that reason; the rafters too are so high that
we shall be quite safe in that direction. And we are far from the
windows and the place is therefore much safer as far as revealing
our secrets is concerned; furthermore no man living has the power
to open them, any more than the wind can, without breaking them.
In short this place has no ear-hole whatever, and no one can hear
your voice, except for me alone. Therefore I beg you piteously by
our love that you have enough confidence in me to tell me what
it is.'

" 'Lady,' he says, 'may God be my witness, not for anything 16429
would I tell it, for it is not a thing to tell.'

" 'Aha!' she says, 'my fair sweet lord, do you suspect something 16432
of me, your faithful wife? When we came together in marriage,
Jesus Christ, whom we have not found mean or stingy of His
grace, made one flesh of us two, and when we have only one flesh
by the right of common law, there can be only a single heart on the
left side of one flesh. Our hearts are then both one; you have mine
and I yours. You can then have nothing in yours that mine should
not know. Therefore I pray you to tell it to me both as a reward

and because I deserve it, for I shall never have joy in my heart until I know what it is. And if you don't want to tell it to me, I see well that you are deceiving me, and I know with what kind of heart you love me, you who call me sweet lover, sweet sister, and sweet companion. For whom are you peeling this chestnut? Certainly if you don't reveal it to me, it appears indeed that you are betraying me, for I have confided myself to you so much since you married me that I have told you everything that I have en-

16463 closed within my heart. And for you I left father and mother, uncle, nephew, sister and brother, and all my friends and relatives, as is very clear. I have certainly made a very bad exchange when I find you so distant toward me. I love you more than anyone living, and it's all not worth a shallot to me. You think that I would misbehave toward you to the extent of telling your secrets, but that is a thing that could not happen. By Jesus Christ, the celestial king, who better than I should protect you? May it please you at least to consider, if you know anything about loyalty, the pledge that you have of my body. Doesn't this pledge suffice you? Do you want a better hostage? Then I am worse than all

16483 others if you dare not tell me your secrets. I see all these other women who are sufficiently mistresses of their houses so that their husbands confide in them enough to tell them all their secrets. They all take counsel with their wives when they lie awake together in their beds, and they confess themselves privately so that there is nothing left to them to tell. Truth to tell, they even do so more often than they do to the priest. I know it well from them themselves, for many times I have heard them; they have revealed to me everything, whatever they have heard and seen and even all that they think. In this way they purge and empty themselves. However, I am not the same sort. None of them is comparable to me, for I am no loose, quarrelsome gossip, and at least, however it may be with my soul and God, I am an honest woman in my body. You have never heard it said that I have committed any adultery unless the fools who told you such a tale invented it maliciously. Have you tested me well? Have you found me false?

16511 " 'Next, fair sir, consider how you keep your faith with me. Certainly you made a bad mistake when you put a ring on my finger and pledged your faith to me. I don't know how you dared do so. If you dare not confide in me, who made you marry me?

" 'Therefore I beg that your faith may be safe with me at least 16519
this time, and I assure you loyally, and promise and pledge and
swear, by blessed Saint Peter, that this will be a thing buried under
stone. Now certainly I would be a big fool if from my mouth came
any speech that would shame or do harm to you. I would be
shaming my own family, which I have never defamed on any
occasion, and myself first of all. There is a customary saying that is
true without fail: "He who is fool enough to cut off his nose dishonors his face forever." Tell me, and may God help you, what
troubles your heart. If not, you will have me dead.'

"Then she uncovers her chest and head, kisses him again and 16537
again and between the feints at kissing she weeps many tears over
him. Then the unfortunate wretch tells her his great sorrow and
shame and with his words hangs himself. When he has said it he
repents; but once a speech has taken wing it cannot be called back.
Then he begs her to keep quiet, for he is more uneasy than he
had ever been before, when his wife knew nothing about it. She
in turn tells him without fail that she will keep quiet, no matter
what happens. But what does the wretch think he can do? He
cannot keep his own tongue silent. Is he going to try now to restrain another's? What result does he think to arrive at? Now the
lady sees that she has the upper hand, and she knows that at no
time whatever will he dare get angry at her or grumble at her
about anything. Since she has something definite to work with,
she will make him keep mum and quiet. Perhaps she will hold to
her agreement until they get angry with each other. She will have
his heart in balance still more if she waits that long, but she will
scarcely ever wait so much that it will not be a great burden to him.

"If anyone loved men he would preach this sermon to them 16569
and would do well to say it in all places so that every man might
see himself mirrored in it and be drawn back from his great danger.
But such a man could perhaps be displeasing to the women, with
their gossip. Truth, however, does not seek corners.

"Fair lords, protect yourselves from women if you love your 16577
bodies and souls. At least never go to work so badly that you reveal
the secrets that you keep hidden inside your hearts. Fly, fly, fly, fly,
fly, my children; I advise you and urge you without deception or
guile to fly from such an animal. Note these verses of Virgil, but know
them in your heart so that they cannot be drawn out therefrom: O

child who gather flowers and fresh, clean strawberries, here lies the cold serpent in the grass. Fly, child, for he poisons and envenoms every person that comes near. O child, seeking along the earth for flowers and new strawberries, the evil chilling serpent, who goes about here hiding himself, the malicious adder who covers up and conceals his venom, and hides it under the tender grass until he can pour it out to deceive and harm you; O child,

16605 give thought to avoiding him. Don't let yourself be seized if you want to escape death, for it is such a venomous animal in body, tail, and head, that if you approach it you will find yourself completely poisoned, for it treacherously corrodes and pierces whatever it reaches, without remedy. No treacle may cure the burning of that venom. No herb or root is worth anything against it. The only medicine is flight.

16617 "However, I do not say, and it was never my intent to say, that you should not hold women dear or that you should flee from them and not lie with them. Instead I recommend that you value them highly and improve their lot with reason. See that they are well clothed and well shod, and labor always to serve and honor them in order to continue your kind so that death does not destroy it. But never trust them so much that you tell them anything to keep quiet about. Certainly allow them to go and come, to keep up the household and the house if they know how to take care of it; or if it happens by chance that they know how to buy or sell they can busy themselves with such activity; or if they know any trade let them do it if they need to; and let them know about the things that are open and that don't need to be hidden. But if you abandon yourself so much that you give them too much power, you will repent later, when you feel their malice. Even Scripture cries out to us that if the woman has lordship she opposes her husband when he wants to say or do anything. Take care in any case that the house does not go to ruin, for one shows to better advantage when it is well kept. He who is wise takes care of his things.

16653 "You, too, who have your sweethearts, be good companions to them. It is a good thing for each of them to know enough about matters of mutual concern. But if you are wise and intelligent you will keep quiet when you hold them in your arms and hug them and kiss them. Stay still, still, still. Think about holding your tongue, for nothing can come to any conclusion when they share secrets, so proud and haughty are they, with such corrosive, venomous, and harmful tongues. But when fools come to be held in their arms and hug and kiss them in the games that are so pleasing to them, then nothing can be hidden from them. There the secrets are revealed; there husbands reveal themselves and afterward they are sorry and chagrined. All of them reveal their thoughts except the wise men who have pondered well.

"Malicious Dalila, through her poisonous flattery, cut off Samson's hair with her scissors as she held him softly close, sleeping in her lap. As a result, this man who was so valiant, worthy, strong, and fierce in battle, lost all his strength when she thus sheared off his locks. She revealed all his secrets, which the fool, not knowing how to hide anything, had told her. But I don't want to tell you any more examples; one can very well suffice you for all of them. Even Solomon speaks of it, and because I love you I will tell you quickly what he says: 'In order to flee from danger and reproach, guard the gates of your mouth against her who sleeps in your bosom.' Whoever hold men dear should preach this sermon so that they may guard against women and never confide in them. 16677

"Now I have not said these things on your account, for without contradiction you have always been loyal and steadfast. Even Scripture affirms that God has given you such pure sense that you are wise without end." 16701

Thus Genius comforted her and exhorted her by any means that he could to abandon her sorrow entirely. For no one, he said, could overcome anything in sorrow and sadness; sorrow, he said, is a thing that wounds and that profits nothing. When he had said what he wanted to, without making any longer plea, he sat down upon a seat placed next to his altar; and Nature immediately kneeled down before the priest. However, it was undoubtedly true that she could not forget her sorrow; and he, for his part, did not want to plead with her any longer, since he would have wasted all his trouble. Instead he kept quiet and listened to the lady, who, with great devotion and weeping many tears, made her confession. I bring it to you here in writing, word for word, just as she said it. 16707

"When that most fair God who abounds in beauty created the world of beauty whose fair form, pondered upon forever in eternity, He carried within His thought before it ever existed outside, nothing ever moved Him to do so except His own sweet-tempered 16729 will, broad, courteous, free of envy, the fountain of all life; He took His exemplar and whatever was necessary from His thought, for if He had wished to seek elsewhere, He would have found neither heaven nor earth nor anything with which He might help Himself, since nothing existed outside. He in whom there can be

16747 no lack made everything spring from nothing. In the beginning He created only a mass that was in confusion, without order or distinction, and then divided it into parts that afterward were not split up. He enumerated everything by number, and He knows how many there are altogether. By rational measures He completed all their shapes and made them round so that they might move better and contain more, as they were to be mobile and capacious. He put them into places that He saw were suitable for them; the light ones flew on high, the heavy went to the center, and those of medium weight to the middle. Thus the locations were ordered with true measurement, with right spacing.

16768 "When God Himself, through His grace, had placed His other creatures according to His plans, He so honored and valued me that He established me as chambermaid. He lets me serve there and will let me do so as long as it shall be His will. I ask no other right, but I thank Him for loving me so much that He, a great lord, should so value me, a very poor girl, that He has taken me as chambermaid in so large and beautiful a house. As chambermaid! Certainly indeed as constable and vicar, positions of which I am not worthy except through His benign will.

16785 "Thus, since God has honored me so much, I keep the beautiful golden chain that binds the four elements, all of them bowing before my face. And He gave me all the things that are enclosed within the chain and commanded me to guard them and to continue their forms, and He wanted them all to obey me and learn my rules so that they might never forget them, but hold them and keep them always to eternity. In truth, things commonly do so; all give their attention to this task except one creature alone.

16801 "I should not complain of heaven; it turns forever without hesitation and carries with it in its polished circle all the twinkling stars, powerful over all precious stones. It goes along diverting the world; beginning its westward journey, it sets out from the east and does not stop turning backward, carrying all the wheels that ascend against it to retard its movement. But they cannot hold it back enough that it ever, on their account, runs so slowly that it does not take 36,000 years to come exactly, with an entire circle completed, to the point where God first created it. It follows the extent of the path of the zodiac with the great heavenly circle, which turns on it as on a form. It is the heaven that runs so exactly that there is no error whatever in its course; and therefore those who found no error whatever there called it *aplanos*, for *aplanos* in Greek means the same as 'a thing without error' in French. This other heaven that I speak of to you here is not seen by men, but reason proves it thus to him who finds the demonstrations there.

"I do not complain of the seven planets, each of them bright, shining, and clean, throughout the whole of its course. It seems to men that the moon may indeed not be clean and pure, because in some places it shows up dark. But it is because of its double nature that it appears opaque and cloudy in some places, shining in one part and ceasing to shine in another, because it is both clear and opaque. Thus what makes its light fail is the fact that the clear part of its substance cannot reflect the rays that the sun throws out toward it; instead they pass on through and beyond. But the opaque part, which can resist the rays well and overcome its light, shows the light. In order to make this matter better understood, one can very well, instead of a gloss, give an example in a brief word, the better to clarify the text. 16833

"When rays pass through transparent glass, there is nothing opaque, in front or behind, that may reflect them; thus transparent glass cannot show shapes, since the eye-beams cannot encounter there anything that may retain them, by which the form might come back to the eyes. But if one took lead, or something dense that does not allow rays to pass through, and placed oneself on the side opposite to that from which the sun's rays come, the form would return immediately. Of if there were some polished object that could reflect light, and it were opaque of its own nature or through some other material, it would return an image, I know well. In the same way the moon, in its clear part, in which it re-sembles its sphere, cannot retain the rays by which light might come to it; instead they pass beyond. But the opaque part, which does not let them pass beyond, reflects them back strongly instead, and makes the moon have light. Therefore the moon appears light in parts and seems dark in parts. 16855

16881   "The dark part of the moon represents to us the shape of a very marvelous animal, a serpent that keeps his head always bent toward the west and whose tail finishes toward the east. On his back he carries an upright tree that extends its branches toward the east but that in doing so turns them upside down. On this upside-down arrangement dwells a man, leaning on his arms, who has pointed both his feet and thighs toward the west, as it appears by the looks of them.

16895   "These planets perform a very good function. Each of them works so well that none of the seven is delayed in any way. They turn through their twelve houses and run through all of their steps and remain just as they should. To perform their task, they turn by a motion contrary to that of the heaven and each day occupy the positions of the heaven that they should in order to complete their circles. Then they begin again without end, slowing down the speed of the heaven so as to give help to the elements; for if the heaven could run freely, nothing could live under it.

16911   "The beautiful sun that gives rise to the day—for it is the cause of all brightness—keeps its place in the middle like a king, all flaming with rays, and has its house in the middle of them. It is not without reason that God the beautiful, the strong, the wise, wanted his dwelling to be there; for if it had run lower, there is nothing that would not have died of heat, while if it had run higher, the cold would have condemned everything. There the sun divides its brightness among the stars and the moon and makes them appear so beautiful that in the evening, when Night sits down to her table, she makes of them her candles so as to be less frightful before her husband Acheron, whose heart is afflicted with chagrin for this reason. He would have preferred to be with a Night who was completely black, without any light, as they had been together before, when they first had known one another. It was then, in their wild abandon, that Night conceived the three
16939   Furies, the cruel, fierce girls who are justices in hell. Nevertheless Night thinks, when she looks at herself in her pantry, her storeroom, or her cellar, that she would be too hideous and pale and would have too dark a face if she didn't have the joyous brightness of the heavenly bodies, reflecting the rays of light, shining through the darkened air as they turn in their spheres just as God the father established them. There they create among themselves

their harmonies, the causes of melodies and of differences of tone which we put together in concord in all sorts of song. There is nothing that does not sing according to their music.

"They also, through their influences, change the accidents and substances of things that are beneath the moon. Through their common diversity clear elements become dark, and they also make the dark ones clear. They make cold and hot, dry and moist, enter into every body as into a container, to hold their parts together. Although the elements may struggle against each other, the heavenly bodies go about binding them together. Thus they make peace among the four enemies when they put them together in suitable proportions, with dispositions according to reason, in order to form in the best shape all things that I form. And if it happens that they may be worse, that is because of the defect in their materials. 16955

"But no matter how great care one may know how to take, the peace among the elements will never be so good that heat may not suck up humidity and, without stopping, destroy and eat it up from day to day, until the death that is due them by my just establishment may come, if death does not come to them in some other way. It may be hastened for some other reason before the humidity is destroyed; for although no one, with any medicine that one may find, or anything with which one may know how to anoint oneself, can prolong the life of the body, I know well that each one can easily shorten it. Many, indeed, shorten their lives, before their moisture fails, by getting drowned or hanged or by undertaking some dangerous adventure in which they get burned or buried before they can flee. Or they get themselves destroyed through some accident brought about foolishly by their own deeds, or through their private enemies, who have such false and wicked hearts that they have put many guiltless people to death by the sword or by poison. Or they fall into sicknesses through bad management of their lives—through sleeping too much or staying up too late, resting or working too much, or getting too fat or too thin; for one can sin in all these respects, in fasting too long, in having too many delights or wanting too much discomfort, in enjoying oneself too much or sorrowing to excess, in drinking or eating too much, or in changing one's characteristics too much. These situations show up particularly when 16975 16991 people suddenly get too hot or feel too cold; then, later, they repent of their excesses. Or they change their habits, and many people have been killed when they changed their habits suddenly; many have given themselves a lot of trouble and many have killed themselves, for sudden changes of this sort are very harmful to Nature, and as a result they make me waste all my pains to lead

17027 them to a natural death. And although they commit great wrongs in opposing me by bringing about such deaths, they still give me a great burden in any case when they stop short on their road like surrendered captives, conquered by the misfortune of death; and they could easily protect themselves from death if they wanted to hold back from the excesses and follies which shorten their lives before they have attained and taken the good that I have prepared for them.

17039 "Empedocles took poor care of himself. He looked in his books so long and loved philosophy so much, full, perhaps, of melancholy, that he never feared death but threw himself alive into the fire. With feet joined he jumped into Etna in order to show that those who want to fear death are indeed of weak mind. Therefore he wanted to throw himself in voluntarily. He valued neither honey nor sugar but chose his own sepulchre there among the boiling sulfur.

17052 "Origen, who cut off his testicles, also valued me lightly when he cut them with his own hands so that he could serve the religious ladies with devotion and so that there would be no suspicion that he might ever lie with them.

17059 "Men say that the fates had decreed such deaths for them and had set up such destinies from the times when they were conceived. And since they took their births under such constellations that by strict necessity, without any other possibility, they have no power to avoid such a death, however much it should grieve them, they must accept it. But I know very well that it is quite true that however the heavens work to give them those natural ways that incline them to do those things that drew them to this end, obedient to the material that goes about to bend their hearts in this way, even so, they can, through teaching, through clean, pure nourishment, by following good company that is endowed with sense and virtues, or through certain remedies, provided that they are good and pure, and also through goodness of understanding, they can, I say, obtain another result, provided that, like intelligent people, they have bridled their natural ways. For when a man or woman wants to turn his spirit away from its own nature, against his good and against right, Reason can turn him back, provided that he believes in her alone. Then the situation will go in another way. It can indeed be in another way, whatever the heavenly bodies do, and they certainly have very great power as long as they don't go against Reason. But they have no power against Reason, for every wise man knows that they are not the masters of Reason, nor did they bring her to birth.

"But to solve the question of how predestination and the divine foreknowledge, full of all providence, can exist with free will is a difficult thing to explain to lay people. Anyone who wanted to undertake the task would find it hard to make it understood, even if he had solved the arguments brought up in opposition. But it is true, whatever it may seem to the lay, that predestination and free will accord very well together. Otherwise those who lead good lives should never have any recompense for them, while those who take trouble to sin should never have any punishment, if it were true that everything occurred by necessity. He who wanted to do good could not wish otherwise, and he who wanted to do evil could not withdraw from it. Whether he wished to or not, he would do it, since it would be his destiny. In fact, anyone could say, in arguing the question, that God is not deceived by the deeds that He has foreknown, and that they undoubtedly will happen just as they exist in His knowledge. But He knows when they will happen, how, and what result they will work toward, for if it could be otherwise than that God knew it beforehand, He would not be all-powerful, all-good, or all-knowing, nor would He be sovereign, the fair, sweet, the first of everything. He would not know what we do, or, along with men, who live in doubtful belief, He would believe without the certainty of knowledge. To attribute such an error to God would be to commit the devil's work; no man who wanted to enjoy Reason should hear it. Hence, when man's will exerts itself in any direction, he must perforce, in whatever he does, perform it, think, say, wish, or obtain it in just that way. Then the thing that cannot be deflected is destined. It seems that it should follow from this argument that nothing may have free will.

17101

17119

17155   "And if destinies bound all things that happen, as this argument proves by the appearance that it finds in it, then what reward should God have in mind for him who works well or what punishment for him who works badly, when neither of them can do otherwise? Even if one had sworn the opposite, he couldn't do anything else. Then God would not be doing justice in rewarding good and punishing vice, for how could he do so? If one wanted to consider the question well, there would be neither virtue nor vice, nor celebration of the mass in the chalice of suffering. To pray to God would be worth nothing if vice and virtue were lacking. Or if God did justice, in the absence of vice and virtue, it would not be just; instead, He would declare usurers, thieves, and murderers acquitted. He would weigh all, the good and the hypocrites, with an equal weight. Thus those who exerted themselves to love God would be shamed indeed if in the end they lacked His love. And they would have to lack it, since the argument comes to the conclusion that no one could obtain the grace of God through good works.

17187   "But He is without doubt just, for all goodness shines in Him; otherwise there would be a defect in Him in whom there is no lack. Then He returns either gain or loss to each according to his deserts. Then all works are recompensed and the destinies annihilated, at least as laymen feel, who ascribe all things to destiny, good, evil, false, and true, as necessary occurrences; and free will, which such people go around treating so badly, is seen to exist.

17201   "But suppose that someone wanted to raise another objection in order to glorify the destinies and shatter free will. Many have been tempted to do so. About some possible thing, however unlikely, he would say, at least when it happened, 'If anyone had foreseen it and said, "Such a thing will be, and nothing will deflect it," wouldn't he have told the truth? Thus this would be necessity. For it follows, from the interchangeability of truth and necessity, that if the thing is true, then it is necessary. Hence a thing must perforce be when it is constrained by necessity.'

17219   "How could one who wanted to reply escape from this reasoning? Certainly he would be speaking about something true, but not therefore necessary. For although he may have foreseen it, the thing did not happen as a necessary occurrence, but only as a possible one. If one examines the case well, it is conditional necessity, not simple necessity. Thus the reasoning is not worth a wimple. If a thing to come is true then it is necessary, for such contingent truth cannot be interchanged with simple necessity, as can simple truth. Such reasoning cannot avail to destroy free will.

"On the other hand, if one were to follow this logic, he should never seek people's advice on anything or do any work on earth; for why should one get advice or do any work if everything were predestined and predetermined? There would never be more or less, and there could not be any better or worse, because of any advice or manual labor, whether it was a thing born or to be born, done or to be done, something to be said or something to keep silent about. No one would need to study; he would know without study whatever arts he will know if he studies with great labor for his whole life. But this idea is not to be conceded: one should deny completely then that the works of humanity happen by necessity. Instead people do good or evil freely through their will alone. To tell the truth, there is nothing outside of themselves that may make their will choose in such a way that they cannot take or leave it, if they wished to use their reason. 17239

"But it would be difficult to reply to and confute all the arguments that can be brought up in opposition. Many have wanted to trouble themselves and have said, in a distilled judgment, that divine prescience lays no necessity whatever on the works of humanity. They go around pointing out that because God knows them beforehand, it does not follow that the works of men are forced to take place or that they hold to such ends. But because they will happen and will have this or that result, therefore, they say, God knows them beforehand. But these people untie the knot of this question badly. For if one sees the trend of their argument and wants to follow out their logic, and if they are giving a true idea, then the things that are to come are the causes of God's foreknowledge and cause it to be necessary. But it is a great folly to believe that God's understanding is so weak that it depends on the deeds of others, and those who follow such an idea wage an evil battle against God when, by creating such fables, they wish to enfeeble his foreknowledge. Reason cannot understand that one might teach anything to God; certainly He could not be perfectly wise if He were found so deficient that this instance were proved against Him. This reply then, which hides God's foreknowledge 17267

17290

and conceals His great providence under the shadows of ignorance, is worth nothing. This much is certain: His providence can learn nothing from the works of humanity; and if it could, such a characteristic would come from impotence. Such an idea remains painful to relate and even sinful to think.

17313   "Others will feel otherwise about it and reply according to their ideas; they will certainly agree that however it may happen with things that go by free will, just as choice gives them out, God knows whatever will happen with them and toward what end each one will tend. But they make this small addition: He knows the way in which they are to happen. With this argument they want to uphold the idea that there is no necessity, but that things go according to possibility. Thus God knows what ends things will come to and whether they will take place or not. He knows all this, that everything will hold to one of two ways. One thing will go by negation, another by affirmation, but not so finally that it may not perhaps turn out otherwise, for if free will wants to insist, it may turn out otherwise.

17337   "But how did anyone dare make this argument? How dared he despise God so much that he gave Him the kind of foreknowledge with which He knows nothing except in a doubtful way, when He cannot perceive the truth absolutely? When He knows the end of a deed, He has not known it to be so if it can turn out otherwise; if He sees something keep to a result other than that which He knew, his foreknowledge would be deceived, an uncertain situation like a deceptive opinion, as I have shown before.

17352   "Still others have gone by another route and many still hold to this idea. They say of the deeds that take place by possibility here on earth that they all come by necessity as far as God is concerned, but not otherwise. For however it may be with free will, He knows things finally, forever, without any mistake, before they have taken place, whatever ends they may have, and He knows
17364   all this through necessary knowledge. They undoubtedly speak the truth in so far as they agree in the idea, which they develop as a truth, that God's knowledge is necessary, eternal, and free of ignorance, and that He knows how things will happen. But He lays no constraint upon them, either as far as He is concerned or as far as men are concerned. To know the whole of things, with the details of all their possibilities, all this comes to Him from His great

power, from His goodness and His knowledge, from which nothing can be hidden. If one wanted to reply that according to this reasoning He lays necessity upon our deeds, he would not be saying the truth, for I insist that things do not exist because He foreknows them and that the fact that they occur afterward will never make them foreknown. But because He is all-powerful, all-good, and all-knowing, therefore He knows the truth about everything, so that nothing can deceive Him, and nothing can exist that He does not see. If one wanted to understand the matter and stick to the straight way—and it is not an easy thing to understand—he could set a rough example to lay people, who don't understand writing. Such people want something general, without any great subtlety of a gloss.

"Our case could be something like this: suppose that a man 17397 did something, whatever it might be, by free will, or abstained from doing it because, if we examine the case, he would be ashamed of it; and suppose that someone else knew nothing of it before the first had done it or, if he preferred to refrain from the deed, before he had omitted to do it. Then this second person, who knew about the thing afterward, would never on that account have contributed necessity or constraint to the situation. And if he had also had foreknowledge of it, as long as he did not go interfering but simply knew it, that fact would not have prevented the first person from doing what pleased or suited him or from abstaining from doing it, if he were allowed by his will, which is so free that he can flee the deed or follow it.

"In the same way God, only more nobly and in a completely 17421 absolute way, knows things to come and the ends to which they must keep, no matter how the thing may exist through the power of its human master, who holds the power of choice in his subjection and is inclined to one side by his sense or his folly. And God knows how the things that have occurred were done and accomplished. He knows too about the people who abstained from some deeds, and He knows if they omitted to do them out of shame or for some other cause, reasonable or unreasonable, just as their will leads them. I am completely certain that there is a great plenty of people who are tempted to do evil and who omit to do it; some of them abstain in order to live virtuously and only for the love of God; they are people with ways of grace, but they

17447   are scattered few and far between. The others, who plan to sin
if they think that they will not find it forbidden, subdue their
hearts for fear of pain or shame. God sees all this open and present
before His eyes, along with all the conditions of deeds and intentions. Nothing can be kept from Him, no matter how one may
try to delay; for there will never be a thing so far away that God
may not hold it before Him as if it were present. Let ten years
go by, or twenty or thirty, in fact five hundred or a hundred
thousand, and whether the event occurs in the country or the city,
whether it is honest or something that one should not do, still God
sees it from this very moment as if it had taken place. And He
has seen it always in true detail in His eternal mirror, which no
one, except Him, can polish without taking away his free will.
This mirror is the same one from which we took our beginning.
In this beautiful polished mirror, which He keeps and has always
kept with Him, in which He sees all that will happen and will keep
it always present, He sees where the souls will go who will serve
Him loyally; He sees also the place of those who have no concern
for loyalty or justice, and in His ideas He promises them salvation or damnation for the deeds that they will have done. This is
predestination, this the divine prescience that knows all and divines
nothing, that is accustomed to extend its grace to men when it sees
them directed toward good, and that has not, for all that, sup-
planted the power of free will. All men work by free will, either
for joy or sorrow. This predestination is His present vision, for
if one unbinds the definition of eternity, it is the possession of life
which cannot be grasped by an end, a life that is a complete whole,
without any division.

17499   "But one must trace out to an end, as far as universal causes are
concerned, the government of this world that God, by His great
Providence, wanted to establish and regulate. These causes will
perforce be such as they should be in all times. The heavenly
bodies will make all their transmutations according to their revolutions, and they will use their powers, through necessary influences, on individual things that are enclosed in the elements when
these things receive upon themselves the heavenly rays as they
should receive them. For things that can be engendered will always
engender similar things, or they will make their combinations by
natural dispositions, according to the properties that they have in

common with each other. The one that is to die will die, and he will live just as he can. The hearts of some, by their natural desire, will want to lie in idleness and in delights, these in virtues and these in vices.

"But perhaps events will not always take place as the heavenly bodies direct, if things protect themselves from them, things that would always obey them if they had not been deflected by chance or by will. They will all always be tempted to follow the inclination of the heart, which does not cease to draw them toward such an end, as toward a thing that is destined. Thus I grant that destiny may be that disposition, under predestination, that is added to changeable things, insofar as they are capable of being inclined in one direction or another. 17527

"Thus a man can have the fortune to be, from the time of his birth, successful and bold in his affairs, wise, generous, and good-natured, surrounded by friends and wealth, and renowned for great ability; or he can have perverse fortune. But he must take care how he lives, for everything can be hindered either by virtue or by sin. If he feels that he may be mean and miserly, for such a man cannot be wealthy, he should oppose his habits with reason and keep only enough for himself. Let him take good heart, give and spend money, clothes, and food, provided that by doing so he does not get the reputation of being foolishly generous. He who excites people to heap up treasure, makes them live in such martyrdom that nothing can suffice them, and so blinds and overwhelms them that he leaves them no good to do—he will have no liking for avarice. And when they wish to attach themselves to him he makes them lose all virtues. In the same way, if one is not stupid, one can guard against all the other vices, or turn away from virtues if one wants to turn toward evil. For free will is so powerful, if one knows oneself well, that it can always be maintained if one can feel within one's heart that sin wants to be its master, no matter how the heavenly bodies may go. For he who could foreknow the things that heaven wished to do could certainly prevent them. If heaven wanted to dry out the air until all people would die of heat, and if the people knew it beforehand, they would construct new houses in damp places or near rivers, or they would dig out great caverns and hide themselves underground, so that they would not mind the heat. 17543

17569

17590 "Or if, however late, it happened that a flood of water came, those who knew the places of refuge would leave the plains beforehand and flee to the mountains. There they would build such strong ships that they would protect their lives against the great inundation, as Deucalion and Pyrrha did in former times when they escaped by the boat into which they entered when they were not seized by the flood. When they had escaped and come to a safe harbor and saw, when the seas had gone away, the marshy plains throughout the valleys of the world, and saw that there was no lord or lady in the world except Deucalion and his wife, they went away to confession at the temple of the goddess Themis, who adjudged the destinies of all things that were fated. There they went down on their knees and asked for Themis's counsel on how they could set about to revive their line.

17617 "When Themis heard their request, a very fair and honest one, she advised them to go away and immediately throw their great mother's bones behind their backs. This reply was so bitter to Pyrrha that she refused it and excused herself from her fate by saying that she should not destroy or break her mother's bones. She continued until Deucalion told her the explanation of this advice.

17629 " 'We must seek another meaning,' he said. 'Our great mother is the earth, and the rocks, if I dare name them, are certainly her bones. We must throw them behind us to revive our line.'

17635 "Just as he said, so they did, and men sprang up from the rocks that Deucalion threw with good aim, and from Pyrrha's rocks sprang women in body and soul, exactly as lady Themis had put in their ear. They never sought another father, and the hardihood of rock will never fail to appear in their race. Thus they worked wisely when they saved their life from the deluge in a boat. Those who knew about such a deluge beforehand could also escape.

17651 "Or if famine should spring up and cause a dearth of goods so that people had to die of hunger because they had no wheat, they could hold out enough grain two years, or three or four years, before it could happen, so that, when the famine came, all the people great and small could defeat the hunger, just as Joseph did in Egypt, when by his sense and his merit he created so great a store that they were able to provide from it without hunger and without discomfort.

"Or if they could know beforehand that an extraordinarily 17666
unusual cold wave were to occur in winter, they would give their
attention ahead of time to providing themselves with clothing and
with great cartloads of logs to make fires in the fireplaces. And
when the cold season came they would strew their house with
fair, clean, white straw that they could gather on their farm. Then
they would close up doors and windows, and the place would be
more secure.

"Or they would build hot bathhouses, in which, quite naked, 17679
they could hold their gay dances when they saw the weather grow
furious and hurl stones and tempests that would have killed the
beasts in the fields, and then seize the rivers and freeze them. No
matter how much the weather might threaten them with tempests
or ice, they would laugh at the threats. They would carol within,
free of danger; indeed they could mock the weather by providing
for themselves in this way. But unless God worked a miracle
through a vision or oracle, there is no one, I have no doubt, unless
he knew by astronomy the strange complexions and various positions of the heavenly bodies, and observed which climates they
had influence over, there is no one, I say, who may know these
things beforehand, for any knowledge or wealth.

"Although the body has such power that it flies from the dis- 17703
temper of the heavens and thus disturbs them at their work by
protecting itself so well against them, the force of the soul, I
aver, is more powerful than that of the body. For the soul moves
and carries the body; if it did not exist, the body would be a dead
thing. Free will then, by the exercise of good understanding, could
better and more easily avoid whatever can make it suffer. It has no
concern that it may sorrow over anything, provided that it does
not wish to consent to it and that it knows by heart that one is
the cause of one's own discomfort. Outside tribulation can only be
the occasion of it. Neither has a man any concern over destinies, if
he observes his nativity and knows his situation. What is this preaching worth? Free will is above all destinies, no matter how destined
they are.

"I would speak more about destinies, I would settle the subject 17727
of Fortune and chance, and I would like very much to explain
everything, to raise more objections, reply to them, and give many
illustrations for them, but I would spend too much time before I

finished everything. The good is decided elsewhere. He who does not know it may ask a clerk who had studied it and who may understand it.

17737　　"I would never yet have spoken of this question, if I should have kept silent about it, but it belongs to my subject; for my enemy could say, when he heard me complain of him in this way and in order to make nothing of his disloyalties and to blame his creator, that I want to defame him wrongfully. He himself is accustomed to say often that he does not have the free will to choose, because God, with his foresight, holds him in such subjection that he directs every human thought and deed by destiny. Thus if he wants to draw toward virtue, God makes him do so by force, and if he strives to do evil, it is again God who forces him to do it. God does more than hold him by the finger, so that he does whatever he must—sinning, almsgiving, speaking well or cuttingly, giving praise or detraction, thieving, killing, making peace or marriage—either reasonably or foolishly. 'Thus,' he says, 'it must be. God caused this woman to be born for this man, and he could not have another for any reason or for any possession. She was destined for him.' And then if the match is badly made, since he or she may be a fool, and someone in conversation may condemn those who agreed to the marriage and arranged it, the senseless fellow will then reply to the critic: 'Apply to God,' he will say, 'who wants the affair to go in this way. Without fail, he made all of this take place.' And then he will confirm by oath that it could not go otherwise.

17779　　"No, no, this reply is false. The true God, who cannot lie, does not serve men such a sauce that he makes them consent to evil. The mad thinking that gives birth to the evil consent which moves them to deeds from which they should have refrained—this thinking comes from them. For they could indeed have refrained, provided only that they had known themselves. Then they would have called upon their Creator, who would have loved them if they had loved Him; for he alone loves wisely who knows himself entirely.

17793　　"Without doubt, all dumb animals, empty and bare of understanding, are by nature incapable of knowing themselves, for if they had speech and reason with which to understand one another, so that they could instruct each other, it would be an evil occurrence for men. The beautiful chargers with their manes would never let themselves be subdued, nor allow knights to mount them; the ox would never put his horned head beneath the yoke of the cart. No donkey, mule, or camel would ever carry a load for man or consider him worth a cake. No elephant would ever carry a castle upon its tall backbone (the elephant sounds a trumpet with his nose, and with his nose, as a man does with his hand, he also feeds himself night and morning). No dog or cat would serve him, for they could very well get along without him. Bears, wolves, lions, leopards, and wild boars would all want to strangle man; even the rat would strangle him when he was little in his cradle. For no call would any bird ever put its skin in danger; instead it could harm man very much by putting out his eyes while he was sleeping. If one wanted to reply to this reasoning that he thought he could overcome them all, because he knew how to make armor, helmets, hauberks, hard swords, bows, and crossbows, the other animals could do so also. Don't they have monkeys and marmots that would make them good coats of leather and iron, doublets in fact? They would never wait for hands, for they would work with their own and would be in no way inferior to man; they could be writers. They would never be so empty-headed that they might not all exercise their wits over how to oppose these arms and over what devices they might make as well to give great trouble to men. Even fleas and earwigs, if they were enclosed in their ears while they were sleeping, would annoy them wondrously. Even lice, mites, and nits would often give them so many struggles that they would make them leave their jobs, bend and get down, turn, flinch, jump, skip, scratch themselves and fuss around, and take off their clothes and shoes, so hard could these insects pursue them. Even flies could often give them great difficulty at their meals and attack them in their faces; it wouldn't matter if they were kings or pages. Ants and small vermin would do them a great deal of injury if they knew about them. But it is true that the animals' ignorance comes from their nature. However, if a reasonable creature, whether mortal man or divine angel, all of whom should give praise to God, is foolish and does not know himself, this defect comes to him from his vice, which troubles and fuddles his sense, for such a creature can indeed follow reason and can use free will; there is nothing that can excuse him from

17813

17853

doing so. It is for this reason that I have said so much to you about it and brought up arguments to quell men's gossip on the subject, for nothing can defend them against it.

17875   "But in order to follow out my intention, from which I want to be freed, and because of the sorrow that I recall and that troubles me in body and soul, I do not want to say anything more on this subject now. I turn back now to the heavens, which indeed do whatever they must do to creatures, who receive the celestial influences according to their different substances.

17885   "These influences make the winds blow against one another, make the air break out in flame, yell and cry out, and burst out in many parts with thunder and lightning that rumble, drum, and trumpet until the clouds are burst open by the vapors that they have raised. Then the heat and movement rend the bellies of the clouds with their horrible struggles, and the tempest rages, throws out thunderclaps, raises up clouds of dust on the earth, even beats down towers and steeples and so wrenches many old trees that they are torn from the earth. They were never so strongly attached that the roots were always good enough to keep them from going down to the ground or to keep a part or all of the branches from being broken off.

17905   "Men might say that devils do these things with their crooks and battering rams, their claws and hooks, but such an opinion is not worth two turnips. They are mistaken, for no one has harmed anything except the tempests and the winds that go in pursuit. These are the things that harm them, those that blow over the wheat and cut down the vines and beat down the flowers and fruit from the trees. The winds blow them and beat them so much that they cannot stay on the branches long enough to mature.

17919   "Indeed the heavens also make the atmosphere weep great tears at different times, and the clouds have such great compassion for it that they unclothe themselves until they are quite naked; they don't give a straw for the black cloak in which they are clothed. They feel such sorrow that they tear it completely to pieces and help the sky to weep, as if it were to make them perish as a result. They weep so deeply, so strongly and heavily, that they make the rivers overflow their banks and strive with their raging floods against the fields and nearby forests. Then floods often make the grain die and living become expensive, and as a

result the poor people who work the fields weep over the hopes
that are lost. When the rivers overflow their banks, the fish, who   17939
follow their rivers, as is right and reasonable, since they are their
own homes, go off like lords and masters to feed on fields, meadows, and vineyards. They run into oaks and pines and ash trees;
they steal the manors and inheritances of the wild beasts and thus
go swimming everywhere. Then Bacchus, Ceres, Pan, and Cybele
all go around raging passionately when the fish with their fins
go trooping around through their delightful pastures. The satyrs
and fairies are very sorrowful when through such floods they
lose their pleasant groves. The nymphs weep for their fountains
when they find them full of rivers, overflowing and covered up,
as if they wept their loss. The elves and dryads also have hearts   17963
so sick with grief that they think themselves lost when they see
their woods invaded, and they complain of the river gods who
bring them fresh troubles, undeserved and unrecompensed, although they have really lost nothing. The fish are also house
guests in the nearby low-lying towns, which they find wretched
and mean. There remains no grange or cellar, no place so valuable
and fine that they do not go installing themselves everywhere.
They go into temples and churches, where they rob the gods of
their services and harry from their dark rooms the private gods
and images.

"And when at the end of the play the fair weather scatters the   17981
foul—for stormy, rainy weather is displeasing and harmful to the
heavens—the atmosphere takes off all its anger and laughs and
rejoices. And when the clouds also see the skies rejoicing, then
they too rejoice, and, in order to be pleasing and beautiful after
their sorrows, they make dresses of all their beautiful colors. They
put out their fleeces to dry in the pleasant warmth of the beautiful
sun and in the clear, resplendent weather, they go about teasing
and carding them. They spin, and when they have spun, they set
flying, with their spinning, great spindlefuls of white thread as if
it were for sewing up their sleeves.

"Then when they again take courage to go afar on pilgrimage,   18001
they harness their horses, climb and pass along mountains and
valleys, and flee like madmen; for Aeolus, the god of winds, is the
one they call upon, and when he has harnessed them well, for
they have no other charioteer who knows how to deal with their

horses, he puts on their feet such good wings that no bird has anything like them.

18013   "Then the sky takes up its blue cloak, which it wears very willingly in India, and decks itself out and strives to adorn itself and be festive to wait in fine array until the clouds return. To comfort the earth as well as to go hunting, the clouds are accustomed to carry a bow in their hand, or two or three when they wish; these are called celestial bows, and no man, unless he is a master good enough to teach optics, knows how the sun varies their colors, how many or what colors they have, nor why there are so many and these particular ones, nor the cause of their shape. One would have to take the trouble to be a disciple of Aristotle, who made better observations of nature than any man from the time of Cain. Alhazen, the nephew of Huchain, was neither a fool nor a simpleton, and he wrote the book of *Observations*, which anyone who wants to know about the rainbow should know about. The student and observer of nature must know it and he must also know geometry, the mastery of which is necessary for the proofs in the

18044   book of *Observations*. There he will be able to discover the causes and the strength of the mirrors that have such marvelous powers that all things that are very small—thin letters, very narrow writing, and tiny grains of sand—are seen as so great and large and are put so close to the observers—for everyone can distinguish among them—that one can read them and count them from so far off that anyone who had seen the phenomenon and wanted to tell about it could not be believed by a man who had not seen it or did not know its causes. This would not be a case of belief, since he would have the knowledge of the phenomenon.

18061   "If Mars and Venus, who were captured in the bed where they were lying together, had looked at themselves in such a mirror before they got up on the bed, provided that they held their mirror so that they could see the bed in it, they would never have been captured or bound in the fine, thin nets that Vulcan had placed there and that neither of them knew anything about. Even if he had made the nets finer than spider web, they would have seen them and Vulcan would have been deceived. They would not have entered the trap because every net would have appeared to them thicker and longer than a large beam, and cruel Vulcan, burning with jealousy and anger, would never have proved their adultery. The gods would never have known anything about them if they had had such mirrors, for they would have fled from the place when they saw the nets stretched out there and run to lie in some other place, where they might better hide their desire. Or they would have worked some expedient to avoid their misfortune without being shamed or troubled.

"Now by the faith that you owe me, do I tell the truth in what you have heard?" 18090

"Yes, certainly," the priest told her. "It is quite true that these mirrors were very necessary to them then, for they could have come together elsewhere when they knew the danger. Or perhaps Mars, the god of battle, would have taken revenge on jealous Vulcan by cutting the nets with his sword that cuts so well. Then he could have satisfied his woman at his ease in the bed, without seeking any other place, or near the bed, even on the floor. And if by any chance—and it would have been a cruel, hard one— Dan Vulcan had come upon them there, even when Mars held her, then Venus, a very discreet lady—for there is a great deal of fraud in women—if she could have enough time to cover her loins when she heard the door open, would have certainly had excuses, through some caviling, and would have made up some other reason for Mars's presence in the house. And she would have sworn whatever you like until she had robbed him of his proofs, and she would have forced him to believe that the affair was never true. Even if he had seen it, she would have said that his sight had been dark and confused. Thus would she have used double talk in different convolutions to find excuses, for nothing swears or lies more boldly than a woman, and Mars would have gone off completely cleared." 18092

"Certainly you speak well, sir priest," she said, "like a worthy, courteous, wise man. Women have too many devious and malicious ways in their hearts, and he who does not know that is a foolish ignoramus. However, we do not excuse women for their ways. Certainly they swear and lie more boldly than any man, particularly when they feel themselves guilty of some misdeed, and they will be especially careful never to get caught in such a deed. Thus I can truthfully say that anyone who sees a woman's heart should never be proud of doing so. He would not do so safely, since some misfortune would happen to him otherwise as a result." 18130

18147   Thus, it seemed to me, Nature and Genius agreed with each other. Still, since I want to stick to the truth, Solomon says that a man who found a good woman would be blessed.

18153   "Mirrors still have many other great and wonderful powers," said Nature. "Large, bulky objects set very close seem set so far away that even the largest mountains between France and Cerdagne can be seen so small, so tiny, that one could hardly distinguish among them, no matter how long one kept at it.

18163   "Other mirrors, if you look carefully in them, show truly the right amounts of things that one sees in them. There are others that burn things when directed at them, if one knows how to adjust them rightly in order to collect the sun's rays together when they are shining on the mirrors and reflecting from them. Others make different images appear in different situations—straight, oblong, and upside down in different arrangements. Those who are masters of mirrors make one image give birth to several: if they have the right form ready, they create four eyes in one head, and they make phantoms appear to those who look within. They even make them appear, quite alive, outside the mirror, either in water or in the air. One can see the images play between the eye and the mirror, by means of different angles, either compound or single, of one sort or another in which the form is reversed and continues, by the appropriate means, to multiply itself until it comes to the eyes, appearing along with the reflected rays that the medium receives in so many different ways that it deceives the observers.

18197   "Aristotle himself bears witness. He was certainly one who knew about this matter, for he valued all knowledge. A certain man, he tells, was sick, and his disease had very much weakened his sight. The atmosphere was dark and troubled, and because of these two conditions he saw his face in the air in front of him, going from place to place. In short, mirrors, if they have no impediments, make many miracles appear.

18209   "Different distances, in fact, with mirrors, create great deceptions. They make things that are far apart from each other seem to be closely joined; depending on their differences, they make one thing seem to be two, or three six, or four eight, if one wants to amuse himself with such sights, or one may see more or less. One's eyes may be so placed that several things seem one if one arranges them well so as to bring them together. Mirrors may make a man that is so small as to be called a dwarf appear to the eye as if he were larger than ten giants, and to appear to stride over the woods, without bending or breaking a branch, so that everyone trembles with fear. This resemblance of dwarfs to giants is the result of the eyes' error when they see them so differently.

"And after these people have been thus deceived, after they have seen such things in mirrors or because of distances, which have created such illusions for them, then they go to other people and boast, and their sight has been so deceived that they say, not in truth but falsely, that they have seen devils. 18231

"Infirm and troubled eyes indeed make one thing seem double, make a double moon appear in the sky, or make one candle seem to be two, and there is no one who guards himself so well that he may not often make faulty observations. As a result many things are judged to be quite other than they are. 18239

"But I do not now want to take the trouble to clarify the shapes of mirrors, nor do I want to tell how rays are reflected or to describe their angles. Everything is written elsewhere in a book. Nor do I wish to say why the images of mirrored things are reflected to the eyes of those who look at themselves when they turn toward the mirrors; nor do I want to talk of the places of their appearance or the causes of the deceptions, or, fair priest, about where such images have their being, either inside the mirror or outside. I will not now tell about other marvelous sights, either pleasant or sorrowful, that one sees happen suddenly, or about whether they come from outside or only from fantasy. I will not and must not explain these things in detail now, but instead will pass over them in silence, along with the things I mentioned before, which I shall never describe. I have a very long subject, and it would be a burdensome thing to tell and very difficult to understand, even if someone knew how to teach it without speaking generally, especially to lay people. They could not believe that the things were true, particularly the things about the mirrors that work in such different ways, unless they saw them with instruments, provided that the students who knew this wonderful science through demonstration wanted to let them use their instruments. 18247 18273

"No more readily could they grant the types of visions, so strange and wonderful are they, no matter who wanted to explain 18287 them, nor the deceptions that such visions bring, either waking or sleeping, and that have dumbfounded many people. Therefore I want to pass over these things here; I don't want to tire myself with talking nor you with hearing. It is a good thing to flee prolixity. Women are very troublesome and contrary about talking. But I beg you not to be displeased if I don't keep completely quiet on the subject, if indeed I stick to the truth. In any case I want to say in this connection that many are so deceived by these dreams that they are moved out of their beds; they dress and put on their shoes and get ready with all their gear while their common senses sleep and their individual senses are all awake. They take up staffs and sacks, or stakes, sickles, or pruning hooks, and they go off on long journeys without knowing where. They even get up on horses and pass along mountains and valleys, by dry roads or muddy, until they come to strange places. Then when their common senses awake, they are completely amazed, and they marvel. Afterward, when they come back to their right senses and are with people, they aver, not to tell stories, that devils have taken them from their houses and brought them there. But they themselves brought themselves.

18327   "It still happens very often that when people are seized by some great sickness, the sort that shows up in a frenzy, and when they don't have sufficient protection, or are lying alone in the house, they jump up and start traveling, never stopping until they find some wild place, meadows, vineyards, or groves, and there let themselves fall down. Afterwards, if someone comes by there, no matter how much later, he can see them, dead from cold and exposure, because they had no protection whatever, except perhaps foolish or evil people.

18343   "One sees a great number of people who, even when they are well, are many times, through natural habit, given to think too much in an unregulated way when they are very melancholy or irrationally fearful; they make many different images appear inside themselves, in ways other than those we told about just a short time ago when we were speaking about mirrors. And it seems to them then that all these images are in reality outside them. Or there are those who, with great devotion, do too much contemplating and cause the appearance in their thought of the things on which they have pondered, only they believe that they see them

18311

quite clearly and outside themselves. But what they see is only a trifling lie, just as with a man who dreams. He sees, I think, the spiritual substances in their actuality, as Scipio did formerly. He sees hell and paradise, heaven, air, sea, and earth, and all that   18368 one may seek there. He sees the stars appear, birds flying through the air, fish swimming in the sea, and beasts in the woods, playing and describing pretty turns. He sees different kinds of people, some enjoying themselves in their rooms, others out hunting through woods, mountains, and rivers, through meadows, vineyards, and fallow fields. He dreams about law pleas and judgments, wars and tournaments, balls and carols, and viols and citoles. He recognizes odorous spices, tastes savory dishes, and feels his sweetheart in his arms, even though she is not there. Or he sees Jealousy coming, holding a pestle at her neck; she finds them there in the act, by means of Foul Mouth, who makes up things before they take place and brings constant dismay to all lovers. Those who call themselves pure lovers, when they burn with love for one another and have great toil and trouble, when at night they have gone to sleep in their beds or have thought a great deal—I know their characteristics—then they dream of the beloved things that they have asked for so much by day; or they dream of the adversaries who make so much trouble and opposition for them.

"If they are in a state of deadly hatred, they dream, either di-   18405 rectly or by contraries, of anger and quarrels, of struggles with the enemies who have set off their hatred, and of the things that follow on war.

"Again, if by some great mishap, they are put in prison, they   18411 dream of their release, if their hopes are good, or of the gibbet or rope if during the day their hearts have told them about these things; or they dream about other unpleasant things that are not outside, but within. However, they think at that time that the truth is that they are outside; they make of everything an occasion for sorrow or joy, and they carry everything inside the head, which thus deceives the five senses with the phantoms that it receives. As a result, many people, in their folly, think themselves sorcerers by night, wandering with Lady Abundance. And they say that in the whole world every third child born is of such disposition that three times a week he goes just as destiny leads him; that such people push into all houses; that they fear neither keys nor bars, but enter by cracks, cat-hatches, and crevices; that their souls leave their bodies and go with good ladies into strange places and through houses; and they prove it with such reasoning: the different things seen have not come in their beds, but through their souls, which labor and go running about thus through the world; and they make people believe that, as long as they are on such a journey, their souls could never enter their bodies if anyone had

18449 overturned them. But this idea is a horrible folly and something not possible, for the human body is a dead thing as soon as it does not carry its soul; thus it is certain that those who follow this sort of journey three times a week die three times and revive three times in the same week. And if it is as we have said, then the disciples of such a convent come back to life very often.

18461 "But this is a matter that has been well dealt with, and I dare say without gloss that no one who must run out his life to his death has more than one death to die. And he will never return to life until his judgment day, except by a special miracle of God in heaven, like what we read of Saint Lazarus. We do not deny these occurrences.

18471 "When, on the other hand, they say that after the soul has parted from the body, which is thus denuded, it does not know how to come back to it if it finds it overturned, who can support such fables? For it is true, and I recall it well, that the soul that is severed from the body is clearer, wiser, and cleverer than when it is joined to the body. With the body, it follows the body's disposition, which clouds the soul's aim. Thus then the entry into the body is better known than the exit, and the soul would find it sooner, no matter how overturned it found the body.

18487 "Again, in connection with the idea that a third of the world goes with Lady Abundance in this way, silly old women prove it by the visions that they find. Then it must be, without fail, that the entire world goes that way, for there is no one, whether he lies or tells the truth, who does not dream many visions, not just three times a week, but fifteen times in two weeks, or perhaps more or less, according to the strength of his fantasy.

18499 "I do not want to say any more about dreams, about whether they are true or lies, whether one should distinguish among them or if they should all be despised, about why some are more horrible, others more beautiful and peaceful, according to their appearances in different dispositions or according to the various inclinations of the hearts in different ways and times, or about whether God sends revelations through such visions or the malign spirits do so, to put people in danger. I will not undertake all this, but will come back to my subject.

"I say to you then that when the clouds are tired and worn   18515
out from shooting their arrows through the air, more of them moist than dry, for the clouds have sprinkled them all with rain and dew, unless some heat dries them to draw out something dry—then, when they have shot as long as it seems good to them, they unstring their bows together. But the bows that these archers use have very strange ways, for all their colors flee when they are unstrung and sheathed. Never afterward will they shoot with the very same bows that we have seen; if they want to shoot another time, they must make new bows which the sun can paint with many colors. They must not shape them in any other way.

"The influence of the heavens does still more, for they have   18535
great power by sea and land and air. They cause comets to appear. Comets are not placed in the heavens, but kindled in the atmosphere; they last for a short time after they are created, and many fables are taken from this circumstance. Those who never stop divining predict the deaths of princes on the basis of comets. But comets do not spy out the poor more than the rich or the rich more than the poor, nor do their influences or rays lie more thickly on one than on the other. We are certain that they operate on the regions of the world according to the dispositions of climate, men, and animals, that are subject to the influences of the planets and stars that have greater power over them; the comets bear the import of celestial influences and they disturb complexions as they find them obedient.

"I do not say or affirm that kings should be called rich, any   18561
more than the little people who go on foot through the streets; for sufficiency creates wealth and covetousness creates poverty. One may be a king where there is nothing worth two peas, and he who covets more is less rich. If you want to believe what is written, kings resemble paintings. He who wrote the Almagest for us affords us an instance of this idea, if anyone who looks at paintings knew how to give good attention to them. They may please if one does not approach them, but close up, the pleasure stops; from

far off they seem very delightful, but from close they are not so. Powerful friends are the same. When one does not know them, their help and acquaintance are sweet, through the lack of trial; but if anyone tested them well, he would find there so much bitterness that he would fear very much to push in that direction, so much is their favor to be feared. Thus Horace assures us about their love and favor.

18589   "Princes are not worthy that the heavenly bodies should give signs of their deaths rather than those of other men. The body of a prince is worth not one apple beyond that of a plowman, a clerk, or a squire, for I make them all alike, as it appears at their birth. Through me they are all, strong and weak, great and small, born alike and naked. As far as the condition of humanity is concerned, I put them all on an equal footing. Fortune does the rest. She does not know how to be permanent; she gives her benefits at her pleasure and takes no care about which person she gives to, and she takes back or will take back as many times as she wants.

18607   "And if anyone who boasts of his nobility dares contradict me and say that noblemen—those whom people call noblemen—are, through their nobility of birth, of better standing than those who cultivate the earth or live by their labor, then I reply that no one is noble unless he is intent on virtue, and no man is base except because of his vices, which make him appear unbridled and stupid.

18619   "Nobility comes from a good heart, for nobility of ancestry is not the nobility of true worth when it lacks goodness of heart. For this reason a nobleman must display the prowess of his ancestors, who conquered their nobility by means of the great labors that they gave to it. When they passed from the world, they carried all their virtues with them and left their possessions to their heirs, who could have nothing more of them. They have the possessions, but nothing else is theirs, not nobility or valor, unless they act so that they may be noble through the sense and the virtues that they themselves possess.

18635   "Learned men have a greater opportunity than have princes or kings, who know nothing of what is written, to be noble, courteous, and wise, and I will explain why. In the things that are written, clerks see, with proved, reasonable, and demonstrated information, all the evils from which one should withdraw and all the good things that one can do. He sees all the things of the world written down, just as they are done and said. In the lives of the ancients he sees the villainies of all the villains, all the deeds of courteous men, the *summae* of all courtesies. In short, he sees written in books whatever one should flee or follow. Thus all learned men, disciples or masters, are noble or should be; those who are not should know that the reason is that they have wicked hearts, for they have many more advantages than those who run after the wild stags.

"Thus clerks who do not have noble and gentle hearts are worth   18659
less than any gentleman when they avoid the good things that they know about and follow vices that they have seen. Clerks who abandon themselves to vices should be more punished before the celestial emperor than should lay people, simple and ignorant, who do not have described for them in writing the virtues that the clerks consider low and despicable. Even if princes know how to read, they cannot undertake to study and learn a great deal, since they have too much to attend to elsewhere. Therefore you may know that learned men have a finer and greater advantage in gaining nobility than have earthly lords.

"In order to conquer nobility, which is very honorable on earth,   18677
all those who wish to gain it must know this rule: whoever turns his desire toward nobility must guard against pride and laziness, must give himself to arms and to study and must empty himself of baseness. He must have a heart that is humble, courteous, and gentle in all places and toward all people, except, of course, toward his enemies when no agreement can be reached. He should honor ladies and girls, but not confide too much in them, since he could indeed be unfortunate as a result, for no one is very good to see through completely. Such a man should have praise and esteem, without blame or reprimand, and he, not others, should receive the name of nobility.

"Consider the knights who are brave at arms, strong in deeds   18697
and courteous of speech, as in former times was Monsieur Gawain, who was unlike weak men, and as was the good Count Robert of Artois, who from the time that he left his cradle frequented generosity, honor, and chivalry all the days of his life and who was never pleased by idle periods, but rather became a man before

his years. Such a strong, valiant knight, generous, courteous, and bold in battle, should be welcomed, praised, loved, and held dear by everyone.

18711   "One should also honor a clerk who wants to labor well with his mind, who thinks of following the virtues that he finds written about in his book. And certainly they did so in former times. I could easily name ten of them, indeed so many that if I numbered them, you would be bored at hearing the number.

18719   "Formerly, the valiant noblemen, as they are called in writing, the emperors, dukes, counts, kings, of whom I will never tell here, used to honor the philosophers. They even gave poets towns, gardens, places of honor, and many delightful things. Naples, a more delightful city than Paris or Lavardin, was given to Virgil, and in Calabria Ennius had beautiful gardens that were given to him by people of that time who knew him. But why should I find more of them? I would prove the case to you by several who were born of low ancestry and had hearts more noble than those of many a son of a king or a count; I will never tell you about them here, but they were considered noble. Now, however, times have come to the point where the good people who work at philosophy all their lives, who go off to foreign lands to win sense and worth, who suffer great poverty and go begging or in debt, perhaps barefoot and naked, are neither loved nor held dear. Princes don't value them at an apple, and yet—may God keep me from having fevers—they are more gentlemen than those who go out chasing hares and than those who are in the habit of remaining on their paternal dung-heaps.

18755   "And is he who wants to carry off the praise and renown of another person's nobility, when he has neither the worth nor prowess of that other, is he noble? I say no; he should rather be called base and considered vile, and loved less than if he were the son of a tramp. I shall never go around flattering any of that sort, even if he were the son of Alexander, who dared to undertake so many feats of arms, and who continued his wars until he was lord of all lands. After all those who fought against him obeyed him, and after those who had not defended themselves had surrendered, he was so tormented by pride that he said this world was so cramped that he could scarcely turn around; he did not wish to delay, but thought of seeking another world to begin a new war.

He went off to break open hell, so that he might be esteemed everywhere. When I told the gods of hell about his coming, they all trembled with fear, for they thought that it would be He who, for the sake of souls dead through sin, was to break open the gates of hell with the crossed sticks of wood and to crush their great pride in order to draw His friends from hell.

"But let us assume something that cannot be, that I cause some 18787 to be born noble and that I don't care about the others whom they go around calling base. What good is there in nobility? Certainly, if one puts his wits to a good understanding of truth, he who may have the quality of nobility can understand nothing other than that people should follow their parents' prowess. He who wants to be like a noble man must always live under this burden if he does not want to steal his nobility and have praise without deserving it. For I make known to all that nobility gives no other good thing to men than this burden alone. They know quite certainly that no man should have praise because of the virtue of some person alien to him. And it remains unjust that one blame any person for another's fault. He who deserves it may be praised. But it is not just, I dare well say, for anyone to have the praise that belongs to his parents when he himself serves no good, when one finds in him wickedness, meanness and bad humor, boasting and bluster, and when he remains deceitful and treacherous, stuffed with pride and insolence, devoid of charity and generosity, or neglectful and lazy—for one finds too many of this sort—even though he may be born of parents in whom every virtue appeared. Instead he should be considered lower than if he had come of a wretched line.

"All men capable of understanding know that, as far as doing 18827 what one wishes is concerned, the acquisition of large dwellings and great amounts of money and adornments is not the same thing as the acquisition of sense, nobility, and renown through one's prowess, for he who desires to work in order to acquire money, adornments, or land for himself, even though he may have amassed a hundred thousand marks of gold or still more, can leave everything to his friends; but when he has put all his work into the other things we have spoken about, as long as he gains them by his merits, no love can force him to the point where he might ever leave them anything. Can he leave knowledge? No,

nor nobility nor renown. But he can indeed teach them about these
things if they want to take him as an example. He can do nothing
else about it, nor can they draw anything more out of him.

18851   "There are many who do not attach much importance to these
things, who would not give a husk for anything except gaining possessions and wealth. They say that they are gentlemen because they
are so reputed; because their good parents were (but they were
such as they should have been); because they have dogs and birds
so as to seem noble young men; because they go hunting by the
rivers, through woods, fields, and briars; and because they idle
away their time in amusements. But those who boast because of
others' nobility are villainous vassals. They do not speak the truth;
they lie and they steal the name of nobility when they do not
resemble their good parents. For when I cause likenesses to be born,
they acquire fresh nobility if they have so much ability and if they
want to be noble with a nobility other than that which I give to
them. This nobility is a very beautiful one. Its name is natural
freedom, and I have put it into everyone equally, along with the
reason that God gives them and that is so wise and good that it
makes them like God and the angels, if it were not that death made
them different. By means of this difference of mortality, death
18883   brings about the separation of men. But if men do not acquire
these new, noble qualities by themselves, they will never be noble
through the efforts of others, and I do not except kings or counts.
Besides, it is more shameful for the son of a king to be stupid and
full of wild ways and vices than if he were the son of a carter,
a swineherd, or a cobbler. Certainly it would be more honorable
for the good fighter Gawain to have been engendered by a coward
who sat by the fire, all covered with ashes, than to have been a
coward with Renouart for his father.

18897   "But without fail, it is no fable that the death of a prince is
more notable than that of a peasant, when one finds him lying
dead, and the speeches about it go on longer. And therefore the
foolish people think, when they have seen comets, that they may
have been created on account of princes. But if there were never
a king or prince in all kingdoms and provinces, and if all on earth
were equal, in peace or in war, still the heavenly bodies would cause
the comets to be born in their time, when they had entered under
the influences in which they were to perform such labors, provided

that there was enough material in the atmosphere for them to work with.

"The heavenly influences also make the stars appear to be 18915 dragons and sparks flying through the air and falling down from the heavens, as foolish people think. But reason cannot see that anything might fall from the heavens, for there is nothing corruptible in them. Everything is solid and strong and stable. They do not receive forms that may be impressed upon them externally. Nothing could break them, nor would they allow anything to pass, no matter how subtle or piercing, unless, perhaps, it were spiritual. Their rays, certainly, pass through them, but neither harm them nor break them.

"Through their various influences the heavenly bodies produce 18931 the hot summers and cold winters, the snow and the hail, large at one time, fine at another, and all the other impressions upon us. They do so according to their oppositions, according to whether they are far from each other, approaching, or in conjunction. For this reason many men often become dismayed when they see eclipses in the heavens. They think that they are in bad situations because they have been deprived of the influence of the planets that they had seen before, but have now lost sight of so suddenly; but if they knew the causes of eclipses, they would never be upset by them in any way.

"By means of the combats of the winds that raise the waves of 18947 the sea, the heavens make the floods kiss the clouds; they pacify the sea again until it dares not grumble or make its waters leap, except for those that the moon always causes to move by necessity, making them ebb and flow. Nothing can hold this movement back.

"And if someone wanted to inquire more deeply into the miracles 18957 that the stars and heavenly bodies perform on earth, he would find so many beautiful ones that if one wanted to put them down in writing he would never have written them all. Thus the heavens discharge their debts toward me; by their goodness they bring so much benefit that I can easily see that they do their whole duty well.

"I do not complain about the elements. They keep my com- 18967 mandments well; they make their mixtures among themselves, turning into their different solutions. For well I know that whatever is beneath the influence of the moon is corruptible. Nothing there can nourish itself so well that it will not have to rot entirely. All things by their dispositions, through natural direction, have a rule which neither fails nor lies: everything goes back to its beginning. This rule is so general that it does not want to fail in the case of the elements.

18981   "Neither do I complain of the plants, for they are not slow to obey. They are very attentive to my laws and, as long as they live, they produce their roots and leaves, their stems and branches, fruits and flowers. Every year each one, like the grass, the trees, and the woods, bears whatever it can until it dies.

18990   "Nor do I complain of the birds or the fish, which are very beautiful to look upon. They know well how to keep my rules, and they are such very good scholars that they all pull in my collar. They all produce their young in their different ways and do honor to their ancestry. They do not let their lines perish, and it is very comforting to see it so.

18999   "I do not complain about other beasts that I have made, beasts with heads that are bent, all looking down toward the earth. They have never started war against me; they are all on my side and do as their fathers did. The male goes with his female, and they make a suitable, fair couple. All beget young, coming together at all times that seem good to them, and they make no market of it when they agree together; instead, one likes to do things for the other with good-natured courtesy. And they all consider themselves repaid by the benefits that come to them through me. My beautiful insects, my ants, butterflies, and flies, act in this way. Worms born of rot do not cease to keep my commandments, and my snakes and adders are all diligent in my works.

19021   "But man alone, for whom I had made all the benefits that I knew how; man alone, whom I create and ordain to carry his face on high toward the heaven; man alone, whom I shape and cause to be born in the very form of his master; only man, for whom I struggle and labor, acts worse toward me than any wolf. He is the end of all my labor, and except for what I give him, he has nothing that is worth a pomander as far as his body is concerned, either in the whole body or in the limbs, nor in fact as far as his soul is concerned, except for one thing only. From me, his lady, he has received three powers, of body or of soul, for I can indeed say without lying that I make him exist, live, and feel. The wretch has many advantages, if he wanted to be worthy and wise. He abounds in all the virtues that God has put into this world. He is companion to all things that are enclosed in the whole world, and he shares in their bounty. With the stones he has existence, with the thick grass he lives, and with the dumb animals he feels. He is capable of still much more in that with the angels he understands. What more can I recount to you? He has whatever one can think of. He is a new little world, and he acts worse toward me than any wolf.

"Certainly I know truly that I did not give him his understanding; that is not my area of responsibility. I am neither wise nor powerful enough to create anything so capable of knowing. I never made anything eternal; whatever I create is corruptible. Plato himself bears witness to this fact when he speaks of my task and of the gods who have no concern over death. Their creator, he says, keeps and sustains them eternally by his will alone, and if this will did not maintain them they would all have to die. My deeds, he says, can all be dissolved, so poor and obscure is my power in comparison with the great power of the god who in his presence sees the three aspects of temporality under a moment of eternity. 19055

"He is the king, the emperor, who tells the gods that he is their father. Those who read Plato know this fact, for such are the words there; at least this is the meaning in the French language. 19077

" 'O gods of gods whose maker, father, and creator I am, and who are my creatures, my works, and my products, you are by nature corruptible but eternal through my will. For there will never be anything made by Nature, however great care she gives to it, that may not fail at some time; but whatever God, strong, good, and wise without equal, wishes to bring together and regulate with reason, He will never wish nor has ever wished to dissolve. Corruption will be powerless against it. Therefore I draw this conclusion: since you began to exist through the will of your master, who made you and engendered you and by whom I hold you and will hold you, you are not entirely free of mortality nor of corruption, since I would have seen you all die if I had not maintained you. By nature you can die, but by my will you will never 19083 die, for my will has lordship over the bonds of your life, the bonds that hold together its compositions, and from my will eternity comes to you.'

19113   "This is the meaning of the words that Plato wanted to put into his book when he dared to speak better of God. He valued and glorified Him more than did any earthly being among the ancient philosophers. He could still not say enough, for he was not capable of understanding very perfectly what nothing except a virgin's womb could ever comprehend. But it is true without fail that she whose womb swelled understood more than Plato, for she knew from the time that she bore Him and rejoiced in doing so, that He was the wondrous sphere that can have no end, that shoots its center through every place and whose circumference has no fixed place. She knew that He was the wondrous triangle whose unity creates three angles, but whose three angles make only one

19137   whole. He is the triangular circle, the circular triangle who harbored in the virgin. Plato did not know as much as that; he did not see that the triple unity in this simple trinity, the sovereign deity clothed in a human skin, is God who is called Creator. He created man's understanding and in making it, gave it to man. But to tell the truth, man has repaid Him badly, for afterward he thought to deceive God; but he has deceived himself. For this deceit my Lord received His death when, without me, He took on human flesh to remove the wretch from his suffering. He did so without me, for I do not know how He did, except that He can do everything by His commandment. Instead I was very deeply amazed when for wretched man He was born in the flesh of the Virgin Mary and afterward was hanged in the flesh. It could never be through me that anything might ever be born of a virgin. In former times this Incarnation was foretold by many prophets, Jewish and pagan, so that we might better calm our hearts and strive to believe that the prophecy might be true. In Virgil's *Bucolics* we read this voice of the Sibyl, taught by the Holy Spirit: 'Already a new line is sent down to us on earth from high heaven to guide the people, who have lost their way. With this line the age of iron will perish and the age of gold will spring up in the world.'

19177   Even Albumazar, however he knew about the matter, testifies that within the sign of the virgin would be born a worthy maiden who will be, he says, virgin and mother and will give suck to her

father, and whose husband will be near her without touching her at
all. Anyone who wants to have Albumazar can know this sentence,
since it lies all ready in the book. Every year in September Christian people who remember such a birth hold a feast for it.

"But our Lord Jesus knows that, with everything that I have   19191
talked about, I have labored for man; it is for this wretch that I
take this trouble. He is the end of all my work, and he alone works
against my laws. This disloyal, forsworn creature does not consider
himself repaid in any way; there is nothing that can satisfy him.
What is the good of it? What more could one say? The honors
that I did him could not be withdrawn, and he in turn shamed
me so much that one could not measure or count how much. Fair
sweet priest, fair chaplain, is it then just that I love him, that
I hold any more reverence for him, when I find him lacking when
he is tested? So help me God on the cross, I repent very much
of having made man. But by the death suffered by Him whom
Judas offered the kiss and whom Longinus struck with his lance,
since he has done so much against me, I will tell the story of his
fall before God, who gave him to me when he created man in his
image. I am a woman and cannot keep silent; from now on I want
to reveal everything, for a woman can hide nothing. Man was
never better vilified than he will be now. It was an evil hour for
him when he wandered so far from me. His vices will be recounted; I shall tell the whole truth.

"He is a proud, murderous thief, cruel, covetous, miserly, and   19225
treacherous. He is desperate, greedy, slanderous, hateful, and
spiteful; unfaithful and envious, he lies, perjures himself, and
falsifies; he is foolish, boastful, inconstant, and senseless; he is a
quarrelsome idolator, a traitorous, false hypocrite, and a lazy
sodomite; in short he is such a stupid wretch that he is slave to all
the vices, and harbors them all within himself. See with what
shackles the miserable creature chains himself. Does he do well to
go buying his death by giving himself to such evils? And since all
things must return the gift that they receive at the beginning of
their existence, how will man dare, when he comes before his
Master, to look at Him? He should always have served and
honored his Master as much as he could, and he should have kept
himself from evil. With what eyes will his Judge look at him
when the miserable creature, with a heart so apathetic that he has

no desire to do well, is proved so wicked toward his Judge that he is found out in such vices? Great and small do the worst that they can as long as they keep their honor, and it seems that they have sworn an agreement with each other to do so. However, each one's honor is not often safe through agreement; instead, they receive

19263   very great suffering, or death, or great worldly shame. What can the wretch think if he wants to recount his sins, when he comes before the Judge who weighs all things rightly, without error and without twisting or turning anything? What reward can he expect except the rope for leading him off to be hanged on the sorrowful gibbet of hell, where he will be taken and put in iron, riveted into eternal shackles, before the prince of devils? Or he will be boiled in a copper, roasted in front and behind on coals or on grills, or like Ixion, held with large pegs on cutting wheels that the devils turn with their paws. Or he will die of thirst and hunger in the marshes, along with Tantalus, who always bathes in water up to his chin but will never approach it with his mouth no matter how much his thirst drives him on. The more he follows the water, the lower it goes. Such strong hunger torments him that it can never be satisfied; instead he dies enraged by hunger. He cannot pick the apple that he always sees hanging at his nose, for when

19295   he pursues it with his mouth, the apple raises itself higher. Or he will role the millstone along the surface of the rock, then go find it to roll it again, never to cease, as you did, O wretched Sisyphus, who were put there for that task. Or he will try to fill the bottomless cask and never succeed in filling it, as the Belidians did on account of their ancient follies. You know, fair Genius, how those vultures strove to eat Tityus's liver; nothing could drive them away from it. In that place there are also many other great torments, cruelties, and villainies into which, perhaps, man will be put to endure tribulation, with great suffering and torture, until I am well revenged on him. In faith, if the Judge I spoke of before, who judges everything in word and deed, were only compassionate, the usurers' loans would perhaps be good and delightful; but he is always just and much to be feared. To enter into sin is evil.

19323   "Of course, I leave to God all the sins with which the wretch is stained; let God take care of them and punish when He pleases. But of those of whom Love complains (for I have indeed heard the complaint), I complain myself, as much as I can, and I should do so because they have denied me the tribute that all men have owed me, and always do and always will owe me as long as they receive my tools. O Genius with the gift of speech, go among the army to the God of Love, who strives mightily to serve me and who, I am certain, loves me so much that with his open, good-natured heart he wants to draw close to my works more than iron does to a magnet. Tell him that I send greetings to him and to my friend, the lady Venus, and to his entire barony as well, except False Seeming alone, because he always goes congregating with those proud criminals, those dangerous hypocrites of whom Scripture says that they are pseudoprophets. And I consider Abstinence very suspect of being proud and like False Seeming, however humble and charitable she seems.

"If False Seeming is found any more with such proved traitors,   19355 may neither he nor his friend Abstinence take part in my salvation. Such people are very much to be feared. If Love had not known certainly that they were so necessary to him that he could do nothing without them, he should have shoved them out of his army if it pleased him. But if there are advocates to lessen their wickedness in the case for pure lovers, I pardon them their fraud.

"Go, my friend, to the God of Love, carrying my complaints   19369 and outcries, not so that he may do me justice but so that he may take comfort and solace when he hears this news, which should be very pleasing to him and harmful to our enemies, and so that he may cease to be troubled by the worry that I see him occupied with. Tell him that I send you there to excommunicate all those who want to work against us, and that I send you to absolve the valiant ones who work with good heart to follow strictly the rules that are written in my book, those stalwarts who strive mightily to multiply their lines and who think about loving well. I must call them all my friends and give delights to their souls. But they are to guard themselves well against the vices that I have told you about before, for they destroy all goodness. Give them a pardon that is fully effective, not for ten years, for they would not think it worth a penny, but a full pardon forever for everything that they have done when they know fully how to confess their sins.

"When you come into the army, where you will be held very   19399 dear, and after you have greeted them for me as you know how, announce in their hearing the pardon and judgment that I wish to be written here."

19406   Then he wrote it at her dictation, and afterward she sealed it, gave it to him, and begged him to go off immediately as long as she might be absolved for what had been taken off her mind.

19411   As soon as the goddess Lady Nature had confessed, then straightway, as law and custom wish it, the valiant priest Genius absolved her and gave her a penance that was suitable and good, one that accorded with the magnitude of the fault that he thought she had committed. He enjoined her to remain within her forge and labor as she was accustomed to do when she had no sorrow; he told her always to perform her service in this way until the King who can arrange everything and make and destroy everything might give some other counsel.

19427   "Sir," she said, "I will do so willingly."

"And meanwhile," said Genius, "I will go off very quickly to bring help to pure lovers. But first I will take off this silk chasuble, this alb and surplice."

19434   Then he went to hang everything on a hook and dressed in his less cumbersome worldly clothing, as if he were going off to a carol. He then took wings for immediate flight.

10

GENIUS'S SOLUTION

Nature remained in her forge, took her hammers and struck out and shaped everything as she had done before, while Genius, with no more delay, beat his wings faster than the wind. He came quickly to the army, but did not find False Seeming there. He had left in a hurry as soon as the Old Woman was captured, the one who opened the door of the enclosure for me and helped me advance to the point where I was allowed to speak to Fair Welcoming; he had not wanted to wait any longer, but had fled without asking leave. There is no question, however, that Genius found Constrained Abstinence, who, when she saw the priest coming, got ready with all her might to run after False Seeming in such great haste that she could hardly be held back; for, provided that no one else saw her who would give her four bezants, she would not have taken up with the priest unless False Seeming were there.

At that same time, Genius, with no more delay, greeted them all as he was supposed to and, forgetting nothing, told them the reason for his coming. I shall not try to make a story out of the great joy that they showed when they heard this news; instead I want to shorten my account and lighten your ears; many times, when a preacher does not dispatch briefly, he makes his audience leave by being too prolix in his speaking.

Straightway the God of Love put a chasuble on Genius. He gave him a ring, a crosier, and a mitre clearer than crystal or glass. They had so great a desire to hear his judgment read that they sought no other preparation. Venus, who was so delighted and gay that she could not stop laughing, could not keep quiet. In Genius's hand she placed a burning torch, not of virgin wax, the more to enforce his anathema when he would have finished his theme.

Without taking any more time, Genius then mounted a large platform, the better to read the text, according to the things told about before. The barons sat on the ground and didn't want to seek any other seats. Genius unfolded the charter, made a sign with his hand all around him, and called for silence. Those whom his words pleased looked at and nudged one another. Then they quieted down immediately and listened while the definitive sentence began:

19505 "By the authority of Nature, who has the care of the whole world, as vicar and constable of the eternal emperor, who sits in the sovereign tower of the noble city of the world, of which he made Nature the minister; Nature who administers all good things through the influence of the stars, for they ordain everything according to the imperial justice that Nature executes; Nature, who has given birth to all things since this world came into being, who gives them their allotted time for growth and increase, and who never for nothing made anything under the heaven that continues without delay to turn around the earth, as high below as above, and never stops, night or day, but turns always without rest—by the authority of Nature, let all those disloyal apostates, of high rank or low, who hold in despite the acts by which Nature is supported, be excommunicated and condemned without any delay. And let him who strives with all his force to maintain Nature, who struggles to love well, without any base thought, but with lawful labor, go off to paradise decked with flowers. As long as he makes a good confession, I will take on me all his deeds with such power as I can bring to them, and he will never have to bear the smallest pardon for them.

19543 "It was an evil hour when Nature, in accordance with her laws and customs, gave to those false ones of whom I have been speaking their styluses and tablets, hammers and anvils, the plowshares with good sharp points for the use of their plows, and the fallow fields, not stony but rich and verdurous, that need to be plowed and dug deep if one wants to enjoy them; it is an evil hour when they do not want to labor at serving and honoring Nature, but wish rather to destroy her by preferring to flee from her anvils, her tablets and fallow fields, which she made so precious and so dear in order to continue things so that Death might not kill them.

19561 "These disloyal creatures of whom I tell should be greatly ashamed when they do not deign to put their hands to the tablets to write a letter or make a mark that shows. The tablets have a very cruel future, since they will become all rusty if they are kept idle. Now that they let the anvils perish without striking a blow with the hammer, the rust can bring them down, and no one will hear them hammered or beaten. If no one thrusts the plowshare into the fallow fields, they will remain fallow. These people might as well be buried alive when they dare to flee from the tools that God shaped with his hand when he gave them to my lady. He wanted to give them to her so that she would know how to fashion similar ones in order to give eternal existence to creatures subject to corruption.

"It seems certain that these disloyal creatures work great evil, 19583 because if all men together wished to avoid their tools for sixty years, men would never engender. If this situation is pleasing to God, then he certainly wants the world to fail or the lands to remain bare, peopled with dumb animals, unless he made new men, if it pleased him to make them again, or revived the others to repopulate the earth. Then if these people kept themselves virgin for sixty years, they would perish again, so that, if God should please, he would always have to make them again.

"And if there were anyone who wanted to say that God in his 19599 grace took the desire away from one and not from another, then, since his renown is so great and he has never ceased to do good, it should be pleasing to him to create everyone the same, so that he might put such grace in them. Thus I come back to my conclusion that everything would go to perdition. I do not know how to reply to this position, unless faith wants to explain belief. At their beginnings, God loves all equally and gives reasonable souls to men as well as to women. And I believe that he would want each soul, not only one, to keep to the best road, the one by which it might most quickly come to him. If then God wants some to live as virgins in order to follow him better, why will he not wish it for others? What reason will deter him? It seems then that it wouldn't matter to him if engendering were to cease. Let him reply who wants to; I know nothing more of the matter. May they who divine it become divine and not cease their divining.

"But those who do not write with their styluses, by which mortals 19629 live forever, on the beautiful precious tablets that Nature did not prepare for them to leave idle, but instead loaned to them in order that everyone might be a writer and that we all, men and women, might live; those who receive the two hammers and do not forge with them as they justly should on the straight anvil; those who are so blinded by their sins, by the pride that takes them off their road, so that they despise the straight furrow of the beautiful, fecund field and like unhappy creatures go off to plow in desert land where their seeding goes to waste; those who will never keep to the straight track, but instead go overturning the plow, who confirm their evil rules by abnormal exceptions when they want to follow Orpheus (he did not know how to plow or write or forge in the true forge—may he be hanged by the throat!—when he showed himself so evil toward Nature by contriving such rules for them); those who despise such a mistress when they read her rules backward and do not want to take them by the good end in order to understand their true sense, but instead pervert what is written when they come to read it; since all these want to be of that party, may they, in addition to the excommunication that sends them all to damnation, suffer, before their death, the loss of their

19669   purse and testicles, the signs that they are male! May they lose the pendants on which the purse hangs! May they have the hammers that are attached within torn out! May their styluses be taken away from them when they have not wished to write within the precious tablets that were suitable for them! And if they don't plow straight with their plows and shares, may they have their bones broken without their ever being mended! May all those who want to follow them live in great shame! May their dirty, horrible sin be sorrowful and painful to them; may it cause them to be beaten with sticks everywhere, so that one sees them as they are.

19687   "For God's sake, my lords, you who live, take care not to follow such people. At the works of Nature, be quicker than any squirrel, lighter and more mobile than a bird or the wind may be. Do not lose this good pardon; provided that you work well at this, I pardon you all your sins. Move, skip, leap; don't let yourself get cold or let your limbs become tepid. Put all your tools to work; he who works well keeps warm enough.

19701   "Plow, for God's sake, my barons, plow and restore your lineages. Unless you think on plowing vigorously, there is nothing that can restore them. Tuck up your clothes in front, as though to take the air; or if you please, be quite bare, but don't get too cold or too hot. With your two hands quite bare raise the guideboards of your plows; support them stoutly with your arms and exert yourself to push in stiffly with the plowshare in the straight path, the better to sink into the furrow. And for God's sake never let the horses in front go slowly; spur them harshly, and when you want to plow more deeply give them the greatest blows that you can ever give. Couple horned oxen to the plow yokes, and wake them up with goads. Then we will receive you with our benefits. If you spur them well and often, you will necessarily plow better.

"And when you have plowed so much that you are tired out and it comes to the point where you have to rest—for nothing can last long without rest—you will not be able to begin again immediately to advance the job farther; but do not let your desire flag. 19727

"Cadmus, at a word from lady Pallas, plowed more than an arpent of ground and sowed the teeth of a serpent. From these, armed knights sprang up and fought one another until they all died on the spot except five who were his companions and wanted to give him help when he had to build the walls of Thebes, the city that he founded. With him they laid the stones and populated his city, one of great antiquity. This sowing of Cadmus was very good; he thus advanced his people. If you also begin well, you will advance your lines a great deal. 19736

"And you also have two very great advantages in saving your lines: if you don't want to be the third, you have addled wits. You have only one difficulty; defend yourself vigorously. You are attacked from one direction. Three champions are very slack—and they well deserve to be beaten—if they cannot conquer the fourth. 19753

"If you do not know, there are three sisters, two of whom help you; only the third harms you, for she cuts short all lives. You should know that Cloto, who carries the spindle, and Lachesis, who draws out the thread, are of great comfort to you. But Atropos breaks and cuts off whatever these two can spin. Atropos seeks to trick you. If you don't dig deep, she will bury your whole race, and she goes around spying on you yourself. We have never seen a worse animal, nor do you have a greater enemy. My lords, thank you, thank you, my lords. Remember your good fathers and your old mothers. Conform your deeds to theirs, and take care that you do not degenerate. What did they do? Pay good heed to it. 19763

If you consider their prowess, you see that they defended themselves so well that they have given you this existence. If it weren't for their chivalry, you would not be alive now. They had great compassion for you. With love and amity think of the others who will come and who will maintain your line.

19793   "Don't let yourselves be overcome. You have styluses; think about writing. Don't leave your arms in muffs; hammer away, use forge and bellows; help Cloto and Lachesis so that if Atropos, who is so villainous, cuts six threads, a dozen more may spring from them. Think about multiplying yourself, and you will thus be able to trick the cruel, unyielding Atropos, who hinders everything.

19805   "This miserable wretch, who strives against lives and whose heart is so full of joy over deaths, nourishes the knave Cerberus. He craves their deaths so much that he quite fries in lechery over it; if the wench had not helped him he would have died of raging hunger, for, if she had not done so, he could never have found anyone who could. She does not stop feeding him, and in order to feed him pleasantly, she hangs the cur at her breasts, which are triple, not double; he hides his three snouts in her breasts and butts and pulls and sucks on them. He never was weaned and never will be. He never asks to be given any other milk to drink, nor to be fed on any other meat except bodies and souls alone. And she throws men and women by mounds into his triple gullet. She feeds it all alone, and she always thinks that she can fill it; but she always, no matter how much she tries to fill it, finds it empty. The three cruel pursurers, the avengers of crimes, Alecto, Thesiphone—for I have the name of each—and the third, whose name is Megara, are all in great torment over Atropos's food. Megara alone will eat you all, if she can.

19839   "These three await you in hell. There, before the three provosts therein, sitting in full consistory, they bind those who committed crimes when they had life in their bodies, and beat them, switch them, hang them; they strike them, rain blows on them, skin them, and stamp on them; they drown, burn, grill, and boil them. By means of these tortures, the provosts wring from them the confessions of all the wicked things that they ever did from the time that they were born. All people tremble before them, and I am a coward, it seems, if I dare not name these provosts here.

They are Rhadamanthus and Minos, and the third, their brother Æacus. Jupiter was the father of these three. In the world these three had the reputation of being such worthy men and of maintaining justice so well that they became judges in hell. This was the reward that Pluto gave them; he was so eager for them that their souls left their bodies, and they filled the office of judge in hell.

"For God's sake, my lords, do not go there. Fight against the   19865
vices that Nature, our mistress, has just told me about today at my mass. She told me them all, and I never sat down afterward. You will find twenty-six of them, more harmful than you think. If you are indeed empty of the filth of all these vices, you will never enter the enclosures of the three wenches I named before, who have such evil reputations, and you will not fear the judgments of the provosts filled with condemnation. I would tell these vices to you, but to do so would be an excessive undertaking. The lovely Romance of the Rose explains them to you quite briefly; please look at them there so that you may guard against them better.

"Think of leading a good life; let each man embrace his sweet-   19885
heart and each woman her lover and kiss and feast and comfort him. If you love each other loyally you should never be blamed for doing so. And when you have played enough, as I have recommended here, think of confessing yourselves well, in order to do good and avoid evil, and call upon the heavenly God whom Nature calls her master. He will save you in the end, when Atropos buries you. He is the salvation of body and soul and the beautiful mirror of my lady, who would never know anything if she did not have this beautiful mirror. It is he who governs and rules her, and my lady has no other rule. He taught her whatever she knows when he took her for his chamberlain.

"Now, my lords, I wish, and my lady also orders that each   19907
of you take in this sermon, word for word, just as I preach it. One does not always have one's book and it is a great trouble to write down. Take it in so that you retain it by heart and are able to recite it, in whatever place you come to, fortresses, castles, cities, and towns, winter and summer, to those who were not here. It is a good thing to remember the lecture when it comes from a good school, and a better thing to tell it again; as a result, one may

rise in the esteem of others. My lecture is full of great virtue, a hundred times more precious than sapphires, red rubies or pink ones. Fair lords, my lady, for her law, needs preachers to chastise the sinners who transgress her rules when they should maintain and keep them.

19931   "And if you preach in this way, upon my word and promise and as long as your deeds accord with your words, you will never be prevented from entering the park of the lovely field where the son of the virgin ewe in all his white fleece leads his flock with him, leaping over the grass. They follow after him, not in a crowd, but in a scattered company, along the narrow calm path that is so little traveled and beaten down that it is covered with flowers and grass. The little white ewes, good-natured and open, go along grazing and eating on the young grass and flowers that spring up there. But you must know that they have a pasture of such a wondrous nature that the delightful little flowers that spring up fresh and clean, all in their spring maidenhood, are as young and new as stars winking through the green grass in the morning dew. Throughout the whole day they keep their own early beauty, their pure colors, fresh and live, and in the evening they are not aged, but can be gathered the same then as in the morning, if anyone wants to put out his hand to collect them. You may know for certain that they are neither too closed nor too open, but shine through the grass at the best stage of their growth. For the sun shining therein is not harmful to them and does not consume the dew with which they are sprinkled; it so sweetens their roots that it keeps the flowers always in pure beauty.

19975   "I tell you too that no matter how much of the grass and flowers the little sheep can nibble and eat, for they will always want to eat them, they cannot eat as much as they will always see spring up again. I tell you further, and don't think it a fable, that the flowers and grass cannot decay no matter how much the sheep graze on them. And their pastures cost the sheep nothing, for their skins are not sold at the end, nor their fleeces used up to make woolen cloth or coverings for people strange to them. They will never be taken away, nor will their flesh be eaten in the end, or decay or rot or be overtaken by disease. But certainly, whatever I say, I do not doubt that the Good Shepherd, who leads them grazing before him, may be clothed in their wool; but he neither skins them nor plucks from them anything that costs them the price of one feather. But it pleases and seems good to him that his robe resemble theirs.

"I will say more, but not to bore you: they never saw night born. They have only one day with no approach whatever toward evening, and morning cannot begin there, no matter how far the dawn can advance. Evening is like morning, and morning resembles evening. I tell you the same thing about every hour. The day dwells forever in a moment and cannot darken, however much the night may struggle against it. It has no temporal measure, the day that is so fair, that lasts forever and smiles with present brightness. It has neither future nor past, for, if I sense the truth well, all three times are present there, and the present encompasses the day. But it is not a present that passes away, in part, to form an end, nor of which part is still to come; for past was never present there. Moreover, I say to you, the future is of such stable permanence that it will never have presence. For the shining sun always appears and establishes the day at a certain point such that no man ever lived in an eternal spring so beautiful and so pure, not even when Saturn reigned as ruler over the ages of gold. His son Jupiter did him a great outrage and injury when he cut off his testicles.

"But certainly, if we tell the truth, anyone who castrates a worthy man does him a very great shame and injury; for, even though I may say nothing about his great shame and discomfort, still anyone who takes away a man's testicles robs him at least, I have no doubt at all, of the love of his sweetheart, no matter how closely she was bound to him. Or if he is perhaps married his affairs will go so badly that he will lose the love of his loyal wife, no matter how good-natured she was. It is a great sin to castrate a man. Anyone who castrates a man robs him not just of his testicles, nor of his sweetheart whom he holds very dear and whose fair face he will never see, nor of his wife, for these are the least; he robs him especially of the boldness in human ways that should exist in valiant men. For we are certain that castrated men are perverse and malicious cowards because they have the ways of women. Certainly no eunuch has any bravery whatever in him, unless perhaps in some vice, to do something very malicious. All women are very bold at doing deeds of great devilishness, and eunuchs resemble them in

20001

20037

20058

this respect. In particular, the castrator, even though he may not be a murderer or a thief nor have committed any mortal sin, at least he has sinned to the extent of doing Nature a great wrong in stealing the power of engendering. No one, no matter how well he had thought about it, could excuse him for his act; at least I couldn't, for if I thought about it and told the truth, I could wear out my tongue before I could excuse the castrator for such a sin, such a wrong as he has committed toward Nature.

20083   "But whatever sin it may be, Jupiter made no point of it, provided only that he succeeded in holding the ruling power in his hand. When he became king and was considered the lord of the world, he gave out his commandments, laws, and statutes, and immediately he had his proclamation called out openly in everyone's hearing in order to teach them how to live. I will tell you the import of this proclamation:

20095   " 'Jupiter, who rules the world, commands and establishes as a rule that each one think of living comfortably. If anyone knows of something which may please him, let him do it, if he can, in order to bring solace to his heart.'

20101   "He did not preach anything else, but gave general permission that everyone individually might do whatever he himself saw to be delightful. As he said, delight is the best thing that can exist and the sovereign good in life; everyone should desire it. And in order that all might follow him and take their example for living from his acts, the gay Dan Jupiter, who valued delight so highly, did for his body whatever pleased it.

20115   "And as he who wrote the *Bucolics* says in the *Georgics*—for he found in Greek books how Jupiter acted—before Jupiter came there was no one who held a plow; no one had ever plowed, spaded, or cultivated a field. The simple people, peaceable and good, had never laid down boundaries. Together they sought for the good things that came at their wish. Jupiter commanded that the earth be parceled out, and he divided it into lots, but no man knew how to look for his portion. He put venom into snakes and raised malice so high that he taught wolves to ravin; he cut down the oaks with honey in them and stopped the brooks of wine. He grew so ingenious at tormenting people that he extinguished fire everywhere, and he was such a subtle deceiver that he made them search for it in rocks. He created various new arts: he named and

numbered the stars, had snares, nets, and lime traps stretched to
capture wild animals, and cried the first dogs after them, a thing
no one had done before. With the malice that torments men he
subdued the birds of prey. On battle sites he set up attacks by sparrow hawks on partridges and quail, he arranged tournaments in
the clouds between goshawks, falcons, and cranes, and he made
them return to the lure. To keep their favor, so that they would   20152
return to his hand, he fed them night and morning. Thus this
young man made slaves of the cruel birds and put them into bondage so that, like horrible ravishers, they were the enemies of the
other, peaceable birds. He did so because he could not pursue
them through the air, and he did not want to live without their
flesh; he was so much a gourmand and was so fond of fowl that
he wanted instead to eat them. He put ferrets into rabbits' burrows
to attack them and make them leap out into his nets. He was so
fond of his body that he had the fish from the seas and rivers
scaled, roasted, and skinned, and he made entirely new sauces of
different kinds of spices and many herbs.

"Thus have the arts sprung up, for all things are conquered by   20175
labor and hard poverty; through these things people exist in great
care. For difficulties incite people's ingenuity because of the pain
that they find in them. Thus said Ovid, who, as he himself tells,
had a great deal of good and ill, honor and shame, as long as he
lived. In short, when Jupiter set out to take the earth, he intended
nothing other than changing the state of the empire from good to
ill and from ill to worse. He was a very lax manager. He diminished the time of spring and divided the year into four parts, as it
is divided now: summer, spring, autumn, and winter, the four
different seasons that all used to be contained in spring. But Jupiter
no longer wished it so. When he set himself up to rule, he destroyed the ages of gold and created the ages of silver. These afterward were those of brass, for men did not then cease becoming
worse, so close to evil did they want to draw. Now their estate
has become so alien that the age of brass is changed to that of iron,
and the gods of the halls that are forever dark and filthy are very
happy, for they are jealous of men as long as they see them alive.
They have the black sheep tied up in their stable, from which they   20209
will never be released, the sorrowful black sheep, worn out,
wretched, mortally sick, who did not want to go along the path

that the white lamb offers, the path by which they would all have been freed, and their black fleeces made white, at the time when they took the large broad road by which they brought themselves to their dwelling there, in so plentiful a company that it occupied the whole road.

20221   "But no beast that goes therein ever carries a fleece that is worth anything or from which one might make cloth, unless it is some awful hair shirt, sharper and more piercing, when it is next to the ribs, than a coat made of the hides of bristly hedgehogs would be. But anyone who wanted to card the wool of the white animals, soft and smooth and sleek, and make cloth of the fleece, provided that he had such an abundance of it, certainly emperors or kings— angels in fact, if they wore woolen clothing—would be dressed in it for festal occasions. Therefore, you may know that he who could have such robes would be very nobly dressed, and for this reason he should hold them especially dear, for there are very few such beasts.

20243   "The shepherd who keeps the flock in this beautiful park is not stupid, and it is a fact that he would not allow any black animal to enter for any begging that it could do, so much does it please him to keep the white ones separate. They know their shepherd well, and for that reason go to shelter with him; and since he knows them well, they are the better received.

20253   "And I tell you that the most compassionate, beautiful, and delightful of all these worthy animals is the leaping white lamb who by his work and his suffering leads the sheep to the park, for he knows that if one strays off and the wolf only sees her, the wolf who seeks no other thing than that she stray from the path of the lamb intent on leading them, then he will carry her off without a struggle and eat her alive, and nothing alive can keep him from doing so.

20267   "My lords, this lambs awaits you, but we will say no more about him except to pray to God the father that, through his mother's request, he grant that he may so guide the sheep that the wolf may not harm them and that you may not fail, because of sin, to go and play in that park that is very beautiful and delightful, redolent with grass, flowers, violets and roses, and all good things. If any- one wanted to draw a comparison between the lovely square gar- den, closed with the little barred wicket, where this lover saw the

carol where Diversion dances with his people, and this fair park
that I am describing, as wondrously fair as one could wish it, he
would make a very great mistake if he did not draw the comparison
as one would between a fable and the truth. Anyone who was inside this park or who only cast his eye within would dare to swear
safely that the garden was nothing in comparison with this enclosure. This is not built in a square, but is so round and carefully made that no beryl or ball was ever so well rounded a shape.
What do you want me to tell you? Let us speak of the things
that the Lover saw at that time, both inside and outside, and in
order not to tire ourselves, we will pass over them in a few words.

"Outside the garden he saw ten ugly images called portraits. 20303
But if one sought outside this park one would find there the
figures of hell and all the devils, most ugly and terrifying, all
the faults and excesses that they commit in hell, their dwelling
place, and one would find Cerberus, who keeps everything closed.
One would find the whole earth, with its ancient riches and all
earthly things. One would see the sea itself, all salt-water fish, all
things of the sea, fresh waters, cloudy and clear, and the great
and small things that are contained in fresh water. One would see
the air and all its birds, the flies, butterflies, and everything that
hums through the air. One would see the fire that entirely sur-
rounds the possessions and dwellings of all the other elements.
Then one would see all the stars, clear, shining, and beautiful,
either wandering or fixed, attached in their spheres. Anyone there
would see all these things, shut out from this fair park, as openly
portrayed as if they appeared there themselves.

"Now let us go back to the garden and speak of the things inside. 20335
The Lover said that he saw Diversion leading his farandole on
the fresh grass, and his people with him, caroling on the sweet-
smelling flowers. The young man said too that he saw plants, trees,
animals, birds, brooks and springs babbling and singing over the
gravel, and the fountain under the pine; and he boasts that since
the time of Pepin there was not such a pine, and that the fountain
was also filled with very great beauty.

"For God's sake, my lords, take care. If anyone looks at the 20349
truth, the things contained here are trifles and bagatelles. There is
nothing here that can be stable; whatever he saw is corruptible.
He saw carols that will pass away; all those who dance them will

disappear, and so will all the things that he saw enclosed therein. For when Cerberus's nurse Atropos wants to use her power, and she uses it forever without getting tired, there is no human practice that can keep her from consuming everything. She refuses nothing; from behind she spies on all, except the gods, if there are any, for certainly divine things are not subject to death.

20369   "But now let us talk of the beautiful things that are enclosed in this lovely park. I shall speak of them in general, for I want to stop soon. If anyone wants a correct account, I cannot speak properly of it, since no heart could conceive nor mouth of man tell of the great beauty and worth of the things that are contained in that place, the lovely games, the great joys, eternal and true, that the carolers who dwell in that enclosure experience. All who divert themselves therein possess all things that are delightful, true, and eternal. It is indeed right that it should be so, for all good things well forth from the same fountain, one that waters the entire enclosure; from its streams drink the animals who wish and deserve to enter there after they are separated from the black sheep. The fountain is so precious and health-giving, so beautiful and clear, clean and pure, that after they have drunk from it, they can never be thirsty, and they will live as they wish without sickness or death. They will enter the gates in good time, in good time they will see the lamb that they followed along the narrow path under the protection of the wise shepherd who wanted to harbor them with him. No man who could drink once of that fountain would die.

20405   This is not the fountain beneath the tree, the one that the Lover saw in the rock of marble. One should scorn him when he praises that fountain. It is the perilous fountain, so bitter and poisonous that it killed the fair Narcissus when he looked at himself in it. The Lover himself is not ashamed to recognize its peril, but bears witness to it. He does not conceal its cruelty when he calls it the perilous mirror, and he says that when he looked at himself in it, he found himself so heavy and full of grief that many times thereafter he sighed over it. You see what sweetness he feels in the water! God! What a good and pleasing fountain, where the well become sick! And how good it is to bend over and look at oneself in the water!

20425   "He says that the fountain comes in great waves from two deep springs. But I know well that its springs and waters do not come of itself. There is nothing about it that does not come to it from elsewhere.

"Then he says also, since it never stops, that the fountain is brighter than pure silver. Now see what trifles he urges on you. In fact it is so cloudy and ugly that no one who puts his head there to look at himself sees a drop. They all struggle and go to great pains there in order not to know themselves at all. 20431

"At the bottom, he says, there are two crystals which the unclouded sun causes to shine so brightly, when it throws its rays there, that he who watches them always sees half of the things that are enclosed in the garden; so bright and powerful are the crystals that if he wants to turn to the other side he can see the rest of the things in the garden. On the contrary, these stones are murky and cloudy. Why don't they show everything together when the sun throws its beams at them? In faith, they cannot, it seems, because of the darkness that obscures them. They are so murky and dark that they cannot be effective by themselves for him who looks at himself therein, since they get their brightness from elsewhere. If the sun's rays do not strike far enough to meet the crystals, they have no power to show anything. But the fountain that I am describing to you is as beautiful as one could wish. Now prick up your ears a little to hear me tell some wonderful things about it. 20439

"The fountain that I have spoken of, with its beauty and its usefulness as a cure for all tired-out animals, always rolls its delicious waters, sweet, clear, and lively, from three fine springs. Each is so close to the other that they all form one, so that when you see them all, if you want to take the time to count them, you will find both one and three in them. You will never find four there, but always three and always one. Such is their common characteristic. 20465

"We have never seen such a fountain, for it issues from itself. Other fountains, issuing from alien veins, do not produce it. It runs all by itself and has no need of any other channel; it keeps to its living course, staying firmer than native rock. It needs no marble stone nor the covering of a tree, for the water, never ceasing, comes from a source so high that no tree can grow so tall that the height of the water is not greater. However, without fail, you see a little lowly olive tree on a slope, as if it were descending, and 20479 all the water passes away underneath it. When the little olive tree feels the fountain of which I tell, and when the fountain waters its roots with its sweet, pure waters, it takes such nourishment from it that it grows heavy with both leaves and fruit. It becomes so tall and broad that the pine he told you about never grew so tall from the earth, nor extended its branches so far, nor gave such beautiful shade.

20509   "Standing erect, this olive extends its branches over the fountain. Thus it shades the fountain, and there the little animals hide in the coolness of the lovely shade and sip the sweet dews that the pleasant coolness spreads over the flowers and the tender grass. On the olive tree hangs a small scroll with little letters on it, saying to those who read them as they lie in the shade of the olive tree: 'Here runs the fountain of life beneath the leafy olive tree that bears the fruit of salvation.' What pine is worth as much?

20525   "I say to you, and foolish people will hardly believe this and many will consider it a fable, that in this fountain there shines a carbuncle that is marvelous beyond all marvelous stones, completely round and with three facets. It sits in the midst so tall that one sees it plainly glowing throughout the park. Neither wind nor rain nor cloud can deflect its rays, so beautiful and noble is it. Know too that the virtue of the stone is such that each facet is worth as much as the other two, such are their powers between them. Two are worth only that one, however beautiful each may be. No matter how well he can apply himself, no one can distinguish the facets nor so join them by thinking that he may not find them separate. But no sun illumines it; it has a color so pure, so bright and shining, that the sun that brightens the twin crystals in the other water would be dark and murky beside it. In short, what should I tell you? No other sun shines within but this glowing carbuncle. This is the sun that they have within, a sun that abounds

20559   more in splendor than does any sun in the world. This sun sends night into exile, this creates the day that I said lasts eternally, without end and without beginning, maintaining itself spontaneously at a single point without passing a zodiacal sign, a degree, or midnight or some other division into which time may be separated. It has such wondrous power that as soon as those who go there to see it bend toward it and see their faces mirrored in the water, they always, no matter where they may be, see all things in the

park and understand them rightly, themselves as well. After they
have seen themselves there, they become such wise masters that
they will never be deceived by anything that can exist.

"I will teach you about another wonder: the rays of that sun   20579
do not confuse or weaken or dazzle the eyes of those who look at
them, but they strengthen, make joyful, and reinvigorate their
sight by means of their beautiful clarity, full of temperate warmth
that, by its wondrous worth, fills the whole park with the sweet
odor that comes from it. And in order not to detain you too long,
I want in a brief word to remind you that whoever saw the form
and matter of the park could say that in former times Adam was
not formed in so beautiful a paradise.

"For God's sake, my lords, how do the park and the garden   20597
seem to you together? Give in reasonable statements both accidents and substances; say by your loyalty which is of greater
beauty, and consider which of the fountains gives out water of
greater health, virtue, and purity. Judge the nature of the springs
and say which have the greater virtue. Judge the precious stones,
the pine, and the olive that covers the living fountain. If you give
a just judgment in accordance with the evidence that I have read
out to you, I stand by your judgment. For I say to you without
flattery that I do not submit myself entirely to it; if you wanted
to do wrong, to speak falsely or keep the truth silent, I do not
seek to hide from you that I would appeal immediately elsewhere.
In order to bring you the sooner to an agreement, I want briefly
to recall, according to what I have told you, their great virtue and
goodness. The other makes the living drunk with death, while this
fountain makes the dead live again.

"My lords, know for certain that if you act wisely and do what   20627
you should, you will drink from this fountain. And in order that
you may retain all my instruction more easily—for a lesson given
in a few words is more easily remembered—I want to go briefly
over everything that you should do.

"Think how to do honor to Nature; serve her by working well.   20637
If you get anything from someone else, give it back, if you know
how, and if you cannot give back the good things that are spent
or played away, have the good will to do so when you have benefits in plenty. Avoid killing; keep both hands and mouth clean.
Be loyal and compassionate, and then you will go by the delectable

fields, following the path of the lamb, living eternally to drink from the beautiful fountain that is so sweet and bright and healthful that as soon as you drink its water you will never die but go in gladness, forever singing motets, conductuses, and chansonettes on the flowers among the green grass, as you carol beneath the olive tree. What do I see you chattering about here? It is right for me to sheath my flute, for beautiful songs often get boring. From now on I could keep you too long, and I want to finish my sermon to you at this point. Now here it will become apparent what you are to do when you are raised up on high to preach from the balcony."

20668   Genius preached to them thus, delighting and comforting them. Then he threw down his candle on the spot, and its smoky flame spread among everyone. There is no lady who might protect herself from it, so well does Venus know how to spread it, and the wind caught it up so high that all living women have their bodies, their hearts, and their thoughts permeated with that odor. Love in turn spread the news that was read from the document so that no man of worth ever disagreed with the judgment.

20683   When Genius had read everything, the barons were moved with joy. As they said, they had never heard such a good sermon nor ever from the time that they were conceived had they had so great a pardon, or heard as well so just an excommunication. In order that they might not lose the pardon, they all sided with his sentence and replied immediately in lively tones: "Amen, amen; fiat, fiat."

20695   As the matter was at that stage, there was no delay whatever thereafter. Everyone who liked the sermon noted it word for word in his heart, for it seemed to them very salutary because of the good, charitable pardon, and they heard it very willingly. Genius vanished so that no one knew what had become of him.

11

VENUS'S CONFLAGRATION AND THE
WINNING OF THE ROSE

Then more than twenty in the host cried out: "Now to the assault   20704
with no more delay, all who understand the meaning of this sermon! Our enemies are mightily discomfited." Then all rose to
their feet, ready to continue the war, to take everything and level
it to the earth.

Venus, ready for the assault, first demanded that the enemy   20711
surrender. And what did they do? Shame and Fear replied to her:

"Venus," said Shame, "that is clearly impossible. You will never
set foot in here, not even if there were only me. I shall never fear."

When the goddess had heard Shame, she said, "Get out, you   20719
filthy slut. Where will it get you to resist me? You will see everything in a whirlwind if the castle is not surrendered to me. It will
never be defended by you. You would defend it against us! By
God's flesh, you will give it up or I will burn you alive like miserable prisoners. I will set fire to the whole enclosure and raze the
towers and turrets. I'll warm up your rump; I'll burn the pillars,
walls, and posts. Your moat will be filled with the wreckage of all
your outworks; however high you erect them, I will lay them flat
to the ground. And Fair Welcoming will let the rosebuds and
roses be taken at will, one hour by sale, another hour by gift. No
matter how proud you are, all will strike in there. Everyone, with
no exception whatever, will be able to go in procession among the
rosebushes and the roses when I have opened the enclosures. To   20747
trip up Jealousy I will lay the meadows and the pastures low
everywhere, so greatly will I widen the passages. Everyone, lay
or cleric, religious or secular, will there gather buds and roses
without hindrance. No one can avoid it; all will perform their
penance, but the methods will not be without difference: where
some come secretly, others will be very open. Moreover, those
who come secretly will be considered fine men, but the others will

be defamed, called rioters and whoremongers, although their fault is smaller than that of others whom nobody blames.

20765 "It is still true that some evil men (may God and Saint Peter of Rome confound them and their works!) will pass up the roses to follow a worse course; and the devil who so pricks them will give them a chaplet of nettles, for Genius, speaking for Nature, has put all of them under sentence, along with our other enemies, for their vile, filthy ways.

20775 "And as for you, Shame, if I don't trip you up, I hold my bow and my wits at little worth; and I shall never complain of anything but them. Certainly, Shame, I shall never love you nor your mother, Reason, who is so bitter toward lovers. Whoever would believe you and your mother would never love *par amour*."

20783 Venus had no desire to say more, since this much satisfied her well. Then she drew herself up tall and seemed a woman in a towering rage. She drew the bow and engaged the brand, and, when she had well nocked it, brought the bow, no longer than a fathom, up to her ear and aimed, like a good archer, at a tiny narrow aperture which she saw hidden in the tower. This opening was not at the side, but in front, where Nature, by her great cunning, had placed it between two pillars.

20797 These pillars were of very fine silver and supported, in place of a shrine, an image neither too tall nor too short, neither too fat nor too thin in any respect, but constructed, in measure, of arms, shoulders, and hands that erred in neither excess nor defect. The other parts were also very fine. But within there was a sanctuary, more fragrant than pomander, covered by a priceless cloth, the finest and richest between here and Constantinople. If anyone, using reason, were to draw a comparison between this and any other image, he could say that this image was to Pygmalion's as a mouse is to a lion.

20817 Pygmalion, a sculptor who worked in wood, stone, and metals, in bone, wax, and in all other materials suited to such a craft, wished to divert himself in producing a likeness that would prove his skill (for no one was better than he) and also gain him great renown. He therefore made an image of ivory and put into its production such attention that it was so pleasing, so exquisite, that it seemed as live as the most beautiful living creature. Neither Helen nor Lavinia, however well-formed, were of such perfect complexion or development, nor did they have a tenth the beauty. When Pygmalion saw the image, he was amazed. He took no heed for himself, and lo, Love enmeshed him in his nets so securely that Pygmalion didn't know what he was doing. He mourned to himself, but could not stanch his grief.

"Alas! What am I doing?" he said. "Am I sleeping? I have many images that could not be priced, and I never fell in love with them, but I am badly tripped up by this one. She has deprived me of my wits. Alas! Where did this thought come from? How did the idea of such a love come about? I love an image that is deaf and mute, that neither stirs nor moves nor will ever show me grace. How did such a love wound me? There is no one who heard of it who should not be thunderstruck. I am the greatest fool in the world. What can I do in this situation?

"Faith, if I loved a queen, I could at least hope for grace, since it is a possibility. But this love is so horrible that it doesn't come from Nature. I am acting despicably in this case. Nature has a bad son in me; she disgraced herself when she made me. But I should not blame her because I love insanely, nor should I put the blame anywhere but on myself. Since my name was Pygmalion and I could walk on my own two feet, I have never heard such a love spoken of. But I do not love too foolishly, for, if writing does not lie, many have loved more dementedly. Didn't Narcissus, long ago in the branched forest, when he thought to quench his thirst, fall in love with his own face in the clear, pure fountain? He was quite unable to defend himself and, according to the story, which is still well-remembered, he afterward died of his love. Thus I am in any case less of a fool, for, when I wish, I go to this image and take it, embrace it, and kiss it; I can thus better endure my torment. But Narcissus could not possess what he saw in the fountain.

"Besides, many lovers in many countries have loved many ladies and served them as much as they could, without a single kiss from them, although they exerted themselves strenuously. Has Love treated me any better? No, for those lovers, however uncertain they may have felt, had in any case the hope of a kiss and other favor; but I am completely cut off from the delight expected by those who hope for the diversions of Love. When I want to ease myself, to embrace and to kiss, I find my love as rigid as a post

20843

20859

20889

and so very cold that my mouth is chilled when I touch her to kiss her.

20907   "Ah! I have spoken too rudely. I ask your grace, sweet friend, and beg that you will accept amends for my wrong, for as much as you deign to look sweetly upon me and to smile, this much, I think, should suffice me. Sweet looks and tender smiles are most delightful to lovers."

20915   Then Pygmalion knelt, his face wet with tears, and offered his gage as amends to her. But she cared nothing for the gage; she neither heard nor understood anything, either of him or of his present. As a result, he feared that he was wasting his effort in loving such a thing. He didn't know how to recover his heart, for Love had robbed him of his intelligence and wisdom, so that he was completely desolated. He didn't know whether she was alive or dead. Softly he took her in his hands; he thought that she was like putty, that the flesh gave way under his touch, but it was only his hand which pressed her.

20931   Thus Pygmalion strove, but in his strife was neither peace nor truce. He could not remain in any one condition. He either loved or hated, laughed or cried; he was either happy or distressed, tormented or calm. He would dress the image in many ways, in dresses made with great skill of white cloths of soft wool, of linsey-woolsey, or of stuffs in green, blue, and dark colors that were fresh, pure, and clean. Many of the fabrics were lined with fine furs, ermine, squirrel, or costly gray fur. Then he would undress her and try the effect on her of a dress of silk, sendal, or *melequin*, of a *moiré* in indigo, vermilion, yellow, or brown, of samite, variegated material, or camelot. Her countenance was so simple that a little angel would have been nothing beside her.

20952   At another time he would put a wimple on her, and a coverchief over both wimple and head. But he didn't cover her face, for he did not want to follow the custom of the Saracens, who are so full of jealous rage that they veil the faces of their wives so that passersby will not see them when they walk along the roads. At another time his heart led him again to take off everything and put on head-ornaments of yellow, vermilion, green, and indigo, or of silk and gold with seed pearls. Then he would fasten the ornaments with a very precious pin and place, on top of it, a delicate little crown with many precious stones in settings of squares with semicircular arcs on each of the four facets. Besides the settings, there were other tiny gems, too many to count, sown thick around the crown. And on her two little ears he hung two earclips with tiny gold pendants. To hold her collar he placed two gold clasps at her neck, and he put another in the middle of her chest and a girdle around her waist. But it was so very rich a girdle that no girl ever encircled herself with anything like it. At the girdle he hung a precious and expensive purse, and in it he put five stones chosen from the seashore, of the sort that girls use for play-hammers, when they find pretty, round ones. He gave careful attention to dressing her feet. On each foot he put a shoe and a stocking cut off prettily at two fingers' length from the pavement. He did not gratify her with a present of boots, for she was not born in Paris; a boot is much too coarse for the footwear of so young a girl. Then, that she might be better dressed, he took a well-pointed needle of fine gold, threaded with gold thread, and sewed up her two sleeves so that they were snug. He brought her fresh flowers, the kind that pretty girls make chaplets of in the springtime; he brought balls and little birds and various novel little things that bring delight to young ladies. Out of the flowers he made chaplets, but not fashioned like any that you have seen, for he put his whole attention on them. He put gold rings on her fingers and said, like a fine, loyal husband:

"Fair sweet one, I here take you as wife, and I become yours and you mine. May Hymen and Juno hear me and wish to be at our wedding. I seek for it neither clerk nor priest nor the mitres and crooks of prelates, for Hymen and Juno are the true gods of weddings."

Then in a loud, clear voice full of great gaiety, he sang, instead of the Mass, songs of the pretty secrets of love. He made his instruments sound so that one might not hear God thundering. He had many kinds of instruments and, for playing them, hands more dextrous than Amphion of Thebes ever had. Pygmalion had harps, *gigues*, and rebecs, guitars and lutes, all chosen to give pleasure. Throughout his halls and chambers he had made his clocks chime by means of intricately contrived wheels that ran forever. He had excellent organs that could be carried in one hand while he himself worked the bellows and played as, with open mouth, he sang motet or triplum or tenor voice. Then he turned

20977

20999

21014

21021

his attention to the cymbals, then took a *fretel* and fluted on it, then a pipe, and piped; he took drum, flute, and tambourine, which he drummed, fluted, and struck; he took *citole*, trumpet, and bagpipes and played on each of them, then on psaltery and viol; he took his musette, then worked away at the Cornish pipes. He danced various dances, the *espingue*, the *sautelle*, the *balle*, and kicked up his heels throughout the hall. He took the image by the hand and danced with her, but he had a great weight at his heart because she did not wish, for all his prayers and exhortations, to sing nor to respond.

21059   Then he took her in his arms again and laid her down on his bed and embraced her and kissed her again and again, but the situation was not that of a good school, when two people kiss each other, and the kisses did not please the gods.

21065   Thus the deceived Pygmalion, captive of his foolish thought and led on by his deaf image, fell into a suicidal madness. In every way he could he decked her out and adorned her—for he turned his attention entirely to serving her—nor did she appear less beautiful without clothes than when she was dressed.

21073   At that time it happened that in that country they celebrated a feast on which many marvelous things occurred, and all the people came to the vigils of a temple that Venus had there. The young man, in great confidence that he might get counsel about his love, came to watch at the feast: he complained to the gods and bewailed the love which so tormented him.

21083   "O fair gods," he said, "if you are all-powerful, please hear my request. And you, Saint Venus, who are the lady of this temple, fill me with grace. For when Chastity is elevated, you are greatly angered, and I have deserved great punishment for having served her so long. But now, with no more delay, I repent and beg that you pardon me and, by your pity, your sweetness, and your friendship, grant me, on my promise to flee into banishment if I do not avoid Chastity from now on, that the beautiful one who has stolen my heart, who so truly resembles ivory, may become my loyal friend and may have the body, the soul, and the life of a woman. And if you hasten to grant this request and if I am ever found chaste, I consent that I may be hanged or chopped up into pieces, or that Cerberus, the porter of hell-gate, may swallow me alive and pulverize me within his triple gorge or bind me with ropes or iron bands."

Venus, who heard the young man's prayer, was overjoyed be- 21109 cause he was abandoning Chastity and striving to serve her as a truly repentant man, ready, in his penitence, to make his sweetheart quite naked within his arms, if he might ever possess her alive. Straightway she sent a soul to the image, who became so beautiful a lady that no man in any country had ever met one so beautiful. Pygmalion, since he had made his request, stayed no longer in the temple but returned to his image in very great haste, for he could no longer wait to hold her and gaze on her. He ran in little bounds until he came to her. Although he knew nothing of the miracle, he had great confidence in the gods, and the closer view he got of her the more his heart burned and fried and grilled. Then he saw that she was a living body; he uncovered her naked flesh and saw her beautiful shining blond locks, rippling together like waves, he felt the bones and the veins all filled with blood, and he felt the pulse move and beat. He didn't know if she were a lie or the truth. He drew back, not knowing what to do; he dared not draw near her for fear of being enchanted.

"What is this?" he said. "Am I being tempted? Am I awake? 21144 No, not awake, but dreaming. But no one ever saw so lifelike a dream. Dream! In faith, I do not dream, but wake. Then where does this wonder come from? Is it a phantom or demon who has been put into my image?"

Straightway the girl, beautiful and pleasing with her lovely 21151 blond hair, replied to him:

"I am neither demon nor phantom, sweet friend, but your 21154 sweetheart, ready to receive your companionship and to offer you my love if it please you to receive such an offer."

When he heard for certain and saw the miracles manifested, he 21159 drew near to reassure himself. Since it was certain, he gave himself willingly to her as if he were entirely hers. They united themselves to one another with promises of love and thanked each other for their love. There was no pleasure that they did not make for each other: they embraced one another in their great love and kissed each other as if they were two doves. Each loved and gave pleasure wholeheartedly to the other. Both of them returned thanks to the gods who had granted such a favor to them, especially to Venus, who had aided them more than anyone.

21175 At last Pygmalion was happy. There was nothing to displease him, for she refused nothing that he might wish. If he raised objections, she surrendered herself, reduced to her last argument; if she commanded, he obeyed. For nothing would he refuse to accomplish all her desires for her. At last, since she neither resisted nor complained, he could lie with his sweetheart. They played so well that she became pregnant with Paphus, whose fame gave the island of Paphos its name. From him was born King Cynaras, a good man except for one instance, whose happiness would have been complete if he had not been deceived by his daughter, the fair Myrrha, whom the old woman—may God confound her for having no fear

21195 of sin—brought to the king in his bed by night. The queen was at a feast and the king took the girl in haste, without knowing by any word that he was to lie with his daughter. It was a strange trick for the old woman to allow the king to lie with his daughter. After she brought them together, the beautiful Adonis was born of them and Myrrha was changed into a tree. Her father would have killed her if he had discovered the trick, but it could not happen so, for, when he had candles brought, she who was no longer a virgin escaped in swift flight, since otherwise he would have destroyed her. But all this is very far from my matter, and I must draw back from it. By the time you have finished this work you will know what it means.

21215 But I won't keep you any longer on this subject; I should return to my story, since I must plow another field. Whoever, then, would wish to compare the beauties of these two images could, it seems to me, compare them by saying that as much as the mouse is smaller than the lion in body, strength, and worth, and less to be feared, so much was the one image less beautiful than that which I here esteem so greatly.

21228 Dame Cypris looked well upon the image which I have described, the one placed between the pillars, within the tower, right in the middle. Never yet have I seen a place where I would so gladly gaze, even go down on my knees to adore. For no archer, bow, nor brand would I have relinquished the sanctuary and its aperture and the right to enter there at my pleasure. At least I would do everything in my power, whatever end I might come to, if I could find someone who might offer it to me or, if nothing more, might allow me there. For I am dedicated by God to the relics of which you have heard and which I shall seek out, equipped with sack and staff, as soon as I find time and place. May God keep me from being tricked or prevented in any way in my enjoyment of the rose.

Venus waited no longer: she let fly the feathered brand, covered with burning fire, to bring panic to those in the castle. But so subtly did Venus launch it that no man nor woman of them, however long they might have looked, had the power to see it. **21251**

When the brand had flown, those in the tower fell into panic. Fire blazed out in the whole area, and they had to acknowledge their capture. They all cried out: "Betrayed? Betrayed? All dead! Woe! Woe! Let us fly the country." Each threw down his keys where he was. When Resistance, the vile devil, felt himself burned, he fled faster than a stag over a heath. Nor did anyone wait for another; each one, with his clothes pulled up to his middle, thought only of flight. Fear fled, and Shame shot forth; flaming, all left the castle. From that moment no one wanted to put to the test what Reason had taught them. **21259**

At this point Courtesy came forth. When the noble, the beautiful lady of high esteem saw the rout, she came out into the fray, with Pity and Openness, to take her son away from the fire. They did not abandon Fair Welcoming to the flames; they stopped at nothing till they came to him. Courtesy spoke to him first, for she was not slow to speak out. **21277**

"Fair son, I have been full of sorrow and grief of heart because you have been held in prison. May evil fire and flame burn him who put you into such confinement. But now that Foul Mouth the slanderer, along with his Norman drunkards, lies dead in the moat, you are, thank God, delivered. He can neither see nor hear. Jealousy is not to be feared. One should not, on Jealousy's account, neglect to lead a happy life or to comfort one's lover in private, especially when it comes to the point where one can neither hear nor see anything. There is no one who might tell her, and she hasn't the power to find you here. The others, too, those presumptuous oppressors, have lost heart and fled into exile. The field is completely cleared. **21288**

"O sweet lovely son, for the grace of God, don't let yourself be **21311** burned here. In true friendship we beg you, I and Openness and Pity, to grant this loyal lover, this free spirit who has long suffered for you and who has never played you false nor tricked you, that his lot may be better through your efforts. Receive him and whatever he has; indeed, he even offers you his soul. For the love of God, sweet son, do not refuse his offer, but rather receive it by the faith you owe me and by Love who impels it and who has given it such great power.

21327   "O fair son, Love conquers everything; everything is held in by his key. Even Virgil confirms this idea in a powerful and courtly saying. When you look through the *Bucolics* you will find that 'Love conquers all' and that 'we should welcome it.' Indeed, he spoke well and truly when he tells us all this in a single line; he could not tell a better tale. My fair son, rescue this lover so that God may rescue both. Grant him the gift of the rose."

21340   "Lady, I grant it to him," said Fair Welcoming, "very willingly. He may pluck it while only we two are here. I ought to have received him long ago, for I see that he loves without guile."

21346   I gave him a hundred thousand thanks for his gift, and straightway after that delicious boon, I set out like a good pilgrim, impatient, fervent, and wholehearted, like a pure lover, on the voyage toward the aperture, the goal of my pilgrimage. And I carried with me, by great effort, the sack and the staff so stiff and strong that it didn't need to be shod with iron for traveling and wandering. The sack was well-made, of a supple skin without seam. You should know that it was not empty: Nature, who gave it to me, had cleverly forged two hammers with great care at the same time that she first designed it. No man, it seems to me, works as diligently and in so coördinated a way; she knew better how to work than Daedalus ever did. And I believe that she made them because she planned that I would shoe my horses when I went wandering, as indeed I shall do if I may have the possibility, for, thank God, I know how to forge. I tell you truly that I count my two hammers and my sack dearer than my citole or my harp.

21377   Nature did me a great honor when she equipped me with this armor and so taught me its use that she made me a good and wise workman. She herself had made me the gift of the staff and wished to put hand to its polishing before I was taught to read. But it wasn't important to shoe it with iron; it was worth none the less without shoeing. And since I have received it, I have always had it near me, and have never since lost it. If I can, I shall never lose it; for I would not want to be deprived of it for five hundred times a hundred thousand pounds. She made me a fair gift of it, one to be cherished. I am supremely happy when I gaze on it, and when I feel it content and happy, I give her thanks for her present. Since then it has often comforted me in many places where I have carried it. It serves me well; and do you know how? When, in my travels, I find myself in a remote place, I put it into the ditches where I can see nothing, to see if they can be forded. That way, I can congratulate myself that there's no delay to fear, so well do I know how to deal with the fords, to trust the banks and brooks. But again I find some so deep, with banks so far apart, that it would be less trouble to swim two leagues along the sea shore; even then I would be less tired than if I crossed so perilous a ford. I know; I have tried many great gulfs. True, I have come to no trouble, for if, after I had made ready to enter, I tested them and found them such that you couldn't touch bottom with pole or oar, I went along on the outskirts and kept near the banks so that I was able to come out at the end. But if I had not had the arms and armor that Nature gave me, I would never have been able to get out. But let us leave these wide roads to those who travel them willingly, and let those of us who lead a light-hearted life keep gaily to the seductive bypaths, not the cart roads but the intriguing footpaths. 21397

Still, an old road is more profitable than a new path; you find more property there, and more to bring in further gain. Juvenal declares in fact that if a man wants to gain a great fortune he can take no shorter road than to take up with a rich old woman. If he takes up his servitude gladly, it propels him immediately into high station. Indeed, Ovid affirms, in a tried and weighty maxim, that he who wants to ally himself with an old woman can get a rich return. By trafficking thus he acquires great wealth straightway. 21435

But he who petitions an old woman must be careful not to do or say anything that might look like a ruse when he wants to steal her love or even to bring her honestly into the snares of Love. Those old women are hard to trap who have passed the time of youth when they were flattered, taken in, and tricked. When they were more often deceived, these fraudulent old tricksters see more 21451 readily through the sweet lies they hear than do those tender young girls who suspect no trap whatever when they listen to flatterers. In fact, they think that hypocrisy and guile are as true as gospel, for they have not yet been scalded. The wrinkled old cynics, however, malicious and cunning, are so well instructed in the art of fraud, the knowledge of which they have gained through time and experience, that they know what to do when the sweet-tongued talebearers come. These deceivers are those who detain the ladies with lies and drum into their ears their pleas for grace, who sigh and abase themselves, clasping their hands and crying out for favor, who bow down and kneel and flood everything with their tears, who cross themselves before their ladies so that they will have greater trust in them, who promise in sham their hearts, bodies, possessions, and services, who pledge themselves and swear by all the saints that ever were, are, or shall be, and go around thus, deceiving with words that are only wind. They operate just as the birdcatcher does. Like a thief, he hides in the thickets and spreads his net for the bird and calls him with sweet sounds to make him come to the snare so that he can be taken captive. The silly bird approaches but does not know how to reply to the sophism which has deceived him through a figure of speech, as the quail-catcher deceives the quail so that the bird may leap into the net: the quail listens to the sound, draws near, and throws himself into the net that the quailer has spread on the grass, fresh and thick in the springtime. But there is no old quail that longs to come to the quailer. She is scalded and beaten; she has seen many nets before, from which, perhaps, she escaped when she should have been captured among the fresh grass.

Just so, the old women I spoke of, those whose favors were implored and whose implorers trapped them, recognize the ambushes from afar by the speeches that they hear and the faces they see put on. As a result, they entertain these tricks less trustingly. But if, indeed, the tricks are performed in earnest, to have the rewards of Love—if the petitioners are those who are taken in the same snare, the comfort of which is so pleasant and the burden so delightful that nothing is so agreeable to them as the heavy hope which so pleases and torments them—then the old women are very afraid of being hooked, and they listen and study to determine if they are being told truth or fables. They go around weighing each word, so much do they fear the presence of fraud, because of those who have passed before and whose memory is still fresh. Every old woman thinks that everyone wants to deceive her.

If it please you to incline your hearts to such a course in order   21539
to enrich yourselves more quickly or to discover delight there, you can indeed trace that road, to delight and comfort yourselves. And you who want the young girls will not be traduced by me on that score, however my master commands me—and all his commands are very beautiful. Indeed I tell you the truth, believe me who will, that it is good to try everything in order to take greater pleasure in one's good fortune, just as does the good lover of luxury who is a connoisseur of tidbits and tastes of several foods— simmered, roasted, with dressing, in a pasty, fried or in a galantine —when he can go into a kitchen; he knows how to praise and to blame, to say which are sweet, which bitter, for he has tasted several. In this way know, and do not doubt, that he who has not tried evil will hardly ever know anything of the good, any more than will he who does not know the value of honor know how to recognize shame. No man knows what is easy if he has not experienced difficulty before, nor does he deserve to have his ease if he is not willing to accept his hardships; no one should offer comforts to anyone who does not know how to suffer.

Thus things go by contraries; one is the gloss of the other. If   21573
one wants to define one of the pair, he must remember the other, or he will never, by any intention, assign a definition to it; for he who has no understanding of the two will never understand the difference between them, and without this difference no definition that one may make can come to anything.

It was my wish that, if I could bring my entire harness, just as   21583
I carried it, up to the harbor, I might touch it to the relics if I were allowed to bring it so close to them. And I had done so much and wandered so far, my staff entirely unprotected by ferrule, that, vigorous and agile, I knelt without delay between the two fair pillars, for I was very hungry to worship the lovely, adorable sanctuary with a devoted and pious heart. Everything had been razed by the fire, with which nothing can war, so that nothing remained standing except the unharmed sanctuary. I partly raised the curtain which covered the relics and approached the image to know the sanctuary more intimately. I kissed the image very de-

voutly and then, to enter the sheath safely, wished to put my
staff into the aperture, with the sack hanging behind. Indeed I
thought that I could shoot it in at the first try, but it came back
out. I replaced it, but to no avail; it still recoiled. By no effort
could it enter there, for, I found, there was a paling in front,
which I felt but could not see. It had formed the fortification of
the aperture, close to its border, from the time when it was first
built; it gave greater strength and security.

21617   I had to assail it vigorously, throw myself against it often, often
fail. If you had seen me jousting—and you would have had to
take good care of yourself—you would have been reminded of
Hercules when he wanted to dismember Cacus. He battered at his
door three times, three times he hurled himself, three times fell
back. His struggle and labor were so great that he had to sit down
three times in the valley, completely spent, to regain his breath.
I had worked so hard that I was covered with the sweat of anguish
when I did not immediately break the paling, and I was indeed,

21633   believe it, as worn out as Hercules, or even more. Nevertheless,
I attacked so much that I discovered a narrow passage by which
I thought I might pass beyond, but to do so I had to break the
paling. By this path, narrow and small, where I sought passage,
I broke down the paling with my staff and gained a place in the
aperture. But I did not enter halfway; I was vexed at going no
farther, but I hadn't the power to go on. But I would have relaxed
for nothing until the entire staff had entered, so I pressed it through
with no delay. But the sack, with its pounding hammers, remained
hanging outside; the passage was so narrow that I became greatly

21655   distressed, for I had not freed any wide space. Indeed, if I knew
the state of the passage, no one had ever passed there; I was absolutely the first. The place was still not common enough to collect
tolls. I don't know if, since then, it has done as much for others
as it did for me, but I tell you indeed that I loved it so much that
I could hardly believe, even if it were true, that the same favors
had been given to others. No one lightly disbelieves what he loves,
so dishonored would it be; but I still do not believe it. At least I
know for certain that at that time it was not a well-worn, beaten
path. Since there was no other place whatever where I might enter
to gather the bud, I hurled myself through that path.

21673   You shall know how I carried on until I took the bud at my pleasure. You, my young lords, shall know both the deed and the manner, so that if, when the sweet season returns, the need arises for you to go gathering roses, either opened or closed, you may go so discreetly that you will not fail in your collecting. Do as you hear that I did, if you know no better how to come to your goal; for, if you can negotiate the passage better, more easily or deftly, without straining or tiring yourself, then do so in your way when you have learned mine. At least you will have the advantage that I am teaching you my method without taking any of your money, and for that you should feel grateful.

Cramped as I was there, I had approached so near to the rose-   21695
bush that I could reach out my hands at will to take the bud from the branches. Fair Welcoming had begged me for God's sake to commit no outrage, and, because he begged me often, I promised him firmly that I would never do anything except his will and mine. I seized the rosebush, fresher than any willow, by its branches, and when I could attach myself to it with both hands, I began very softly, without pricking myself, to shake the bud, since I had wanted it as undisturbed as possible. However, I could not help making the branches stir and shake, but I never destroyed any of them, for I wished to wound nothing, even though I had to cut a little into the bark; I did not know how otherwise to possess this gift, for which my desire was so strong.

Finally, I scattered a little seed on the bud when I shook it, when   21719
I touched it within in order to pore over the petals. For the rosebud seemed so fair to me that I wanted to examine everything right down to the bottom. As a result, I so mixed the seeds that they could hardly be separated; and thus I made the whole tender rosebush widen and lengthen. All this I should not have done. But then I was quite certain that the sweet fellow who had no evil thought would bear me no ill will for it, and that he would agree to it and allow me to do whatever he knew might please me. He reminded me of the agreement and said that I was doing him a great wrong, that I was too unbridled; but he did not forbid me to take, to reveal and pluck the rosebush and branches, the flower and the leaf.

When I saw myself raised to such high degree, an estate gained   21743
so nobly that my methods were not suspect, because I had been loyal and open toward all my benefactaors, as a good debtor

should be—for I was very much bound to them, since through them I had become so rich that (I declare it as the truth) there was no wealth as rich—when I saw myself thus, I rendered thanks, among the delicious kisses, ten or twenty times, first to the God of Love and to Venus, who had aided me more than anyone, then to all the barons of the host, whose help I pray God never to take away from pure lovers. But I didn't remember Reason, who gave me a lot of trouble for nothing. My curse on Riches, the shrew, who showed no pity when she refused me entry by the path which she guarded. She took no care of that path by which I entered, secretly and precipitantly, here within. My curse too on those mortal enemies who held me back so long, especially on Jealousy, crowned with her marigolds of solicitude, who protects the roses from lovers. She is still keeping a very good watch.

21775 Before I stirred from that place where I should wish to remain forever, I plucked, with great delight, the flower from the leaves of the rosebush, and thus I have my red rose. Straightway it was day, and I awoke.

Notes to the Text

NOTES

THE notes provide a guide to the principal recent bodies of annotation and discussion and short comments on questions of interpretation and, occasionally, of translation. There is no attempt to provide full explanatory notes; to indicate sources other than major ones or to refer to detailed parallels; to give more than summary reference for many lengthy passages of discussion in the works referred to; or to document the *Romance*'s influence on subsequent writers. I have indicated, very briefly, a few passages that show some influence upon Chaucer, but even there I would refer the interested reader to Robinson's notes for more detailed parallels.

The headings of the notes refer to line numbers of the Langlois edition, indicated in this translation by marginal figures. The following abbreviations refer to works frequently cited:

F   Fleming 1969
G   Gunn 1952
Lc   Lecoy edition 1965–
Ln   Langlois edition 1914-24
P   Paré 1947
R   Robertson 1962
T   Tuve 1966

Reference is to page except in the case of Ln and Lc, where it is to the line number of the note-heading unless otherwise specified. Full references may be found in the Bibliography. I have translated most of the quotations in foreign languages without further comment; where I have quoted a translation, that fact is noted, either implicitly through the bibliographical reference or explicitly in the note itself.

CHAPTER 1

1-1680   (Chapter 1) On the structure of the poem, see Introduction; R 96-98, 196; Friedman 1965; F 99-103 and *passim*. Chapter 1 establishes the allegorical dream-framework and the first stage in the process of the Lover's involvement, the appeal to the senses, corresponding to the first of the traditional three stages of any sin: suggestion to sense, delight of the heart, consent of the reason. The emphasis in this chapter on sense imagery is thus central to the overall development. Cf. 4377-88 and n.

1-85   See G 95-98 on the rhetorical structure.

1-20   On true and false dreams, cf. Virgil (*Aeneid*, VI. 893-96) and Homer (*Odyssey*, XIX. 560-67). Chaucer, *House of Fame* (*HF*),

1-65, speculates on the kinds of dreams and seems to echo some such dream classification as that of Macrobius (see below); cf. 18499-514. Robinson 1957, pp. 779-88, details other parallels to *HF*. Cf. also *Nun's Priest's Tale, Canterbury Tales* (*CT*), VII. 2922-41; *Troilus and Criseyde*, v. 358-85, 1275-88.

1-2   Ln quotes parallels to the idea that dreams are empty falsehoods. But such dreams are only one of Macrobius's five kinds. Cf. 21780 n., 7-10 n.

6-7   Ln

7-10   Ln Lc; Dahlberg 1953, pp. 136-39; R 196-97. Ambrosius Theodosius Macrobius flourished in the late fourth and early fifth centuries, wrote the *Commentarii in somnium Scipionis* and *Saturnalia*; see Stahl 1952, pp. 5-9. The dream material comes from the *Commentary*, I. ii-iii.

37-44   *it is the Romance . . . should be called Rose*: Guillaume immediately sets out to fulfill Macrobius's concept of the *somnium*, or enigmatic dream, "one that conceals with strange shapes and veils with ambiguity the true meaning of the information being offered, and requires an interpretation for its understanding." See 38 n., 44 n.

38   *in which the whole Art of Love is contained* (Ou l'Art d'Amors est toute enclose): G 97, 143. "Art of Love" is an ambiguous phrase: 'complete method of seduction' and 'organized inquiry into all the kinds of love' are two of the possible, complementary meanings. Note the ambiguous reference where *in which* (Ou) may have as antecedent either *rose* or *Romance of the Rose*.

40-41   Ln

44   On the ambiguities of the rose, see 895-96 n.; cf. R 95-96; T 233-34, 239, 242.

45-63   Ln thinks that these lines influenced Rutebeuf in *Voie de Paradis*, 1-8. See the ed. of Faral and Bastin (1959-60, 1, 341), who think that the influence is not proved. The important point is that similar spring openings are used in a poem of veiled allegory (*Romance*) and one of overt allegory (*Voie*); the pilgrimage motif is another common feature, direct in the *Voie*, ironic in the *Romance*. Cf. 21347 n. Rutebeuf (fl. ca. 1250-80), wrote shortly before Jean de Meun, and they both supported Guillaume de Saint-Amour and the antimendicant faction at the University of Paris. See 11488 n.

45-47   Cf. Chaucer, *Book of the Duchess* (*BD*), 291-92. Chaucer speaks directly of the *Romance* in lines 332-34. For further specific parallels with the *BD*, see Robinson's notes (1957, pp. 773-78).

59-66   On the robe of grass and flowers, Ln quotes Alanus de Insulis, *De planctu naturae*, *PL* 210, cols. 447 D-448 A; subsequent references will be to *De planctu*, col.—.

76   *enjoy themselves* (se deduit): Ln. The verb *deduire* is cognate with the proper noun *Deduit*, the name of the owner of the garden; see 590 n.

78 Ln. On gardens, cf. 635-68 n. See also Robertson 1951; 1962, pp. 69-72, 91-93, 386-88, 421-22. Langlois notes that a four-teenth-century reader of MS Me (Paris, B. N. fr. 1560) calls atten-tion in a marginal note to the parallel with Matthew of Vendôme's description of a garden; the reader of that manuscript thus associates Guillaume's garden with Cicero's characterization of Verres as seduced to adultery by the beauties of Sicily's landscape (*Ars versificatoria*, 110-11, ed. Faral 1962, pp. 147-49); and this association would support Robertson's understanding of the garden imagery.

81 *He has a very hard heart . . . May*: A marginal note to this line in MS Paris, B. N. fr. 803 reads "pour le temps bel et doulœureux." This reader's perception of the pain, where the text refers, overtly, only to the sweetness of the weather, shows a characteristically medieval mode of reading. Cf. 4279-358.

90-98 Ln

98 *zigzag lacing* (cousdre a videle): Ln

119 Ln quotes *Hueline et Aiglentine*, v. 7-10, which refers to a garden containing a fountain beneath a pine and a brook flowing there-from. Cf. lines 1425-38 ff.

129-462 P 292. Cf. 20267-334, Figs. 2-10. See Kuhn 1913-14, pp. 50-58, on the relation between the MS illuminations and contem-porary representations of the Vices; Katzenellenbogen 1939 (1964); R 91-93, 197-98, Figs. 13, 56-58, 68, 70; F 31-34; Lewis 1936, pp. 126-27. In general, the portraits represent not so much the qualities that would exclude a lover from the garden and its activities as at-tributes that are complementary to those represented within. Youth in the garden leads to Old Age without; Wealth leads to Poverty, Love to Hatred; Openness becomes mingled with dissembling (Pope-Holi-ness), and so on. Cf. 727-1284, 4293-334, 20933-34.

132 Ln

136-38 G 102-4 compares 691-700, 796-800, 2225-28, 2265-68, 2751-55, 3797-99, as examples of Guillaume's "artistic prudence" in passages of summary; the list might be extended (e.g., 3499-510, 2057-76). It would be misleading to assume that Jean de Meun's ability does not extend to such "careful indexing of the poem" (cf. 4113-220, 10526-678, 15133-302; see G 21-28), but it is clear that such passages are more complex in terms of scale and ironic method than are Guil-laume's.

139 Ln

139-51 Guillaume's use of Hatred for his first portrait may well suggest the state of discord that is characteristic of fallen man, the opposite of the harmony in the garden of Eden before the Fall. Far from suggesting anything more than a purely literal opposition between hatred and love, the figure suggests the close connection between the Hatred on the outside of the garden and the kind of love characteristic of the garden. Cf. Duhem 1913-59, I, 76; R 243.

152, 156 Ln

156-68 The usual MS illustration for Villainy (not represented in the series reproduced here from B. N. fr. 378) is one of the most definite of the series and shows a seated female figure kicking the kneeling young man who offers her a vessel. Cf. R 197-98, Figs. 56, 70; Kuhn 1913-14, pp. 51-53. Katzenellenbogen 1964, p. 76, calls the figure Malignitas; Mâle 1958, pp. 123-25, opts for "ingratitude" or "hardness of heart." The important point is that a vice-portrait from a standard theological cycle is used to illustrate the *idea* represented in the text.

156 *Villainy* (Vilanie): The Late Latin etymon *villanus* 'inhabitant of a farm' accounts for the later meanings 'peasant, boor, churl, base or lowborn fellow.' Although the Modern English derivatives *villain* (*-y,-ous*) may sometimes be misleading (cf. 165, 736, 1209, 1931-38, 6577-82), the highly pejorative nature of this important passage suggests that to retain *villainy* as a technical term, rather than to seek a more "precise" translation, may establish a clearer frame of allusion; here and at 2077-86 I retain the derivative.

169-234 On the distinction between Avarice and Covetousness, cf. 9578: "The latter acquires [possessions] and the former locks them up." Cf. Figs. 4, 5.

180 Ln

205 Ln quotes parallels to "bread kneaded with . . . caustic."

213 *clothespole*: Ln compares 8874, 13774. The MS illustrations usually show the pole; see Fig. 5.

235-90 Ln calls the portrait of Envy an enlargement of Ovid's description of *Pallor, Metamorphoses (Met.)*, II. 775-82. Fleming 1963, p. 106, notes Ln's error: *Pallor* is a characteristic of *Invidia* (Envy). Lc also notes the Ovidian source. On the iconography, see Fig. 6; R 207-8; F 33.

246, 265-66, 274, 282, 283, 296-97, 298, 323, 324 Ln

339-406 *Old Age* (Vieillece): Ln. On old-ness in general, see R 127-32, 379-82. Cf. the Old Woman (Chapter 7), who aids the Lover's suit. Thus the portrait here represents only a superficial contrast to the "Youth" that enter the garden. She is the end result of "whatever is begotten, born, and dies," as the passage on Time reminds us.

355, 357, 358 Ln

361 ff. *Time, who goes away* . . . : See P 288 on the scholastic distinction between time and eternity.

363-81 Ln quotes specific parallels, which I omit, to Ovid, *Ex Ponto*, IV. ii. 42, and IV. viii; *Fasti*, VI. 771-72 (not 711-12); *Ars amatoria*, III. 62-64; *Met.*, XV. 179-85, 234-36.

371-72 *for before* . . . *passed*: Lc numbers these lines 370 a-b; they do not appear in his base MS, and he supplies them from a control MS. In references to the Lc notes I shall use the Ln numbering; for conversion to Lc numbering, see Appendix.

384, 386, 388, 396   Ln

407-40   *Pope-Holiness* (Papelardie): Cf. False Seeming, 10952-12014, particularly 11524. Again we have a case of the close connection between the portrait and the activity within the garden. See Fig. 9.

414-15, 418   Ln

436-37   *as the Gospel says . . . faces*: Lc quotes the text, Matt. 6: 16 ("And when you fast, be not as the hypocrites, sad. For they disfigure their faces, that they may appear unto men to fast."). Guillaume de Saint-Amour was later to use this traditional text on hypocrisy in his antimendicant writings; cf. *Responsiones*, No. 10, ed. Faral 1951, p. 343, where the Scriptural reference is used with the gloss to reinforce the idea that pride may be caused by humble clothing.

441-62   Cf. 11245-54. On the connection between poverty and the activities of the garden, cf. 1017-1126, 10051-267 n.

443, 463, 485, 506   Ln

524   *hornbeam* (charme): There may be a pun with *charmes* 'enchantments, spells'; cf. 9151, 13237.

525-94   *a very sweet and lovely girl . . .* : On Idleness (Oiseuse), see R 92-93, 198, for a detailed literary pedigree which shows how "impossible" it is "to make Oiseuse an innocent forbear of modern 'leisure.'" Cf. F 73-81. At 11519-24 we see that idleness is a characteristic of False Seeming.

530-31, 541, 554   Ln

555   *chaplet . . . of fresh roses*: Cf. 895-96 n.

557   *in her hand she held a mirror*: The mirror and the implied comb of line 568 are the conventional attributes of the vice *luxuria* (lechery). See R 92-93, 95, 198; Kuhn 1913-14, pp. 25-27, Figs. 10-14. In the Angers tapestries, a fourteenth-century series on the *Apocalypse*, the Whore of Babylon is pictured with the mirror and comb. See Planchenault (n.d.), Pl. 64.

563-64   *gloves . . . Ghent* (ganz . . . Ganz): In the Old French we have a case of identical rhyme, or *rime riche*, a common technique; cf. P 81 on Jean's use of such rhyme. Here the selection of the place-name may be due partly to iconography. F 76, 85-86 suggests that illustrators used the glove as an emblem of sexual cupidity—in one case, along with the mirror, as an attribute of the character Carnalité in the *Roman de Fauvel* (MS Paris, B. N. fr. 146, fol. 12, reproduced Kuhn 1913-14, p. 27). Cf. 14694 n.

582   Ln quotes Ovid, *Remedia amoris*, 139, on the idea that Idleness leads to love. See R 92-93, n. 69-70.

583   Ln

590   *Diversion* (Deduit): Ln v, 335: "Divertissement personifié." Two senses of *diversion*, 'having a good time' and 'turning away from a (right) course,' are implicit. The Chaucerian translation, 'Sir Mirth,' probably conveyed such overtones.

592   *Saracen land* (la terre as Sarradins): So Ln. Lc reads (follow-

ing his base MS) *la terre Alixandrins* 'the territory of Alexander's empire.' In either case the trees are those of the infidel.

607-8   Ln

631-1614   P 292

635-68   *Believe me . . . a melody*: Ln quotes parallels in *Tornoiement Antecrist, Image du Monde, Flamenca.* On the *locus amoenus* 'pleasure grove' or 'garden,' Lc cites Curtius 1948, pp. 200-205 (1953, pp. 195-200), who notes that "Peter Riga (d. 1209), makes the *locus amoenus* the theme of an entire poem" (*De ornatu mundi*, PL 171, cols. 1235-38) in which "the pleasure grove is the rose of the world. But it fades: turn ye to the heavenly rose" (1953, p. 198). Cf. 78 n. F 55-73 explores the nature of Guillaume's garden, particularly in its relation to Eden and the *hortus conclusus* of the Song of Songs, and gives a summary of the fifteenth-century interpretation in the prose gloss on the *Echecs amoureux.*

643   See R 127-28 on the singing birds and their symbolic relationship to the theme of love.

663, 664, 667, 683   Ln

691-700   See 136-38 n.

711   Ln

727-1284   The carol (*querole*) is a round-, or ring-, dance. The portraits of the characters form a general complement to those of the garden wall; see 129-462 n. On the significance of the portraits, see R 130 and Figs. 41-42; F 81-89 deals with the MS illustrations and with the origins of the carol in peasant life and the associations that help "to explain how the carol could easily become a figure or icon for sexual cupidity" (p. 83). F refers to Sahlin 1940 for the historical background.

733, 750-52   Ln

796-800   See 136-38 n.

809   Ln

829-30   *chaplet of roses*: This attribute, which appears in Fig. 12, associates Diversion with other followers of Venus. See 895-96 n.

856, 879 ff.   Ln

892   *or any yellow, indigo, or white flower*: Ln chose a reading other than that of Lc's base MS, Paris, B. N. fr. 1573, which has two extra lines plus a slightly different reading of 892. The Lc text would read, in translation: "or any flower, black or white, yellow, indigo, or greenish-blue—any flower, no matter how varied." See Appendix.

895-96   *chaplet of roses*: Cf. Idleness's chaplet, 555, as well as the later use of such a chaplet to gain "Fair Welcoming," 12439 ff., and to adorn the young friends of Wealth on their way to the stews, 10102. Cf. Wisdom, 2:6-8: "Come therefore, and let us enjoy the good things that are present, and let us speedily use the creatures as in youth. Let us fill ourselves with costly wine, and ointments: and let not the flower of the time pass by us. Let us crown ourselves with roses, before they be withered: let no meadow escape our riot" (the Douai chapter heading reads: "The vain reasonings of the wicked"); R 192, Fig. 59; F 174-75 identifies the rose-chaplet as an iconographical attribute of Idleness or of Venus.

909 Ln quotes, Lc cites sources and parallels for the bows and arrows, in particular, Ovid, *Met.*, I. 468-71.

916, 921 Ln

924-25, 935 ff. On the relationship between the five arrows and the five senses, see Dahlberg 1969, pp. 575-76; cf. 1693-95 n. The parallel tradition of the "five points of love" (*quinque lineae amoris*: sight, conversation, touching, kissing, *coitus*) is related in terms of sight, hearing, and touch. Ln quotes *Carmina Burana* on the five points, or steps; Lc notes the distinction from the five arrows of the *Romance*. Cf. Chaucer, *Pars T*, x. 852-62; Adler 1952; Curtius 1953, pp. 512-14; R 407, n. 26; Friedman 1965; Dronke 1965-66, I. 49, 62; II. 488-89; F 100-102.

976, 977, 1010, 1021, 1023, 1026 Ln

1033 *power* (dangier): Cf. 2827 n.

1045-47 *and decry those who are praised . . . have denounced many good men*: Lc's base MS omits the two lines, numbered 1045-46 by Ln, which fall between 1044 and 1045 of the Lc numbering; they appear in his *Variantes* II; see Appendix. A translation of the Lc text, 1042-47: "But secretly their flatteries so pierce men to the bone that these flatterers, by their flattery, make many turn their backs, for they alienate from court those who should be intimate."

1069-83 Ln

1093 Lc

1097 *jargons* (jagonces): a reader has kindly pointed out that these are the ordinary green or brown variety of zircon, distinct from the *jacinth* or hyacinth, the reddish-orange zircon.

1119, 1124, 1136-38 Ln

1194 *an Orleans nose*: To judge from Ln's note, a flat nose.

1213, 1217-20, 1227 Ln

1228 *Windsor's lord*: Ln. Perhaps King Arthur is meant.

1236 *excess* (outrage): P 71-75 discusses other uses in the poem of the words *outrage, outrageous, outreement*, and relates them to the idea of the mean as the position of virtue.

1241, 1258 Ln

1279-88 G 101

1308, 1312 Ln

1323 Ln quotes extracts from the description of the garden in *Floire et Blancheflor*, which he had noted at 78 n. Cf. 635-68 n., 119 n.

1326, 1331-32, 1343, 1346, 1348, 1350 Ln

1369-74 *The branches were long and high . . . one hour*: Cf. 20479-524; Robertson 1951, pp. 33, 41-42.

1393, 1408   Ln

1425-1614   On Narcissus and the fountain, see P 293, R 93-95, F 89-96; cf. Frappier 1959, Köhler 1963, Goldin 1967, pp. 52-59. Jean de Meun has his Pygmalion compare himself, favorably, with Narcissus; see 20876-88 and note. See Fig. 13. Several illustrations, including Fig. 59, show Narcissus as a knight, kneeling at the fountain, with his horse standing nearby; cf. MSS Paris, Arsenal 5209, fol. 11 b; B. N. fr. 19157, fol. 10 c. See also Ancona and Aeschliman 1949, Pl. LXXX and p. 141. On the iconography of the horse, cf. 19787 n.

1425-38   Cf. 119 n.

1433-34   *Nature . . . under the pine*: On the role of Nature, see 15891-19438 n. Cf. R 94.

1434   Ln

1439-1506   Ln Lc note the source of the Narcissus story in Ovid, *Met.*, III. 344-503. Lc considers Guillaume's contribution the identification of the Fountain of Narcissus with the fountain of love; cf. 1425-1614 n. For an interpretation of Narcissus, current in mid-thirteenth-century Paris, see John of Garland, *Integumenta Ovidii*, ed. Ghisalberti 1933, p. 49: "Narcissus is the youth filled with desire and deceived by the glory of worldly things, which flower and like shadows pass away." Cf. Arnulfe d'Orléans, *Allegoriae fabularum Ovidii*, III, 5-6, ed. Ghisalberti 1932, p. 209, and note. On John of Garland, see Paëtow 1927; on Arnulfe, see also Ghisalberti 1946, pp. 18-19.

1456, 1472, 1499, 1536   Ln

1538   *two crystal stones*: R 95: "These are . . . [the Lover's] own eyes, which . . . transmit colors and forms from outside into the well, just as mirrors do." Cf. F 93-95.

1543-70   Lc

1547, 1551   Ln

1571-1614   R 95: "The well . . . is that mirror in the mind where Cupid operates. It has been tainted by Cupid ever since the Fall, when cupidity gained ascendancy over the reason."

1588   *Venus*: On the understanding of Venus in the poem, see 10749-826 n. For a guide to MS illustrations of classical, historical, and Biblical subjects, see Fleming 1963, pp. 236-47. See also F 175, n. 77.

1591-94   *stretched his nets . . . birds*: R 94-95; Koonce 1959.

1595   Lc

1597-99   *in books*: Lc suggests parallels; cf. 78 n., 635-68 n.

1607   *I admired myself there* (m'i mirai): The present translation (and the parallel with Narcissus) is buttressed by the fact that Jean de Meun uses the same verb and construction with reference to Narcissus at 20412 (Quant il se mirait iqui sus). Cf. Goldin 1967, p. 57, "I *saw* myself there." See his n. 10. Cf. R 95.

1615 ff.   On the roses, see 895-96 n.

1619-25 *I was seized . . . rosebushes*: Guillaume does not have his dreamer turn away from the fountain toward the rosebushes. The impression left is that he pursues the roses within the fountain. While such a conclusion is illogical, it does in fact accord with the dream-situation, with "the madness," with lines 1571-1602, with the legendary fate of Narcissus, and with Robertson's analysis, p. 95, of the well as "that mirror in the mind where Cupid operates."

1623-24, 1629, 1643, 1644, 1647, 1649, 1650, 1669-70   Ln

CHAPTER 2

1681-2970   (Chapter 2) See 1-1680 n.

1693-95   Ln Lc document the notion of the arrows of love entering the eyes; cf. 1743-44. See Figs. 14, 60, from the two earliest illustrated MSS. The latter, from B. N. fr. 1559, departs from the letter of the text in showing the arrow striking the Lover not in the eye or heart but in the genital region; it is thus more accurate symbolically than literally; and, in showing the God of Love's goal, it provides a clear contemporary gloss to the text. Cf. 924-25, 935 ff. n.

1710-20, 1719, 1735   Ln

1784, 1785   Ln Lc

1877, 1940, 1945-54, 1991   Ln

1994, 1998   P 73

1999-2007   Ln and Lc note that the key had appeared in Chrétien de Troyes; see *Yvain*, 4626 (ed. Roques) and *Perceval*, 2636.

2029   Ln Lc

2043   *for the grace of God*: Ln notes that this is a curious expression to use to the God of Love. It may well be used ironically.

2052-56   G 334

2053-56   Ln

2062   *for the romance improves from this point on*: G 66, 114 takes this line as an indication that for Guillaume, as for Jean, the major interest of the poem may have been expository or didactic. I would take the line as referring to more than the God of Love's discourse, which is probably to be viewed as irony.

2062, 2063-64, 2067-69   Ln

2067-76   G 114

2071-72   *explain the dream's significance* (espoigne . . . dou songe la senefiance): P 22 takes this phrase as parallel to *gloser* 'gloss,' as a scholastic term; see 7153-80 n. Cf. also Phanie's gloss to Croesus's dream, 6489-622.

2077-2232   On the parallels between the God of Love's commands to the Lover and the Old Woman's advice to girls (through Fair Welcoming, 13011 ff.), see F 176-78. Lc thinks that Guillaume did not intend a parody of the Ten Commandments, but, as he points out, Jean de Meun so regarded them; see 10396-412. "For Jean de Meun," says Lc, "lines [2175-210] constitute a single precept." He notes that this interpretation is natural and that Jean has the Old Woman say that there are ten; cf. 13011-31.

2077-86 Lc's base MS omits this paragraph; he therefore supplies the ten lines from a control MS and numbers them 2074 a-j. See Appendix. On the term *villainy*, see 156 n.

2087-98, 2093, 2099 Ln

2109-14 Cf. 5713-16.

2131-76, 2135-74, 2148, 2149, 2158, 2169 (?) Ln

2173-74 *a love contrary to Nature*: Contrast this concept, which more or less follows Alanus de Insulis, *De planctu naturae*, with that developed later by Genius, in which the chaste are included among those who act "against Nature." Cf. 4343-45 n., 16272-20703 n.

2175-2210 See 2077-2232 n.

2183-84 *At one hour . . . bitter* (Amant sentent le mal d'amer / Une eure douz e autre amer.): The first *amer* is the verb, from Latin *amare*, the second the adjective, from Latin *amarum*. The rhyme was common in Old French and of course lends itself to the thematic development of the *Romance*, where it appears here and at 3483, 4233, 13011, 13639, 14611 (see Ln, I, 71, 121). For the thematic development, cf. 4293-334, 21573-82. The pun *l'ameir* (love), *l'ameir* (bitterness), *la meir* (the sea) appears in Chrétien de Troyes, *Cligés*, 541-44 (ed. Micha 1965, p. 17); Thomas, *Tristan* (ed. Bédier 1902-5, I, 155); Gottfried von Strassburg, *Tristan*, 11985-92 (ed. Ranke 1961, p. 150).

2183, 2184, 2185, 2188, 2189-2210, 2203-5 Ln

2225-28 Cf. 136-38 n. On brevity, Ln quotes Horace, *Ars poetica*, 335-36.

2245-46, 2263 Ln

2265-2580 Lc (on the description of the effects of love, in large part adapted from Ovid)

2265-68 Cf. 136-38 n.

2278, 2288, 2295, 2302-13, 2305, 2309, 2317, 2327, 2341-42 Ln

2358 Lc

2391 Ln

2417-18 *This is the battle . . . last forever*: Ln notes that Jean repeats the idea (and construction) at 5085-86. The context of course is quite different; in the later passage, the speaker, Reason, hardly presents a "delightful" torment, as does the God of Love. The parallel then is ironic.

2423 ff. R 97 compares Alixandre in Chrétien de Troyes, *Cligés*, 1615-24.

2432   Ln; Lc cites M. D. Legge, "Toothache and Courtly Love," *French Studies*, 4 (1950), 50-54.

2433-48, 2442, 2459   Ln

2465-66   Lc's base MS omits these two lines, which he supplies from a control MS and numbers 2452 a-b. See Appendix.

2470   Ln; P 73

2519-20   Ln Lc

2536   *sanctuary*: Lc notes the religious tone; cf. 2727, 20915 n. and the passages cited there.

2544   *conversations* (parlers): Ln chooses *parlers* over *pensers* (thoughts), which, as he admits, suits sense if not rhyme (*alers* / *parlers*); Lc's base MS has *pensers*.

2548, 2563, 2569, 2571   Ln

2577-78   G 334

2587, 2594   Ln

2601-2   Ln Lc

2611-17   Ln

2627   Ln Lc

2628, 2631-34, 2635-36   Ln

2677-78   Ln Lc

2695-96   *with her beauty . . . countenance*: Lc omits these two lines, which do not occur in his base MS, but would fall between 2680 and 2681 of his numbering; he notes their MS basis in his Variantes II. See Appendix.

2704, 2751   Ln

2751-55   Cf. 136-38 n.

2768   Ln

2792   *Fair Welcoming* (Bel Acueil): An important figure because he regulates access to the rose. He is imprisoned by Jealousy (3911-24), is wooed through the mediation of the Old Woman (12401-14678), and grants final access to the rose (21277-345). As a result, he often seems to be identified as female, and the MS illustrations show him with either sex; but his masculinity is chiefly grammatical, since the word *acueil* was masculine. Cf. T 322-23; F 43-46; Lewis 1936, p. 122.

2827   *Resistance* (Dangier): For the basic meaning of *dangier*, 'lordship, dominion, power,' cf. 1033; see Lewis 1936, pp. 123-24, 364-66. The choice in translation is to leave the name in the original and explain its meaning or to translate it with a term that may unduly limit the meaning. I choose a term which seems best suited to cover both the inner quality and overt manifestations of *dangier* in Lewis's Sense B, 'power to withhold.' For the meaning 'restraint,' see F 187-89. See also Dahlberg 1969, pp. 579-81; Introduction, "The Illustrations."

2836   Ln

2840 ff.   *daughter of Reason*: Cf. 3028, 14962, 20779.

2854-56, 2894, 2922-23   Ln

2965-67   *No heart . . . sorrow*: P 78 cites 1 Cor. 2:9, calling this passage an adaptation "to the sufferings of love" of the Pauline epistle. Lc, in addition, quotes Virgil, *Aeneid*, VI. 625, and calls the locution a "banale" hyperbole from classical rhetoric.

CHAPTER 3

2971-4058 (Chapter 3) See 1-1680 n. Chapter 3 carries the Lover into the third of the three steps, the consent of reason, represented in the colloquy with and rejection (3073-98) of Reason. Cf. 4377-88 n. The subsequent action follows naturally, and there is little reason to expect that Guillaume's ending would have been different, in terms of overt action, from Jean's; the style of course is quite different.

2971 ff.   P 81 notes that Jean de Meun reintroduces the character Reason. See Introduction on the unity of the two parts. Cf. 4221-7230 n.; R 98, 199.

2975-80   Cf. 4233-36 n.

2976   *tower*: Cf. 4227.

2981-82   Ln

2984-95   *She looked . . . that he believe her*: Ln provides two parallels for the idea that Nature could not form Reason and that she was made in paradise. On Nature as God's vicar, or chamberlain, see Chapter 9, particularly 16729-800. On Reason as the image of God in man, P 78 cites Gen. 1:26-28 and notes that the "letter" (2989) is that of the Bible. He sees a parallel between 2991 (*A sa semblant e a s'image*) and 2985 (*A son semblant e a son vis*), a parallel which the translation obscures. Cf. 19025-28, 19191-95, 19214-16, 18875-77, all passages from Nature's confession, where she complains that man, made in the image of God, is the only one of her creatures who acts unreasonably. Cf. R 44; Augustine, *De civitate Dei*, XII. xxiv.

The agreement between Guillaume and Jean in their concept of Reason and the centrality of that figure in the poem are arguments for its unity. See Introduction.

2987-88   *For Nature would not have known how to make a work of such regularity*: Nature makes the same point about herself at 19055-62. Cf. Augustine, *De trinitate*, XII. iv (4).

2996   *While I was thus lamenting*: Cf. 4221-22 n.

2997   Ln

2998-99   *Fair friend . . . dismay*: Again, both Guillaume and Jean agree, in the words of Reason, that the Lover is foolish. Cf. 4229-52, 5791-92, 6741-52.

3004   Ln

3015   Ln Lc

3028   Cf. 2840 ff., 14962, 20779.

3031, 3033, 3038   Ln

3041-42   G 335

3050   Ln notes that the white monks are the Cistercians.

3051-52   Ln

3057-58   G 335

3062, 3064   Ln

3067   *Take the bit hard in your teeth*: For the iconography, cf. 19787 n.

3089   *idleness*: Ln suggests the play on words with the name of the character Idleness.

3093-94   Ln suggests the sense: "I want to persevere in loving well and only at the end to be praised or blamed for doing so."

3096-98   G 335

3134, 3145, 3167   Ln

3209-10   Ln Lc

3211, 3216, 3223, 3228, 3281-82   Ln

3311   Lc

3345-46   *If he had . . . so*: Omitted in Lc between 3328 and 3329. See Appendix. A translation of the Lc text would read: "Fair Welcoming saluted me sweetly and showed me an appearance fairer than he had ever shown before."

3353-54   *fallen . . . from deepest hell to paradise* (cheoiz . . . / De grant enfer en parevis): Guillaume underlines the inverted state of the Lover's reasoning by the verb *cheoir*, normally used of a fall from paradise to hell.

3394, 3400-8   Ln

3414-15   Ln Lc

3427   *quaint* (cointe): the diction, with its sexual implications, fulfills in its word-play the idea of the previous sentence. Cf. 8841-44.

3473-936   P 137

3473-74   *breath* (aier *Ln*, eer *Lc*): I have adopted Lc's suggestion that the word is a form of *air*, rather than of *aidier* 'help,' as Ln thought.

3479   Ln

3483-84   *love . . . bitter*: See 2183-84 n.

3517, 3523, 3537, 3550, 3552, 3574-76, 3582, 3588, 3635, 3636, 3639, 3646   Ln

3651-53   *in which we can do nothing. April and May have passed many times* (De ce don nos ne poon mais. / Maintes foiz est avris e mais / Passez): Lc notes the common occurrence of the second phrase, and Ln notes its later appearance in Rutebeuf, *La complainte de Guillaume*, line 56; Faral and Bastin 1959-60, I, 260, note that in line 54 of the same poem we have the same construction (*ne pouvoir mais*) as in the first of the two phrases, a construction that reappears in the *Romance*, 3690. In sum, Rutebeuf's verbal echo of Guillaume de Lorris's poem is stronger than Ln and Lc indicate, and it occurs in the same poem that offered Jean de Meun the name False Seeming (Faux Semblant). Faral and Bastin date the poem 1259. See 10459 n.

3660   Ln

3689   Lc

3690   Cf. 3651-53 n.

3697   Ln

3702-3   Ln Lc

3731, 3732   Ln

3761   *situation*: literally, "verse." See Ln's note, and gloss, v, 325.

3761-66   On the use of the present tense and the ambivalent point of view that such use suggests, see Strohm 1968, pp. 6-7.

3791, 3796   Ln

3797-99   Cf. 136-38 n.

3839   Lc

3840-41   Ln

3869 ff.   Ln quotes a passage from Thibaut of Champagne which names the three porters Fair Seeming, Beauty, and Resistance (Biaus Semblanz, Biautez, Dangier). The first two of the three correspond, not to Guillaume's porters but to the last and first of the arrows of love (935-56). The Thibaut passage is interesting because of its differences from Guillaume. It shows the direct use of personification in allegory, for Fair Seeming, Beauty, and Resistance are waiting to seize the lover and put him in prison. Guillaume's method is ironic, for he distributes the three characters into seemingly opposite forces: Beauty and Fair Seeming lead to Fair Welcoming, but Resistance (apparently) keeps the Lover away from Fair Welcoming; and it is Fair Welcoming, not the Lover, who is put in prison. But the Lover is as surely trapped in one case as in the other; Guillaume inverts only part of the picture.

3888, 3891   Ln

3893-900   Ln. Lc's text would produce a slightly different translation: "Foul Mouth . . . had soldiers from Normandy. He guarded the door behind, and you may know too that he often came and went at the other three. When he knew that he was to be on lookout at night, he would mount up . . ."

3898   *discords* (descorz): Ln says simply "a kind of song." It was apparently a form of *lai*, which in turn was "constructed on the plan of the ecclesiastical sequence." While scholars have been unable to trace the "discordance" which gave the *descorz* its name, Friedrich Gennrich believes that it consisted in a rhythmic variation in the repetition of a series of notes (Reese 1940, pp. 225-26).

3920   *an old woman*: For Jean's extensive elaboration of this character, see 12381-14807. Cf. R 131.

3925-30   Ln

3927-36   *for there was no . . . the old dance*: Lc supplies these lines (3908 a–j in his numbering), which his base MS omits, from a control MS. See Appendix.

3930 Ln

3936 *She knew the whole of the old dance*: See R 131-32. Ln's interpretation—that to know the old dance means to be cunning or crafty—is clear but neglects the figurative context. Cf. Chaucer's Wife of Bath, *CT*, 1. 476.

3940, 3951, 3966, 3978 Ln

3981-91 *It is just as with Fortune . . . who is so turned*: The comparison between the instability of Love and that of Fortune is picked up by Jean de Meun and developed—in Reason's speech—at great length. See 4837-974 n.

4047-58 Cf. Strohm 1968, pp. 3-4, 8-9, who suggests that Guillaume's ending is suitable as a complaint, which "is really the conclusion of a finished poem."

4049-50 *and to influence you . . . line*: Ln notes the palaeographical reason for the omission of these two lines by the scribe of MS Ha, Lecoy's base; Lecoy, however, has decided to omit them from his edition, preferring the reading (in translation): "I know in truth that they hope to deceive you, and perhaps they have already done so." See Lc, Variantes II, line 4020; and Appendix.

4058 Ln gives the 78-line text of the anonymous conclusion that appears in several MSS. Since it exhibits a marked lessening of literary skill, I omit a translation; see Robbins 1962, pp. 89-90. Briefly, Dame Pity brings Fair Welcoming, Beauty, Loyalty, Sweet Looks, and Simplicity from the tower while Jealousy is sleeping. Beauty gives the rosebud to the Lover, and he spends the night with it on the grass, under rose-petal coverlets. In the morning, Beauty laughs at Jealousy, asks the Lover's promise of faithful service, and returns with the rosebud to the tower.

PART II

4059-21780 (Part II) Cf. R 198: "In Jean de Meun's continuation, the organization is, if anything, more explicit than that of the earlier part of the poem, and, at the same time, there is a much more thorough effort at exemplification. With reference to the first point, the poem may be seen to fall into well-defined sections devoted to explicit exposition by the principal characters, each of whom, in effect, reveals his or her own nature. The 'characters' thus serve as rubrics under which the various ideas and attitudes relevant to the subject of love may be developed." Dunn 1962, p. xiii, compares the poem to "some great

French cathedral, conceived by its first architect in early Gothic . . . and then extended on a grandiose plan and executed in an advanced and ornate style." The simile is stylistically apt and recognizes the poem's basic unity. See R 202-7 for a discussion of stylistic differences between Guillaume and Jean. Cf. T 237: "Jean de Meun was firmly interested in the relation of eternal beatitude to heavenly and earthly love, but the riotous gallop of his ironies shows that while the blasphemously 'loyal' Lover can be deceived into thinking his plucked Rose will teach him something about a paradise other than an earthly one with a serpent in it, Jean de Meun is not so deceived; and he is using every device of writing to make us notice the Lover's deception with amusement." Her discussion of the *Romance* occupies pp. 233-84. For a characteristic older view, see Lewis 1936, e.g., pp. 137-42; cf. Cohn 1961.

CHAPTER 4

4059-7230 (Chapter 4) Although in one way or another Jean de Meun manages to recapitulate the whole of the Lover's experience in Guillaume's portion, he has chosen to emphasize the third step, the consent of reason; accordingly Chapter 4 is a large-scale amplification of the colloquy between the Lover and Reason at 2971-3098. Cf. 4221-7230 n.

4059-221   P 81
4059-60   G 136; cf. 10595-96.
4059   P 136
4067, 4070   Ln (Cf. 2631-39.)
4071, 4078   Ln
4084-92   *For when she constructs . . . dare blame her*: P 35-36, 27 explains the scholastic terminology. "The worse" is a negative, "the better," an affirmative conclusion to the formal scholastic disputation (*querelle*), a syllogistic form. Cf. 17101-2 n.
4097   Ln
4114-19   Ln; cf. 2640-750.
4130, 4134   Ln
4181-84   Ln (4185 n.); cf. 2025-28.
4190   Lc
4221-7230   P 81-135 gives a *seriatim* analysis of Reason's speech but thinks (p. 82) that "most of the ideas in this chapter have no direct connection with the progress of the *Roman*." He does not, apparently, connect the character Reason with his discussion (pp. 34-35) of *reason* as a scholastic term, which he limits to the relatively minor meaning 'rational proof.' Reason, however, is of central importance in the poem. The 3000 lines of her discourse open Jean's continuation; she gives a

lengthy analysis of the central theme, love; and the basic contrast between her rationality and the varying degrees of irrationality in the major personifications and in the Lover sets her apart as a central figure. Cf. 2971 ff. n.; F 112-40.

4221-28 G 168-69

4221-22 *While I raved . . . suffering*: Langlois 1890, pp. 94 ff., indicates that Jean de Meun echoes Boethius and Alanus in these lines. However, he could just as easily be echoing Guillaume (2996), and both of them Boethius and Alanus.

4233-36 *How do the woes . . . and sufficiency*: See P 71-75 for a discussion of the scholastic theme "virtue resides in the mean" (*in medio stat virtus*). Cf. 2975-80, 4402, 5744-50, 5760, 11269-76; P 50. At 11275, *sufficiency* is defined as "the mean."

4233-34 *love . . . bitter*: See 2183-84 n.

4263-65, 4268-71, 4274-92 G 336-37

4279-358 Ln quotes the source, Alanus de Insulis, *De planctu naturae, PL* 210, cols. 455 A-456 B. Cf. Lc; P 82. The well-known oxymoronic description of love (4293 ff.) is Reason's opening description (see Introduction), and readers and scribes of the MSS often drew attention to it as well as to Andreas Capellanus's definition which follows at 4377-86. Opposite this passage in MS London, British Museum Egerton 881, fol. 29 b, is a note by two different readers, "descri[ption] dam[our] folle." The word "folle" is in a hand at least a century later than that which wrote the other two words. The note thus provides a kind of chronological stratification: it may be inferred that a thirteenth-century reader would have known, without the note, what kind of love was involved. Even when the first annotator made his comment, he did not find it necessary to qualify the word "amour."

There is evidence that scribes saw the definition in much the same way. MS Arras, Bibliothèque municipale 532 (845), contains extracts from the *Romance* with explanatory rubrics at the heads of columns or pages. Fol. 251 b is headed "Nota Raison cont*r*e fol amo*r* carnel"; the next page contains the Alanus description and is headed "Raison description damo*r* carnel"; the first column of the next folio (252 a) is headed "Raiso*n* de le difini*t*ion damo*r* carnel" and contains Andreas Capellanus's definition of love (4377-88); and finally, to make the point of contrast perfectly clear, the next column (252 b) has the heading "de lamo*r* de dieu" and contains the long interpolation which occurs in many MSS at 4400-1 (see note). Cf. 4377-88 n.

4279-84 P 38 discusses the scholastic terms *demonstration, science, opinion, belief* (creance). Cf. 6697-98, 16829-32, 17348-51, 18059-60, 18640-43.

4285-88 Lc offers a translation which differs from mine, approximately as follows (I translate his modern French): "[. . . what cannot be known, demonstrated, or understood,] and that [i.e., you shall have such knowledge] in order that every man who consecrates his heart to love may have a better understanding of it, without, at the same time, having his suffering diminished as a result, unless he is capable of renouncing it."

4329   Ln Lc

4333-34   Ln

4343-45   *whom Genius . . . Nature*: Ln points out that the source is Alanus, *De planctu, PL* 210, cols. 482 B, 432 A. The later development of Genius in the *Romance*, 16272-20703, is based upon that of Alanus but incorporates important differences which depend upon Jean's ironic method. The basic meaning of Genius is *naturalis concupiscentia* 'natural concupiscence, natural desire or inclination' (R 199-202, citing Guillaume de Conches, quoted in Jeauneau 1958, p. 46). In Alanus, Genius quite properly excommunicates those who act *un*-naturally; and Reason, at this point, so uses him. But later, when Nature and Genius operate allegorically as mirrors of the Lover's condition, this natural inclination becomes the servant, in episcopal robes, of the God of Love, the very one whom Reason, in this context, warns against. The hilarious result is that Jean's Genius puts the chaste into the same category that Alanus's Genius had put the perverted. That Jean did not misunderstand Alanus is perfectly clear in this passage. For background, see Knowlton 1920 and 1922-23; Lewis 1936, pp. 361-63, and 1966, pp. 169-74. Cf. 16272-20703 n., 2173-74 n.

4357-58   Ln

4369   *make a public lecture of the whole thing* (lire en tout comunement): P 18-19 discusses the scholastic terms *lire, congié de lire*. Cf. 5037, 5757, 7099-101, 12350-53, 12817, 13503-6, 13919, 13928, etc.

4371-76   G 339; P 83

4376-628   P 97

4377-88   Ln quotes the source, Andreas Capellanus, *De amore*, I. i-ii. Cf. Lc; P 83-84. See Introduction on the correspondence between this definition and the traditional analysis of the three stages of sin: suggestion, delight, and consent; see Dahlberg 1953, pp. 166-69 for evidence that the definition is one of cupidity. Cf. R 84-86 and (for an extended analysis of the *De amore*) 391-448. See 4279-358 n.; and contrast 5443-54.

4379   Ln

4389-97   P 85

4391   Ln

4400   *to be deceived,*: Lc's punctuation supports the translation; Ln has a semicolon, probably in error.

4400-1   Langlois 1910, p. 425, notes that a long interpolated passage appears between these two lines in many of the MSS. In addition to those he lists, three other MSS contain the passage, one (Paris, B. N. fr. 802) on the last folio, another (B. N. fr. 1559) on a folio (37) inserted after the original text had been made up into a book, and the third (Arras, Bibl. mun. 532 [845], described but not classified by Langlois) within the text of some fragments of the *Romance*, fol. 252. Cf. 4279-358 n.

The passage is an extended definition of charity, and its appearance in MSS as early as the thirteenth century shows a) that readers saw charity as a background of Reason's exposition and b) that Jean's artistry had no need at this point of making this assumed background explicit. For text of the interpolation, see Méon 1814, pp. 19-22, or Dahlberg 1953, pp. 249-51. The text appears as a separate poem, with the rubric "Un petit trestie damour en rime," in MS Paris, B. N. fr. 1136, fols. 130 d-132 a.

4402 *the mean*: Ln (i.e., neither to deceive nor to be deceived); cf. 4233-36 n.

4403-21 G 245-46 notes the parallel with 5763-76 and cites the two passages as statements of the "principle of replenishment," one of the doctrines that he sees as part of Jean de Meun's "philosophy of plenitude." P 57-58 cites this passage as an expression of ideas relating to the Aristotelian doctrine on the relation between individuals and species in the material world; and he adduces Thomas Aquinas, *Summa*, II-II, 151, 3, as a contemporary Aristotelian parallel. But the idea is orthodox in Christian tradition and closely related to the idea of the Fall. R 86 cites Augustine, *De genesi ad litteram*, XI. 32. 42: "Once [Adam and Eve] had given up the condition [in which they had existed before the Fall], their bodies took on a diseased, death-bringing quality, which exists naturally in the flesh of beasts; and in order that births might succeed deaths, their bodies also took on that same impulse that brings about in beasts the appetite for copulation." Cf. *De trinitate*, XIII. xii (16), quoted by Peter Lombard, *Sentences*, III, d. xx, c. I, where Augustine distinguishes between two natures, one as it is "rightly created from the beginning," the other as it is "depraved in sin." Cf. 6965-78, 15891-19438 n., 15893-16016, 16625-28; 16005-12 n.

4415-20 P 58

4416, 4422 Ln

4422-24 P 85

4430-32 Ln (Cf. Cicero, *De senectute*, XII.). F 120 points out that the phrase "the root of all evil" is not in Cicero but, of course, in I Tim. 6:10, and that Reason's addition of the Scriptural phrase is a further means of identifying the Lover's love as cupidity.

4430-31 *concludes* (determine): P 23-27 discusses the terms *sentence, doner sentence, determiner*; cf. 5488-89, 7099-7104, 7190, 8306, 10681-83, 11375-80, 15177-83, 17282-88, 17421-23, 17727-28, 19079-82, 19113-14, 20597-99, 20611-14, 20771-73.

4433-4544 P 86

4444-63 *He may go into some convent . . . the virtue of patience*: P 86, 187 considers this passage an attack on the life of the monastery and relates it to the antimendicant passages (e.g., 10467 ff.). But we can distinguish between monks, who "mew themselves up" (4448), and the mendicant friars, "the divines who walk the earth" (5101). Reason complains here of the false monks who enter the religious life for the wrong reasons; note the contrast between remaining in the monastery because of shame and remaining there, through grace, in a state of patience and obedience. Cf. the apparently similar passage at 13967-78 and note.

4447 *pluck the crane from the sky* (prendre au ciel la grue): Ln, v, 219, glosses as 'faire une belle affaire' (make a good thing for himself). The phrase occurs in Rutebeuf, *Vie de Sainte Elysabel*, 388, and Faral and Bastin 1959-60, II, 112, take the phrase to mean 'to perform a miracle.' Cf. Dante, *Inferno*, v. 46: "E come i gru van cantando lor lai." Those who wail like the cranes are the shades of the "peccator carnali, / che la ragion sommettono al talento" ("the carnal sinners who subject reason to desire," *Inferno*, v. 38-39, ed. and trans. Sinclair 1939, pp. 74-75). Among these, of course, the most famous are Paolo and Francesca. To pluck the crane from the sky would be to overcome desire in an impossibly easy way, thus to "get to heaven" without working, or, as in line 5423, to "fly with the cranes."

4463-65   P 73
4469, 4471-72, 4484, 4512   Ln
4540   *sovereign good*: P 50
4545-50, 4559-78   P 86
4560, 4563-68   G 387 (Cf. 13695 ff.)
4599   *any more than by bodily pleasures*: Lc's note suggests this translation.
4600-80   P 86
4624-25   *recover it, if indeed . . .* : The translation here depends upon lighter punctuation than the periods that both Ln and Lc use at the end of 4624 (Ln: Mais recouvrer ne le pourras. / Encor, se par tant en eschapes,).
4635   Ln
4663-85   G 339-40
4667   P 32
4680-768   P 87, 97
4685-762   Lc (The ultimate source is Cicero, *De amicitia*; cf. 4748.)
4685-774   Ln quotes parallels from Cicero, *De amicitia*, v, vi, xii, xiii, xiv, xvii. See Friedman 1962 for evidence that Jean de Meun's source for specific passages—and possibly for much of the Ciceronian material in general—was Aelred of Rievaulx's *De spirituali amicitia*; cf. 4924-40 n.
4712-14, 4739   Ln
4747-48   Ln; P 46
4769-836   P 87, 97

4807-8   Ln (Cf. 5235-36.)

4836-5356   P 88

4837-974   See P 115-32 for a discussion of the theme of Fortune in the poem as a whole, F 123-32 for an iconographical analysis of the theme and figure of Fortune. The major passages, besides this, are 3981-91, 5877-6900, and 8005-154; see also 4975-5588 n. For background, see Patch 1927, Courcelle 1967. The present passage, as Ln and Lc note, is a translation and development from Boethius, *De consolatione philosophiae* (*De cons.*), II, pr. 8.

4842-48   P 34-35 discusses *raison* as a scholastic term and compares 6300-3, 6335-37, 17237-38, 18440. See 4221-7230 n.

4863, 4894, 4920, 4941-42, 4942, 4943-44   Ln

4924-40   Friedman 1962, pp. 140-41 documents a specific source in Aelred of Rievaulx.

4947-48   Ln Lc

4949, 4966   Lc

4975-5588   P 98-115 takes this long passage somewhat out of the context of Fortune and discusses it under the heading of "social and political morality." The objection here is not a mere quibble, since Jean's treatment makes this passage on riches and poverty, justice and nobility, subordinate to the topic of Fortune, which is in turn subordinate, as one form of love, to the full discussion of the different kinds of love. By treating the material in this passage separately, Paré has encouraged his conclusion that "in this matter [of social and political morality], Friend speaks exactly as Reason does, Nature as Friend does, False Seeming as Reason, Friend, and Nature do, which indicates clearly where the author's preferences lie" (p. 98). Aside from questions of literal accuracy, we have a set of strange bedfellows here, for the alignment ignores even the overt disposition of forces in the Lover's battle. The most misleading assumption is that Jean shares the attitudes of each of the characters, for such an assumption neglects the possibility of irony. The passages that Paré adduces in comparison are 18561-885 (Nature), 20123-29 (Genius), 8447-48, 9521-664 (Friend); the collocations are useful, but often, when differences in speaker are taken into account, more to reveal irony than agreement. Cf., for example, 20033 n., 5535-54 n., 8355-9634 n.

4991   Ln Lc

5020   Cf. 8128 n.

5025-32   Ln Lc (Calcidius, CXXXVI, ed. 1962)

5029   Cf. 8128 n.

5035-40   Ln Lc; G 53. *De cons.*, I, pr. 5. Jean had not yet done the translation (ed. Dedeck-Héry 1952) that he proposes at 5039-40.

5037   Cf. 4369 n.

5045   Ln

5049   *La Greve*: Ln; the unloading ramp for the Seine river-freight, on the site of the present-day Place de l'Hôtel de Ville in Paris. Cf. Rutebeuf, *Dit des Ribauds de Greve*, ed. Faral and Bastin 1959-60, I, 531.

5052, 5053, 5054, 5063   Ln

5085-86   Ln (Cf. 2417-18.)

5101-18   *the divines who walk the earth*: the mendicant friars. Cf. P 187 and 4444-63 n.

5127-32   Ln Lc

5143-44   P 46

5159-66, 5173-74   Ln

5185-87   Lc

5196-202, 5221-25, 5226   Ln

5235-36   Ln. Cf. 4807-8.

5269-79, 5280-84   Ln

5280   Lc (Juvenal, *Satire* x. 22)

5315-45   P 124

5315-19   Lc (Boethius, *De cons.*, II, pr. 5. 14)

5319   Ln

5320   P 303 (Cf. 7072.)

5325   Ln

5388-403   Ln

5395   Lc

5405-11   Ln Lc (Cicero, *De amicitia*, IV)

5417-18   Ln

5423   *cranes*: Cf. 4447 n.

5424-26   *Socrates' swan*: Ln Lc (John of Salisbury, *Polycraticus*, II. 16)

5435-58   P 88-89

5443-54   *He must love generally . . . to take toward you*: Lc (to 5451-52, 5453-54). P 43-44 discusses the terms *generaument, en generalité, en especialité*; cf. 18274-78, 20371; 18305-20 n. P 88-89 notes the connection between "loving generally" and the Christian precept of charity. My translation of the phrase *dou comun* ('of what is common to all') does not entirely agree with Ln's gloss of *comun* 'le peuple, la foule.' It is somewhat surprising that neither Ln nor P note any parallel to the Golden Rule, not even the most obvious one; Lc quotes Matt. 7:12 and one proverbial formulation of the very widespread negative form of the rule in 5453-54. With the entire passage, contrast the definition of cupidinous love at 4377-88.

5459-695   P 89

5467   Ln

5488-89   See 4430-31 n.

5495   Ln

5527-31   P 90

5532   *It is for this reason that I call love the better*: Lc. See also his article, Lecoy 1964.

5535-54 Fleming 1963, p. 228, points out that according to the First Vatican Mythographer, "the birth of Venus was not a happy moment in the history of the human race," and notes that the birth was coincident with the disappearance of the Golden Age (see 5537-42 n.); cf. F 146. Thus the use of the Golden Age motif by Friend and Genius, both in the service of Venus, is additionally ironic. Cf. 4975-5588 n., 8355-9664 n., 20033 n.

5537 P 132, 135

5537-42 *Saturn, whose testicles . . . as the book tells*: Cf. 20034-36, 10827-30. The "book," as Ln notes, may well be the First Vatican Mythographer (ed. Bode 1834, I, 33, 34, 64); but Lc's suggestion of the Second and Third Mythographers (Ibid., I, 84, 155) or of Servius's commentary on the *Aeneid* (III. 707 and v. 801) is less appropriate, since Jean is not following the Hesiod tradition that these writers do. In that tradition Kronos (Saturn), rather than Zeus (Jupiter), is the one who castrates his father. Jean's version may well go back to Fulgentius (see Liebeschütz 1926, p. 58; cf. Third Mythographer, ed. Bode, I, 155). Bode (II, 35-36) accounts for the shift from Saturn to his son Jupiter through a confusion between the castration of the Sky, by his son Saturn, and the struggle against the Titans, in which Jupiter overthrew his father Saturn and banished him to Tartarus. See Hesiod, *Theogony*, 154-210, 617-819; Ovid, *Met.*, I. 113-15; *Servii . . . commentarii*, ed. Thilo and Hagen 1881, I. 457, 649-50.

5543 Ln

5562-63 *. . . absolutely . . .* (simplement): P 40-41 discusses the terms *simplement, necessité simple, necessité en regart.* Cf. 17228-29.

5571 Ln

5589-658 Ln Lc give the reference in Livy, *Annals*, I. iii. 44-58. Ln quotes parallels at 5600-14, 5616, 5618-23, 5635-39, 5649-56. Cf. Chaucer, *Physician's Tale, CT*, VI. 1-286.

5659-92 P 91
5660-62 Ln Lc
5683-84 Ln

5695-96 *the reasons which seem to me appropriate to this judgment* (les raisons . . . / Qui me semblent a ce meües): Ln's gloss on *movoir* construes *a* as auxiliary with *meües*. This reading involves a lack of concord with *qui*, whose antecedent is *raisons*. I therefore translate *a* as a preposition and *meües* (past participle as adjectival modifier of *raisons*, literally 'moved') as 'appropriate.' Cf. Foulet 1930, section 113.

5696-763 P 92
5697-724 Cf. 6928-7228.
5700-3 Ln (Cf. 5537.)
5710 Ln; G 342
5712-16 G 342
5713-16 *My master . . . ribaldry*: The prohibition occurs at 2109-14.

5713, 5715-16   G 169

5737-39   Ln Lc

5744-50, 5760   Cf. 4233-36 n.

5757   Cf. 4369 n.

5763-94   On this important passage, see Dahlberg 1969, pp. 572-75. G 245-47 sees it as evidence for the "principle of replenishment," and P 92, 97 identifies it with the "*appetitus naturalis* or *amor naturalis* of the scholastics." Cf. 4403-21 n.

5769   P 32

5777-850   P 92-95

5837-38   Ln (Cf. 1453-66.)

5847-62   *Solinus*: Third-century author of *Collectaneum rerum memorabilium*. Ln Lc quote the passage on Socrates.

5848   Ln

5869-74   Ln quotes the Solinus passage on Heraclitus and Diogenes.

5877-6900   See 4837-974 n.; P 119-22. Cf. 8005-154 n.

5914-15   Ln Lc quote Juvenal, *Satire* x. 365-66, and Ln adds Alanus, *De planctu*, PL 210, col. 464 A.

5921-6118   Lc cites, Ln quotes the source for the description of the island of Fortune, a long passage from Alanus, *Anticlaudianus,* VII. 405-VIII. 14, ed. Bossuat 1955. Cf. Patch 1927, pp. 123-46 (not 42-49, as in P 119, n. 1); P 119-20.

5938, 5941, 5942   Ln

5945   P 50

5978-6078   With the two rivers, cf. the two springs of Narcissus's fountain (1532), Jupiter's two tuns (6813-42 n.), and Venus's two fountains (Claudian, *De nuptiis Hon.*, 69-70, quoted Lc, 1, 276).

5978, 6041, 6080, 6085   Ln

6119-72   Ln Lc (*Anticlaudianus*, VIII. 45-57)

6157-60   *And when she sees . . . in a whorehouse*: Lc (6129 n.) asks where Jean de Meun got the comparison between Fortune and a whore. To the two rather remote parallels that he lists we may add those in Patch 1927, pp. 12, 56-57. Boethius and Alanus offer sufficient basis, if not a clear parallel, for the concept. The figure is common in Shakespeare (e.g., *Hamlet*, II. ii. 239, 515).

6166-70   Ln

6185-272   For the episode of Nero's cruelty, Lc summarizes Jean's borrowings from Boethius, *De cons.*, II, pr. 6 and m. 6, along with other sources. Ln quotes the parallels in his notes to 6188-202, 6203-6 (Suetonius), 6208 (John of Salisbury), 6211-13, 6246-50, 6251-72, 6263-65. Chaucer uses much of the Nero material in the *Monk's Tale*, *CT*, VII. 2463-550.

6194-96   On Nero's opening his mother's womb (not in Boethius), see Ln, Lc (6155-242 n.), and Jean de Meun 1952, p. 200, where he adds this detail to Boethius, II, m. 6.

6220   P 303

6229-45 Ln
6251-342 P 109-14
6265, 6275-77 (Lc also) Ln
6278 P 50
6280-81 Ln
6291-342 Lc and Ln note that the "text" mentioned at 6293 and 6299 is the *De cons*. Lc summarizes the parallels to III, pr. 12 and IV, pr. 2; Ln quotes passages in his notes to 6291-99, 6304-12.

6300-3 P 15-18 discusses the terms *aucteur, auctorité, autentique*; cf. 6627-28, 9187-88, 15217-18, 16196-98; on *reasons*, cf. 4842-48 n.

6332 P 50
6335-37 Cf. 4842-48 n.
6355-70 Ln quotes, Lc cites the passage from Claudian, *In Rufinum*, I. 1-23.

6361 P 28
6370, 6381-412, 6392, 6408 Ln
6413-88 Lc (Suetonius, *Nero*, XLVII-XLIX); Ln gives details in notes to specific passages.

6422, 6430, 6458 Ln
6458 P 303
6489-630 Ln and Lc both note that the Croesus story is suggested by Boethius, *De cons*., II, pr. 2; for further details, Ln suggests the First and Second Vatican Mythographers, ed. Bode 1834, I, 59-60, 137, where the dream and the connection with Fortune are explicit. Cf. Chaucer, *Monk's Tale, CT*, VII. 2727-66.

6528-32 Ln
6568-70 Instead of *Fall (Cheance)*, Lc suggests *Chance (Hasard)*, and quotes the parallel in *Anticlaudianus*, VII. 397-400, where the corresponding word is *Casus*. Langlois's gloss, "chute personifiée" (V, 334) seems strengthened, if anything, by this parallel, but of course the notions of "fall" and "chance" are both present and closely related in the word *casus*.

6569, 6570-71 Ln
6579-92 See T 43. Cf. 18607-896.
6581-92 P 103
6592, 6594-95 Ln Lc
6600 P 73
6608-10 *For know . . . letter*: Cf. 7153-80 n.
6627-28 Cf. 6300-3 n.
6631-740 Jean's account of the contemporary struggle between Manfred and Charles of Anjou for the kingdom of the Two Sicilies is important in dating the poem; see Introduction. For the historical details and sources, see the notes of Ln and Lc. Briefly, Charles of Anjou killed Manfred at the battle of Benevento, Feb. 26, 1266, and assumed the throne which Pope Urban had offered him; and when

Conradin, Manfred's nephew, took up the struggle, Charles defeated him at the battle of Tagliacozzo, Aug. 23, 1268. Henry of Castile had been Charles's supporter, but betrayed him and fomented the revolt of 1268.

6631-98   Cf. Chaucer, *BD*, 617-86.

6631   Ln notes that Jean de Meun alludes to Charles's victory over Conradin in his translation of Vegetius, *L'Art de Chevalerie*, II. xvii, ed. U. Robert, Paris, 1897 (SATF).

6650   *in the front ranks of his army* (En la prumeraine bataille): Lc (1, 287) quotes historical justification for this translation; Ln (6637-45 n.) assumes "in the first battle," i.e., the battle of Benevento, a reasonable interpretation but not as well supported.

6662   Ln

6664   *fools* (fos): The fool was equivalent—in chess—to the modern bishop.

6684   Lc

6691-98   Ln and Lc cite John of Salisbury, *Polycraticus*, I. 5, ed. Webb 1909, p. 35.

6697-98   Cf. 4279-84 n.

6723   Lc

6769, 6772, 6774, 6778-79, 6803-4   Ln

6813-42   On Jupiter's two casks or tuns, cf. 10627-34. Ln and Lc (6747-824 n.) note the parallel in *De cons.*, II, pr. 2. 13, and the fact that Boethius does not cite Homer (*Iliad*, XXIV. 527), the early source. For further history of the figure in Plato, the neo-Platonists, and medieval commentators, see Bieler 1957, p. 20; Courcelle 1967, pp. 106, 131, 145, 166-67, 281, and Pl. 68. The idea behind the two tuns is similar to that behind the two rivers of Fortune in Alanus, *Anticlaudianus*, VII. 439-80; Jean uses the passage at 5978-6078.

6823   *sweetened wine* (piment): Ln (specifically, wine, honey, and spices); cf. 8379.

6855-61   P 132. On Fortune's wheel, see Patch 1927, pp. 147-77; Courcelle 1967, pp. 141-52 and, for a collection of MS illustrations, Pls. 65-86.

6858   *the conjuror's strap-folding trick*: Ln. A strap can be folded so that no matter which loop the player places his finger in, the "conjuror," by pulling on the suitably arranged ends of the strap, can leave the player's finger free of or, alternatively, enclosed within the loop.

6866, 6867-68   Ln

6900-6   G 179

6901-78   P 133-34

6901-27   T 260. Cf. 7185-228.

6909, 6916   Ln

6917-24   Ln Lc (Cf. 4218-20.)

6928-7228   Cf. 5697-724.

6928-29   G 169
6929   Ln (See 5537.)
6940   Ln
6943-78   G 229
6943-44, 6956-58   Cf. 7153-80 n.
6951-58   Ln
6965-78   Cf. 4403-21 n.
6988   Ln Lc
7016, 7022   Ln
7037-57   Cf. Chaucer, *Manciple's Tale, CT*, IX. 329-33.
7037-43, 7053-54   Ln Lc
7061-62   On the utility of pagan literature, see Augustine, *De doctrina christiana*, II. xviii-xlii, particularly xl, where he uses the simile of Egyptian gold for useful pagan learning.
7072   P 303 (Cf. 5320.)
7078-82   Cf. 7153-80 n.
7081-86   *oppose, reply* (oposer, respon) : terms relating to scholastic disputation. P 28-29 discusses these, *obicier* 'object,' and *soudre* 'solve, resolve.' Cf. 7106-7, 8889-90, 17101-2, 17108-10, 21497-21500.
7099-105   *Timaeus*: Ln Lc note that the source is Calcidius's translation of Plato's *Timaeus*, ed. 1962, p. 44. Cf. also 4430-31 n.
7099-101   Cf. 4369 n.
7104-18   G 230-32
7106-7   Cf. 7081-86 n.
7121-22   *God . . . well done* (E Deus, qui est sages e fis. / Tient a bien quanque je fis,) : Lc corrects Ln's errors in punctuation and supports this translation.
7131-47   Ln
7137   Ln Lc
7143   Ln
7147   Lc
7153-80   Ln quotes Alanus, *De planctu, PL* 210, col. 451. On the subject of the medieval understanding of poetry and of pagan poetic materials, see R 61, 286-317, 337-65; F 134-35; Hill 1966, p. 114. In the *Romance*, says Robertson (p. 61), "it is appropriate that Raison should be the source of instruction on the subject of poetic appreciation." Cf. P 19-23; Paré, Brunet, Tremblay 1933, pp. 116-20. The point here is that the poetic theory developed by Reason follows the traditional Christian pattern, with the distinction between the letter, the obscure fable or the integument, and the verity which lies hidden by this dark exterior (7162-68); Reason enunciates the Horatian combination of the pleasing and the useful in a way which reflects Augustine's ideas on these categories (7169-80); cf. *Soliloquiorum*, II. xi (19) : "a fable is a lie composed for utility and delight"; *De diversis questionibus*, XXX: "Many visible things are useful; but in anything useful, the true utility

from which we benefit and which we call divine providence, that utility is invisible." *De doctrina christiana*, III. x (16): "Utility is what charity does for one's own benefit." Cf. Quain 1945, pp. 215, 220.

P 19-23 discusses several of these matters in connection with his examination of the terms *glose, gloser, espondre, integumenz, moele, escorce*. Cf. 2071-72, 6943-44, 6956-58, 7078-82, 7181-84, 7190-92, 7559-61, 11858-60, 15148-50, 17627-28, 21574.

7168 Ln Lc
7171-76 Ln (Horace, *Ars poetica*, 333-34)
7212-22 G 179-80
7228 Ln
7229-33 Ln (Cf. 3096-110.)

CHAPTER 5

7231-10002 (Chapter 5) R 199: "The discourse of Amis, who is a worldly friend not exactly of the kind advocated by Cicero, is an essay in worldly wisdom. Flattery, hypocrisy, force, deceit, a contempt of marriage, and bribery are strongly urged as proper weapons of a lover. If Raison gives us a wise attitude toward love, Amis furnishes a wily approach to the same subject." Cf. Introduction. On Cicero's advice concerning friends, see Reason's account at 4685-768. On Friend, see F 140-60; T 241-45, 247-48. We should note that, following Reason's overt and wide-ranging examination of love, "we find ourselves," as Miss Tuve observes (262), "building a definition for love by negatives, as we progress through the ironic presentation of unrelieved inadequacies and deceptions and rationalizations and errors." The process continues to the end of the poem; cf. T 239. P 136-54 gives an analysis of this chapter but tends to take it seriously as a direct expression of Jean de Meun's thought, leading toward a supposed Aristotelian naturalism (p. 341); cf. 8005-154 n., 4975-5588 n. I omit further specific references to P's discussion in the pages noted or to G's *seriatim* discussion of this chapter, pp. 345-51.

7233, 7261, 7268 Ln
7307-794 The passage, as Lc notes, is "strongly inspired by Ovid's *Ars amatoria*." Both Lc and Ln cite and quote specific passages, and I omit further references to such notes. The main passages in Ovid are as follows: I. 149-52, 277-78, 343-90, 441-44, 657-78, 705-20; II. 161-66, 198-211, 429-32; III. 485-86, 497-98. There is a minor *erratum* in Lc, I, 290, line 9 from bottom: for *IV, 485-86*, read *III, 485-86*.

7315 Lc

7352 Ln Lc

7355-56 *and Foul Mouth is a trickster* (boulierres). *Take away the tricks* (bou), *and he remains a thief* (lierres): The play on words is reinforced by the rhyme, *boulierres / lierres*.

7365-69 Ln Lc

7369 Ln

7392-93 Ln Lc

7405-7, 7408 Ln

7410-14 Lc Ln

7415, 7534, 7541-42 Ln

7555-58 G 75

7559-61 Cf. 7153-180 n.

7605-6 Ln

7625 Lc

7670, 7762 Ln

7761-66 Cf. Chaucer, *Manciple's Tale, CT*, IX. 183-86.

7764-66 Ln Lc

7768-70 Ln

7791-94 G 180

7847-48 Ln Lc

7863-66 Ln

7887 ff. Lc notes that the long development on poverty expands Ovid, *Ars amatoria,* II. 161-66.

7911, 7912 Ln

7914 Ln (See 10040.)

7932 P 73

7940 Ln

7954-56 P 73

7985-86 Ln Lc (Ovid, *Remedia amoris,* 749)

8003-4 Ln Lc (Cf. 3015.)

8005-154 P 117-19 discusses this passage as one of Jean's statements on Fortune, parallel to those at 3981-91 (Guillaume), 4837-974, and 5877-6900. "The ideas of Friend on the subject of Fortune," he says, p. 118, "coincide perfectly with those of Reason" (cf. 4975-5588 n.). That the correspondence is somewhat less than perfect is apparent when we consider the nature of the speaker, Friend, and the context of the remarks on Fortune, for it is *against* Poverty that Friend is warning, and the seemingly good doctrine about how Fortune reveals one's true friends becomes utterly hollow in such a context. Cf. 7987-8004 and 8155-206 as well as the entire thrust of Friend's speech. Embedding sound doctrine in unsound argument is one of Jean's favorite techniques of irony. Cf. 4343-45 n., 19931-20667 n., 7231-10002 n., 8355-9634 n.

8005 Ln

8047-53   Ln Lc

8059-60, 8073, 8081   Ln

8099-114   Ln notes (8100 n.) that the *beggars* (*li mendiant*) are the mendicant orders, particularly the Minorites (Franciscans) and Preaching Friars (Dominicans); Lc thinks that the beggars may be simply professional beggars. Ln is probably right; the phrase *sound of body* (*poissant de cors*; cf. 11408 *forz on de cors*) recalls the Latin *validus corpore* which recurs frequently in the antimendicant writings of Guillaume de Saint-Amour. See, e.g., *Responsiones*, Nos. 7, 8, 11, ed. 1951, pp. 341-44; *De periculis*, xii, *Opera* 1632, pp. 48, 52; *Collectiones catholice canonice scripture*, p. 218. Ln quotes these texts at 11317-23 n., 11345-49 n., 11366-74 n. See also *De valido mendicante quaestio*, pp. 80-87. False Seeming develops the theme of manual labor and the cases in which one may beg; see 11317-508. Cf. P 187-88.

8128   Ln. P 303, in comparing 5020, 5029, again neglects the distinction in Jean's literary method between direct and ironic development; the contexts, with Reason as the speaker in one case and Friend in the other, establish the distinction.

8143   Ln

8148-54, 8174-78, 8185-88   Ln Lc

8199-354   Ln Lc note several parallels to Ovid, *Ars amatoria*, ii. 13, 107-8, 111-20, 143-44, 261-70, 273-78; I omit their specific references.

8216   Ln

8223-26   P 73-74

8240-42   Ln Lc

8244   Ln

8245-56   G 194-95

8252-56   G 181

8279   Ln

8287-92, 8293-96   Ln Lc note parallels to Juvenal, *Satire* vi. 53-54, 209-10.

8306   Cf. 4430-31 n.

8312-13   *figure* (fourme): On the use of *fourme* 'shape,' see P 65; cf. 9059-60, 16038, 16755-56, 16109-11.

8324   Ln

8351   Ln Lc

8353   Ln

8355-9664   Lc notes that the description of the Golden Age is interrupted by the passage on the Jealous Husband and the satire on marriage (8455-9492). The principal "writings" that Jean de Meun may have used for the Golden Age motif were, according to Ln and Lc, Ovid, *Met.*, i. 89-115, 127-50; *De cons.*, ii, m. 5. I omit specific references to such parallels. The motif, Lc notes, was a commonplace in classical rhetoric. On Jean's use of it, cf. 5535-54 n., 20033 n.; T 241,

260-61. In this and the later case, Jean achieves irony through incongruous juxtaposition of speaker (Friend and Genius) and motif (Golden Age). Here the contrast is between the ideal situation of the Golden Age and the far-from-ideal situation of the Jealous Husband as well as between the general tenor of Friend's advice and the picture of the Golden Age. Cf. 4975-5588 n., 8005-154 n. Friedman 1959 argues for a reading of the passage in context and against the assumption that the Jealous Husband expresses Jean de Meun's opinions. Cf. Introduction.

8355-8393   There are several parallels to this passage in Chaucer, *The Former Age*; for details, see Robinson 1957, pp. 859-60. Boethius is, of course, a common source.

8369   Ln

8379   Ln (Cf. 6823 n.)

8380   Ln

8386-89, 8393, 8399-402   Ln quotes Juvenal, *Satire* VI. 2-3, 5-7.

8423-24   Ln

8447-48   Cf. 4975-5588 n.

8451-53   Ln Lc (Ovid, *Met.*, II. 846-47)

8463   Lc

8465-66   *to have control over the body . . . of his wife* (la maistrise aveir / Dou cors sa fame): F 155-56 notes the parallel to 1 Cor. 7:4, "The wife hath not the power of her own body, but the husband," a parallel that casts doubt on the validity of Friend's analysis of marital relationships.

8480   Lc

8486-87   Ln

8488-89   Ln Lc quote, or cite, evidence to indicate that to strike someone in the face with an inflated bladder indicated that he was a simpleton, or was wool-gathering.

8509   *For whom . . . chestnuts?*: Ln. "Who do you think you're fooling?" has the same sense but not the imagery. Cf. 8502.

8560   Ln

8561-832   Ln Lc note that Theophrastus's *Aureolus* is lost, that our knowledge of it comes principally through Jerome, *Adversus Jovinianum* (I. 47), and that Jean's version of Jerome probably came through John of Salisbury, *Polycraticus*, VIII. xi. The "Valerius" passages are from Walter Map, *De nugis curialium*, IV. 3, ed. 1914, pp. 143-58, entitled *Dissuasio Valerii ad Rufinum philosophum ne uxorem ducat*. Lc notes that Map had earlier presented this section of the *De nugis* separately as the work of the fictitious "Valerius," who was then supposedly identified with Valerius Maximus (Delhaye 1951, pp. 79-82). Jean also borrows from Juvenal's *Satires* VI and VII. I omit specific references to parallels, which are detailed in the notes of Ln and Lc.

8561   P 95-96

8579-600   Cf. Chaucer, *Wife of Bath's Prologue, CT,* III. 248-56.

8603-4   Ln

8608-50   Ln Lc quote and cite Livy, I. lviii ff.

8690, 8756   Ln

8759-832   Ln Lc note the source as Abelard's *Historia calamitatum,* ed. 1962, pp. 75-76, 114.

8759, 8769   P 96, 52

8784, 8789-90   Ln

8801   *another abbey*: Ln (Saint-Gildas, in Brittany)

8822, 8827-30, 8834-35, 8836-38, 8870   Ln

8874   Ln (Cf. 213 n.)

8889-92   Cf. 7081-86; see P 51.

8899, 8900   Ln

8908   Lc. On dung-heaps, cf. 18754 n.

8911-12   Ln

8921-56   Ln Lc (Boethius, *De cons.,* III, pr. 8.10)

8929   *explicate the sophism* (le sofime deviser): P 29 discusses this scholastic phrase in connection with the terms *distinter, distinction.* Cf. 11063-64; P 52.

8944-45   Ln

8957-58   Ln Lc

8968-70   Ln

9009-12   Ln Lc (Virgil, *Aeneid,* VI. 563)

9015, 9020-30, 9039-70   Ln

9040   Lc

9059-60   Cf. 8212-13 n.; P 52.

9081   *camelot*: Ln defines it as "a kind of costly fabric." The *New (Oxford) English Dictionary,* s.v. *camlet,* is uncertain of origin, noting that it was early associated with *camel,* but that it may spring from Arabic *Khaml, Khamlat* 'nap or pile on cloth.' Camelot appears to have been a rich fabric, sometimes with a velvety or plushy pile, but it has varied widely in materials and weave. Cf. 12045 n.

9131   Ln

9143-54   Ln Lc (Juvenal, *Satire* VI. 133-35)

9155-56   *All you women . . . desire*: See Friedman 1959; 8355-9664 n.

9185   Ln

9187-90   *Solinus*: Cf. 5847-62 n. Ln Lc quote the passage.

9187-88   Cf. 6300-3 n.

9191-206   Cf. Chaucer, *Wife of Bath's Prologue, CT,* III. 721-26.

9191-202   Ln

9191, 9203   Lc

9204   Ln Lc

9267   See 9081 n.

9282-84, 9306   Ln
9313-60   Ln Lc (Juvenal, *Satire* VI. 231-41)
9328-56   G 389-90
9329   Ln
9330   *that mackerel, that pimping whore* (Maquerele e charaier-resse): Levy 1952 translates *charaierresse* as '*putain*,' rather than as '*sorcière*' (Langlois 1924, v, 148).

9336, 9339, 9340, 9343, 9361-504, 9366, 9416-20   Ln
9416   Ln Lc (Prov. 9:13)
9417-20   Ln Lc (Map 1914, p. 153)

9427   *his equal and his companion*: A parallel may be suggested to Robert de Sorbon's sermon *De matrimonio*: "Again, woman was made from man's rib, not from a lower part but from the middle; thus this circumstance signifies that a woman should be her husband's equal" (quoted by Mariella 1938, p. 252, from B. Hauréau, *Notices et extraits de quelques Mss. latins de la Bibliothèque Nationale* [Paris 1890], I, 189; cf. Chaucer, *Parson's Tale, CT*, x. 926-28). Robert de Sorbon was a popular preacher and lecturer in Paris during the period, 1250-74, when he was developing the college associated with his name (Glorieux 1933-34, I, 340-41; Glorieux 1966, p. 48), the period, moreover, when Jean de Meun was probably in the same neighborhood. In any case, the idea "was a commonplace in medieval religious literature" (Mariella, p. 252).

9436   Ln
9439-473   G 354-56
9467   Ln
9474   Ln Lc
9483, 9484-87   Ln
9497-500   Ln Lc
9498, 9501-3   Ln
9505   Ln (Cf. 13229 ff.)
9509-12   Ln
9521-664   Cf. 4975-5588 n.
9526, 9528-34, 9549-54, 9557-60, 9565, 9569-74, 9587, 9593   Ln
9603 ff.   Lc (Horace, *Satires*, I. iii. 98 ff.)
9633-36   P 345
9658-59, 9659-61   Ln
9679-938   Lc and Ln note specific parallels, which I omit, to passages in Ovid, *Ars amatoria*, II. 121-642. Cf. P 136, n. 1.
9693-95, 9740   Ln
9921-24   Ln Lc (Eccles. 7:29)
9969-70   Ln Lc
9976   P 73
9987-99   G 181-82

CHAPTER 6

10003-12380 (Chapter 6) R 199: "To elaborate the ideas set forth by Amis, we are introduced to Faus-Semblant, for, as Amis has indicated, the successful follower of the God of Love must be a 'seemer.'" Cf. T 248-50, 256, 258-59; Dahlberg 1953, pp. 145-53; F 161-70. On the propriety of self-revelation in an allegory, see T 255. On the parallel between False Seeming and the Lover, see notes to 7153-80, 11216. See P 155-91; note, however, that he thinks that the antimendicant passages have no direct relation to the plot (p. 160).

10040 Ln (See 7914.)

10042, 10083-84 Ln

10051-267 The primary significance of this episode is perfectly clear, but added point arises from the juxtaposition of Wealth, with her emphasis on poverty, and False Seeming, a hypocritical friar, since the major distinguishing feature of the fraternal orders was a radical form of poverty: communal poverty as well as the individual poverty that the older monastic orders practiced. Cf. 10687-928, where the God of Love *pretends* to be the champion of poor men against Wealth, who has spurned the Lover, and appropriately grants False Seeming permission to be in his court; cf. also 11037-82, 11238-424, two passages in False Seeming's speech that reveal his profession of poverty and his practice of cultivating wealth.

We may note a contrast between the Lover, who is urged to get money and to abhor poverty, and the rich ruler whom Christ urged to sell all he had, give to the poor, and follow Him (Luke 18:22; see 11327, 11375-77). This contrast reveals a strong family resemblance among Wealth, the God of Love, the Lover, False Seeming, and the Old Woman, all of whom have the same basic attitude toward wealth and poverty. Cf. 11553-76, 13695-724.

10056 *elm tree* (ourme): Alanus de Insulis associates the elm (*ulmus*) with "the worldly mind, which bears no spiritual fruit as long as it is subject to earthly concerns" (*Distinctiones dictionum theologicalium, PL* 210, col. 984). The association is obvious in Fig. 33.

10094 P 73

10095-98 Ln

10102 *chaplets of flowers*: Cf. 895-96, 12439-41, 7435.

10124-26, 10140 Ln

10152-90 Lc Ln (Ovid, *Met.*, VIII. 784-808)

10154, 10173, 10183, 10206, 10208, 10210-15 Ln

10244-46 *beech . . . folly* (fou . . . fou): Ln and Lc note that in the play on words a third meaning, *fou* for *feu* 'fire,' is probably present.

10248-60, 10278-306, 10311-670 G 360-72

10325-37 Ln (Cf. 4069-154.)

10344-47, 10353 Ln

10364-412 P 156-57

10371-76 P 297 regards the ending of the poem as the fulfillment of this declaration.

10403-12 Ln Lc (See 2077-264.)

10430-918 P 157-60

10449 Ln

10459 *False Seeming*: Lc and P 158, n. 2, note that Jean gets the name from Rutebeuf, *Complainte de Guillaume* [de Saint-Amour], 78, 86, ed. Faral and Bastin 1959-60, I, 261-62; the context is an anti-mendicant poem, and the selection of the name establishes from the outset the basis for the specific satire that develops later. Cf. 11293 ff. n., 3651-53 n.

10508-18 Ln Lc (Ovid, *Amores*, III. ix. 7-12, 15.)

10514 Ln

10522-25 Ln Lc (Cf. 10508-18; Ovid, *Amores*, III. ix. 61-64.)

10526-678 See G 22-29, 134, 183-84, 322-25; Dahlberg 1953, pp. 134-35; T 254-55. The passage, as P 159 points out, is important for our knowledge of the composition and authorship of the entire *Romance*, but we must approach it with caution, not because we have any reason to dispute the data but because it is easy to neglect the ironic framework. If, as we have suggested, Guillaume sees the Lover as headstrong and foolish, the God of Love's speech is another fine example of dramatic irony, where the reader understands it quite differently. Moreover, this view still implies a fundamental unity between Guillaume and Jean. Cf. 10650-51 n.

10555-60 Ln Lc (See 4053-58.)

10567, 10582 Ln

10595-96 Ln Lc (See 4059-60.)

10599-604 Ln (Cf. the end of the poem.); Lc

10605-8, 10616 Ln

10627-34 Ln Lc (Cf. 6813-42 n.)

10641-44, 10645 Ln

10650-51 *should call this book* The Mirror for Lovers: G 28. The speaker at this point is the God of Love, and he clearly understands the book as a model *Mirror*, one for lovers to emulate. Fleming 1963, pp. 162-63 suggests that, from the point of view of Jean and the reader, the book is a warning *Mirror*, like the *Mirror for Magistrates*, rather than a model. Fleming shows that both senses of the word *mirror* were current, and we here see another example of Jean's ironic technique, the exploitation of a double symbolic significance. Cf. 10526-678 n.

10681-83 Cf. 4430-31 n.

10687-928 Cf. 10051-267 n.

10735 Ln

10749-826 See Lewis 1936, p. 121, on the comparison between Venus and her son Cupid. The text at this point justifies considerably more than his description of Venus as "the sexual appetite—the mere natural fact . . . the generative force in nature whom the school of Chartres had taught men to contemplate philosophically." Such a characterization is more appropriate to Genius than to the Venus that the God of Love describes here; cf. 4343-45 n. A more nearly Chartrian view is that in Bernardus Sylvestris's distinction between the two Venuses, the "legitimate Venus who, we say, is the music of the world" and "the shameless Venus, the lascivious goddess" whom we call "carnal concupiscence because she is the mother of all fornication. . . . Where you find that Venus is the wife of Vulcan and the mother of Iocus and Cupid, you are to understand the desire of the flesh. . . . Where however you read that Venus and Anchises had a son Aeneas, you are to take Venus as the music of the world, Aeneas as the human spirit" (1924, pp. 9-10). F 192 quotes a parallel in the fifteenth-century prose gloss to the *Echecs Amoureux* (MS B. N. fr. 9197, fol. 197ʳ-197ᵛ).

10765-826 Lc (Cf. 4559-78, 8273-80; Andreas Capellanus, *De amore*, II. ix; Ovid, *Amores*, I. x. 43-46.)

 10765-82 Ln
 10765-68 G 373
 10817-20 G 374
 10827-30 Cf. 5537-42 n.

10830-31 Ln gives the text of a 40-line interpolation, still with the God of Love as speaker, on Saturn, Jupiter, Venus; Neptune, Pluto, Juno; Phoebus, Marsyas, Midas. See David 1974.

 10836 Lc
 10838 Ln
 10839-43 Lc (Cf. Servius's *Commentary* on the *Aeneid*, VI. 324.)
 10842, 10863, 10869, 10904, 10915, 10938 Ln
 10951 P 48
 10982 P 173

11006 ff. Ln Lc note a general parallel with John of Salisbury, *Polycraticus*, VII. xxi (*De ypocritis* . . .), but a clearer dependence upon the contemporary identification, principally in Guillaume de Saint-Amour and Rutebeuf, of the friars as hypocrites. See 10459 n., 11293 n., 11488 n.

11006-291 See P 169-74 for a *seriatim* discussion of this passage.

11008 *world . . . cloister* (siecle . . . cloistre): Ln says that *siecle* means "secular clergy," and that at 11015-16 *religieus* and *seculer* mean "the cloister" and "the world." I would suggest that the meaning is the same in both cases, "world" and "cloister," and that the sense of the passage is that False Seeming is found everywhere but more in the cloister than in the world. The phrase "in no place except these two" is thus an understatement.

11013-36 On the clothing imagery, see Dahlberg 1953, pp. 39-40, 149-50; cf. 11054-58, 11071-72, 11096-101, 11123-26, 11522-24, etc. Such imagery parallels the literary metaphor of chaff (of grain) or cortex (of nucleus); cf. 11216 n., 7153-80 n., 7190-92.

11015 Ln

11017-22 P 46-47 discusses the term *religion*, which I have translated here as "the religious" and "the religious calling." The implication is that of a life lived according to a rule (*regula*), usually in a distinctive garment, or habit. P compares lines 13968, 14127, 14138, 15254, 17056. Cf. Ln (11018 n.); 13967-78 n.

11023 Ln

11037-82 Cf. 10051-267 n.

11045-46, 11049 Ln

11051-62 Cf. 12138-46 n.

11057 Ln

11058 Ln Lc

11059-62 *Nevertheless . . . thirteen branches*: P 36-37 notes that an *elenchus* is a "mode of argumentation and refutation designed not so much to demonstrate objective truth as to convince or put down an adversary"; that Aristotle's *De sophisticis elenchis* was on the program of the Faculty of Arts in Paris around 1255; that in it Aristotle does in fact divide sophisms into thirteen categories; and that the razor image "alludes to the scholastic procedures of distinction and division in the refutation of sophisms." Cf. Ln Lc (11061-62 n.). The image of the razor follows readily from the "knife of privet" at 11057; and I suspect that it is some such "razor" with which False Seeming cuts out Foul Mouth's tongue (12367). But the razor is a traditional simile for the maliciously deceitful (Ps. 51:4); and this association establishes the context for the irony in which we see False Seeming in the very character of the one whom he mutilates and kills. Cf. F 170-71.

11063-64 *distinctions*: P 29. Cf. 8927-30.

11068, 11077, 11106 Ln

11111 *the eleven thousand virgins*: Ln identifies as the companions of Saint Ursula.

11123-25, 11134 Ln

11134 *your new apostles*: Lc identifies these as the mendicant orders and notes that the traditional metaphor for a hypocrite, the wolf in sheep's clothing, goes back to Matt. 7:15, a text much used by Guillaume de Saint-Amour (*De periculis*, pp. 28, 36). We may note a clearer reason for the phrase "your new apostles." One of Guillaume's main points was that the friars were *not* apostles: "they are neither apostles or their successors, that is the bishops, nor are they among the Lord's seventy-two disciples, their successors the parish priests, or their helpers the vicars." They are Paul's brothers "walking disorderly and not according to the tradition which you have received of us." (*Responsiones*, No. 14, ed. 1951, p. 345; see 2 Thess. 3:6 and, for the "seventy-two disciples," Luke 10:1). Guillaume takes this tradition to be the apostolic tradition of the secular clergy; and he argues that when the friars take on the secular office of teaching and preaching, they violate their vows and become "pseudo apostles." (*Responsiones*, Nos. 24-27, pp. 349-50; *De periculis*, pp. 24, 34, 35-36, 47, 57-72; see Dahlberg 1953, pp. 34-36.) The reference to the "new apostles" is thus clearly ironic.

11160, 11181   Ln

11199   Ln points out that Robin was a lower-class, Robert an upperclass name.

11200   *Cordeliers*: Franciscans (Fratres minores or Minorites); *Jacobins*: Dominicans (Fratres praedicatores or Preaching Friars)

11215-16   Cf. 11013-36 n.

11216   *I leave the kernel of religion and take the husk* (J'en lais le grain e preing la paille): Ln. The metaphor is often applied to literary works. Cf. 7153-80 n., 11013-36 n. The word *paille* (straw, chaff, husk) may involve a pun: (1) chaff (2) the cloak of religion. The Old French *paile* (masc. from Lat. *pallium*) was in fact the technical name for one of the ecclesiastical vestments worn by archbishops and bishops; cf. Dahlberg 1953, pp. 149-50. The word-play may thus satirize the pretensions of the friars to the duties of the prelatical status. On the vestment *pallium* see Rabanus Maurus, *De clericorum institutione*, I. xxiii, *PL* 107, col. 309.

11222-23   Between these two lines there appears in various MSS an interpolation that varies in length from MS to MS. Langlois gives a text, based upon a group of nine MSS, that runs to 98 lines, and he adds 60 more lines of variant interpolations from other MSS: for details, see Ln, III, 310-15. The passage deserves attention because it reflects clearly, in the form of blatant self-confession, the abuses which the secular clergy condemned particularly in the friars, the assumption of the duties of preaching, teaching, and hearing confessions, the seculars' traditional duties. But the passage seems to show a particular emphasis on the bishops; False Seeming, after saying that he has the whole world in his nets, that he can confess and absolve, points out that no "prelaz" can get rid of him (line 4), except the Pope alone, and he is the very one who has established the privileges in the first place (7-8^1). No "prelat" dares criticize or grumble, for he, False Seeming, has shut the prelate's mouth (8^2-8^4). He boasts of his wealth and power, his easy life, all gained through the stupidity of the prelates, who were very fearful of his snares (8^9-8^{16}). After a long passage on how he impairs the confessional relationship between priest and parishioner, with the result that priests lose their flocks to him, False Seeming concludes: "And if the prelates dare to grumble—for indeed they should become furious when they lose their fat sheep—I shall give them such blows on their heads and raise such bumps that they will lose both mitres and croziers. Thus, so powerful are my privileges, have I tricked them all" (91-98). This emphasis upon the prelates suggests that the interpolation belongs to the period 1282-90, which Glorieux (1925, p. 309) has labeled as the period of episcopal opposition to the friars. Confirmation lies in what appears to be a reference (9-12[1]) to the bull of Pope Martin IV, *Ad fructus uberes* (Dec. 13, 1281) which gave friars the right, with the permission of bishops or parish priests, to preach and hear confessions, provided that the parishioner confess at least once a year to his parish priest (as had been provided in the statute *Omnis utriusque sexus* of the Fourth Lateran Council, 1215). Cf. Congar 1961, pp. 48-50; Dahlberg 1953, p. 36. This bull, as Glorieux and Congar show, gave rise to a period of strong opposition from the French bishops, and it seems safe to conclude that the interpolation reflects a period very shortly after Jean de Meun's continuation and thus provides a kind of contemporary comment or gloss on his text.

11235-36 Ln
11238-424 Cf. 10051-267 n.
11254-55 Ln
11254 Ln Lc
11269-76 Cf. 4233-36 n.
11277-90 Ln Lc (Prov. 30:8-9)

11293 ff. *I can swear to you without delay . . .* : Lc says that from this point False Seeming's speech attacks the mendicant orders directly; the attack had of course been implicit in the selection of the name; see 10459 n., 11488 n. The basis of the antimendicant attack was the mid-century quarrel between the secular masters at the University of Paris and the friars (principally Dominican and Franciscan), who had begun to get teaching chairs in the Theology faculty and who thus seemed to represent a professional threat to the seculars. In this controversy, Guillaume de Saint-Amour was the leader of the seculars, and his treatise of 1255, *On the Perils of the Last Times* (*De periculis novissimorum temporum*) was the most violent attack upon the friars. These, in turn, appealed for the support of King Louis IX and made complaints to Pope Alexander IV, citing Guillaume's treatise in particular; and the Pope, in June 1256, deprived Guillaume and others of their clerical appointments and asked Louis IX to banish them from the kingdom of France, which at that time did not include Guillaume's native region of the Jura. By October 1256, a papal commission had recommended condemnation of the *De periculis*, the Pope had so ordered, and Guillaume had left for Rome with a deputation of the Parisian masters to reply to the friars' charges. Although the other masters retracted their positions, Guillaume persisted in his replies to the charges (*Responsiones*, ed. Faral 1951), and was eventually acquitted by the four cardinals who heard his defense. The Pope, however, maintained the decree of June 1256, and Guillaume returned to Saint-Amour where he apparently lived the rest of his life in exile. See Fleming 1965 b for an aspect of his contribution to the debate during the period of his exile.

Rutebeuf, from whom Jean de Meun got the name False Seeming, preceded Jean by several years in giving vernacular literary support to the secular masters, particularly Guillaume de Saint-Amour. His poems of the latter 1250s and early 1260s include a good dozen that are pro-secular and antimendicant. See Rutebeuf 1959-60, I, 238-335.

For accounts of the controversy between the seculars and the friars at the University of Paris during the 1250s and for guides to the primary material and to further secondary material, see the notes of Ln (11488, 11506, 11513, 11551-52) and Lc (11263, 11761-866); P 161-69; Faral 1951, pp. 361-68; Faral and Bastin 1959-60, I, 68-82; Glorieux 1957. The controversy widened to a more clearly doctrinal matter during the rest of the century and in the fourteenth; see Congar 1961; Glorieux 1925, 1934, 1935; Schleyer 1938; Dahlberg 1953, pp. 29-77. For literary reflections of the secular position, see Dahlberg 1953, pp. 79-128.

11293-524   P 174-78 discusses False Seeming's inverse attack on the institutions of communal poverty and mendicancy. Ln and Lc quote the relevant passages in Guillaume de Saint-Amour, and I summarize them without giving the specific parallels: *De periculis*, pp. 25, 48-53, 67; *Responsiones*, Nos. 7, 11, ed. 1951, pp. 341, 343; *Collectiones*, p. 218.

11316-17   Ln. See 11414-91 n.

11317-508   Cf. 8099-114; Dahlberg 1953, pp. 41-42.

11324-26   Ln (See 11437-87.)

11331-32   In the margin of MS Paris, B. N. fr. 24390, fol. 77 a, opposite these lines, appears the notation "xiij. q. 1 ecclesias," a refer-ence to the *Decrees* of Gratian, *PL* 187, col. 935 A ("We have given individual churches to individual priests"). Guillaume uses the same citation in *Responsiones*, No. 6, ed. 1951, p. 341.

11332, 11334, 11351, 11357   Ln

11366 ff.   Cf. Chaucer's Friar, *CT*, I. 243 ff.

11368-69   Ln

11374   Ln Lc

11375-80   Cf. 4430-31 n.

11408   *a man . . . strong of body* (Forz on de cors): Cf. 8100, 8099-114 n.

11414-91   Ln Lc point out that Jean's material comes from Au-gustine's *De opere monachorum* through Guillaume's citations; they quote the relevant passage from *Responsiones*, No. 7, p. 341. Jean fol-lows Guillaume's listing of the cases in which a man may beg. The importance of the *De opere monachorum* to the medieval reader's under-standing of the *Romance* is indicated by the interpolation which ap-pears in two MSS, between 11316 and 11317, and which cites the work in support of the contention that the religious should engage in manual labor.

11417, 11418   Ln notes that the white monks are Cistercians, the black Benedictines, and the canons regular the Augustinian canons.

11434   Ln (Cf. 16576.)

11440-42, 11479-82   P 47, 50

11479-80, 11480-81   Ln Lc point out that the representations of the two hands are probably authentic. The figures come from the Ln edition; Lc, in spite of the fact that his base MS contains them, omits them from his text.

11488   *the man from Saint-Amour*: Cf. 4058-59 n., 11293 n. Guillaume de Saint-Amour (1202-72), as Ln notes, was a native of the Jura and taught at the University of Paris, where he was one of the most vociferous defenders of the secular masters against the encroachments of the friars. See Dahlberg 1953, pp. 9-11, 31-44. On the life and works, see Perrod 1902; Amann 1939; Glorieux 1933-34; for further bibliography, consult Congar 1961, n. 21, pp. 44-45.

11506   Ln Lc. See 11293 ff. n.

11513, 11514   Ln. The book is the *De periculis*. See 11293 ff. n.

11519-24   On False Seeming's idleness, cf. the portrait of Idleness, 525-94 and note; with *pope-holiness* (papelardie), cf. the portrait of Pope-Holiness, 407-40. On the *foxlike nature* (renardie), cf. the use of the fox image for the friars in Rutebeuf, *Renart-le-Nouvel*, and later poems: see Dahlberg 1953, pp. 100-116; Faral and Bastin 1959-60, I, 533-35; Glorieux 1925, pp. 480-81.

11528-786   P 178-80

11551-52   Ln

11553-790   Lc

11553-76   Cf. 10051-267 n.

11566   Cf. Chaucer, *CT*, I. 256.

11568-69   Ln

11587-90   Ln Lc (Cf. *De periculis*, p. 32.)

11591-92   Ln (*De periculis*, p. 30)

11592, 11597   Ln

11601-36   Ln Lc (Matt. 23:2-8; cf. 23:13-15, etc.)

11637-49   Ln (*De periculis*, p. 69)

11641, 11650, 11655-56   Ln

11679-92   Lc (*De periculis*, pp. 48, 68)

11681   Ln

11693-700   Ln Lc (*De periculis*, p. 21)

11708   Lc

11717-18   Ln (Matt. 7: 15)

11724-25   *heretics* (bougre): Ln. Cf. Orr 1947-48.

11742, 11744, 11746, 11748, 11758, 11780-81   Ln

11791-896   Ln, Lc, and P 180-86 summarize the history of the controversy over the *Liber Introductorius in Evangelium Aeternum*, published 1254 (not 1255) by the Franciscan, Gerard de Borgo San Donnino. The book is now lost, but it appears that what Gerard called the *Evangelium Eternum* were three works of Joachim of Flora, who, according to Paré, did not think of them as replacing the Bible. Apparently, however, Gerard so presented them in his *Liber Introductorius*, and brought upon himself and the Franciscans a storm of controversy which resulted in the condemnation of the book by Alexander IV in 1255. The secular masters, Guillaume de Saint-Amour in particular, led the attack, and it is from the *De periculis* that Jean drew most of the material for this section. The relevant sections of the *De periculis* are VIII, p. 38; XIV, pp. 68-69; I omit specific parallels. Cf. also *Responsiones*, No. 15, ed. 1951, pp. 346-47, and Faral's note, p. 390.

11841   Lc

11858-60   On *rind* and *marrow*, cf. 7153-80 n.; Dahlberg 1953, pp. 147-49.

11866   *preachers*: Lc thinks that Jean may be playing on the meaning 'Dominicans' (Preaching Friars).

11897-976   P 186

11903-4   Ln

11911   Lc (Guillaume de Saint-Amour, *Responsiones*, No. 35, ed. 1951, p. 352)

11936, 11940-42, 11941   Ln

11967-68   Ln Lc (Prov. 26:11; 2 Peter 2:22)

11989   P 50

11996-98   Ln Lc

12033-80   P 190-91

12045   *cameline*: "A fabric of wool mixed with silk or other fibers" (*Middle English Dictionary*). Distinguish *sauce cameline*, 13416. The *New (Oxford) English Dictionary* suggests that the word is related to *camlet* (*camelot*, see 9081 n.).

12049   Cf. the portrait of Papelardie, 423.

12053-64   Ln; Lc (Faral and Bastin 1959-60, I, 275, note to Rutebeuf, *Des Regles*, 154-74)

12063-64   Ln (Rutebeuf, *Des Regles*, 172-73)

12066-74   Ln Lc (Apocalypse 6:8); G 272. Faral and Bastin 1959-60, I, 262, note to Rutebeuf, *Complainte de Guillaume*, 86 ("Faus Samblant et Morte Color"), give parallels in Guillaume de Saint-Amour: *De periculis*, p. 29; *Responsiones*, No. 34; *Sermo in die sanctorum apostolorum Jacobi et Philippi*, p. 496. Lc notes the last.

12084   Ln Lc

12088, 12094-96, 12113, 12126, 12129   Ln

12131-67   P 188

12135-37   Ln (The barred friars are the Carmelites, the friars of the sack the Frères de la Pénitence, both so called from the appearance of their habits.) On the relevance of this passage for the poem's date, see Introduction; Lecoy 1968.

12138-46   P 32 discusses the terms *argumenz, conclusion, conséquence, sofime, aparence.* Cf. 11051-62.

12179-83   Ln Lc

12214   Ln (See 6167.)

12227, 12232, 12234, 12240, 12260   Ln
12277-78   Ln Lc
12324   P 73
12345-51   Ln (*De periculis*, p. 30)
12350-53   Cf. 4369 n.
12353   Ln
12361-67   Cf. 11059-62 n.

CHAPTER 7

12381-14807   (Chapter 7) R 199: "A set of worldly-wise instructions for the ladies is furnished by La Vieille, who condemns constancy and advises the use of 'love' as a means of gaining wealth. This descendant of Ovid's Dipsas [*Amores*, I. viii] and ancestress of the Wife of Bath and Celestina is hardly a spokesman for the author." Cf. T 241-45; F 171-84; 13710-24 n.

12381-740   P 191
12411   Ln
12439-41   *And now take this chaplet . . . to Fair Welcoming*: The acceptance of the chaplet would make Fair Welcoming a follower of Venus; cf. 895-96 n. There the chaplet appears as the God of Love's crown, later (10102) as an attribute of the friends of Wealth on their way to the stews. Idleness (555) and Diversion (829-30) had also worn rose-chaplets. Cf. 12592-735.

12551-52   Ln
12570   *the senile old whore* (la pute vieille redoutee): for background to the medieval tradition of the "old whore," see Haller 1960; F 171-74. Cf. Dahlberg 1953, p. 157.

12641   P 73
12666-67   Ln
12738-14622   G 374-95; P 192-99. Cf. 12381-14807 n.
12761 ff.   Cf. Chaucer's Wife of Bath, *CT*, I. 445-76; III. 1-856.
12761-855   Ln Lc (Ovid, *Ars amatoria*, III. 59-88)
12775-76   Ln (Horace, *Odes*, I. xxv. 1-8)
12781   *other company*: Cf. Chaucer, *CT*, I. 461.
12790   Ln Lc (Cf. 16171.)
12801-11   The emphasis on experience as opposed to theory makes the Old Woman suspect, from a rational point of view, to a medieval audience. Cf. Chaucer, *Wife of Bath's Prologue*, *CT*, III. 1 ff., 187; R 317-31.

12803   P 50
12817   Cf. 4369 n.

12818-21   Ln Lc (Ovid, *Met.*, VI. 28-29)
12833-37   Ln (Horace, *Odes*, I. xxv. 1-8)
12889-92   Ln Lc (Calcidius's trans. of Plato's *Timaeus*, ed. 1962, pp. 16-18)
12907   Ln
12924-28   Cf. Chaucer, *Wife of Bath's Prologue*, *CT*, III. 469-79.
12924, 12925, 12939-42   Ln
12984, 12990   Ln Lc
13007   Ln
13011 ff.   See 2077-2232 n. The teaching which follows is directed largely at gaining wealth.
13011-12   *loving . . . bitter*: See 2183-84 n.
13019-20   Ln
13021-26   Ln Lc (Cf. 2077-2232, 10403-12.)
13036, 13046, 13053   Ln
13061   Ln Lc (Cf. 915 ff.)
13075   Ln
13079-88   Cf. 20818-21191, particularly the passage on clothing, 20931-21013.
13085-88   G 311; Ln. Lc hypothecates a separate poem on Pygmalion by Jean de Meun and goes on to speculate on the possibility that he alludes to it here and had not perhaps decided to insert it later (20817-21191); there is no evidence for such a separate poem, and it seems clear that Lc has been led to his speculation by the assumption that the Pygmalion passage "is only an *hors d'œuvre.*" But see 20811-21227 n.
13109-22   Ln (Ovid, *Ars amatoria*, III. 591-92)
13123-28   Ln Lc (Ibid., I. 632-36)
13124   Lc
13146-47   Ln
13148-49   Ln Lc
13149   Ln
13150-52   Ln Lc
13160, 13164-72, 13167, 13169-70   Ln
13173-264   Ln Lc note parallels with Ovid, *Ars amatoria*, III. 31-40; *Met.*, VII. 1-403; *Heroides*, II; V; VII. 184, 195-96. I omit specific references to passages in the *Romance*. Chaucer, *BD*, 726-34, uses several of these examples.
13200-3   Ln (*Roman d'Eneas*, 2032-33)
13204-5, 13211-14, 13257   Ln
13279-374   Ln Lc note that this passage of instructions uses Ovid, *Ars amatoria*, III. They note specific parallels, which I omit, to III. 163-66, 199-200, 209-10, 261-62, 271-87, 291-92, 307-8, 315-16, 367-68.
13297-300   Ln Lc give references on headpieces with horns.
13336, 13340   Ln

13375-84   Ln Lc

13385-474   Ln Lc note that this passage is a development from Ovid, *Ars amatoria*, III. 749-68. I omit specific parallels.

13401   *who shares her plate*: Ln (Two people used to eat from one trencher.)

13408-32   A source for Chaucer's description of the Prioress's table manners, *CT*, I. 127-36.

13414   Ln (The use of forks was unknown.)

13416   Ln. *Sauce verte* (green sauce): a bread sauce flavored with vinegar, ginger, and parsley, which presumably gives it its color. *Sauce cameline*: Ln suggests that it is so-called from its color; presumably the color is that of cinnamon (*canelle*). His recipe and that given in the *Middle English Dictionary* (s.v. *camelin*) suggest a bread sauce spiced with ginger, cloves, and cinnamon, with or without nuts and raisins, guinea-pepper, mastic, or hot pepper. *Sauce jausse*: Ln says that *jausse* also may indicate a color (yellow?); it may be a garlic-flavored sauce.

13427-32, 13427, 13446   Ln

13449-60   Ln cites Juvenal, *Satire* VI. 300-4, in addition to Ovid, cited above.

13450-51   Ln (Prov. 31: 4)

13452-56   Cf. Chaucer, *Wife of Bath's Prologue*, *CT*, III. 467-68.

13466   Lc

13468-74   Ln Lc (Virgil, *Aeneid*, v. 833-71)

13475-600   Ln Lc give specific parallels, which I omit, with Ovid, *Ars amatoria*, III. 59-70, 133-54, 298-306, 387-98, 417-26.

13499-516   P 51 notes the prevalence of scholastic diction in this passage.

13503-6   Cf. 4369 n.

13506-7   Ln

13517-28   Cf. Chaucer, *Wife of Bath's Prologue*, *CT*, III. 555-58.

13517, 13562   Ln

13584   *wants to steal*: Ln notes the variant *vait*, and Lc's text shows *vet*, which would give the translation "*goes to steal.*"

13600   Ln; P 52, 67

13619-20   Ln Lc (Ovid, *Ars amatoria*, II. 279-80; cf. *Amores*, I. viii. 61.)

13621-24   Ln Lc (Ovid, *Heroides*, XVII. 191 [not 193, as in Lc])

13631-77   Ln Lc give specific parallels, which I omit, with Ovid, *Ars amatoria*, III. 433-36, 441-50, 461-62, 469-78.

13635-38   Ln Lc

13639-40   *bitter . . . love*: See 2183-84 n.

13683, 13691   Ln

13695-724   Cf. 10051-267 n.

13699-708   Ln (Cf. 2599-602.)

13703-4   Lc

13710-24   Ln Lc (Ovid, *Amores*, I. viii. 87-92). Lc notes that this entire elegy, the portrait of the old bawd, Dipsas, underlies the portrait of the Old Woman, even though there are not many verbal parallels. Ovid's word for "old woman," *anus* (*anus, -ūs*, fem.) may pun with *ānus, -ī*, masc. 'the fundament, anus.' Cf. 12381-14807 n.

13721, 13730   Ln

13741-52   Ln Lc (*Amores*, I. viii. 101-2)

13758-59   Lc (Andreas Capellanus, *De amore*, I. ix, ed. 1964, p. 228)

13759, 13773-74, 13792   Ln

13795-840   Ln Lc (Ovid, *Ars amatoria*, III. 601-6, 675-80)

13808, 13820-21   Ln

13840-71   Ln Lc (Ovid, *Ars amatoria*, II. 561-92). The account of Venus and Mars continues at 14159, and Jean has Nature allude to the same story at 18061-129. Hill 1966 quotes Fulgentius, Arnulf of Orléans, and the Third Vatican Mythographer in support of the conclusion that "in mythological commentary the story of Mars and Venus is consistently taken to signify the bondage of the 'chains' of illicit and irrational desire." Cf. Miller 1959, pp. 470-76; 13875-14160 n.

13870   Ln Lc

13875-14160   This passage, on women's "natural" desire for freedom, occurs as an apparent digression from the story of Mars and Venus but relates at the same time, by way of contrast, to Reason's conception of nature and to the full-length portrait of Nature in Chapter 9. The alternation between human and animal examples in lines 13936-14160—all designed to illustrate the inescapable power of nature —also illustrates the Augustinian conception of Nature after the Fall. See 4403-21 n. Cf. P 194-96, G 468-72. Hill 1966 shows that, in the light of medieval commentaries on the Mars-Venus story (see above), the Old Woman's defense of unrestrained sensuality becomes ironic: the Old Woman, like Venus, is herself "bound" by the chains of love and also, unaware of the bondage, argues for more of the same. The "digression" is thus structurally relevant in that it completes the ironic framework for the reader's understanding of the Mars-Venus story and of the Old Woman's advice to Fair Welcoming.

13880-84   Ln

13919   Cf. 4369 n.

13921-22   Ln. Cf. also 6300-3 n.

13923-28   Ln Lc (Horace, *Satires*, I. iii. 107-10)

13924   *con* (con): Female genitalia. Cf. 15138-42 n.

13928   Cf. 4369 n.

13941-58   Ln Lc (Boethius, *De cons.*, III, m. 2. 17-26). Cf. Chaucer, *Manciple's Tale*, *CT*, IX. 163-74.

13967-78   G 468 thinks that the Old Woman's ideas express the poet's view, and P 187-88 puts this expression of opposition to the religious life, on the grounds that it destroys natural liberty, on the same footing as the apparently similar passage in Reason's discourse (4444-63). But the speakers are different, each representing an abstract idea, and their speeches are different. In the Old Woman's there is no hint whatever of any legitimate value in the religious life, such as we find in Reason's acknowledgement of grace, obedience, and patience. To the Old Woman the religious life is a final, inescapable trap; "the will is not moved on account of any habit . . . ," she says, and omits any mention of the will's being moved through grace. Cf. 13875-14160 n.

13979-14006 Ln Lc
14008-11, 14015 Ln
14019-25 Ln Lc (Horace, *Epistles*, I. x. 24)
14027-30 P 44 discusses the terms *violent, violence.*
14027 Ln
14037-38 Ln Lc
14039-52 Lc. Cf. Chaucer, *Manciple's Tale, CT*, IX. 175-80.
14060, 14083, 14112, 14136, 14144, 14152 Ln
14159-86 Ln (Ovid, *Ars amatoria*, II. 561-92; cf. 13840-71.)
14163, 14180, 14193 Ln
14203-408 Lc notes the return to the development at 13823, and he and Ln give specific parallels, which I omit, with Ovid, *Ars amatoria,* III. 579-80, 585-86, 593-94, 607-58, 683-85, 752, 797-803, 807-8; II. 99-105, 725-28.
14209, 14220 Ln
14244-45 *since . . . in mind*: the translation follows Lc's text rather than Ln's; see Lc 14214 n.
14247 Ln
14267 *when it is all right for him . . .*: Lc. Again the translation follows the Lc text (Ln: *and order him*).
14284, 14371-72 Ln
14399 Ln Lc (On Balenus, "supposed author of a certain number of treatises on magic," see Thorndike 1923-58, II, 234-35.)
14403, 14404, 14418-19 Ln
14420-28 Lc
14504-7 Ln (Ovid, *Ars amatoria*, II. 459-62)
14531, 14544 Ln
14611-12 *love . . . bitterness*: See 2183-84 n.
14673-75 P 74
14679-15104 P 199-200
14693 Ln
14694 *in time for the gloves*: Ln suggests that gloves were traditionally a form of tip in return for good news. In view of what F 85-86 says about the glove as a sexual symbol (see 563-64 n.), we may suspect further word-play here, particularly in the light of the Lover's reply, 14697-701.
14708, 14731, 14736, 14793-94, 14807 Ln

14808-15890   (Chapter 8) For a comparison of differing tastes on the *psychomachia* that constitutes the central action of this chapter, see P 200-2 and T 250-52; for an analysis in terms of moral categories, see F 187-89.

14816   Ln

14817   Ln Lc

14829-63   Lc; Ln (14831 n.)

14840, 14846, 14866, 14885, 14887   Ln

14898   Ln Lc

14908   Ln

14962   *and born of Reason's race*: Cf. 2840, 3028, 20779.

14989, 14997, 15030   Ln

15135-53   G 24

15136-302   P 189-90. Cf. 13967-78 n.

15138-42   The figure of the dogs chasing the rabbit is common in marginal illustrations of the MSS and stands, as in this passage, for the hunt of sexual love. The parallel depends in part on the French pun *conin* 'rabbit' / *con* 'female genitalia.' Cf. Ln (15140 n.); R 113; F 186-87.

15143-44   G 27

15146-53   Ln

15148-50   Cf. 7153-80 n.

15177-83   Cf. 6300-3 n., 4430-31 n.

15178-92   Ln Lc

15195-302   See Introduction on techniques of irony in the passage. Pierre Col, a late fourteenth-century writer and one of the more perceptive early critics of the poem, says that Jean de Meun speaks in his own person only in this passage of the poem. See Ward 1911, pp. 74-75; Col's entire letter occupies pp. 56-76. Cf. P 190; G 46, 50, 52, 55, 57-58, 84; Dahlberg 1953, pp. 95-97.

15217-18   Cf. 6300-3 n.

15241-42   Ln Lc (Horace, *Ars poetica*, 333-34)

15243-302   Ln Lc (Guillaume de Saint-Amour, *De periculis*, p. 20)

15329   Ln (*Biere* is an old name for the forest of Fontainebleau.)

15334-37   P 201

15346-47   *Renouart de la Pole* (Renoart / Au tinel): Ln (A courageous character from the Narbonnais epic cycle)

15384   Ln

15388   See Fig. 38 and Introduction, "The Illustrations."

15392   *misericord*: Ln notes a play on two meanings, 1) pity and 2) a kind of dagger.

15395   Ln

15397-98   Lc
15406, 15429   Ln
15441   Lc. The translation here follows Lc's text.
15487   Cf. R 35, Fig. 10.
15521   *beryl*: In the lapidaries, beryl is associated with the sun, with fire, with love between man and woman, with a simple round shape, with strength and humility. See, e.g., the *Peterborough Lapidary*, ed. Evans and Serjeantson 1933, pp. 72-73. The simile thus implies an iconographical melioration.
15559-60, 15563   Ln
15573-83   Ln Lc (Virgil, *Aeneid*, VIII. 193-267)
15605   Ln
15627   P 201
15637-38   Ln
15661-890   P 201-2
15663   Ln
15675-750   Ln and Lc identify the basis of the Venus and Adonis material as Ovid, *Met.*, x. 529-723, and Ln quotes parallels to various specific passages; I omit references. It is from the same book of the *Met.* that the Pygmalion story comes (see 20811-21227 n., 20816 n., 21201-3 n.). On the hunt imagery, see R 113, 253-55, 263-64; Miller 1954; F 186-87.
15766   Ln
15840-52   G 131
15874   Ln
15877-90   T 267 calls attention to the deliberately shocking quality of the oath: images of the "intrinsically holy"—relics, the Trinity—are juxtaposed with phallic images—arrows, darts, torches. Cf. 7103-36 and the imagery of Chapter 11, the "sanctuary" and the pilgrim's sack and staff.
15887-90   G 232. Cf. 20695-700.

CHAPTER 9

15891-19438 (Chapter 9) R 199-200: "The wisdom of Amis and La Vieille is insufficient for purposes of seduction without Venus. As a personification of sexual delight she represents an element which, since the Fall, comes from Nature. The long confession of Nature to Genius, or natural inclination, serves to show why Venus operates as she does. Nature's function is to replenish the ravages of death at her forge, but Nature is disturbed, just as she is in the *De planctu* of Alanus, by a fault. Man alone among all creatures violates her laws . . . through his own free will." Cf. Jean de Meun's Preface to his translation of Boethius,

1952, pp. 168-71; T 264-75; F 191-204; and the various views on Nature of Reason (4403-21, 4444-63, 5763-90), the Old Woman (13875-14160), Genius (Chapter 10), and the Lover (2985-88, 20792-96, 21357-427). Perhaps no other *character* illustrates so fully Jean's method of achieving irony through subtle contrasts in point of view; love, of course, as a *concept*, receives more complex treatment, and indeed that concept controls the development of Nature. See T 323-27.

P 203 notes the two principal divisions in this chapter: 1) the presentation of Nature, her functions and characteristics, 2) the confession proper, 16279 ff. His long analysis of Nature's confession, pp. 203-278, is an important contribution, but his neglect of Jean's literary method leads him to conclude (pp. 301-3) that this chapter contains a direct exposition of the philosophy of the *Romance*, that is of Jean de Meun, and that "the developments of Nature are manifestly digressions which have no direct relationship with the plot" (p. 303). The same difficulty marks his summary, "The Allegory of Nature," pp. 327-40.

15893-16016 Lc; G 133, 245; P 53-61. Cf. 4403-21 n.

15894 *beneath the heavens*: The limitation contrasts Nature's sphere with that of Reason. Cf. 2985-88; P 53. The distinction is parallel to that which underlies Alanus's between Nature and Reason (or Prudence); see the prose *Summarium* to the *Anticlaudianus*, ed. Bossuat 1955, p. 199 (trans. Cornog 1935, p. 49). But the character Nature, and her priest Genius, conveniently—for the Lover, of whom they are of course reflections—forget this limitation and elevate their subordinate role into man's final purpose. Cf. T 270.

15895-16016 *was entered within her forge . . . coins of different monies*: Ln shows that the passage was inspired by Alanus, *De planctu*, *PL* 210, col. 456 D; he gives detailed quotations of parallels, the bulk of which occur from this point up to 16813 and from 18981-19663. I omit any separate indications of these parallels. We should note that, as many have agreed, Jean's Nature is different from Alanus's (P 206-7; Knowlton 1920, 1922-23), but Jean's variations are undoubtedly made for ironic purposes and not because of any misunderstanding of Alanus; see 15894 n.; T 268-69; F 190-98. For broader treatments of the concept of nature, see Knowlton, as cited; Lewis 1960 (1967), pp. 24-74; Scaglione 1963; Collingwood 1945 (1960), for early and modern, but not medieval, theories.

15921 Ln (Cf. 15939.)

15925-28 Cf. 16016-148 n.

15930 Ln

15939-42 P 188

15959-61 Ln

15965-16016 G 247-49

15973-74 Cf. 20592-96 n.

15975-16004 Ln Lc; P 56-58. For a recent brief account of the phoenix tradition and its association with death and resurrection themes, see Blake 1964, pp. 8-16. The motif is curiously placed here, for in one important way ("there cannot be two of them together") it lies outside the usual workings of Nature; in fact, this characteristic of the phoenix legend probably helped to make the phoenix a symbol for Christ's resurrection. This very curiosity recalls the reader to the difference between reproduction after the Fall (cf. 4403-21 n.) and the supernatural resurrection and establishes the framework for the understanding of Nature's relationship to God; cf. 15894 n.

15983, 15995   Cf. 20592-96 n.

16005-12   P 59-61 discusses the theme of generation and corruption. Cf. 16281-82, 18971-72, 19062 ff., and 4403-21 n.

16014-18   Cf. 20592-96 n.

16014-16   Lc (Alanus de Insulis, *De planctu*, col. 453)

16016-148   P 203-4. On pp. 65-68, P discusses the background of the *art-nature* relationship. As he notes, p. 67, "It is a question not only of the fine arts but of every human creation." In any case, the attitudes expressed are clearly consistent with a hierarchial concept of the universe. For *art* in the sense of "discipline of making," see 17253-54, 15925-28, 20139, 20175. Ln (16018 n.) quotes Albertus Magnus, *De mineralibus*, I. i. 3; and Lc (16031 n.) cites Curtius 1948, p. 524; Dante, *Inferno*, XXIX. 139.

16035 ff.   Ln

16038   Cf. 8312-13 n.

16042-43   Ln

16065-148   On the *art* of *alchemy*, see Ln and Lc, who quote parallels and cite background material, and P 68-71. Their principal sources are Vincent of Beauvais, *Speculum naturale*, VIII, Chapters 4, 13, 60, 63, 67, 81-82, 84-85; *Summa perfectionis magisterii*, Chapters 6, 8, 10, 13, 17; *Breve breviarium de dono dei*, pp. 99, 130-31 of *Sanioris medicinae magistri Rogerii Baconis Angli de Arte chymiae scripta . . .* (Frankfurt 1608). I omit specific references.

16069-70   Cf. 20592-96 n.

16070   *prime matter*: Lc notes that, in principle, this was supposed to be a particularly pure form of mercury, or quicksilver, from which, in combination with sulfur, other metals were formed.

16075-81   Cf. 21573-82 n.

16077-78   Cf. 20592-96 n.

16102-5   P 71

16109-11   *These are . . . shape*: Cf. 16955-57 n., 20592-96 n., 8312-13 n.

16109, 16112, 16113, 16115-16   Ln

16126, 16129   *spirits . . . bodies*: Ln Lc (*Spirits* were volatile substances like mercury, sulfur, arsenic, sal ammoniac; *bodies* were metals with which the spirits might combine, metals like iron, pewter, lead, gold, silver, bronze.)

16133, 16140   Ln

16141-43   Cf. 20592-96 n.; see also P 61.

16146   P 70

16152-53   Ln Lc (*De planctu,* col. 475). Cf. Jean de Meun 1952, pp. 168-69.

16165-248   Ln Lc note that Jean has not copied the description of Nature from *De planctu*, cols. 432-39. Lc notes that this passage is an example of the "inexpressibility topoi" that Curtius discusses, 1953, pp. 159-62.

16167, 16169   Ln

16171   Ln Lc

16179-85, 16180   Ln

16196-98   Cf. 6300-3 n.

16196-97   Ln Lc

16233-48   G 199, 239, 436-37; P 204

16248   The Lc text (16218 of his numbering) supports the assumption that Ln's quotation mark is an error.

16249-72   P 204

16249   Ln Lc (See 15877-90.)

16272-20703   For the difference between Jean's development of Genius and that of his source, Alanus, see 4343-45 n.; P 279-86 and ff. Cf. R 200: "To understand [the] confession [of Nature] it is necessary to remember that Genius, the Father Confessor, is not a Christian priest. . . . Genius is not grace; he is merely the inclination of created things to act naturally. Hence Genius is, as it were, the 'conscience' of Nature. Since he is not grace, he does not know the solution to Nature's problem. . . . He absolves Nature, who is obviously not responsible for man's peculiar transgressions, and approaches the God of Love, who, since his dominance at the Fall, has been eager to turn natural inclination to his own purposes and so invests Genius in epis-copal robes. Nature is, as it were, the great authority of cupidinous desire and has probably been cited as such ever since the first damsel showed some reluctance." Cf. T 268-78; F 193-94.

16272-322   P 204-5

16272-84   The iconography reveals Genius as a pretender to priestly status. His service is not a "new Mass," i.e. it is unregenerate, terrestrial rather than celestial; he "recited . . . the representative shapes of all corruptible things." Cf. R 127-29, 200, Fig. 69; T 268-69, 327-28. Certain illustrators used a motif from else-where in the poem to indicate Genius's pretensions to priestly status. In Fig. 61, for example, we see Genius, dressed as a friar, seated on Nature's anvil and hearing her confession as she kneels at the right; cf. B. N. fr. 798, pp. 238 a, 242 b. The parallel with False Seeming indicates that, to the illustrator or his programmer, Genius is a "pseudo apostle" and the confession a false one; cf. 11134 n., 11216 n., 11293 ff. n.

16272   Ln Lc (*De planctu*, col. 476)
16277-84   Ln Lc (Ibid., col. 479)
16281-82   Cf. 16005-12 n.
16323-706   P 205-6. Cf. 19218-20.
16325-28   Ln Lc (Virgil, *Aeneid*, IV. 569-570)
16330-33   Ln Lc (Ecclus. 25: 22-23, 26)
16337-43   Ln Lc (Livy, I. 9)
16344-46   Ln (1 Tim. 6:10)
16359, 16401   Ln
16456   Ln (See 8509.)
16507-8, 16524   Ln
16532-33   Ln Lc
16545-46   Ln Lc (Horace, *Epistles*, I. xviii. 71; *Ars poetica*, 390)
16569-70   Ln (Cf. 16697-98.)
16576   Lc
16576, 16577, 16583-84   Ln
16582-616   Ln Lc (Virgil, *Eclogues*, III. 92-93)
16625-28   Cf. 4403-21 n.
16645-48   Ln Lc (Ecclus. 25:30)
16677-88   Ln (Judges 16)
16693-96   Ln Lc (Micah 7:5)
16697-98   Ln (Cf. 16569-70.)
16707-28   P 206
16729-800   On Nature as God's vicar, cf. 2985-90. See P 207-17; G 232-35.
16729-92   Ln (*De planctu*, col. 453. *De cons.*, III, m. 9; IV, m. 6)
16749-67   G 242
16751-67   Cf. Wisdom 11:21: "but thou hast ordered all things in measure, and number, and weight." The text was a favorite in the medieval conception of *ordo*, hierarchial order, and it influenced numerical composition in music, literature, and architecture (Curtius 1953, pp. 504-5; von Simson 1956, p. 22).
16755-56   Cf. 8312-13 n.
16768-84   P 328-29
16785-97   G 243-44, 249-50
16793-813   Ln (*De planctu*, col. 448)
16798-801   G 130, 517
16801-954   P 217-26
16801-13   Ln (16811-13 n.) notes the contrary motion of the heaven (Macrobius, I. xviii; Calcidius, XCVII, ed. 1962; *De planctu*, col. 443).
16807   Ln
16816   *36,000 years*: the "Great Year." Ln quotes Albertus Magnus, *De celo et mundo*, I. iv. 1, and notes that Macrobius, II. xi, gives 15,000 years as the period of the Great Year. P 220 says that "most of the thirteenth-century masters speak of a duration of 36,000 years"

and quotes Guillaume d'Auvergne (*De universo*), who was bishop of Paris from 1228 to 1248. On the Great Year, see Duhem 1913-59, I, 275-96; II, 447-53. In III, 240, he records a curious collocation (Joannes de Sacrobosco [fl. ca. 1225], *Computus ecclesiasticus*) of a Great Year of 15,000 years and a "perfect year" of 36,000 solar revolutions.

16829-32   Cf. 4279-84 n.

16833-35   Ln (*De planctu*, col. 448)

16833   G 130

16834-35, 16843-46, 16848-50, 16855-80, 16865   Ln

16867-80   Ln (Macrobius, I. xix)

16869   Ln

16881-94   Ln (Albertus Magnus, *De celo et mundo*, II. iii, chap. 8)

16895-910   Ln (*De planctu*, col. 448)

16907-10   G 250

16911-15   Ln (Macrobius, I. xvii; I. x)

16929-38, 16936   Ln

16943-48   G 307

16947   P 303

16955-17058   P 227-30. This passage on the sublunary world leads to the long discussion (17059-874) on free will and predestination and back again to the sublunary world (17875-19112).

16955-60   P 217

16955-57   P 30-31 discusses the terms *accidents* and *substances*. Cf. 16109-11, 20599-600; and P 227.

16987, 16990   Ln

16991, 17014-17   P 49

17030, 17039-51   Ln

17052-58   On Origen's self-castration, Ln cites Eusebius, *Ecclesiastical History*, VII. vii; Abelard's 1st and 7th letters, ed. Cousin, pp. 32, 150; John of Salisbury, *Polycraticus*, VIII. vi. See Fig. 40. Fleming 1963, p. 190, points out that "it is a spiritual more than a physical action he performs." Cf. Matt. 19:12; Miller 1955, pp. 182-86; F 212-13.

17059-874   P 231-52 discusses this passage *seriatim* under the heading "Human liberty and divine foreknowledge." See 16955-17058 n. The views are basically traditional; see Dahlberg 1953, pp. 161-62; 17101 n.

17101   Ln notes that "the entire chapter which follows, on divine foreknowledge and free will, is borrowed from Boethius." He notes specific parallels, which I omit, to *De cons.*, V, pr. 3, pr. 4, pr. 6; I, m. 5; the parallels run from 17113 to 17526.

17101-792   P 131

17101-6   P 125

17101-2   P 27-28 discusses the terms *question, dispute, disputation.* Cf. 17125-27, 17282-83, 4089-91. On *solve* (*soudre*), cf. 7081-86 n.

17106   P 311

17108-10 Cf. 7081-86.

17125-27 Cf. 17101-2 n.

17139 Ln

17156 P 34

17195 P 311; Ln

17201-38 P 42

17201 P 28

17205-6 *possible thing* (chose possible): P 41-43 discusses the terms *possible, chose possible, vérité possible*; cf. 17224-26, 17233-36.

17212-15 *interchangeability* (convertibilité): P 39-40 discusses this term and its adjectival form, *convertible*. Cf. 17233-36.

17219 P 28

17224-30 On *necessary, simple* and *conditional necessity*, see 5562-63 n.; Ln (*De cons.*, v, pr. 6.27-29); Jean de Meun 1952, p. 273. On *possible*, see 17205-6 n. See also P 43, n. 1.

17233-36 On *interchanged*, see 17212-15 n.; on *contingent* (*possible*), see 17205-6 n.

17237-38 On *reasoning*, cf. 4842-48 n. See also P 42-43.

17253-54 Cf. 16016-148 n.

17257-60 *concede, deny* (otreier, neier): P 29 discusses these terms from scholastic disputation. Cf. 17538-40.

17261 Ln

17267 P 28

17282-88 Cf. 4430-31 n.

17282-83 Cf. 17101-2 n.

17303 P 28

17307 Ln

17314 P 28

17348-51 Cf. 4279-84 n.

17375-76 Ln

17394 P 311

17422 Cf. 4430-31 n.

17426, 17431 Ln

17451-72 P 307

17472 G 238

17506-22 G 251

17506-12 P 217

17513 Ln

17538-40 Cf. 17257-60 n.

17549 Ln

17550-52 P 48

17582, 17597 Ln

17598-645 Ln notes the source as Ovid, *Met.*, I. 318 ff. and records specific parallels, which I omit. Cf. G 257.

17624 Ln

17627-28 Cf. 7153-80 n.

17651   Ln

17727-36   P 130-31

17728   P 121. Cf. also 4430-31 n.

17752-62   P 74

17793-874   Ln (*De cons.*, II, pr. 5)

17794, 17834, 17868   Ln

17875-19112   P 252-71 discusses this passage under the heading "The sublunary world (continued)." See 16955-17058 n.

17879   Ln (See 11160.)

17880-904   Ln (*De planctu*, col. 449)

17889, 17920   Ln

17934   P 73

17935-38   Ln (Ovid, *Met.*, I. 272-73)

17945   Ln (Ovid, *Met.*, I. 302-3)

17970   Ln

17979   Ln (Ovid, *Met.*, I. 289)

17991-92   G 279, 350

18031   Ln

18034   Ln: "Alhazen ben Alhazen Ibn Alhaitam died in Cairo in 1038." See Duhem 1913-59, II, 119-20.

18059-60   Ln. Cf. 4279-84 n.

18061-129   Ln (Ovid, *Ars amatoria*, II. 561-92; cf. 13840-71 and note.)

18149-52   Ln (Ecclus. 26:1)

18158   *Cerdagne* (Sardaigne): Ln notes that 1) between France and Sardinia there is water, while there are mountains between France and Cerdagne (a valley of the Eastern Pyrenees, on the height of land between the rivers Tet, in France, and Segre, in Spain); and that 2) the form "Sartaigne" designates Cerdagne in several *chansons de geste*. At the same time, the mountains between the "France" of Jean de Meun's day and Sardinia included those of Burgundy and Haute Savoie and were considerably more impressive than those in the direction of Cerdagne. Nevertheless, Ln's textual evidence weighs for *Cerdagne*.

18181-92   P 74

18195   Ln

18200-6, 18213, 18252   Ln

18259-305   G 156-57

18266-67   P 44-45 discusses the term *fantasy*. Cf. 18493-98.

18274-78   Cf. 5443-54 n.

18277, 18289   P 311

18305-20   P 45-46 discusses the terms *common senses* (sen comun) and *particular senses*. Cf. 5443-54 n.

18311   *staffs and sacks*: Cf. 21354 n.

18339   Ln

18343-424   Ln (A development from Macrobius, I. iii, of that one of the five kinds of dream called *enypnion* 'nightmare')

18410, 18427   Ln
18440   On *reasoning*, cf. 4842-48 n.
18460   Ln
18469   Ln (John 11)
18493-98   Cf. 18266-67 n.
18499-514   Cf. 1-20; Chaucer, *HF*, 1-65.
18561-885   Cf. 4975-5588 n.
18572   Ln (The author of the *Almagest* is Ptolemy; see 7037-43 and Ln's note.)
18575-76   Ln
18580-88   Ln (Horace, *Epistles*, I. xviii. 86-87)
18595-600   Ln offers five parallels, including *De cons.*, III, m. 6.
18600   P 121
18607-896   On nobility, cf. 6579-92; T 43. Ln offers several parallels other than Boethius, III, pr. 6, m. 6. Chaucer may have drawn upon these passages for the *Wife of Bath's Tale, CT*, III. 1109-1176, and (with a direct rather than ironic approach) for the ballade *Gentilesse*. Again Boethius is one obvious common source.
18609-12   Ln (*De cons.*, III, pr. 6)
18615-16   Ln (Juvenal, *Satire* VIII. 20)
18615   P 28
18619   P 73
18640-43   Cf. 4279-84 n.
18658   Ln (Only the nobles had the right to hunt.)
18681-710   Ln (Juvenal, *Satire* VIII. 24-30)
18699, 18701, 18706   Ln
18719-26   Ln (Ovid, *Ars amatoria*, III. 405-8)
18720   Ln (Cf. 18610.)
18727, 18729   Ln
18730-33   Ln (Ovid, *Ars amatoria*, III. 409-10)
18752   Ln compares 18658, where he notes that only the nobles had the right of hunting. There may be an additional iconographical overtone, the hare-hunt as sexual hunt. See 15138-42 n.
18754   *paternal dung-heaps*: The phrase may suggest, as an iconographical overtone, "the sins of their fathers." See *Allegoriae in sacram scripturam*, s. v. "Stercus" and "Sterquilinium," *PL* 112, cols. 1052-53; Alanus, *Distinctiones dictionum theologicalium*, s. v. "Stercus," *PL* 210, col. 956.
18771-75   Ln (Juvenal, *Satire* x. 168-69)
18779   P 303
18782   Ln
18790   Ln (Juvenal, *Satire* VIII. 44-45)
18791-805   Ln (*De cons.*, III, pr. 6)
18833, 18870-81   Ln
18875-77   *along with the reason . . . like God and the angels*: P 78-80 shows Jean de Meun's orthodoxy in his development of the idea that

man, in possessing reason and free will, is made in the image of God. Cf. 2984-95 n.

18879 Ln

18886-88 P 74

18891-96 Ln (Juvenal, *Satire* VIII. 269-71)

18902-4 Ln

18919-28 P 217

18953 Ln

18967-72 P 217

18967 G 130

18971-72 Cf. 16005-12 n.

18978 Ln (Cf. 19241-43.)

18981-19022 Ln (*De planctu*, col. 448-49)

18981, 18990 G 130, 131

18995-97 G 252-53

18995 Ln

18999-19001, 19021, 19023-28 G 131

19023-26 Ln (Ovid, *Met.*, I. 83-86)

19025-26 *man alone . . . of his master*: Cf. 2984-95 n.

19041-53 P 75-77 discusses the theme of *microcosme* (little world) and *mégacosme*. See 19053 n.

19043-50 Ln (Alanus, *Sermo I, On the Holy Spirit, PL* 210, col. 222)

19045 P 50

19053 Ln (Macrobius, II. xii; Calcidius, CCII, ed. 1962)

19055-64 P 235

19055-62 Cf. 2987-88.

19062 ff. Cf. 16005-12; see also P 245.

19066 Ln

19074-75 Ln (Calcidius, XXV, ed. 1962)

19077 Ln (Calcidius, CLXXVIII, ed. 1962)

19079-82 Cf. 4430-31 n.

19083-19112 Ln (Calcidius, ed. 1962, p. 35)

19088, 19089-91 Ln

19113-14 Cf. 4430-31 n.

19119-90 *He still could not say enough . . . feast for it*: P 272-77 discusses the relevant Christian traditions. On "the sphere that can have no end" (19129-32), P 273 quotes Alanus, *Theologicae regulae*, 7, *PL* 210, col. 627: "God is an intelligible sphere (*spaera intelligibilis*) whose center is everywhere, circumference nowhere. . . . God is called a sphere because He has neither beginning nor end. . . . But the sphere is not corporeal, but rather a bodiless intelligence (*intelligibilis*)." See Alanus's sermon on this theme, recently ed. d'Alverny 1965, pp. 297-306, and Mlle. d'Alverny's illuminating discussion, pp. 163-80, which clarifies the use of the term *intelligibilis*. Cf. Sneyders de Vogel 1930-31; 1931-32. Gilson 1955, p. 174, shows the relevance to Trinitarian doctrine. Alanus's sermon also establishes the connection between the sphere and the next of Jean's images, the "circular triangle" (19133-39): "Although, according to the natural philosophers, other spheres can be neither squared nor triangulated, in this particular sphere we find the property of an equilateral triangle, that is, a Trinity of persons. Moreover, in this equilateral triangle, it is found that all sides are equal and that all the angles are right angles; and we discover that they are equal not only to two right angles but to one . . . because the three persons are equal to one and one to three, and one is equal to one" (p. 305). The Trinitarian imagery continues in the fountain with three springs, 20465-78, and the carbuncle with three facets, 20525-96; contrast the two crystals in Narcissus's fountain (1538), the two rivers on the island of Fortune (5978-6078), and the two tuns of Jupiter (6813-42, 10627-34). The Trinitarian imagery creates the background for Jean's irony in conveying the aberrant quest of the Lover, who disregards the import of such imagery.

19141-42, 19145 Ln

19169-76 Ln (Virgil, *Eclogues*, IV. 7-10). Courcelle 1957 studies the tradition that took Virgil's Fourth Eclogue as a prophecy of the coming of Christ. For a brief bibliography, see his n. 3, p. 316. Cf. Alanus, *Summa*, ed. 1953, p. 124: "Item Sybilla: Deus summus filium suum misit in mundum."

19177-90 P 277 quotes the parallel from Roger Bacon, *Opus tertium*, which identifies the source as "Herman's translation" of Albumazar's *Majori Introductio*. Heisig 1959, extending the work of Maler 1945-46, duplicates Paré's parallels and identifies Bacon's source (incorrectly) as Hermannus Alemannus, a mid-thirteenth-century translator of Aristotle and his Arabian commentators (Haskins 1924, pp. 15-16). The right source is clearly Herman of Carinthia, the twelfth-century translator. See Thorndike 1923-58, II, 84-85; d'Alverny 1965, p. 21, dates Herman's translation of Albumazar in 1140 and cites R. LeMay, *Abu Ma'shar and Latin Aristotelianism in the Twelfth Century* (Beirut, 1962). Alanus quotes Albumazar in his *Summa* (ed. 1953, p. 124; dated ca. 1160) as a pagan authority on the unity of God; the quotation precedes that of the "Sibyl"; see 19169-76 n.

The phrase "in the sign of the Virgin" (19179) thus corresponds to the feast referred to at 19188-90, that of the Nativity of the Virgin Mary, still celebrated on September 8 (P 277).

19191-436 P 277-78 discusses this résumé of Nature's complaint.

19195-96 *He is the end . . . against my laws*: Cf. 2984-95 n., 19025-26.

19196-19210 Ln (*De planctu*, col. 449)

19204, 19213 Ln

19214-16 *his fall before God, who gave him to me when he created man in his image*: Cf. 2984-95 n. On the Fall, see Introduction.

19218-20 *I am a woman . . . a woman can hide nothing*: Cf.

16374-706 (n.), where Genius develops this idea to Nature at great length.

19221   Ln

19224-37   P 282. Cf. 19870 n.

19244   P 303

19259   Ln (*erreur*, in his note, is probably an error for *eneur*.)

19263   P 303

19278-308   Ln (Ovid, *Met.*, IV. 457-63)

19303   Ln

19305-8   Ln (Virgil, *Aeneid*, VI. 597-98)

19327-30   G 131

19343   *my friend, the lady Venus*: Ln adduces a parallel from *De planctu*, col. 454, in which Nature calls Venus her *subvicaria*. The relationship is different from this, however, in that Venus, in Alanus, is clearly subordinate in a hierarchial sense; she is "meae [Naturae] praeceptionis sub arbitrio" (Moffat 1908: "under my knowledge and guidance"), not a peer, as here. The change is deliberate and shows Nature moving in the direction that Genius and Venus take.

19345-68   P 188. Ln (19349-50 n.) identifies the "scripture" as Matt. 7:15. Cf. 11717-18 n.

19392, 19407   Ln

19419-20   G 134

CHAPTER 10

19439-20703   (Chapter 10) The principal point about Genius's solution is that it is *not* a solution, except from the Lover's point of view. See F 213-26. R 201: "It is the function of Genius's sermon and the events which immediately follow it to explain" how, "if Nature is actually innocent," she comes to be "associated with lechery." "The sermon is an elaboration of the counsel of Gen. 1:28: 'Increase and multiply,' for this, in effect, is what Nature does and what Genius urges her to do." Cf. 4343-45 n., 16272-20703 n.

19439-41   G 134

19453-58   G 402-3

19477-20670   Ln (*De planctu*, cols. 481-82). See 16272-20703 n.; 4343-45 n.

19479   *ring, crosier, and a mitre*: Ln notes that these are the marks of a bishop. The elevation from priest to bishop is an ironic parallel to the switch from the service of God to that of the God of Love and accords with the deliberately shocking effect of the excommunication (of the chaste) and the promised salvation in the Park of the Lamb of those who employ their hammers and anvils, styluses and tablets, plowshares and furrows. Cf. T 256-58, 275-78; R 100. The irony is reinforced in Fig. 42 by the rose-motif in the head of the crosier, a motif that indicates Genius's allegiance to Venus.

19484-90   G 132-33
19487-88   P 47
19498-99   Ln (*De planctu*, col. 480 D)
19504-5   G 405, 481, 494
19505-930   P 279-86 discusses Genius's message, up to the description of the Park of the Lamb, under the heading "the message and its moral."

19505-11   Ln (*De planctu*, col. 476 B)
19521-24   P 213 (Cf. 16755-60, 20327-30.)
19543-60   Ln (*De planctu*, cols. 456-57; for the image of the hammers and anvil, see also cols. 431 B, 450 B, 454 B, 459 C; the image of the stylus and tablets occurs only here; that of the plowshare occurs once again, at 431 B.)

19575-98   G 254
19578-82   Ln (*De planctu*, col. 453 D)
19583-628   P 322-23 adduces as a parallel to this passage one of three arguments that he quotes from Thomas Aquinas, *Summa contra Gentiles*, III, Chapter 136, arguments that Thomas refutes as erroneous: "If it is good that one be continent, it is better that many, best that all be so. But from this it follows that the human race may dwindle away. Therefore it is not good that a man be entirely continent." Paré calls the resemblance "parfaite"; but we cannot assume, with Paré, that the opinion is Jean's or that he is one of the Paris students envisaged in Bishop Tempier's condemnation of 1277; the only evidence for such an association lies in passages of this kind which come from a *persona*, Genius, whose argument goes to some such ridiculous extreme as "If it is good that one be promiscuous, it is better that many, best that all be so." Cf. F 214-20. In fact, of course, Paré is not happy about his own position: he says that by the end of Genius's sermon "the contemplation of the Trinity is promised to those who faithfully observe Nature's laws. No doubt the authentically Christian character of the [*Romance*] doesn't gain a great deal from this development. . . . But such is the teaching that the text presents us; we have to take it as it is" (p. 325). The neglect of irony has unfortunate consequences here. Cf. 19931-20667 n.

19599-628   P 188
19615, 19629, 19636, 19639   Ln
19649-50   Ln (*De planctu*, col. 482)
19651   *when they want to follow Orpheus*: Ln quotes the parallel from *De planctu*, col. 449 C: "Man alone, under the influence of Orpheus's seductive lyre, wanders from the path of reason." The tradition of Orpheus as pederast appears in Ovid, *Met.*, x. 78-85. While Orpheus had a generally favorable significance in medieval commentaries

(cf. R 106-8), the image of unnatural love is related to the Boethian image of Orpheus as one who desires to turn his thought to the clarity of the Sovereign Good but instead fixes his eyes on the gulf of hell, "that is, who turns his thought toward earthly things" and loses all the celestial good that he had. See Jean de Meun 1952, pp. 232-33. The key to Jean's irony lies in Genius's distortion of Alanus's meaning. Where Alanus sees Orpheus as unnatural because of his pederasty, Genius sees "those who follow Orpheus" as including those who follow a life of chastity. Cf. 4343-45 n., 16272-20703 n.

19657-62   G 396-97 (Cf. 19907-35.)

19658-63   Ln (*De planctu*, col. 449; cf. col. 457.)

19663, 19667, 19677-79, 19706, 19710   Ln

19736-48   Ln (Ovid, *Met.*, II. 102-30)

19753-55   Ln's note supplies the translation given.

19760-63   Ln

19787   *chivalry* (chevalerie) : The ambiguity here depends upon the etymological meaning, 'horsemanship, mounted skill,' thus 'skill at engendering.' The use of the term, however, implies the whole complex of virtues traditional to chivalry, among which is the basic ability to control one's mount, to use the rein judiciously. Cf. Genius at 19715-16: "And for God's sake, never let the horses in front go slowly"; Reason at 3067: "Take the bit hard in your teeth"; 21370. See R 253-54, 394, Fig. 6; Miller 1952, pp. 253, 256.

19840-49, 19863   Ln

19870   *You will find twenty-six of them*: "More precisely, twenty-seven (19225-34)," says Ln. Cf. P 282.

19881-84   *The lovely Romance . . . better*: G 21 suggests "an ironical flavor" in these lines but does not specify. Clearly the irony is dramatic. The *Romance* does indeed clarify the vices, and Genius and Nature are themselves exemplary of the Lover's illusion; thus the poetic audience understands Genius's words in a way different from his intention. Cf. Ln (19882 n.).

19900-3   G 238-39

19907-35   G 396-98 (Cf. 19657-62.)

19931-20667   T 329: "The image of the *parc* of the White Lamb . . . shows Jean using the allegorical mode most subtly and powerfully. It is an unmixed straight Christian symbolical image of the Heavenly Paradise, deliberately traditional, to be read mystice, an anagogical figure in the direct stream of Christian religious allegory; it is solely its use in the piece that provides the ambiguity and the irony." T 275: "One of the main objects in [the] introduction [of the Park of the Lamb] is to allow the ludicrous assumption by Nature's priest Genius that entrance into the Heavenly Jerusalem is in *his* gift." Cf. T 245. Paré's discussion of the Park occupies pp. 286-96, but he misses the irony and therefore concludes that Genius's positions are

Jean's. Cf. 4343-45 n., 16272-20703 n., 19439-20703 n., 19583-628 n.

19949-61   Ln

19981-82   P 61

20003, 20024   Ln

20033   *the ages of gold*: R 202 (on "the Golden Age, or the state of Nature as it was created") cites Singleton 1958, pp. 184-203 in support of the idea that "the classical 'Golden Age' was taken to represent the state of nature before the Fall or the restoration of that condition in the Church of the Faithful." The Golden Age appears also in the advice of Friend, 8355-454, in an ironic context (see n.); cf. 9493-664; P 100-1. Here, the allusion proceeds to the rather absurd juxtaposition of 20040 ff.: anyone who takes away a man's testicles robs him of his sweetheart's (or wife's) love. The concepts of "love" and "nature" are thus reduced to trivial dimensions in Genius's treatment. Cf. 5535-54 n., 8355-9664 n.

20034-36   *His son Jupiter . . . testicles*: Ln (Cf. 5537-42 n.). Cf. 10827-30; R 202-3: "The story of the castration of Saturn in Genius's sermon is not a digression, but a narrative exposition of the ideas that are developed there, and it is not, by the standards of Gothic taste, an unseemly mixture of the sacred and the profane." Cf. the interesting development in which the Lover's original prudery about Reason's use of the terms "testicles" and "penis" (6928-7184) becomes swept away in his willing acceptance of Genius's deification of those members through metaphorical (hammer, stylus, plowshare) and eschatological (the Park of the Lamb) argument.

20095-114   Ln

20115-50   Ln (Virgil, *Georgics*, I. 125-46)

20123-29   P 100-1. Cf. 4975-5588 n.

20139, 20175   Cf. 16016-148 n.

20190-95   Ln (Ovid, *Met.*, I. 116-18)

20190   Ln

20196-204   Ln (Ovid, *Met.*, I. 114-15, 125-27)

20249-52   P 291 (John 10:14)

20279-82   Ln

20312-30   G 240-41; P 212, 215 (Cf. 16729-800.)

20371   *in general*: Cf. 5443-54 n.

20373-74   P 50

20409-24   See Goldin 1967, pp. 60-61.

20412   Ln. Cf. 1607 n.

20416, 20426, 20432   Ln (See 1571, 1532, 1527.)

20437-38   See Goldin 1967, p. 61.

20439   Ln (See 1537-38.)

20465-524   P 293-94; T 276-78, 329-30. The fountain and olive tree are of course Christian imagery. Trinitarian doctrine is obvious in the three springs that form one fountain. Tuve clarifies the irony and its function; see Fig. 43 (also reproduced by Tuve, p. 277) for one illustrator's method of revealing the irony. Cf. the carbuncle below, 20525-96, and the circular triangle of 19137-38. See 19119-90 n.

20467   Ln

20479-524   Cf. 1369-74 and note.

20525-96   P 294-95. On the carbuncle (ruby), cf. Augustine, *De doctrina christiana*, II. xvi (24), who emphasizes its virtue of light. The carbuncle appears in *De planctu*, col. 435, as a stone in Nature's diadem, one of seven that represent the seven lowest spheres of the Ptolemaic heaven; as fourth of the seven, it "bears the image of the sun." Here the carbuncle becomes an eternal sun and a trinitarian symbol, "completely round and with three facets." Cf. the fountain above, 20465-524, and the triangular circle of 19137-38.

20528   Ln

20592-96   P 61-65 discusses *form and matter*; cf. 15973-74, 15983, 15995, 16014-18, 16077-78, 16141-42; see also 8312-13 n.

20597-99   Cf. 4430-31 n.

20599-600   Cf. 16955-57 n.

20611-14   Cf. 4430-31 n.

20616   Ln

20631-36   G 398-99

20633-34   Ln (Cf. 2225-28 and n.)

20662   Ln

20664-67   G 399

20668-21780   P 279

20670-82   G 187-88, 133

20670-78   Cf. 20787 n.

20683-21774   G 187-96. See 20704-21780 n.

20683-707   G 400, 404, 406

20694   *fiat*: 'so shall it be,' the usual ending of a sentence of anathema (Ln).

CHAPTER 11

20704-21780   (Chapter 11) The final action of the poem follows out in somewhat more direct fashion the implications of the elaborate ironies of the preceding discourses, particularly that of the last speaker, Genius; but the imagery (torch, sanctuary, Pygmalion's experience, the pilgrimage with sack and staff to the shrine, the penetration of the rose hedge and fertilization of the rose) maintains and heightens the bizarre sense of mingled excitement and detachment that comes to a humorously anticlimactic close with the last line. Cf. P 296-97; G 187-96; F 226-44.

20720 Ln

20769-70 *and the devil . . . chaplet of nettles*: Venus's followers wear chaplets of roses (cf. 555, 895-96 n., 10102, 12439 ff.). The iconography of the nettles is, as we might expect, the reverse of traditional values, for a chaplet of nettles is the sort of headgear that Alanus might well have associated with Venus: "Nettle [*urtica*] . . . means lasciviousness of perverted thinking, . . . the itching of lascivious thoughts." Alanus adduces Isaiah 34:13 (*Distinctiones dictionum theologicalium, PL* 210, col. 988).

20771-73 Cf. 4430-31 n.

20776, 20777 Ln

20779 *your mother, Reason*: Cf. 2840 ff., 3028, 14962.

20783-89 G 405-6, 191-92

20787 *brand* (brandon): Cf. 20670-78. On the iconography of Venus's brand, cf. Fleming 1963, p. 230.

20799, 20806 Ln

20810-11 Ln gives the text of a 52-line interpolation that occurs in two MSS, with portions in others. It is another mythological comparison, this time between the image and Medusa's head. After telling of how Perseus slew her by using Athena's shield as a mirror to avoid looking directly at her, the passage goes on to contrast the image and Medusa's head: "But the image that I speak of surpassed the powers of Medusa, since she served only to kill men, to change them to stone. This one changes them back from stone, maintains their human shapes, better ones in fact than they had before. . . . Medusa's image is harmful, this profitable; that kills, this revives."

20811-21227 See R 99-103; T 262-63, 328; F 228-37.

20811-16 *If anyone . . . lion*: Ln: "Contrary to what we might assume from the construction of the sentence, the 'mouse' represents Pygmalion's statue, the 'lion' the one just described. Cf. 21218-27." If Jean de Meun was aware of the use of small, furry animals in erotic symbolism (see R 113), the simile shows a compounding of the phantasmagorical quality in the imagery: the image is that of a woman, with a "sanctuary" within, which represents the female genitals. But the entire image is placed in an "aperture," which itself stands for the genitals ("an opening . . . in front . . . where Nature had placed it between two pillars"). The terms of the simile compare the image to a mouse, Pygmalion's to a lion, the one a micro-, the other a macro-distortion of the conventional small furry animal, such as cat or rabbit, used as genital-metaphor.

These overtones do not alter or impair the primary use of the simile, to show the Lover's conception of the superiority of his image to that of Pygmalion. Such is clearly the intent at 21218-27, but lines 20811-16 apparently contradict this meaning, and the rhyme *Pygmalion-lion* (20815-16) would seem to preclude obvious textual corruption. The solution may lie in two complementary considerations, a) the controlled development of an aura of irrationality in the Lover's discourse and b) the likelihood that Jean de Meun was aware that the discrepancy between lion and mouse in the old fable was understood as more apparent than real. See Marie de France, *Fables* 1942, pp. 15-16; *Ysopet-Avionnet* 1919, pp. 82-85; *Les fabulistes latins* 1893-99, II, 137, etc.; IV, 261-62.

20817-21214   P 297

20817-21191   Ln notes the source as Ovid, *Met.*, x. 242-99, and remarks on the "jolis développements" that Jean has added. Jean's changes are functional, for they reflect a seeming disregard of Ovid's point, the metamorphosis of Mirrha, to which the "unnatural" love of her great-grandfather Pygmalion furnishes an appropriate prelude rather than the main theme. Jean presents the story from the point of view of the Lover, of course, and the result is a deliberate, ironic distortion. See 20811-21227 n., 20825-21210 n.; cf. the Old Woman's reference to her "song . . . about Pygmalion's image" (13085-88).

In Fig. 62, the parallel between Pygmalion and the Lover was apparent to the rubricator of this carefully illustrated manuscript, B. N. fr. 1565. The illustration shows Pygmalion asleep, with head to left, in the usual position of the dreamer in many of the opening miniatures of the poem (cf. Fig. 1; Kuhn 1913-14, Figs. 2-5; F, Figs. 1-4, 10-11, 15, 40). The rubric reads "Ci commence lystoire de pymalion & de son songe." The story of Pygmalion is only symbolically a dream, but the rubricator thus makes the connection with the main story symbolically clear. The miniatures of this manuscript, like those of several others, are set in medallions somewhat like the gem-settings described at 20972-73, "squares with semicircular arcs on each of the four facets." See Ln (20972-73 n.).

20823-24   Ln

20825-21210   Ln notes specific parallels, which I omit, to Ovid's version of the Pygmalion story, *Met.*, x. 247-513. An indication of Jean's distortion (see 20817-21191 n.) lies in the fact that he devotes 367 lines (20817-21183) to the story of Pygmalion, which in Ovid occupies only 52 (243-94); while the sequel, the account of Pygmalion's descendants, takes 27 lines in the *Romance* (21184-210) and 219 in Ovid (295-513).

20831   Ln (Helen, Menelaus's wife, was carried off by Paris; Lavinia, Latinus's daughter, engaged to Turnus, was married by Aeneas after his victory; see *Iliad, Aeneid*.)

20852   Ln (See 2288.)

20876-88   *Didn't Narcissus . . . in the fountain*: In having Pygmalion compare himself favorably with Narcissus (see 1425-1614),

Jean de Meun reinforces the parallel between the two and between their situations and that of the Lover. Cf. F 231.

20889-92   Cf. Chaucer, *Troilus*, I. 810-12.

20915   *knelt* (s'agenouille): Jean uses religious imagery to underline Pygmalion's idolatry. Cf. 21023 ("instead of the Mass"), 21114 ("in his penitence"); 19479 n., 19931-20667 n., 20465-524 n., 21347 n., 2536 n.

20923-24   *He didn't know . . . intelligence and wisdom*: Cf. Introduction on the three stages of sin; 4377-88 n.

20923, 20928   Ln

20931-21013   Cf. 13079-88.

20933-34   Cf. 4293-334, 129-462 n.

20947   *melequin, of a moiré* (melequins, atebis): Ln glosses *melequin* simply as "étoffe précieuse," but gives a long note on *atebis*, which is English *tabby* 'watered silk.'

20949   *camelot*: See 9081 n.

20963   Ln

20972-73   Ln. See also 20817-21191 n.

20987-90, 20995-98   Ln

21002   *sewed up . . . snug*: Ln compares 90-98, a minor parallel between the Lover and the Pygmalion story.

21026   Ln

21029   Ln (Amphion, son of Jupiter and Antiope, built the walls of Thebes by playing the lyre. Cf. Horace, *Ars poetica*, 394-95.)

21083   "*O fair gods*,": The retable in Figs. 53 and 55 shows three figures, probably Venus, Juno, and Pallas, representing the moral choices (Amorous, Contemplative, and Active lives, according to Seznec) that are available to Pygmalion, as to the Lover; their choice is obvious. See Fleming 1963, pp. 121-22, citing Jean Seznec, *La survivance des dieux antiques* (London 1940), pp. 98-99, and noting the fact that the source for the cover illustration of the Robbins translation of the *Romance* is an illustration to the *Echecs amoureux*, MS B. N. fr. 143, fol. 198 verso, which shows Venus, Juno, and Pallas inside the garden.

21052, 21146   Ln

21171   *thanks to the gods*: See 21083 n. The presence of the bishop in Fig. 55 shows the illustrator's awareness of the parody.

21178   Ln; P 28

21188   Ln

21192-210   Ln identifies Ovid, *Met.*, x. 300-513 as basis. The full passage would, however, begin at 21184, to include Paphos, Cynaras, Myrrha, and Adonis. See 20817-21191 n., 20825-21210 n.

21200-1   Ln

21201-3   *After she brought . . . into a tree*: Adonis's fate furnishes Jean de Meun with other appropriate exemplary material (15675-750 and n.).

21213-14 Ln

21228 *Dame Cypris*: Ln (Venus, from the island of Cyprus, where she was worshipped)

21238 Ln

21247-48 *sack and staff*: Ln. See also 21354 n.

21275-76 Cf. 21760-61, 2996-3098, 7203-30. In a sense, the overthrow of Reason represents the climax of the interior action of the poem.

21275, 21277-80, 21294, 21301 Ln

21332-33 Ln (Virgil, *Eclogues*, x. 69)

21346-780 P 297

21347 *like a good pilgrim*: The religious imagery of the pilgrim (sack and staff, shrine, relics, sanctuary) mingles hilariously—and deliberately ludicrously—with the other elements of the Lover's rationalizations. Cf. 20915 n. and the other passages cited there.

21354 *sack and staff* (escharpe e bourdon): standard attributes of the religious pilgrim here converted into symbols for scrotum and penis. Cf. 18311, 21247-48. See Figs. 57, 63; Fleming 1969, Fig. 42.

21360 *two hammers*: Again, the symbols of labor and of generation (with anvil, 15891 ff.) become symbols for testicles.

21361-62 Ln

21367 Ln (Ovid, *Met.*, VIII. 159)

21370 *horses*: See 19787 n.

21439-44 Ln (Juvenal, *Satire* I. 38-39)

21445-48 Ln (Ovid, *Ars amatoria*, II. 667-68)

21450, 21468 Ln

21497-500 Cf. 7081-86 n.

21498-500 P 28, 37

21514, 21521, 21556, 21563-64 Ln

21573-82 P 31-32 discusses the terms *diffinicion, defenir, especiaus differences, contraires*. Cf. 16075-81.

21574 *gloss*: Cf. 7153-80 n.

21611, 21621-32, 21653, 21663 Ln

21737-40 Ln (Ovid, *Ars amatoria*, I. 665-66)

21738 Ln

21754-55 Ln

21760-61 Cf. 21275-76.

21772 *marigolds of solicitude* (soussie): The French name for the marigold (*soussie*) puns with the word *souci* (care, solicitude, anxiety).

21777-80 G 134, P 297. Fig. 58 illustrates the "plucking of the rose" with a couple in bed; Fig. 64 shows the literal action at the left and the couple in bed at the right; MS Paris, Arsenal 2988, fol. 179 a, shows a couple in standing embrace, with the man's hand on the woman's genital area, in the manner of Chaucer's "hende Nicholas."

21780 *Straightway it was day, and I awoke*: This line suggests that the Lover has experienced a rather elaborate erotic dream. On this level, the dream is an *insomnium*, according to Macrobius's classification, and therefore unworthy of notice. Cf. the Emperor's dream of possessing Fenice in Chrétien de Troyes, *Cligés*, 3309-21, ed. 1965, p. 101. See F 248-49 for a perceptive and—to me—convincing account of the overtones in the Christian concept of "awakening" that are suggested by this passage.

APPENDIX

TABLE OF CONCORDANCES BETWEEN LINE-NUMBERING IN LANGLOIS AND LECOY EDITIONS

LINE NUMBERS IN PARALLEL PASSAGES				DISCREPANCIES IN LINE-NUMBERING	
LANGLOIS EDITION		LECOY EDITION			
DISCREPANT NUMBERING	PARALLEL NUMBERING	DISCREPANT NUMBERING	PARALLEL NUMBERING	SUB-TOTAL	TOTAL
	1-370		1-370		
371-72		370 a-b		2	
	373-892		371-890		2
Omitted**		891-92		-2	
	893-1044		893-1044		0
1045-46		Omitted*		2	
	1047-2076		1045-2074		2
2077-86		2074 a-j		10	
	2087-2464		2075-2452		12
2465-66		2452 a-b		2	
	2467-2694		2453-2680		14
2695-96		Omitted*		2	
	2697-3344		2681-3328		16
3345-46		Omitted*		2	
	3347-3926		3329-3908		18
3927-36		3908 a-j		10	
	3937-4048		3909-4020		28
4049-50		Omitted*		2	
	4051-58		4021-28 (G'me)		30
	4059-21780		4029-21750 (Jean)		

* The omitted passages appear in Variantes II.
** See 892 n.

BIBLIOGRAPHY

THE bibliography is divided into two lists, "Manuscripts" and "Printed Works," and with few exceptions includes only those works referred to in the notes or introduction. Those titles with an asterisk (*) constitute a basic, selective bibliography for the *Romance of the Rose*. The alphabetical arrangement includes cross-references where brief forms of reference differ from the first word of the full entry. Thus, the editions and translations of the *Romance* are entered under "Guillaume de Lorris and Jean de Meun," with a cross-reference under "*Romance.*"

MANUSCRIPTS

Arras. Bibliothèque municipale 532 (845)
London. British Museum (B.M.), Egerton 881
Oxford. Bodleian Library, Douce 195
Paris. Bibliothèque de l'Arsenal 2988
————. 5209
————. Bibliothèque Nationale, fonds français (B. N. fr.)

146	803	1573
378	1136	1575
798	1559	12593
802	1560	19157
	1565	

————. B. N. Rothschild 2800 (IV. 2. 24)
————. 2801 (I. 7. 16)

PRINTED WORKS

Abelard, Peter. *Historia calamitatum*. Ed. J. Monfrin. 2nd ed. Paris: Vrin, 1962
Adler, Alfred. "The Topos *Quinque lineae sunt amoris* used by Ronsard in *Amours* (1552), CXXXVI." *Bibliothèque d'Humanisme et Renaissance*, 15 (1953), 220-25
Aelred of Rievaulx. *Opera omnia. PL* 195
Alanus de Insulis. *The Anticlaudian of Alain de Lille*. Trans. William H. Cornog. Philadelphia: University of Pennsylvania Press, 1935
————. *Anticlaudianus*. Ed. R. Bossuat. Paris: Vrin, 1955
————. *The Complaint of Nature*. Trans. Douglas M. Moffat. New York: Holt, 1908 (Yale Studies in English, 36)
————. *Opera omnia. PL* 210
————. *Summa "Quoniam homines."* Ed. P. Glorieux. *Archives d'histoire doctrinale et littéraire du moyen âge*, 28ᵉ année (1953, published 1954), 113-364

Alanus de Insulis. *Textes inédits*. Ed. Marie-Thérèse d'Alverny. Paris: Vrin, 1965

d'Alverny 1965. See Alanus de Insulis . . . 1965.

Amann, E. "Saint-Amour, Guillaume de." *Dictionnaire de théologie catholique*, 14, 1 (Paris 1939), 756-63

d'Ancona, Paolo, and Erhard Aeschlimann. *Dictionnaire des miniaturistes du Moyen âge et de la Rennaissance dans les différentes contrées de l'Europe*. 2nd ed. Milan: Hoepli, 1949

Andreas Capellanus. *The Art of Courtly Love*. Trans. John Jay Parry. New York: Columbia University Press, 1941

————. *De amore libri tres*. Ed. E. Trojel. 2nd ed. Munich: Eidos, 1964

Arnulfe d'Orléans. See Ghisalberti 1932.

Auerbach, Erich. *Literary Language and Its Public in Late Latin Antiquity and in the Middle Ages*. Trans. Ralph Manheim. New York: Pantheon, 1965

————. *Mimesis*. Trans. Willard Trask. Garden City, N.Y.: Doubleday, 1957

Augustine, Saint. *De doctrina christiana. De vera religione*. Ed. Joseph Martin. Turnhout: Brepols, 1962

————. *On Christian Doctrine*. Trans. D. W. Robertson, Jr. New York: Liberal Arts Press, 1958

————. *Opera omnia. PL* 32-47

Benton, John F. "The Court of Champagne as a Literary Center." *Speculum*, 36 (1961), 551-91

Bernard of Clairvaux, Saint. *Opera omnia. PL* 182-85

Bernardus Sylvestris. *Commentum . . . super sex libros Eneidos Virgilii*. Ed. G. Riedel. Griefswald: Abel, 1924

Bieler 1957. See Boethius . . . 1957.

Blake 1964. See *The Phoenix* . . . 1964.

Bode 1834. See *Scriptores rerum mythicarum* . . . 1834.

Boethius, Anicius Manlius Severinus. *The Consolation of Philosophy*. Trans. Richard Green. New York: Bobbs Merrill, 1962

————. *Philosophiae consolatio (De consolatione philosophiae)*. Ed. Ludwig Bieler. Turnhout: Brepols, 1957

Bossuat 1955 b. See Alanus de Insulis . . . 1955.

*Bossuat, Robert. *Manuel bibliographique de la littérature française du moyen âge*. Melun: Librairie d'Argences, 1951

*————. *Supplément (1949-1953)*. Paris: Librairie d'Argences, 1955

*————. *Second Supplément (1954-1960)*. Paris: Librairie d'Argences, 1961

Calcidius 1962. See Plato . . . 1962.

Chalcidius. See Calcidius.

Chaucer, Geoffrey. *The Works of Geoffrey Chaucer*. Ed. F. N. Robinson. 2nd ed. Boston: Houghton Mifflin, 1957

Chrétien de Troyes. *Cligés.* Ed. Alexandre Micha. Paris: Champion, 1965

Cohn, Norman. *The World-View of a Thirteenth-Century Intellectual: Jean de Meun and the "Roman de la Rose."* Newcastle upon Tyne: University of Durham, 1961

Collingwood, R. G. *The Idea of Nature.* Oxford: Clarendon Press, 1945; London: Oxford University Press, 1960

Congar, Yves M.-J. "Aspects ecclésiologiques de la querelle entre mendiants et séculiers dans la seconde moitié du XIIIe siècle et le début du XIVe." *Archives d'histoire doctrinale et littéraire du moyen âge,* 36e année (1961), 35-151

Cornog 1935. See Alanus de Insulis . . . 1935.

Courcelle, Pierre. *"La Consolation de philosophie" dans la tradition littéraire de Boèce.* Paris: Etudes augustiniennes, 1967

————. "Les exégèses chrétiennes de la quatrième Eglogue." *Revue des études anciennes,* 59 (1957), 294-319

Curtius, Ernst R. *Europäische Literatur und lateinisches Mittelalter.* Bern: Francke, 1948

————. *European Literature and the Latin Middle Ages.* Trans. Willard R. Trask. London: Routledge and Kegan Paul, 1953

*Dahlberg, Charles R. "Love and the *Roman de la Rose.*" *Speculum,* 44 (1969), 568-84

*————. "Macrobius and the Unity of the *Roman de la Rose.*" *SP,* 58 (1961), 573-82

————. "The Secular Tradition in Chaucer and Jean de Meun." Princeton: Ph.D. dissertation, 1953

Dante. *Inferno.* Ed. and trans. John D. Sinclair. New York: Oxford University Press, 1961 (first printed 1939)

Davy, M.-M. 1932. See Pierre de Blois . . . 1932.

————. 1953. See Guillaume de Saint-Thierry . . . 1953.

De cons. See Boethius.

De planctu. See Alanus de Insulis.

Dedeck-Héry 1952. See Jean de Meun . . . 1952.

Delhaye, Philippe. "Le Dossier Anti-Matrimonial de l'*Adversus Jovinianum* et son Influence sur Quelques Ecrits Latins du XIIe Siècle." *Med. Stud.,* 13 (1951), 65-86

Duhem, Pierre. *Le système du monde.* 10 vols. Paris: Hermann, 1913-59

Dunn 1962. See Guillaume de Lorris . . . 1962.

Ellis 1900. See Guillaume de Lorris . . . 1900.

Emery, Richard W. "A Note on the Friars of the Sack." *Speculum,* 35 (1960), 591-95

Evans, Joan, and Mary S. Serjeantson. *English Mediaeval Lapidaries.* London: Oxford University Press for the Early English Text Society, 1933 (reprinted 1960; EETSOS 190)

Ewert and Johnston 1942. See Marie de France . . . 1942.

Les fabulistes latins depuis le siècle d'Auguste jusqu'à la fin du moyen âge. Ed. Léopold Hervieux. 2nd ed. 4 vols. Paris, 1893-99 (reprinted New York: Burt Franklin, 1964)

Fansler, Dean Spruill. *Chaucer and the "Roman de la Rose."* New York: Columbia University Press, 1914 (reprinted Gloucester, Mass.: Peter Smith, 1965)

Faral 1951. See Guillaume de Saint-Amour . . . 1951.

Faral, Edmond. *Les arts poétiques du XIIe et du XIIIe siècle.* Paris: Champion, 1962

————. "Le Roman de la Rose et la pensée française au XIIIe siècle." Revue des deux mondes, 35 (Sept. 15, 1926), 430–57

Faral and Bastin 1959-60. See Rutebeuf . . . 1959-60.

Fleming, John V. "The 'Collations' of William of Saint-Amour Against S. Thomas." *Recherches de théologie ancienne et médiévale,* 32 (1965 b), 132-38

*————. "The Moral Reputation of the *Roman de la Rose* Before 1400." *Romance Philology,* 18 (1965), 430-35

————. The "Roman de la Rose": A Study in Allegory and Iconography. Princeton: University Press, 1969

————. "The *Roman de la Rose* and Its Manuscript Illustrations." Princeton: Ph.D. dissertation, 1963

Foulet, Lucien. *Petite syntaxe de l'ancien français.* 3d ed. Paris: Champion, 1930

Frappier, Jean. "Variations sur le thème du miroir, de Bernard de Ventadour à Maurice Scève." *Cahiers de l'Association internationale des études françaises,* No. 11 (1959), pp. 134-58

*Friedman, Lionel J. "Gradus Amoris." *Romance Philology,* 19 (1965), 167-77

*————. "Jean de Meun and Ethelred of Rievaulx." *L'Esprit Créateur,* 2 (1962), 135-41

*————. " 'Jean de Meung,' Antifeminism, and 'Bourgeois Realism.' " *MP,* 57 (1959), 13-23

Ghisalberti 1933. See John of Garland . . . 1933.

Ghisalberti, Fausto. "Arnolfo d'Orléans, un cultore di Ovidio nel Secolo XII." *Memorie dell' Istituto Lombardo,* 24 (Milan 1932), 157-234

————. "Mediaeval Biographies of Ovid." *Journal of the Warburg and Courtauld Institutes,* 9 (1946), 10-59

Gilson, Etienne. *History of Christian Philosophy in the Middle Ages.* New York: Random House, 1955

————. *The Mystical Theology of Saint Bernard.* Trans. A.H.C. Downes. New York: Sheed and Ward, 1940; London: Sheed and Ward, 1955

Glorieux 1953. See Alanus de Insulis . . . 1953.

Glorieux, P. *Aux origines de la Sorbonne. I: Robert de Sorbon.* Paris: Vrin, 1966

*————. "Le conflit de 1252-1257 à la lumière du Mémoire de Guillaume de Saint-Amour." *Recherches de théologie ancienne et médiévale,* 24 (1957), 364-72

————. " 'Contra Geraldinos,' l'enchaînement des polémiques." *Recherches de théologie ancienne et médiévale,* 7 (1935), 129-55

————. "Les polémiques 'Contra Geraldinos.' " *Recherches de théologie ancienne et médiévale,* 6 (1934), 5-41

————. "Prélats français contre religieux mendiants." *Revue d'histoire de l'Eglise en France,* 11 (1925), 309-31, 471-95

————. *Répertoire des maîtres en théologie de Paris au XIIIᵉ siècle.* 2 vols. Paris: Vrin, 1933-34

Goldin, Frederick. *The Mirror of Narcissus in the Courtly Love Lyric.* Ithaca: Cornell University Press, 1967

Gorce 1933. See Guillaume de Lorris . . . 1933.

Gottfried von Strassburg. *Tristan und Isolde.* Ed. Friedrich Ranke. 5th ed. Berlin: Weidmann, 1961

*Guillaume de Lorris and Jean de Meun. *Le Roman de la Rose.* Ed. Ernest Langlois. 5 vols. Paris: Didot (Vols. 1-2), Champion (Vols. 3-5), 1914-24 (Société des anciens textes français). [Critical edition, with extensive introduction, notes, glossary]

*————. Ed. Félix Lecoy. 3 vols. Paris: Champion, 1965-70 (Classiques français du moyen âge). [Diplomatic edition based on MS Paris, B. N. fr. 1573]

————. Ed. D. M. Méon. 4 vols. Paris, 1814

————. *"Le Roman de la Rose"* dans la version attribuée à Clément Marot. Ed. Silvio F. Baridon and Antonio Viscardi. 2 vols. Milan: Cisalpino, 1954, 1957 ["Preface" contains an essay on the reputation of the *Romance* through the sixteenth century.]

————. *"Le Roman de la Rose." Texte essentiel de la scolastique courtoise.* Ed. M. Gorce, O.P. Paris: Aubier, 1933

————. *The Romance of the Rose.* Trans. F. S. Ellis. 3 vols. London: Dent, 1900 (Temple Classics)

————. *The Romance of the Rose.* Trans. Harry W. Robbins; ed. Charles W. Dunn. New York: Dutton, 1962

Guillaume de Saint-Amour. *Opera omnia.* Constance: Alitophilos, 1632 [In fact, published in Paris]

————. *Responsiones.* Ed. E. Faral. *Archives d'histoire doctrinale et littéraire,* 18 (25ᵉ et 26ᵉ années, 1951), 337-94

Guillaume de Saint-Thierry. *De natura et dignitate amoris.* Ed. M.-M. Davy, *Deux traités de l'amour de Dieu.* Paris: Vrin, 1953

*Gunn, Alan M. F. *The Mirror of Love.* Lubbock, Texas: Texas Tech Press, 1952 [Full discussion of the rhetorical development of the poem]

Haller, Robert. "The Old Whore and Mediaeval Thought: Variations on a Convention." Princeton: Ph.D. dissertation, 1960

Haskins, Charles H. *Studies in the History of Mediaeval Science.* Cambridge: Harvard University Press, 1924

*Hatzfeld, Helmut. "La mistica naturalistica di Giovanni di Meung." *Delta*, 1 (Serie terza, 1962), 1, 25-52

*Heisig, Karl. "Arabische Astrologie und Christliche Apologetik im Rosenroman." *Romanische Forschungen*, 71 (1959), 414-19

Henri d'Andeli. *The Battle of the Seven Arts.* Ed. Louis J. Paëtow. Berkeley: University of California Press, 1914 (Memoirs of the University of California, Vol. 4, No. 1 [History, Vol. 1, No. 1])

Hervieux 1964. See *Les fabulistes latins* . . . 1893-99 (1964).

*Hill, Thomas D. "La Vieille's Digression on Free Love: A Note on Rhetorical Structure in the *Romance of the Rose.*" *Romance Notes*, 8 (1966), 113-15

*Holmes, Urban T., Jr., ed. *A Critical Bibliography of French Literature: Vol. I: The Medieval Period.* 2nd ed. Syracuse: University Press, 1952

James 1914. See Map, Walter . . . 1914.

Jean de Meun. *Li Livres de Confort de Philosophie.* Ed. V. L. Dedeck-Héry. *Med. Stud.*, 14 (1952), 165-275

Jeauneau, Edouard. "L'Usage de la notion d'*Integumentum* à travers les gloses de Guillaume de Conches." *Archives d'histoire doctrinale et littérarire du moyen âge*, 32ᵉ année (1957, published 1958), 35-100

John of Garland. *Integumenta Ovidii.* Ed. Fausto Ghisalberti. Messina and Milan: Principato, 1933

————. *Morale scolarium.* Ed. Louis J. Paëtow. Berkeley: University of California Press, 1927 (Memoirs of the University of California, Vol. 4, No. 2 [History, Vol. 1, No. 2])

John of Ridewall. *Fulgentius metaforalis.* Ed. Hans Liebeschütz. Leipzig: Teubner, 1926

John of Salisbury. *Polycraticus.* Ed. Clemens C. J. Webb. 2 vols. Oxford: Clarendon Press, 1909

Katzenellenbogen, Adolph E. M. *Allegories of the Virtues and Vices in Mediaeval Art from Early Christian Times to the Thirteenth Century.* London: Warburg Institute, 1939; New York: W. W. Norton, 1964

Knowlton, Edgar C. "The Goddess Nature in Early Periods." *JEGP*, 19 (1920), 224-53

————. "Nature in Old French." *MP*, 20 (1922-23), 309-29

*Köhler, Erich. "Narcisse, la fontaine d'amour et Guillaume de Lorris." *Journal des Savants* (1963), 86-103

Koonce, B. G. "Satan the Fowler." *Med. Stud.*, 21 (1959), 176-84

Kuhn, Alfred. *Die Illustration des Rosenromans.* Freiburg i. Breisgau, 1911

*————. "Die Illustration des Rosenromans." *Jahrbuch der Kunst-*

historischen Sammlungen der allerhöchsten Kaiserhauses, 31 (Vienna, 1913-14), 1-66 [with 15 plates and 45 text figures]

Langlois 1914-24. See Guillaume de Lorris . . . 1914-24.

*Langlois, Ernest. *Les manuscrits du Roman de la Rose, description et classement.* Lille: Tallandier, 1910 (Travaux et mémoires de l'Université de Lille. Nouvelle série. I. Droit et lettres. Vol. 7)

*————. *Origines et sources du Roman de la Rose.* Paris: E. Thorin, 1890 (Bibliothèque des écoles françaises d'Athènes et de Rome, 58)

Lecoy 1965, 1966. See Guillaume de Lorris . . . 1965, 1966.

*Lecoy, Félix. "Sur la date du *Roman de la Rose.*" *Romania*, 89 (1968), 554-55

*————. "Sur un passage délicat du *Roman de la Rose* (v. 5532 de l'édition Langlois)." *Romania*, 85 (1964), 372-76

*Levy, Raphael. "Le rôle de la charaierresse dans le *Roman de la Rose.*" *Neophilologus*, 36 (1952), 75-79

*Lewis, C. S. *The Allegory of Love.* Oxford: Clarendon Press, 1936

————. *Studies in Medieval and Renaissance Literature.* Cambridge: University Press, 1966

————. *Studies in Words.* Cambridge: University Press, 1960 (2nd ed., 1967)

Liebeschütz 1926. See John of Ridewall . . . 1926.

Macrobius, Ambrosius Theodosius. *Commentarii in Somnium Scipionis.* Ed. J. Willis. Leipzig: Teubner, 1963

————. *Commentary on the Dream of Scipio.* Trans. William Harris Stahl. New York: Columbia University Press, 1952

Mâle, Emile. *The Gothic Image.* Trans. Dora Nussey. New York: Harper, 1958 [Reprint of trans. originally published in 1913 with the title *Religious Art in France of the Thirteenth Century*]

*Maler, Bertil. "La prophétie d'Albumasar dans le *Roman de la Rose.*" *Studia neophilologica*, 18 (1945-46), 47-48

Map, Walter. *De nugis curialium.* Ed. M. R. James. Oxford: Clarendon Press, 1914

Marie de France. *Fables.* Ed. A. Ewert and R. C. Johnston. Oxford: Blackwell, 1942

Mariella, Sister, O.S.B. "*The Parson's Tale* and the Marriage Group." *MLN*, 53 (1938), 251-56

Martin 1962. See Augustine . . . 1962.

Matthew of Vendôme. See Faral 1962.

McKenzie and Oldfather 1919. See *Ysopet-Avionnet* . . . 1919.

Méon 1814. See Guillaume de Lorris . . . 1814.

Met. See Ovid. *Metamorphoses.*

Migne, J.-P. See *Patrologiae.*

Miller 1916. See Ovid . . . 1916.

Miller, Robert P. "Chaucer's Pardoner, the Scriptural Eunuch, and *The Pardoner's Tale.*" *Speculum*, 30 (1955), 180-99.

Miller, Robert P. "The Double Hunt of Love: a Study of Shakespeare's *Venus and Adonis* as a Christian Mythological Narrative." Princeton: Ph.D. dissertation, 1954

———. "The Myth of Mars's Hot Minion in *Venus and Adonis*." *ELH*, 26 (1959), 470-81

———. "Venus, Adonis, and the Horses." *ELH*, 19 (1952), 249-64

Moffat 1908. See Alanus de Insulis . . . 1908.

Mozley 1939. See Ovid . . . 1939.

Orr, John. " 'Bougre' as Expletive." *Romance Philology*, 1 (1947-48), 71-74

Ovid. *Ars amatoria. The Art of Love and Other Poems.* Ed. and trans. J. H. Mozley. Rev. ed. Cambridge: Harvard University Press; London: Heinemann, 1939 [Contains the *Remedia amoris*]

———. *Metamorphoses.* Ed. and trans. Frank Justus Miller. 2 vols. Cambridge: Harvard University Press; London: Heinemann, 1916

PL. See *Patrologiae.*

Paëtow 1914. See Henri d'Andeli . . . 1914.

Paëtow 1927. See John of Garland . . . 1927.

*Paré, Gérard. *Les idées et les lettres au XIIIe siècle: Le Roman de la Rose.* Montreal: Edition le Centre de Psychologie et de Pédagogie, 1947

———. *Le Roman de la Rose et la scolastique courtoise.* Paris: Vrin; Ottawa: Institut d'études médiévales, 1941

Paré, Gérard, A. Brunet, P. Tremblay. *La renaissance du XIIe siècle: Les écoles et l'enseignement.* Paris: Vrin, 1933

*Paris, Gaston. "*Le Roman de la Rose.*" *La littérature française au moyen-âge.* 5th ed. Paris: Hachette, 1914, pp. 178-90

*Paris, Paulin. "*Roman de la Rose.*" *Histoire littéraire de la France,* 23 (Paris, 1856), 1-61

Parry 1941. See Andreas Capellanus . . . 1941.

Patch, Howard R. *The Goddess Fortuna in Mediaeval Literature.* Cambridge: Harvard University Press, 1927 (reprinted New York: Octagon, 1967)

Patrologiae cursus completus. Series Latina. Ed. J.-P. Migne. 221 vols. Paris: J.-P. Migne, 1844-58 (reprinted Paris: Garnier, various dates; currently at Turnhout, Belgium: Brepols)

Perrod, Maurice. *Etude sur la vie et sur les œuvres de Guillaume de Saint-Amour.* Lons-le-Saunier: Société d'émulation du Jura, 1902

Peter Lombard. *Sententiae. PL* 192, cols. 519-961

Peter Riga. *De ornatu mundi. PL* 171, cols. 1235-38

The Phoenix (Old English poem). Ed. N. F. Blake. Manchester: University Press, 1964

Pierre de Blois. *De amicitia christiana.* Ed. M.-M. Davy, *Un traité d'amour du XIIe siècle.* Paris: E. de Boccard, 1932

Planchenault, René. *Les tapisseries d'Angers.* Paris: Caisse nationale des monuments historiques, n.d.

Plato. *Timaeus a Calcidio translatus commentarioque instructus.* Ed. J. H. Waszink. London: Warburg Institute; Leiden: Brill, 1962

Quain, Edwin A. "The Medieval Accessus ad Auctores." *Traditio*, 3 (1945), 215-64

Rahner, Karl. "La doctrine des 'sens spirituels' au moyen-âge, en particulier chez Saint Bonaventure." *Revue d'ascétique et de mystique*, 14 (1933), 263-99

Reese, Gustave. *Music in the Middle Ages.* New York: Norton, 1940

Riedel 1924. See Bernardus Sylvestris . . . 1924.

Riga, Peter. See Peter Riga.

Robbins 1962. See Guillaume de Lorris . . . 1962.

Robertson 1958. See Augustine . . . 1958.

*Robertson, D. W., Jr. "The Doctrine of Charity in Medieval Literary Gardens." *Speculum*, 26 (1951), 24-49

*———. *A Preface to Chaucer.* Princeton: University Press, 1962

———. "The Subject of the *De amore* of Andreas Capellanus." *MP*, 50 (1953), 145-61

Robertson, D. W., Jr., and Bernard F. Huppé. *"Piers Plowman" and Scriptural Tradition.* Princeton: University Press, 1951

Robinson 1957. See Chaucer . . . 1957.

Romance. See Guillaume de Lorris and Jean de Meun.

Rutebeuf. *Oeuvres complètes.* Ed. Edmond Faral and Julia Bastin. 2 vols. Paris: Picard, 1959-60

Sahlin, Margit. *Etude sur la carole médiévale, l'origine du mot et ses rapports avec l'Eglise.* Uppsala: Almqvist & Wiksell, 1940

Saint . . . . See under proper name.

Scaglione, Aldo D. *Nature and Love in the Late Middle Ages.* Berkeley and Los Angeles: University of California Press, 1963

Schleyer, K. "Disputes scolastiques sur les états de perfection." *Recherches de théologie ancienne et médiévale*, 10 (1938), 279-93

Schoeck, Richard J. "Andreas Capellanus and St. Bernard of Clairvaux: The Twelve Rules of Love and the Twelve Steps of Humility." *MLN*, 66 (1951), 295-300

Scriptores rerum mythicarum latini tres romae nuper reperti. Ed. Georgius Henricus Bode. 2 vols. Cellis, 1834 (reprinted in 1 vol., Hildesheim: Georg Olms, 1968)

Servii grammatici qui feruntur in Vergilii carmina commentarii. Ed. Georgius Thilo and Hermannus Hagen. 3 vols. Leipzig, 1881 (reprinted Hildesheim: Georg Olms, 1961)

Simson, Otto von. *The Gothic Cathedral.* New York: Pantheon, 1956

Sinclair 1961. See Dante . . . 1961.

Singleton, Charles S. *Dante Studies 2: Journey to Beatrice.* Cambridge: Harvard University Press, 1958

*Sneyders de Vogel, Karl. "Le cercle dont le centre est partout, la circonférence nulle part, et le *Roman de la Rose*." *Neophilologus*, 16 (1930-31), 246-50; 17 (1931-32), 211-12

Stahl 1952. See Macrobius . . . 1952.

*Strohm, Paul. "Guillaume as Narrator and Lover in the *Roman de la Rose.*" *Romanic Review*, 59 (1968), 3-9

Thilo and Hagen 1961. See *Servii grammatici* . . . 1881 (1961).

Thomas. *"Le Roman de Tristan" par Thomas, poème du XII⁰ siècle.* Ed. Joseph Bédier. 2 vols. Paris: Didot, 1902-5 (Société des anciens textes français)

Thorndike, Lynn. *A History of Magic and Experimental Science.* 8 vols. New York: Macmillan (Vols. 1-2); Columbia University Press (Vols. 3-8), 1923-58

Thuasne, Louis. *Le Roman de la Rose.* Paris: Malfère, 1929

Trojel 1964. See Andreas Capellanus . . . 1964.

*Tuve, Rosemond. *Allegorical Imagery.* Princeton: University Press, 1966

Vogel, Karl Sneyders de. See Sneyders de Vogel, Karl.

von Simson, Otto. See Simson, Otto von.

Walter Map. See Map, Walter.

*Ward, C. F., ed. *The Epistles on the Romance of the Rose and Other Documents in the Debate.* Chicago: University Press, 1911

Webb 1909. See John of Salisbury . . . 1909.

Willis 1963. See Macrobius . . . 1963.

Ysopet-Avionnet: The Latin and French Texts. Ed. Kenneth Mc-Kenzie and William A. Oldfather. Urbana: University of Illinois, 1919 (University of Illinois Studies in Language and Literature, v, 4)

INDEX

The index lists proper names and a selected group of topics, including major images. The Old French names of characters appear as cross references in a few cases where the translated name may not be readily apparent.

Illustrations

Figures 1 through 28 and 59 through 64 are reproduced here by permission of the Bibliothèque Nationale, Paris. The remaining figures are reproduced with the permission of the Bodleian Library.

Anuoe gent cuidont
que en songes a—
plart ce fables non
fer menconges
Mais on puet
cex songes song.
III ne convent...

1. The Dreamer asleep
(Langlois, line 1)

e ces ymages la samblance
si as mon vient en remembrance

Idevise li auteurs les ymages du
murrer premierement de hayne

2. The author describes
the images on the wall,
Hatred first (139)

3. Felony (155)

A pelee estoit felonnie
B une ymage q̃ vilonie
a noit non . rein delus delbre
oꝛ estoit auqs dautel estre
C om ces . iſ ꝛ dautel fauture

4. Covetousness (169)

G tame qui petit seust
D onorer ce quele deust

A pres fu painte couuoitise
P cest cele qui les genz atise
D e prendre ꝛ de noient donner
ꝛ les granz auoirs abonner

Sle autre ymage i ot aslise
Sdroit encoste de conuoitise
A uarice estoit apelee
L aide estoit z deffiguree
C ele ymage est maigre z chaitiue

5. Avarice (195)

ot l demoraith milt longuemtt
a mons qe en pouith riens traire
aY ais el nauoith de ce que faire
E l naloith pas a ce beant
oY de la bourse ostaith neant

6. Envy (235)

7. Sorrow (291)

8. Old Age (339)

b ien ſauez que ceſt leur nature.

ſte ymage oꝶ apꝛes eſcrite
oꝶ bn ſambloiꝶ eſtre ypocrite

9. Pope-Holiness (407)

t pour ꝟnpou de gloire ꝟaine
a ouꝶ il pdꝛonꝶ dieu ⁊ ſon ꝛaine

ourtanrte fu au daꝛenier
pouuete qui ꞔ ſeul donier
euſꞇ pꝛo ſel ſe deuſꞇ pendꝛe
anꝶ ſeuſꞇ bn ſa ꝛobe vendꝛe
le eſtoiꝶ nue com vns ꝟers
e li tans fuſꞇ ꝟnpou diuers.
eauꝶ q̃ aconꞇ enꞇ de froiꝶ

10. Poverty (441)

11. The Dreamer meets
Idleness (582)

12. Diversion (801)

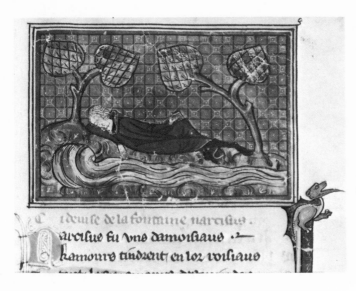

13. The Fountain of Narcissus (1439)

14. The God of Love shoots at the Dreamer-Lover (1681)

la anigome en la pointure
mo mo mti assoage tointure
d' une po moist dame me ault
a insi maio de ainsi me muilt

15. The Lover kneels to the
God of Love (1881)

v ilonme ne mespuison
n enulle maniaise apuson.

16. The lover performs
the act of homage to
the God of Love (1955)

C idenno laucearlome du dieu
d amours e li fist homage

17. Fair Welcoming and
the Lover (2797)

18. Resistance and
the Lover (2943)

A tant es V raisons ymanoe

C pnvle arsons

b raus amns fuliez enbtatoe
o nq mis ton cuer en tel esmoi
a ar veis le biau tans de moi.
os fisq ton cuer si esgare

19. Reason and the
    Lover (2998)

z me onq q tet complole
s e amans p nulle adoison
p astoie outre la clanson.

vanq amns sotz la verite
fl ne ma pas espounte
a inz me disq amns
c omptins oz soiez

20. Friend and the
    Lover (3123)

21. Openness and Pity speak
to Resistance (3255)

22. Venus and Fair
Welcoming (3442)

23. Jealousy and the
    Lover (3535)

Lors la par parole affailli
Garz noienz tp al cuer faitu
on ties aconitte dun garcon

24. Shame and the
    Lover (3568)

pour dieu dame ne crezez pas
ale louche le lofengier
cely vne bone q ment de legier
mait villanty home a vile

25. Shame and Fear waken Resistance (3669)

26. The Lover and Resistance (3755)

27. Tower of Jealousy and
Resistance (3867)

28. The poet at his desk
(4059)

29. The trial and death of Virginia (5595)

30. Fortune and the Lover (5923)

31. Nero has Seneca murdered
(6211)

32. The story of Hercules
(9187)

33. Wealth and the Lover (10051)

34. The God of Love speaks to False Seeming (who appears as the Lover; 10931)

35. False Seeming and
Constrained Abstinence
as pilgrims (12033)

36. The Old Woman speaks
to the messengers (12396)

37. The Old Woman
comes to the Lover
(14694)

38. Pity helps Openness
(against Resistance; 15391)

39. Venus speaks to Adonis (15683)

40. Origen castrates himself
(the better to serve nuns;
Empedocles
jumps into fire; 17039)

41. Albumazar's prediction
of the birth of
Our Lady (19177)

42. The God of Love
vests Genius
as bishop (19477)

43. The "Trinitarian" Fountain of Life (20471)

44. Venus before the Castle of Jealousy (20711)

Duis aduile com bone archiere.
Par vne petite archiere.
Quelle beit en la tour repofte.

45. Venus shoots
at the image
in the sanctuary (20791)

Treftint alz q̃ la regardovent.
Par nul ratin ne len gardovent.
ff ors perlens le filz conus.
Qui par letin la beit ou bis.

46. Three people and image
(at line 9 of the
Medusa-head interpolation;
see 20810-11 n.)

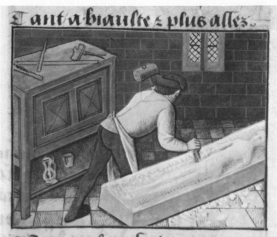

47. Pygmalion carves
an image (20817)

48. Pygmalion
is overcome by the
beauty of the image
(20836)

49. Pygmalion asks
his image
for grace (20907)

50. Pygmalion
dresses the image
(20937)

51. Pygmalion plays his instruments before her (21021)

52. Pygmalion lays her in his bed (21059)

C oe pinnalion faut la reglte a vciy?
D u moult aduenoit de niuaille!
E t vit tout li peuple aur veille!
D ung temple ef venus p ot

53. Pygmalion
makes his petition to
Venus (21075)

De la tenic et retarder

C oe pinnalion la treuue en vie.
I up fen cot les fauld memes.
T at ql eft nulhe la venuz.
D u miracle riens ne fauoit.

54. Pygmalion, finds her
alive (21127)

55. They return thanks
to the gods (21171)

A uv dieuv eulv. ij. graces rednet.
Qui tel courtoisie leur firent
E specialmant a venus.
Qui le ot aydie mieulv q nulz.
De est pymalion a aise.
De nest il ries a luy desplaise.

56. Venus sets fire to the
Castle of Jealousy (21251)

57. The Lover gazes upon the
sanctuary (21587)

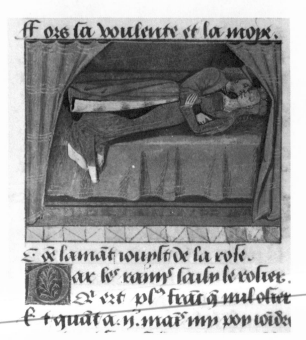

58. The Lover enjoys
the rose (21705)

59. The Fountain of Narcissus
(see 1425-1614 n.)

60. The God of Love
shoots the Lover
(1681; see 1693-95 n.)

61. Genius, dressed as friar
and seated on Nature's anvil,
hears her confession
(16285; see 16272-84 n.)

62. Pygmalion as Dreamer
(see 20817-21191 n.)

63. Rose tree; the Lover,
as pilgrim, approaches the sanctuary
(21619; see 21354 n.)

64. The Lover plucks the rose
(21705; see 21777-80 n.)